POPE JOHN PAUL II SPEAKS ON WOMEN

I0892208

POPE JOHN PAUL II
SPEAKS ON WOMEN

Edited with an introduction by
BROOKE WILLIAMS DEELY

→ Foreword by John P. Hittinger

THE CATHOLIC UNIVERSITY OF AMERICA PRESS
Washington, D.C.

Papal texts copyright © 2014 Libreria Editrice Vaticana
Papal text selection, foreword, introductions, and appendix
Copyright © 2014 Catholic University of America Press
All rights reserved
The paper used in this publication meets the minimum requirements of
American National Standards for Information Science—Permanence
of Paper for Printed Library Materials, ANSI Z39.48-1984.
∞

Library of Congress Cataloging-in-Publication Data
John Paul II, Pope, 1920–2005.
[Works. Selections. English. 2014]
Pope John Paul II speaks on women / edited by Brooke Williams Deely.
pages cm
Includes bibliographical references and index.
ISBN 978-0-8132-2683-5 (pbk. : alk. paper)
1. Women—Religious aspects—Catholic Church. 2. Feminism—
Religious aspects—Catholic Church. I. Deely, Brooke Williams.
II. Title.
BX2347.8.W6J64 2014
282.082—dc23 2014018251

To *Professor Elsa Zambosco-Thomas*
(April 21, 1936–April 1, 2009), who inspired
us all at the University of St. Thomas

CONTENTS

FOREWORD

The question of the status and role of women in contemporary society is a defining one for culture, politics, and religion. The complexity of the issue demands a close attention to the diverse gifts, talents, aspirations of women, the heritage of cultures, and the needs of social organization. Simplifications abound and reductionisms prevail. Authentic answers to the question have become pre-empted by ideology and obscured by intense passion. Thus, Pope John Paul II declares, "After a period marked by a certain ideological confusion and pressure, many today are asking that the relationship between women, the family, and work be dealt with more calmly and objectively."[1] These writings attempt just such a treatment of the issue of women. He gave ample room for the voices and experiences of women to emerge in their authentic voice; these he matched against the biblical teaching of the vocation to love; and he found a deeper account than that provided by either modern liberalism or Marxism in the Augustinian and Thomistic philosophy of human sociability, most adequately expressed as a "communion of persons."

Pope John Paul II was drawn to the issue from many vantages: actor, pastor, philosopher, participant at Vatican II, Supreme Pontiff. John Paul II took the questions head on. He sought to articulate a vision of the dignity of women, as equal to but different from men, whose contributions are vital both to family and to society. Dr. Brooke Deely has rendered a great service in compiling these texts that allow us to see the richness and balance of his account of women.

The pope's writings on women are the fruit of years of a prayerful look at the goodness of God's creation and a thoughtful engagement with social changes and political developments. Constant prayer and political savvy were manifest in the life of John Paul II from his early years as a bishop in

Krakow to his years as pope and world traveler. More hidden from view is the philosophical method worked out by Karol Wojtyła providing him with the tools to cut through ideology, skepticism, and reductionism. Deeply rooted in the study of Aristotle and Aquinas, he also approached the question of the human person through the depth of mystical experience of St John of the Cross and the adumbration of concrete human experience as explored by Polish literature and realist phenomenology. The deep root of John Paul II's account of women is a form of Thomistic "personalism."[2]

This unique approach, combining Thomism and a reflective turn to the historic and concrete phenomena of human experience emerges clearly in his first encyclical, *Redemptor Hominis*: "What is in question here is man in all his truth, in his full magnitude. We are not dealing with the 'abstract' man, but the real, 'concrete,' 'historical' man. We are dealing with 'each' man, for each one is included in the mystery of the Redemption and with each one Christ has united himself for ever through this mystery." What he discovers in the heart of the mystery of human existence is love. Man "cannot live without love. He remains a being that is incomprehensible for himself, his life is senseless, if love is not revealed to him, if he does not encounter love, if he does not experience it and make it his own, if he does not participate intimately in it." The discovery of love and service throughout family, profession, society, and religious life is the key to the question of the status and role of women in contemporary society.

Pope John Paul II's philosophy of woman moves beyond both patriarchy and feminism as ideologies that fail to do justice to the fullness of human experience and suppress the aspiration of men and women to their proper fulfillment in a communion of persons. It is my hope that these readings will display both the need for his approach and method as well as the appeal of his vision for a renewal of human society through a civilization of love.

Feast of St. John the Evangelist
"Perfect love casts out fear"

JOHN P. HITTINGER
Founder and Director, Pope John Paul II Forum
Center for Thomistic Studies, University of St. Thomas

ACKNOWLEDGMENTS

My idea for this book accrued from my correspondence with the Reverend Richard L. Schaefer, theologian, *Censor Deputatus*, and chaplain at Mercy Medical Center, Dubuque, Iowa. This correspondence, in 2004, concerned John Paul II's teaching on women as a frame of reference and perspective for the founding of the Women, Culture, and Society (WCS) program in the contemporary field of women's studies at the University of St. Thomas, Houston. Later, during the period of my direction of the program (2009–2012), I undertook the collaborative task of editing this book, given that the WCS program mission is inspired by this pope's teaching on women. Throughout this editorial process, Fr. Schaefer, with his deep intellectual understanding, worked substantially in helping to cull some key texts, and he also advised on other editorial matters, for which I extend to him my deep gratitude. To further our mission, in this collaborative work of women and men, I greatly appreciate the contribution of Dr. John Hittinger, who wrote the foreword and who concretely supported this work.

For introductions to some of John Paul II's texts (see editorial note at end of each introduction), I offer profound thanks to Dr. Dominic and Mrs. Diane Aquila; Sr. Paula Jean Miller, FSE; Virginia Galloway, who also coordinated the continuity-of-style aspects of this book and did the comprehensive editing of the entire manuscript; Dr. Deborah Savage; and the Rev. Edward J. Baenziger, CSB, who introduced the concluding section, *Divini Amoris Scientia* (The Science of Divine Love), co-authored an introduction with me, prepared the chart in the Appendix, and who also saw me through this protracted project. I give particular thanks to Dr. Kathleen Haney, my successor as director of the WCS program, for her sustaining support; and to Dr. Lois Zamora for her contribution in funding, in memory of her father, Robert Obadiah Parkinson.

For overseeing the comprehensive dimension of the volume in relation to other print sources, and for providing a bibliography of print sources of Vatican Internet sources used in this volume, I owe a deep debt to Dr. Mary Kelleher, chair, Cardinal Beran Library, St. Mary's Seminary, University of St. Thomas School of Theology. I am most appreciative to my student workers, Ivan Earls, who produced the initial working copy for the volume, and Remon Maximos, who helped with technical aspects. Final arrangement of the essays, including formatting and determination of Vatican links to each of the texts, is thanks to the expertise of Dr. John Deely.

Special thanks are due to Richard LeBlanc for his unselfish help on New Year's Eve, when we were in a technical crisis; to Dorothy and Robert Klein and Connie May for their advice and moral support; and to Dr. Gary Shank for his editorial consultation and encouragement.

In the overall context of this work, my thanks go to Dr. Curtis Hancock, Sr. Prudence Allen, RSM, and the Rev. Kieran Kavanaugh, OCD, for their specific helpfulness along the way.

Final thanks go to the students who studied John Paul II with me in the Women, Culture, and Society introductory course.

Never finished, always in process—this book has been a labor of collaborative love and dedication.

POPE JOHN PAUL II SPEAKS ON WOMEN

GENERAL INTRODUCTION

Brooke Williams Deely

John Paul II speaks out courageously, as do the saints in any age, on contemporary problems of his own age that need addressing from the vantage point of Gospel-inspired values. In so doing, he contributes greatly to a developing Catholic tradition, in dialogue with the world. He is the first pope extensively to address the new perspective that the coming of age of women has attained historically. In so doing, he opens a vista wherein his vision has become a beacon in the history and world of ideas aimed at shaping future culture, both within and beyond the Catholic world.

As an historian,[1] I sketch here what is new in the contribution of Pope John Paul II in relation to developing feminist thought, both within and beyond the Catholic tradition. Just as in the late nineteenth century, Pope Leo XIII for the first time championed the historical coming of age of the working class within the development of Catholic tradition as it applied to changed circumstances of the time, so John Paul II champions true insights of the women's revolution in culture begun in the Western world in modern times. Such true insights he distinguishes from mistakes made that counter the human good as integrated in the temporal and spiritual orders of being in conformity with reason. In addressing such a revolution, he thus points out both mistakes and great gains made in this historic journey, gains that promise to transform culture for the better. Since, moreover, this journey is both inclusive of and wider than identities such as race, class, and culture, John Paul II's writings on women are on the boundary, indeed at the cutting edge, of our postmodern era—a new era wherein the pope envisions a paradigm of non-domination as the cultural future of our species.

In meditating on this historical development, John Paul II stands out as encouraging women further to develop insights he brings to the fore. In so doing, he envisions women consciously aware of their own agency as transforming future culture at large in a way that integrates human values that are grounded in woman's unique capacity for being a mother (in her gift of loving service to others) with the larger values of society and culture as a public realm no less accessible in principle and by right to women than to men. Such authentic altruism is to be distinguished from either a historically conditioned one that reduces the personal dignity of woman to a mere function (a restricted social role), or, as in some secular feminist thought, to willfully chosen values contrary to the perfection of human nature as integrated in body and spirit.

John Paul II, hence, deems the participation of women to be *quintessential* in all spheres of influence, as modeling authentically *human* values, for both man and woman, grounded in the highest level of knowing, the mode of knowing through love (contemplative understanding). In this perspective of an integral humanism, he affirms the original unity of man and woman in a shared humanity. He also distinguishes the vocation of woman *along with* that of man, in order that femininity and masculinity be appreciated as embodied differently and yet integrally to humanity as a whole in the composite of body and soul, a composite created to be in reciprocal *relation within* the original unity of a shared humanity.

In deepening understanding and advancing discourse within Catholic tradition and beyond, this pope deeply affirms the *central intuition* of feminist thought, wherein women for the first time in history are empowered, in *both* private *and* public spheres, as persons speaking in their own right, with *full* human rights. At the same time, he addresses the root of the historical problematic concerning the nature of woman *qua* woman that modern feminist thought itself inherited. The problematic was an inheritance, not of the feminists' making, in that feminism found itself entangled within philosophical dualistic presuppositions so construed (or misconstrued) as to privilege the male side of every dualism, such as male/female, public/private, culture/nature, active/passive, and rational/nonrational.

In the early 1970s, women feminists began to challenge such dualisms themselves in the linguistic constructions of woman as the anthropological "other," who, as a subject of inquiry in male-dominant discourse, is nonetheless absent in speaking for herself in such discourse. The various patriarchal traditions all present woman as human indeed, but as a peculiar human who is not a man and who in this sense is nonbeing in such discourse. John Paul II recognizes and seeks to redress this historical, distorted situation of women. Since only human beings, unlike other animal societies, transmit and transform culture over time through linguistic communication as the species-specific human way of modeling the world, he fully appreciates that humans bear moral responsibility for how we have shaped tradition, and that women need to come forward and speak in our own voices publicly in reshaping this human enterprise.

The question, therefore, of how we define the nature of *woman* has been—and still is—the great obstacle to the developing feminist tradition, with so many multiple and often competing schools of thought resulting from such a problematic. An underlying reason for feminisms in the plural is that feminist thought has had to deal first of all with the traditions of men, traditions plural yet unified in virtually excluding collaboration with women in the public sphere as male-defined, higher education included. So "feminists," be they women or men, had first to stand ground against historically male-dominant discourse on the nature of a woman. Pope John Paul II seizes the historic moment himself to call upon women at large to contribute to developing women's history in the making. The long-prevailing exclusion of women from such education, according to him, militated against the good of a woman as a person and her potential contribution to culture.

The task ahead of developing Catholic tradition, in dialogue with the world, remains a formidable one, in view of such obstacles to be overcome in history. Yet we need to bear in mind that the historically grounded women's revolution is a fundamentally new cultural development. This development is one that originated in the modern Western world, yes, but is at the same time a development deeply indebted to the rich heritage of the Classical-Judeo-Christian cultural synthesis which, as a living tradition across the ages, necessarily addresses the needs of a new historical age in a way appropriate to that age. John Paul II recognizes the pressing need for furthering the writing of women's history to meet the need of our age. In this endeavor, I point out, in particular, the work over the decades of Prudence Allen, RSM,[2] which addresses this need by providing an interpretive overview of the concept of woman in Western intellectual tradition.

In looking at history with contemporary eyes (as humans perforce do in seeking what is useful for present understanding), feminist discourse that seeks to realize the full agency of women in cultural transformation has had to go back as far as the writings of Aristotle. For this task of overcoming male privilege is, as the philosopher John Stuart Mill pointed out in his classic *Subjection of Women* (1869), an "arduous task." He explored why. He envisioned a future era when men hear women no longer speaking in whispers but in learned voices of their own, as equally schooled as the voices of men. Later, Virginia Woolf, in her classic feminist essay *A Room of One's Own* (1929), developed such a theme, and, like Mill before her, advised giving the prospect the test of time, in centuries to come (as later did Simone de Beauvoir in her opus, *The Second Sex*).

When we thus move backward in time—in the semiotic spiral of *relation* between future and past texts that shapes future thought—suffice it to say that in early modern times women sought to gain equal rights for women as *individuals*, and in so doing adopted the equal rights paradigm, which is in itself a great advance of Western culture; even so, this paradigm was at that time only male-identified, to the exclusion on principle of female embodiment. Modern feminists of various schools of thought, in an upside-down version of this paradigm, therefore sought *inclusion* within it. The "Declaration of the Rights of Man" during the French Revolution, for example, signified only—as did "universal suffrage"—the male human being as represented in the public sphere. The hegemony of men presupposed the exclusion of women, on the grounds that woman, although equal and complementary to man as a person, is *functionally* unequal as an embodied human animal and hence, in general, "*less rational*" than man and therefore to be governed by him. Woman, as an individual, was dismissed as closer to "nature" than man (ruler of the "cultural" sphere transcending nature), and therefore naturally to be excluded from public representation in the culturally constructed social contract.

To get beyond this impasse, much modern feminist thought imported into feminism the long-prevailing dualistic paradigm wherein the *male* human being was the measure of *perfected* humanity. The thing for woman to do, according to such feminism, was to disown her femininity in order to qualify as perfectly equal "in a man's world." Such feminist rationale thus imported into feminism this now outdated patriarchal rationale, a rationale that retains a stronghold on the subconscious.[3]

In the postmodern era, this original school of feminism sometimes became codified as "sameness feminism." Multiple schools of postmodern feminist thought faulted this frame of reference that linguistically erased sexual differentiation. Yet the newer so-called "difference feminism" itself tripped over the inherited binary logic in order to revalue the female-identified side of the dichotomy, sometimes in a way that promotes the notion of female *superiority*. The central intuition in revalorizing the female-identified side is good in itself, but it requires the rejection of the false option of reducing the frame of reference to what I coin as a "feminocentric" worldview that would devalue masculinity. Such thought sometimes tends to become just as entangled in historically prevailing philosophical dualisms as patriarchy and the older feminism that sought "a piece of the patriarchal pie," so to speak.

In order to clarify the entangled historical roots of this impasse within Catholic tradition and beyond, I turn directly to Jacques Maritain (1882–1973), whose integral humanism deeply influenced the Second Vatican Council. His own stance on the historically problematic male-dominant-over-female dualism[4] cleared the way *historically* for Pope John Paul II's new point of departure from a system of signs which remains no longer trapped in the linguistic and cultural impasse of a biologically based supposition (dating especially to Aristotle and to the medieval theology based on Aristotelian philosophy) of female inequality. Maritain, in seeking to distinguish truth from error in the matter, first redressed the deeply rooted patriarchal justification of male domination by identifying it as a *moral disorder*, something that John Paul II (in a remarkable continuity with Maritain's own insights) emphatically emphasizes as in need of redress when he calls such male domination an outright effect of sin.

In venturing forward, Maritain told us he was well aware that a trailblazing endeavor to escape gender traps required walking on tricky terrain. He made no claim to have "completely worked out" his views (ibid., 156) but only what "seem to be quite necessary to clear up our ideas on a question which today preoccupies everyone's mind and about which the most sincere good will cannot compensate for intellectual confusion."

Maritain proceeded through deepening understanding, for our time and time to come, of the relation between the two accounts in Genesis of creation of the human person as both masculine and feminine. Maritain moved in consonance with Pope John Paul II's later development of complementarity, properly understood as a point of departure *from* (i.e., rejecting) a patriarchal interpretation of complementarity that has reduced woman as a human subject to an object *only* in relation to man. In rejecting the deeply ingrained patriarchal interpretation of the *relation* between man and woman, Maritain acknowledged (ibid., 159) that he was "struggling with words to designate this co-equal complementarity at the very heart of humanity." Maritain nonetheless broke new ground, ground that John Paul II now further develops.[5]

In order to adumbrate the true nature of this gendered relation as defining humanity as an equal whole of equal genders, Maritain found it necessary, first, to mince no words in setting the historical record straight on "the heart of the matter." By "the heart of the matter," he meant precisely what Aristotle, followed by Aquinas and many other "Doctors of the Church," got *wrong* in conceiving of woman, *qua* woman, as "a man that nature accidentally botched up" (ibid., 154), as "a man that did not work out." Although woman is necessary (in the context of the ancient and medieval writings in this area) with respect to the *universal* intention of Nature for procreation, woman is unintended with respect to *particular* nature. So deeply rooted philosophically was—and still is—this presupposition, based on erroneous biology, that all else followed in reinforcing male domination, given man as the "superior" to woman, thus justifying the patriarchal regime: the hegemony of males in the public sphere.

By signaling this capital error as historically transmitted from Aristotle through Aquinas, Maritain remarkably made no attempt either to excuse or even to disentangle earlier Catholic tradition in general (or Thomistic tradition in particular) from this erroneous assertion of "male superiority," which, as Maritain put it, "seemed to go so clearly to the heart of the matter, alas, that St. Thomas thought he had to adopt this assertion" (ibid.). Maritain addressed, as no one so influential within Catholic tradition has before, the *consequence* within tradition of such a mistake: "It followed from this error," he pointed out (ibid.), "that in truth man alone corresponds perfectly to the definition of human nature (whose specific difference is to be endowed with intelligence and reason) … whereas woman is ordained to breed" (ibid.). Maritain told us (ibid., 161) he was "sorry" for this "basic error that I have set out to attack, and which has played its role in the secular enslavement of women—the basic error, that is, to consider the faculty of aiding man to breed as the sole privilege proper to a woman … the one characteristic to which, in the final analysis, her entire femininity is reduced." Of this error both "the Ancients were guilty" and "our most venerable doctors for their part as well." Maritain further pointed out (ibid., 154–55) that the notion of "masculinity as the peak of human nature" continues "to exert its power in our subconscious, even though the correct notion is evidently that of human nature as *shared between masculinity and femininity, while retaining the same value and dignity in the one as in the other*."

Because Maritain insisted on rejecting the deep-rooted patriarchal error, he established a historic turn away from past mistakes and helped open the way for Pope John Paul II's own development of a discourse further integrating truly valid perennial truths in Aquinas and the larger Christian tradition. Indeed, following in the footsteps of Maritain, Pope John Paul II moves in a new direction of *transcending* both patriarchy and late modern feminism as sign systems trapped alike in the false options drawn from the quagmire of philosophical presuppositions prevailing from ancient times through the pre-postmodern cultural eras.

In moving forward, rather than getting stuck in the backwardness that inevitably results from attempting to stand still, John Paul II makes no claim himself to resolve, once and for all, these replicated dualisms used to privilege either man or woman oppositionally as such.

Rather, like Maritain, the pope takes not a *linguistic turn* but a *transcendent turn* toward mystical contemplation, wherein the highest level of knowledge, in the explanation of Aquinas, lies not in discursive reasoning but in the supraratianal mode of knowing through love, the wisdom of the saints.[6] This highest level of knowledge is at the heart of Christianity and is—quite simply—irreducible merely to being a human male or human female and is at the same time inclusive of one's vocation whether as man or as woman. John Paul II concurs with Maritain that a contemplative mode of knowing can prove truly revolutionary in transforming the temporal order toward a fulfillment of the common good, as itself a final end of the human being in the order of nature.

In this moral sense of "revolution," John Paul II dovetails with Maritain (in continuity with Catholic tradition) in stating that, for the integration of faith and reason, the primacy of love as proclaimed in the Gospel is the *sine qua non* for social transformation in the direction of human fulfillment. Such contemplation is not merely for the chosen few (although such a transformation can *originate* from the inspiration of a few) but for all women and men, in a sanctity turned toward the temporal and the secular on behalf of the common good. Such a profound revolution of the heart exercises human agency, wherein the vocation of woman as a mother, in both natural and spiritual senses of "motherhood," is a *sign* of such moral values in the making of history. The good as *common* to men and women requires a human fulfillment that transcends restriction to the private or to the public spheres of culture.

In clarifying this moral sense of "revolution" within our present time, both thinkers converge in drawing deeply upon the doctrine of the sixteenth-century Carmelites and Doctors of the Church, Saint John of the Cross[7] and Saint Teresa of Avila, as well as drawing deeply upon the doctrine of the late-nineteenth-century Carmelite and Doctor of the Church, Saint Thérèse of Lisieux. Maritain[8] applied the words of Saint John of the Cross to the history of civilizations: "By love shall you be judged." The doctrine of Saint Thérèse of Lisieux opened the practice of such spirituality to the world at large with such an original simplicity that John Paul II declared her a Doctor of the Church. That an "unlearned woman," cloistered and hidden from the world, who died so young, would under obedience take up her pen and give voice to her own story of her soul in a way that moved the world is testimony in itself that within the Catholic tradition lie the seeds of contemplation that transcend problematic presuppositions in patriarchy and feminism.

Finally, in relation to a philosophy of *woman*, the essays on woman of the early-twentieth-century Carmelite Saint Edith Stein (Saint Teresa Benedicta of the Cross) so profoundly influenced John Paul II that his meditation on the vocation of woman needs be seen also in relation to her thought.[9] John Paul II offers a deepened understanding of the contemplative tradition, an understanding which clarifies that both woman and man are fully human subjects in their own right, as well as in co-equal relation to each other. This equality in *relation* likewise clarifies the nature of the collaborative stewardship of our whole environment of earth, wherein the nature/culture dualism that had devalued *woman* as signifying *nature* to be dominated gives way to a non-domination paradigm. John Paul II deepens Scriptural understanding of women's vital contribution in this raised consciousness of co-equal stewardship in relation to woman's unique vocation in all spheres of influence. John Paul II thereby moves beyond the dualisms problematic (since Aristotle) for personalism, at least inasmuch as these dualisms have been appropriated traditionally to privilege the male side.

There is clearly a need for such a reconceptualization that integrates both rational and intuitive modes of knowing (inclusive of the *suprarational* mode of knowing through love), in a way that is irreducible to gender, while appreciating the difference gender makes in an integral model of human experience. The further question arises of how to define the human person in a way that singles out neither man nor woman as more or as less perfect by virtue of masculine or feminine embodiment as a human being. In Western culture, the prevailing male-identified philosophical defining of the human as either "rational animal" or "*res cogitans*" now proves problematic for developing an integral humanism that moves beyond subconscious association of "rational" with man as more intellectual in general than woman.

Neither of these phrases, at our current juncture in history, promises any longer to deepen insight into what is distinctively *human* about the integration of the rational mode of intellectual knowing (i.e., knowing through so-called "discursive reasoning") and the suprarational contemplative mode of knowing through love in a way that revalues the latter as the highest of human values. What is needed is precisely a reformulated definition of human being that retains all that is true in the traditional notion of "rational animal," yet does so in a way that clearly and explicitly transcends patriarchy and feminism alike.[10]

John Paul II thus speaks on women in a way that advances discourse in continuity with groundwork laid by Maritain, while also anticipating the emphasis that will be placed by his successor, Pope Benedict XVI, on the centrality of relation to our understanding of person. John Paul II moves decisively beyond any form of feminism that would privilege male-embodiment as the frame of reference by defining woman simply as an *individual,* rather than as a *person* who is embodied as a woman. John Paul II moves forward in covering much more extensive ground in the direction of a newer paradigm, to be further developed practically, in regard to accommodating even—or also—in the public sphere the vital contribution of women who are mothers. Such a standpoint is new in history. It is a viewpoint no longer predicated on the presupposition that while woman is equal to man as a human being, she is functionally unequal in body *and in rationality* to the human being as male, and so she is less fit for the public sphere.

Against this historical backdrop, we can appreciate how surely and decisively this pope moved in recognizing true insights within modern feminist thought, while moving to rectify the mistake in some schools of feminist thought of disowning the female body—albeit precisely in an effort to see woman, too, as a fully human *individual,* in order to overcome women's inequality of rights in the heretofore male-defined public sphere. In order to integrate what he considered to be true insights of the women's movement, in his 1995 letter addressed directly to all women, Pope John Paul II speaks boldly on behalf of women's rights:

> I cannot fail to express my admiration for those women of good will who have devoted their lives to defending the dignity of womanhood by fighting for their basic social, economic and political rights, demonstrating courageous initiative at a time when this was considered extremely inappropriate, the sign of a lack of femininity, a manifestation of exhibitionism, and even a sin!

He *instructs* us, too, in his *World Day of Peace Message* of that same year, that "when one looks at the great process of women's liberation, the journey has been a difficult and complicated one and, at times, not without its share of mistakes, but it has been substantially a positive one, even if it is still unfinished." With his new focus on woman as a subject of inquiry, this pope thus overcomes a historic impasse. He moves beyond the presuppositions about woman's nature that are traceable intellectually to Aristotle's time yet have been transmitted through subsequent human history in culture as a whole, both within and outside of Catholic tradition. This cultural "logic" has imaginatively rendered woman—precisely in her embodiment as a human female in the temporal order—as less perfect compared with the embodiment as a human male. In sharp contrast, we have Pope John Paul II's perspective of an *integral* model of human experience, one that is grounded in the contemplative dimension of love: the Virgin Mary comes to signify not only the vocation of *woman* but also the common *human* values expressive of the deepest spiritual dimension of the human person irrespective of gender.

This pope avoids the triple mistakes of defining woman as inferior, as the same, or as superior. He moves the dialogue forward with his presentation of man and woman as distinct and mutually complementary yet equal when realizing the highest potential of contemplative persons knowing through love.

This pope's writings thus demonstrate a heightened consciousness of the dynamic, interactive, and ongoing *relation* between nature and culture. His writings move us beyond an exclusively linguistic or cultural model that would reduce human experience to the dimension of socially constructed "gender," as well as beyond a model that reduces to the formula: "biology is destiny."

In his teaching specifically on marriage, the pope again moves away from the long-prevailing patriarchal model of male rule toward a bilaterally reciprocal relation of spouses as a gift one to the other. John Paul II thereby brings to the foreground the potential contribution of women, not only in the family and in spiritual motherhood but in the public sphere of education and culture, toward deepening *human* values in transforming culture at large and as a whole.

In short, this pope's historical consciousness is not *retrospective*, in the sense of reinforcing historically prevailing male dominance, but rather *prospective*, in the sense of overcoming—removing—that dominance. The fruitful results of this courageous examination by Pope John Paul II of past ideas on women for the sake of the future are spelled out in the present volume's sifting through of relevant passages from his papal encyclicals, letters, writings, and speeches.

I conclude my sketch with words from his *Letter to Women*:

> Unfortunately, we are heirs to a history which has *conditioned* us to a remarkable extent. In every time and place, this conditioning has been an obstacle to the progress of women. Women's dignity has been unacknowledged and their prerogatives misrepresented; they have been relegated to the margins of society and even reduced to servitude. This has prevented women from truly being themselves, and it has resulted in a spiritual impoverishment of humanity. Certainly it is no easy task to assign the blame for this, considering the many kinds of cultural conditioning which down through the centuries have shaped ways of thinking and acting. And if objective blame for this, especially in particular historical contexts, has belonged to not just a few members of the Church, for this I am truly sorry. May this regret be transformed into a renewed commitment of fidelity to the Gospel vision.... Yes, it is time to *examine the past with courage*...

The time has come for the future to bestow further relevance to John Paul II's writings on women. This book on Pope John Paul II's reflections on woman meets a pressing need of our time for a ready-at-hand reference enabling the reader to see, in full context, what this pope actually said in relation to women's coming of age historically and Catholic tradition. He himself encouraged women, from the vantage point of their own historically situated experiences, further to develop what he has adumbrated in his texts on women.

The principle of organization of this book is both thematic (John Paul II's writings on women) and historically layered (i.e., arranged temporally over the term of his papacy by date). Since this pope addressed the situation of women from the very beginning of his Pontificate, this chronological order or the "historically layering" of his writings best showcases the development in historical context of his thought. Besides this General Introduction to the volume as a whole, six texts (Readings 1, 6, 9, 10, 12, and 23) have their own introductions.

NOVEMBER 1979–DECEMBER 1982

INTRODUCTION TO READING 1 BY SR. PAULA JEAN MILLER, FSE

John Paul II intended, in his *Theology of the Body*, to develop an "adequate anthropology" that would provide a sacramental understanding (a) of creation, (b) of complementary sexual human bodies integral to a theology of marriage, and (c) of foundational principles for sexual morality. Such an adequate anthropology requires the integration of the physical, psychological, intellectual, social, and spiritual aspects of the human person through an integral vision of the human person, an "*integrum*": the Divine Call of every man and woman to eternal life with God and others.

Recognizing that modern philosophy did not provide an adequate understanding of the human person, the Holy Father set out to remedy the situation by providing the Church and the world with a theological, Christological anthropology. Pope John Paul II "re-read" each dimension of the human person in the light of the creation of humanity in the image and toward the likeness of God, as proclaimed in Genesis 1–3. The Pope's insights became more complex because he acknowledged that this *Protoevangelium* was not depicting history as we know it but rather presented humanity in its *Original Innocence* prior to the choice of sin (i.e., when man and woman severed themselves from a relationship with God and thus from immortality).

The *Theology of the Body* is developed within a threefold dynamic: (1) the Garden experience existed on "the threshold" of history and continues to exist within each historical person as an "echo" or a standard of the way life "should be"; (2) the Historical experience is a time of "groaning" and of redemption, of cooperating choice by choice in the restoration of human existence through Christ; of creating an Incarnate communion of persons that is the Image of God: the Perfect Communion of Persons; (3) the Eschatological State is a time of fulfillment: the created communion of persons is divinized and participates in the Divine Communion of Persons. It is the human body, John Paul says, that *links* together all three human experiences: pre-history, history, and post-history. For historical man and woman, there is no "going back" to Original Innocence; human beings can only go forward toward the Eschaton, living into the redemptive process by "tuning in" to the "echo" and responding to God as a "new creation" in Christ.

The first three chapters of Genesis provide a blueprint of the "echo" of the adequate anthropology of Original Innocence; by re-reading it in faith, human persons can develop into images of God in an incarnate communion of persons. The elemental process contained in the blueprint is described by John Paul in a sequence of "Originals": Original Solitude, Original Unity, Original Nakedness and, finally, through the Nuptial Meaning of the Body: redemptive, spousal love.

In a brevity that risks diminishing the profound truth of the Pope's insight, the initial stage of Original Solitude is the experience of "bodiliness" that man and woman hold in common, an experience of being an embodied person that underlies and "preexists" the duality of sexual differentiation as male and female. This Original Solitude is not loneliness, but it is an aloneness that is inherent in the experience of personal transcendence, of not being reduced to a body that can become an object to another rather than a subject in relation with another. Pope John Paul identifies this relationship as "brother-sister," of existing beside each other within the same humanity; the love of the bride and the beloved in the Song of Songs; a time of interpersonal affirmation while awaiting the GIFT of interpersonal Communion.

Original Unity emerges from this common humanity only through the Divine Action, symbolized by "*tardemah*" (i.e., as humanity is immersed in an unconscious, inactive sleep and reemerges as male and female), "two ways of being a body" (*'is* and *'issah*). Male and female are created by God as equal and consubstantial, existing now "for" each other as a GIFT. This physical sexual duality is the foundation for complementarity in the psychological, intellectual, social, and spiritual spheres; it provides the raw material for the fertility of the relationship and thus for an incarnate communion of persons initiated through marriage and the family.

Once established in this relationship, man and woman reach the moment of truth, the moment of choice, the moment of self-determination to be or not to be an image of the Divine Communion of Persons. This is Original Nakedness, the opportunity either for the fullness of interpersonal communication in and through the body in trust, of total vulnerability and self-donation, or for "grasping" and possessing the other as an "object for me," of reducing the other from transcendence to a means for self-pleasure and gratification. The latter constitutes the experience of Shame and distrust, symbolized by covering up the body with fig leaves. Rather than existing "with and for" someone in the nuptial meaning of the body in a mutual exchange of the GIFT, man and woman then become threats to individualized, controlled existences.

To be an Image of God, man and woman must know each other reciprocally in the gift of a "third." The norm of human existence is to live as a GIFT—for each other and for every "third" that is the fruit of their mutual interpenetration in a love that is a participation in the KENOSIS of the Three Persons of God.

We all know the end of the story of our pre-history: Adam and Eve made the wrong choice and were "booted out" of the Garden into History, but with a Promise. If they could "get it together," a Redeemer would come from the fruit of their loins; in other words, the Nuptial Meaning of the body in redemptive, spousal love will be a realized possibility.

Historical existence is the time of learning how to love like God in the mutuality of self-gift in and through the body. It is a time to experience the human body as the revelation of God because the body is created as a sacramental entrance point into an incarnate communion of persons that makes visible the Invisible: the Divine Communion of Persons. The sacramental marriage of man and woman makes visible in an initial way the Invisible Marriage that is the Trinity. In this Grand Plan, the MYSTERY proclaimed by Paul, the body is the *link* that in the True End has been chosen by God to radiate his kenotic, fruitful love, incarnated and divinized forever in Interpersonal Communion.

Sr. Paula Jean Miller, FSE, is the former director of Catholic Studies for the University of St. Thomas, Houston, and is now professor of theology for St. Patrick's Seminary in Menlo Park, Calif. She was appointed by Pope Benedict XVI as Theological Expert for the Synod of Bishops held in Rome, Italy, October 7–28, 2012.

READING 1 (NOVEMBER 7, 1979): Original Unity of Man and Woman[1]

1. The words of Genesis, "It is not good that the man should be alone" (2:18) are a prelude to the narrative of the creation of woman. Together with this narrative, the sense of original solitude becomes part of the meaning of original unity, the key point of which seems to be precisely the words of Genesis 2:24. Christ referred to them in his talk with the Pharisees: "A man shall leave his father and mother and be joined to his wife, and the two shall become one flesh" (Mt 19:5). If Christ quoted these words referring to the "beginning," it is opportune for us to clarify the meaning of that original unity, which has its roots in the fact of the creation of man as male and female.

The narrative of the first chapter of Genesis does not know the problem of man's original solitude. Man is "male and female" right from the beginning. On the contrary, the Yahwist text of the second chapter authorizes us, in a way, to think first only of the man since, by means of the body, he belongs to the visible world but goes beyond it. Then, it makes us think of the same man but through the dualism of sex.

Corporality and sexuality are not completely identified. Although the human body in its normal constitution bears within it the signs of sex and is by its nature male or female, the fact, however, that man is a "body" belongs to the structure of the personal subject more deeply than the fact that in his somatic constitution he is also male or female; therefore, the meaning of "original solitude," which can be referred simply to "man," is substantially prior to the meaning of original unity. The latter is based on masculinity and femininity, as if on two different "incarnations," that is, on two ways of "being a body" of the same human being created "in the image of God" (Gen 1:27).

Dialogue between Man and God-Creator

2. Following the Yahwist text, in which the creation of woman was described separately (Gen 2:21-22), we must have before our eyes, at the same time, that "image of God" of the first narrative of creation. In language and in style, the second narrative keeps all the characteristics of the Yahwist text. The way of narrating agrees with the way of thinking and expressing oneself of the period to which the text belongs.

Following the contemporary philosophy of religion and that of language, it can be said that the language in question is a mythical one. In this case, the term "myth" does not designate a fabulous content but merely an archaic way of expressing a deeper content. Without any difficulty we discover that content, under the layer of the ancient narrative. It is really marvelous as regards the qualities and the condensation of the truths contained in it.

Let us add that up to a certain point, the second narrative of the creation of man keeps the form of a dialogue between man and God-Creator. That is manifested above all in that stage in which man (*'adam*) is definitively created as male and female (*'is-'issah*).[2] The creation takes place almost simultaneously in two dimensions: the action of God-Yahweh who creates occurs in correlation with the process of human consciousness.

God-Yahweh says: "It is not good that the man should be alone; I will make him a helper fit for him" (Gen 2:18). At the same time, the man confirms his own solitude (cf. Gen 2:20). Next we read: "So the Lord God caused a deep sleep to fall upon the man, and while he slept took one of his ribs and closed up its place with flesh. The rib which the Lord God had taken from the man he made into a woman" (Gen 2:21-22). Considering the specific language, first it must be recognized that in the Genesis account, that sleep in which the man is immersed—thanks to God-Yahweh—in preparation for the new creative act, gives us food for thought.

Against the background of contemporary mentality, accustomed—through analysis of the subconscious—to connecting sexual contents with the world of dreams, that sleep may bring forth a particular association;[3] however, the Bible narrative seems to go beyond the dimension of man's subconscious. If we admit, moreover, a significant difference of vocabulary, we can conclude that the man (*'adam*) falls into that "sleep" in order to wake up "male" and "female." In Genesis 2:23, we come across the distinction *'is-'issah* for the first time. Perhaps, therefore, the analogy of sleep indicates here not so much a passing from consciousness to subconsciousness as a specific return to non-being (sleep contains an element of annihilation of man's conscious existence), that is, to the moment preceding the creation, in order that, through God's creative initiative, solitary "man" may emerge from it again in his double unity as male and female.[4]

In any case, in the light of the context of Genesis 2:18-20, there is no doubt that man falls into that "sleep" with the desire of finding a being like himself. If, by analogy with sleep, we can speak here also of a dream, we must say that the biblical archetype allows us to admit as the content of that dream a "second self." It is also personal and equally referred to the situation of original solitude, that is, to the whole process of the stabilization of human identity in relation to living beings (*animalia*) as a whole, since it is the process of man's "differentiation" from this environment. In this way, the circle of the solitude of the man-person is broken, because the first "man" awakens from his sleep as "male and female."

The Same Humanity

4. The woman is made "with the rib" that God-Yahweh had taken from the man. Considering the archaic, metaphorical, and figurative way of expressing the thought, we can establish that it is a question here of homogeneity of the whole being of both. This homogeneity concerns above all the body, the somatic structure. It is also confirmed by the man's first words to the woman who has been created: "This at last is bone of my bones and flesh of my flesh" (Gen 2:23).[5] The words quoted refer also to the humanity of the male. They must be read in the context of the affirmations made before the creation of the woman, in which, although the "incarnation" of the man does not yet exist, she is defined as "a helper fit for him" (cf. Gen 2:18 and 2:20).[6] In this way, therefore, the woman is created, in a sense, on the basis of the same humanity.

Somatic homogeneity, in spite of the difference in constitution bound up with the sexual difference, is so evident that the man, on waking up from the genetic sleep, expresses it at once, when he says: "This at last is bone of my bones and flesh of my flesh—she shall be called woman, because she was taken out of man" (Gen 2:23). In this way, the man manifests for the first time joy and even exaltation, for which he had no reason before, owing to the lack of a being like himself. Joy in the other human being, in the second "self," dominates the words spoken by the man on seeing the woman. All this helps to establish the full meaning of original unity. The words here are few, but each one is of great weight. We must take into account—and we will do so also later—the fact that the first woman, "made with the rib ... taken from the man," is at once accepted as a fit helper for him. We shall return to this same subject, that is, the meaning of the original unity of man and of woman in humanity, in the next meditation.

READING 2 (NOVEMBER 14, 1979): Man Becomes the Image of God by Communion of Persons[1]

1. Following the narrative of Genesis, we have seen that the "definitive" creation of man consists in the creation of the unity of two beings. Their *unity denotes* above all *the identity of human nature; their duality, on the other hand, manifests what, on the basis of this identity, constitutes the masculinity and femininity* of created man. This ontological dimension of unity and duality has, at the same time, an axiological meaning. From the text of Genesis 2:23 and from the whole context, it is clearly seen that man was created as a particular value before God. "God saw everything that he had made, and behold, it was very good" (Gen 1:31). Man was also created as a particular value for himself—first, because he is man; second, because the woman is for the man, and vice versa, the man is for the woman.

While the first chapter of Genesis expresses this value in a purely theological form (and indirectly a metaphysical one), the second chapter, on the other hand, *reveals, so to speak, the first circle of the experience lived by man as value*. This experience is already inscribed in the meaning of original solitude and then in the whole narrative of the creation of man as male and female. The concise text of Genesis 2:23, which contains the words of the first man at the sight of the woman created, "taken out of him," can be considered the biblical prototype of the Canticle of Canticles. If it is possible to read impressions and emotions through words so remote, one might almost venture to say that the depth and force of this first and "original" emotion of the male-man in the presence of the humanity of the woman, and at the same time in the presence of the femininity of the other human being, seems something unique and unrepeatable.

Unity in "Communion of Persons"

2. In this way, the meaning of man's original unity, through masculinity and femininity, is expressed as an overcoming of the frontier of solitude. At the same time, it is an affirmation—with regard to both human beings—of everything that constitutes man in solitude. In the Bible narrative, solitude is the way that leads to that unity which, following Vatican II, we can define as *communio personarum*.[2]

As we have already seen, in his original solitude man acquires a personal consciousness in the process of distinction from all living beings (*animalia*). At the same time, in this solitude, he opens up to a being akin to himself, defined in Genesis (2:18, 20) as "a helper fit for him." This opening is no less decisive for the person of man; in fact, it is perhaps even more decisive than the distinction itself. In the Yahwist narrative, man's solitude is presented to us not only as the first discovery of the characteristic transcendence peculiar to the person, but it is also presented as the discovery of an adequate relationship "to" the person and therefore as an opening and expectation of a "communion of persons."

The term "community" could also be used here, if it were not generic and did not have so many meanings. *Communio* expresses more, with greater precision, since it *indicates precisely that "help" which is derived, in a sense, from the very fact of existing as a person "beside" a person*. In the Bible narrative, this fact becomes *eo ipso*—in itself—the existence of *the person "for" the person*, since man in his original solitude was, in a way, already in this relationship. That is confirmed, in a negative sense, precisely by this solitude.

The communion of persons could be formed only on the basis of a "double solitude" of man and of woman, that is, as their meeting in their distinction from the world of living beings (*animalia*), which gave them both the possibility of being and existing in a special reciprocity. The concept of "help" also expresses this reciprocity in existence, which no other living being could have ensured. All that constituted the foundation of the solitude of each of them was indispensable for this reciprocity. Self-knowledge and self-determination, that is, subjectivity and consciousness of the meaning of one's own body, was also indispensable.

Image of Inscrutable Divine Communion

3. In the first chapter, the narrative of the creation of man affirms directly, right from the beginning, that man was created in the image of God as male and female. The narrative of the second chapter, on the other hand, does not speak of the "image of God," but in its own way it reveals that the complete and definitive creation of "man" (subjected first to the experience of original solitude) is expressed in giving life to that *communio personarum* that man and woman form. In this way, the Yahwist narrative agrees with the content of the first narrative.

If, vice versa, we wish to draw also from the narrative of the Yahwist text the concept of the "image of God," we can then deduce that *man became the "image and likeness" of God not only through his own humanity but also through the communion of persons* which man and woman form right from the beginning. The function of the image is to reflect the one who is the model, to reproduce its own prototype. Man becomes the image of God not so much in the moment of solitude as in the moment of communion. Right "from the beginning," he is not only an image in which the solitude of a person who rules the world is reflected, but also, and essentially, an image of an inscrutable divine *communion of persons.*

In this way, the second narrative could also be a preparation for understanding the Trinitarian concept of the "image of God," even if the latter appears only in the first narrative. Obviously, that is not without significance for the theology of the body. Perhaps it even constitutes the deepest theological aspect of all that can be said about man. In the mystery of creation—on the basis of the original and constituent "solitude" of his being—man was endowed with a deep unity between what is, humanly and through the body, male in him and what is, equally humanly and through the body, female in him. On all this, right from the beginning, the blessing of fertility descended, linked with human procreation (cf. Gen 1:28).

The Body Reveals Man

4. In this way, we find ourselves almost at the heart of the anthropological reality that has the name "body." The words of Genesis 2:23 speak of it directly and for the first time in the following terms: "flesh of my flesh and bone of my bones." The male-man uttered these words, as if it were only at the sight of the woman that he was able to identify and call by name *what makes them visibly similar to each other*, and at the same time *what manifests humanity*.

In the light of the preceding analysis of all the "bodies" which man has come into contact with and which he has defined, conceptually giving them their name (*animalia*), the expression "flesh of my flesh" takes on precisely this meaning: the body reveals man. This concise formula already contains everything that human science could ever say about the structure of the body as organism, about its vitality, and its particular sexual physiology, etc. This first expression of the man, "flesh of my flesh," also contains a reference to what makes that body truly human; therefore, it referred to what determines man as a person, that is, as a being who, even in all his corporality, is similar to God.[3]

Meaning of Unity

We find ourselves, therefore, almost at the very core of the anthropological reality, the name of which is "body," the human body; however, as can easily be seen, this core is not only anthropological but also essentially theological. Right from the beginning, the theology of the body is bound up with the creation of man in the image of God. It becomes, in a way, also the theology of sex, or rather the theology of masculinity and femininity, which has its starting point here in Genesis.

The original meaning of unity, to which the words of Genesis 2:24 bear witness, will have in the revelation of God an ample and distant perspective. This unity through the body—"and the two will be one flesh"—possesses a multiform dimension. It possesses an ethical dimension, as is confirmed by Christ's answer to the Pharisees in Matthew 19 (cf. Mk 10). It also has a sacramental dimension, a strictly theological one, as is proved by St. Paul's words to the Ephesians[4] which refer also to the tradition of the prophets (Hosea, Isaiah, Ezekiel). This is so because that unity which is realized through the body indicates, right from the beginning, not only the "body" but also the "incarnate" communion of persons—*communio personarum*—and calls for this communion right from the beginning.

Masculinity and femininity express *the dual aspect of man's somatic constitution* ("This at last is bone of my bones and flesh of my flesh") and indicate, furthermore, through the same words of Genesis 2:23, *the new consciousness of the sense of one's own body*: a sense which, it can be said, consists in a mutual enrichment. Precisely this consciousness, through which humanity is formed again as the communion of persons, seems to be the layer which in the narrative of the creation of man (and in the revelation of the body contained in it) is deeper than his somatic structure as male and female. In any case, this structure is presented right from the beginning with a deep consciousness of human corporality and sexuality, and that establishes an inalienable norm for the understanding of man on the theological plane.

READING 3 (DECEMBER 19, 1979): Fullness of Interpersonal Communication[1]

1. What is shame and how can we explain its absence in the state of original innocence, in the depth of the mystery of the creation of man as male and female? From contemporary analyses of shame—and in particular of sexual modesty—we can deduce the complexity of this fundamental experience, in which man expresses himself as a person according to his own specific structure. In the experience of shame, the human being experiences fear with regard to his "second self," for example, woman before man. This is substantially fear for one's own "self." With shame, the human being manifests almost instinctively the need of affirmation and acceptance of this "self," according to its rightful value. He experiences it at the same time both within himself and externally, before the "other." Shame is a complex experience. Almost keeping one human being away from the other (woman from man), it seeks at the same time to draw them closer personally, creating a suitable basis and level to do so.

For the same reason, it has a fundamental significance as regards the formation of ethos in human society, and especially in the man-woman relationship. The analysis of shame clearly indicates how deeply it is rooted precisely in mutual relations, how exactly it expresses the essential rules for the "communion of persons," and likewise how deeply it touches the dimension of man's original "solitude." The appearance of shame in the subsequent biblical narration of chapter 3 of Genesis has a pluri-dimensional significance. It will be opportune to resume the analysis in due time. On the other hand, what does its original absence mean in Genesis 2:25: "They were both naked and were not ashamed"?

Misleading Analogies

2. It is necessary to establish in the first place that it is a question of a real non-presence of shame, and not a lack or underdevelopment of it. We cannot in any way sustain here a "primitivization" of its meaning. The text of Genesis 2:25 does not only exclude decisively the possibility of thinking of a "lack of shame" or immodesty; even more, it excludes the possibility of explaining it by analogy with some positive human experiences, such as those of childhood or of the life of so-called primitive peoples. These analogies are insufficient and can even be misleading. The words of Genesis 2:25, "They were not ashamed," do not express a lack, but, on the contrary, serve to indicate a particular fullness of consciousness and experience. Above all, they indicate a full understanding of the meaning of the body, bound up with the fact that they were naked.

The continuation of the Yahwist narrative testifies that this is how the text quoted is to be understood and interpreted. In it, the appearance of shame, and in particular of sexual modesty, is connected with the loss of that original fullness. Taking the experience of shame as a "borderline" experience, we must ask ourselves to what the meaning of the original nakedness of which Genesis 2:25 speaks corresponds? To what fullness of conscience and experience, and in particular to what full understanding of the meaning of the body, does the meaning of original nakedness correspond?

Fullness of Consciousness

3. To answer this question, we must keep in mind the analytical process carried out so far, which has its basis in the Yahwist passage as a whole. In this context, man's original solitude was manifested as "non-identification"

of his own humanity with the world of living beings (*animalia*) that surround him. This non-identification, following upon the creation of man as male and female, made way for the happy discovery of one's own humanity with the help of the other human being. The man recognized and found again his own humanity with the help of the woman (cf. Gen 2:25). At the same time, this act of theirs realized a perception of the world, which was carried out directly through the body ("flesh of my flesh"). It was the direct and visible source of the experience that arrived at establishing their unity in humanity. It is easy to understand that nakedness corresponds to that fullness of consciousness of the meaning of the body, deriving from the typical perception of the senses.

One can think of this fullness in categories of truth of being or of reality, and it can be said that man and woman were originally given to each other precisely according to this truth, since they were naked. In analyzing the meaning of original nakedness, this dimension absolutely cannot be disregarded. This participating in perception of the world—in its "exterior" aspect—is a direct and almost spontaneous fact. It is prior to any "critical" complication of knowledge and of human experience and is seen as closely connected with the experience of the meaning of the human body. The original innocence of "knowledge" could already be perceived in this way.

Meaning of Communication

4. It is not possible to determine the meaning of original nakedness considering only man's participation in exterior perception of the world. It is not possible to establish it without going into the depths of man. Genesis 2:25 introduces us specifically to this level and wants us to seek there the original innocence of knowing. The dimension of human interiority is necessary to explain and measure that particular fullness of interpersonal communication, thanks to which man and woman were naked and were not ashamed.

In our conventional language, the concept of communication has been practically alienated from its deepest, original semantic matrix. It is connected mainly with the sphere of the media, that is, for the most part, products that serve for understanding, exchange, and bringing closer together. Conversely, it can be supposed that, in its original and deeper meaning, communication was and is directly connected with subjects. They communicate precisely on the basis of the common union that exists between them, both to reach and to express a reality that is peculiar and pertinent only to the sphere of person-subjects. In this way, the human body acquires a completely new meaning, which cannot be placed on the plane of the remaining "external" perception of the world. It expresses the person in his ontological and existential concreteness, which is something more than the individual; therefore the body expresses the personal human "self," which derives its exterior perception from within.

Man's Vision of God

5. The whole biblical narrative, and in particular the Yahwist text, shows that the body through its own visibility manifests man. In manifesting him, it acts as intermediary, that is, it enables man and woman, right from the beginning, to communicate with each other according to that *communio personarum* willed by the Creator precisely for them. It seems that only this dimension enables us rightly to understand the meaning of original nakedness. In this connection, any "naturalistic" criterion is bound to fail, while, on the contrary, the "personalistic" criterion can be of great help. Genesis 2:25 certainly speaks of something extraordinary, which is outside the limits of the shame known through human experience. At the same time, it decides the particular fullness of interpersonal communication, rooted at the very heart of that *communio*, which is thus revealed and developed. In this connection, the words "they were not ashamed" can mean *in sensu obliquo* only an original depth in affirming what is inherent in the person, what is "visibly" female and male, through which the personal intimacy of mutual communication in all its radical simplicity and purity is constituted. To this fullness of exterior perception, expressed by means of physical nakedness, there corresponds the interior fullness of man's vision in God, that is, according to the measure of the "image of God" (cf. Gen 1:17). According to this measure, man "is" really naked ("They were naked"—Gen 2:25),[2] even before realizing it (cf. Gen 3:7-10). We shall still have to complete the analysis of this important text during the meditations that follow.

READING 4 (FEBRUARY 13, 1980): Original Innocence and Man's Historical State[1]

1. TODAY'S MEDITATION presupposes what has already been established by the various analyses made up to now. They sprang from the answer Jesus gave to his interlocutors (cf. Mt 19:3-9; Mk 10:1-12). They had asked him a question about the indissolubility and unity of marriage. The Master had urged them to consider carefully that which was "from the beginning." For this reason, so far in this series of meditations we have tried to reproduce somehow the reality of the union, or rather of the communion of persons, lived "from the beginning" by the man and the woman. Subsequently, we tried to penetrate the content of Genesis 2:25, which is so concise: "And the man and his wife were both naked, and were not ashamed."

These words refer to the gift of original innocence, revealing its character synthetically, so to speak. On this basis, theology has constructed the global image of man's original innocence and justice, prior to original sin, by applying the method of objectivization, proper to metaphysics and metaphysical anthropology. In this analysis, we are trying rather to consider the aspect of human subjectivity. The latter, moreover, seems to be closer to the original texts, especially the second narrative of creation, the Yahwist text.

⇝

2. Apart from a certain diversity of interpretation, it seems quite clear that "the experience of the body," such as it can be inferred from the ancient text of Genesis 2:23 and even more from Genesis 2:25, indicates a degree of "spiritualization" of man. This is different from that which the same text speaks of after original sin (cf. Gen 3) and which we know from the experience of historical man. It is a different measure of "spiritualization." It involves another composition of the interior forces of man himself. It involves almost another body-soul relationship, and other inner proportions between sensitivity, spirituality, and affectivity, that is, another degree of interior sensitiveness to the gifts of the Holy Spirit. All this conditions man's state of original innocence and at the same time determines it, permitting us also to understand the narrative of Genesis. Theology and also the Magisterium of the Church have given these fundamental truths a specific form.[2]

Permanent Roots of "*Ethos*" of the Body

3. Undertaking the analysis of the beginning according to the dimension of the theology of the body, we do so on the basis of Christ's words in which he himself referred to that "beginning." When he said: "Have you not read that he who made them from the beginning made them male and female?" (Mt 19:4), he ordered us and he still orders us to return to the depths of the mystery of creation. We do so, fully aware of the gift of original innocence, characteristic of man before original sin. An insuperable barrier divides us from what man then was as male and female, by means of the gift of grace united with the mystery of creation, and from what they both were for each other, as a mutual gift. Yet we try to understand that state of original innocence in its connection with man's historical state after original sin: "*status naturae lapsae simul et redemptae*."[3]

Through the category of the historical *a posteriori*, we try to arrive at the original meaning of the body. We try to grasp the connection existing between it and the nature of original innocence in the "experience of the body," as it is highlighted in such a significant way in the Genesis narrative. We conclude that it is important and essential to define this connection, not only with regard to man's "theological prehistory," in which the life of the couple was almost completely permeated by the grace of original innocence. We must also define this connection in relation to its possibility of revealing to us the permanent roots of the human and especially the theological aspect of the *ethos* of the body.

Ethically Conditioned

4. Man enters the world and enters the most intimate pattern of his future and his history with awareness of the nuptial meaning of his own body, of his own masculinity and femininity. Original innocence says that that meaning is conditioned "ethically," and furthermore, that on its part, it constitutes the future of the human *ethos*. This is very important for the theology of the body. It is the reason why we must construct this theology "from the beginning," carefully following the indication of Christ's words.

In the mystery of creation, man and woman were "given" in a special way to each other by the Creator. That was not only in the dimension of that first human couple and of that first communion of persons but in the whole perspective of the existence of the human family. The fundamental fact of human existence at every stage of its history is that God "created them male and female." He always creates them in this way and they are always such. Understanding of the fundamental meanings contained in the mystery of creation, such as the nuptial meaning of the body (and of the fundamental conditionings of this meaning), is important. It is indispensable in order to know who man is and who he should be, and therefore how he should mold his own activity. It is an essential and important thing for the future of the human *ethos*.

⇻

5. Genesis 2:24 notes that the two, man and woman, were created for marriage: "Therefore, a man leaves his father and his mother and cleaves to his wife, and they become one flesh." In this way, a great creative perspective is opened. It is precisely the perspective of man's existence, which is continually renewed by means of procreation, or, we could say, self-reproduction.

This perspective is deeply rooted in the consciousness of humanity (cf. Gen 2:23) and also in the particular consciousness of the nuptial meaning of the body (Gen 2:25). Before becoming husband and wife (later Gen 4:1 speaks of this in the concrete), the man and the woman emerge from the mystery of creation in the first place as brother and sister in the same humanity. Understanding the nuptial meaning of the body in its masculinity and femininity reveals the depths of their freedom, which is freedom of giving.

From here that communion of persons begins, in which both meet and give themselves to each other in the fullness of their subjectivity. Both grow as persons-subjects. They grow mutually one for the other also through their body and through that nakedness free of shame. In this communion of persons the whole depth of the original solitude of man (of the first one and of all) is perfectly ensured. At the same time, this solitude becomes in a marvelous way permeated and broadened by the gift of the "other." If the man and the woman cease to be a disinterested gift for each other, as they were in the mystery of creation, then they recognize that "they are naked" (cf. Gen 3). Then the shame of that nakedness, which they had not felt in the state of original innocence, will spring up in their hearts. Original innocence manifests and at the same time constitutes the perfect *ethos* of the gift.

READING 5 (OCTOBER 15, 1980):
Gospel Values and Duties of the Human Heart[1]

1. During our Wednesday meetings, we have analyzed in detail the words of the Sermon on the Mount, in which Christ referred to the human heart. As we now know, his words are exacting. Christ said, "You have heard that it was said, 'You shall not commit adultery.' But I say to you that everyone who looks at a woman lustfully has already committed adultery with her *in his heart*" (Mt 5:27-28). This reference to the heart throws light on the dimension of human interiority, the dimension of the inner man, characteristic of ethics, and even more of the theology of the body. Desire rises in the sphere of the lust of the flesh. It is at the same time an interior and theological reality, which is experienced, in a way, by every "historical" man. It is precisely this man—even if he does not know the words of Christ—who continually asks himself the question about his own heart. Christ's words make this question especially explicit: is the heart accused, or is it called to good? Toward the end of our reflections and analyses we now intend to consider this question, connected with the sentence of the Gospel, so concise and yet categorical at the same time, so pregnant with theological, anthropological, and ethical content. A second question goes hand in hand with it, a more practical one: how can and must he act, the man who accepts Christ's words in the Sermon on the Mount, the man who accepts the ethos of the Gospel, and, in particular, accepts it in this field?

Ethos of Human Practice

2. This man finds in the considerations made up to now the answer, at least an indirect one, to two questions. How *can* he act, that is, on what can he rely in his inner self, at the source of his interior or exterior acts? Further, how *should* he act, that is, in what way do the values known according to the scale revealed in the Sermon on the Mount constitute a duty of his will and his heart, of his desires and his choices? In what way are they binding on him in action and behavior, if, accepted by means of knowledge, they already commit him in thinking and, in a certain way, in feeling? These questions are significant for human praxis and indicate an organic connection of praxis itself with *those*. Lived morality is always the ethos of human practice.

Moral Sensitivity

3. It is possible to answer the aforesaid questions in various ways. In fact, various answers are given, both in the past and today. This is confirmed by an ample literature. In addition to the answers we find in it, it is necessary to consider the infinite number of answers that concrete man gives to these questions by himself, the ones that his conscience, his awareness, and moral sensitivity give repeatedly, in the life of everyone. In this sphere, an *interpenetration of ethos and praxis is carried out*. Here the individual principles live their own life (not exclusively "theoretical"). This not only concerns the norms of morality with their motivations which are worked out and made known by moralists. It also concerns the ones worked out—certainly not without a link with the work of moralists and scientists—by individual men, as authors and direct subjects of real morality, as co-authors of its history. On this the level of morality itself also depends, its progress or its decadence. All this reconfirms, everywhere and always, that historical man to whom Christ once spoke. He proclaimed the good news of the Gospel with the Sermon on the Mount, where he said among other things: "You have heard that it was said, 'You shall not commit adultery.' But I say to you that everyone who looks at a woman lustfully has already committed adultery with her in his heart" (Mt 5:27-28).

Need for Further Analyses

4. Matthew's enunciation is stupendously concise in comparison with everything that has been written on this subject in secular literature. Perhaps its power in the history of *ethos* consists precisely in this. At the same time, it must be realized that the history of ethos flows in a multiform bed, in which the individual currents draw nearer to, or move further away from, one another in turn. Historical man always evaluates his own heart in his own way, just as he also judges his own body, so he passes from the pole of pessimism to the pole of optimism, from puritan severity to modern permissiveness. It is necessary to realize this, in order that the ethos of the Sermon on the Mount may always have due transparency with regard to human actions and behavior. For this purpose it is necessary to make some more analyses.

Words Misunderstood

5. Our reflections on the meaning of the words of Christ according to Matthew 5:27-28 would not be complete if they did not dwell—at least briefly—on what can be called the echo of these words in the history of human thought and of the evaluation of *ethos*. The echo is always a transformation of the voice and of the words that the voice expresses. We know from experience that this transformation is sometimes full of mysterious fascination. In the case in question, the opposite happened. Christ's words have been stripped of their simplicity and depth. A meaning has been conferred far removed from the one expressed in them, a meaning that even contradicts them. We have in mind here all that happened outside Christianity under the name of Manichaeism,[2] and that also tried to enter the ground of Christianity as regards theology itself and the *ethos* of the body. Manichaeism arose in the East outside the biblical environment and sprang from Mazdeistic dualism. It is well known that, in its original form, Manichaeism saw the source of evil in matter, in the body, and therefore condemned everything that is corporeal in man. Since corporeity is manifested in man mainly through sex, the condemnation was extended to marriage and to conjugal life, as well as to other spheres of being and acting in which corporeity is expressed.

Affirmation of the Body

6. To an unaccustomed ear, the evident severity of that system might seem in harmony with the severe words of Matthew 5:29-30, in which Christ spoke of "plucking out one's eye" or "cutting off one's hand," if these members were the cause of scandal. Through the purely material interpretation of these expressions, it was also possible to obtain a Manichaean view of Christ's enunciation, in which he spoke of a man who has "committed adultery in his heart ... by looking at a woman lustfully." In this case, too, the Manichaean interpretation aims at condemning the body, as the real source of evil, since the ontological principle of evil, according to Manichaeism, is concealed and at the same time manifested in it. The attempt was made, therefore, to see *this condemnation in the Gospel, and sometimes it was perceived, where actually only a particular requirement addressed to the human spirit had been expressed.*

Note that the condemnation might—and might always be—a loophole to avoid the requirements set in the Gospel by him who "knew what was in man" (Jn 2:25). History has no lack of proofs. We have already partially had the opportunity (and we will certainly have it again) to show to what extent such a requirement may arise solely from an affirmation—and not from a denial or a condemnation—if it has to lead to an affirmation that is even more mature and deep, objectively and subjectively. The words of Christ according to Matthew 5:27-28 must lead to such an affirmation of the femininity and masculinity of the human being, as the personal dimension of "being a body." This is the right ethical meaning of these words. They impress on the pages of the Gospel a peculiar dimension of ethos in order to impress it subsequently on human life. We will try to take up this subject again in our further reflections.

INTRODUCTION TO READING 6 BY DIANE AND DOMINIC AQUILA

Pope John Paul II delivered *Familiaris Consortio* to the Church and the world on November 22, 1981, in the fourth year of his twenty-seven-year pontificate. As is the custom with apostolic exhortations, *Familiaris Consortio* urged Christians to study and take action on an important and pressing issue, in this case the social pressures on the conjugal family and challenges to its definition and cultural position. *Familiaris Consortio* responded to the work of a synod of bishops that met in late 1980 to consider the state of the modern Christian family. The synod produced a lengthy list of proposals that reaffirmed the Church's long-standing teaching on the family, using a language and pastoral concern reflective of current realities and appealing to modern men and women, and especially young people.

John Paul celebrates Christian families whose lives are witness to the enduring values of the Gospel, amid strong and antagonistic social, economic, and ideological forces. The American reader of *Familiaris Consortio* should not infer some sort of functionalism from the English translation of its title, "The Role of the Christian Family in the Modern World." Certainly, the family as the bedrock of the social order has a crucial "role" or "function" in sustaining and strengthening a society during times of moral and cultural crisis, but the reduction of the Christian family to a sociological function does violence to its dynamism as "an educating community" that encourages each of its members "to discern his [or her] own vocation and to accept responsibility in the search for greater justice, educating [each] from the beginning in interpersonal relationships, rich in justice and love."[1]

The word "vocation" occurs thirty-one times in *Familiaris Consortio*, referring to each person's particular natural and earthly vocation and his or her supernatural and eternal destiny, achieved by perfecting the virtue of self-giving love. St. Francis de Sales characterizes vocation simply as "a firm and constant will in which the person who is called must serve God in the way and in the place to which almighty God has called him."[2]

Having fallen into desuetude among lay Catholics, the idea of vocation enjoyed a renaissance at the Second Vatican Council and occupies a central place in Pope John Paul II's thinking on the modern family. In this volume dedicated to the writings of Pope John Paul II on women, it would be fruitful, especially for Americans, to use the history of the idea of vocation as a hermeneutical key to unlock and unpack sections 22 through 24 of *Familiaris Consortio*, in which John Paul addresses the role of women in the family and in society. He will give fuller treatment to the vocation of women in *Mulieris Dignitatem* (1988).

Beyond its importance to women, the idea of vocation as central to the life of the family is the great desideratum for Christians. The importance of vocation to the fulfillment of a Christian life has a long tradition in American Christianity. According to a survey by the Barna Group, a research organization focused on the intersection of faith and culture, the idea of vocation as it applies to the integration of faith and work is under stress. According to one of Barna's researchers, "It's illuminating to learn how few Christians believe they're called to do what they do." Barna's research challenges "the popular Christian understanding of career as calling, since most Christians in the U.S. don't seem to be thinking about their jobs in terms of calling. Most of the data suggests the concept of calling is not on their radar."[3]

Certainly, work is only one dimension of the meaning of Christian vocation, but in early American Christianity it was one of the three senses of the word. God was the subject of all three senses; man was the object. For New England Puritans, for example, as Edmund Morgan points out in his study of *The Puritan Family*, in the first and widest sense, "God called a man to every right action that he did. If the Puritan felt justified in a given act, he perceived a calling or a call to it." Secondly, vocation was integral to "the process of salvation: God called men to salvation," which required a response. The final sense of vocation signified "the occupation by which a man earned his living." Puritans believed that each Christian was obligated to practice his or her particular craft or occupation "as the work of Christ." In early American Christianity, "the choice of a calling was a solemn affair"[4] in which families played the principal role.

In a number of places in *Familiaris Consortio*, there are implied relations between vocation and work. One important instance of this relation is section 23 on "Women and Society." An explication of the relation of vocation and work, for men and women, would be an important step in the reinvigoration of Christian vocation in America.

Diane Aquila served as a consultant for the Fourth World Congress on Women, held in Beijing in 1995; her degree is in social science. Dominic Aquila, her husband, is the provost for the University of St. Thomas. Together, they are the parents of eleven children.

READING 6 (NOVEMBER 22, 1980): *Familiaris Consortio* (On the Role of the Christian Family in the Modern World)[1]

Man, the Image of the God Who Is Love

11. God created man in His own image and likeness: calling him to existence through love, He called him at the same time for love. God is love and in Himself He lives a mystery of personal loving communion. Creating the human race in His own image and continually keeping it in being, God inscribed in the humanity of man and woman the vocation, and thus the capacity and responsibility, of love and communion. Love is therefore the fundamental and innate vocation of every human being.

As an incarnate spirit, that is a soul which expresses itself in a body and a body informed by an immortal spirit, man is called to love in his unified totality. Love includes the human body, and the body is made a sharer in spiritual love.

Christian revelation recognizes two specific ways of realizing the vocation of the human person in its entirety, to love: marriage and virginity or celibacy. Either one is, in its own proper form, an actuation of the most profound truth of man, of his being "created in the image of God."

Consequently, sexuality, by means of which man and woman give themselves to one another through the acts which are proper and exclusive to spouses, is by no means something purely biological but concerns the innermost being of the human person as such. It is realized in a truly human way only if it is an integral part of the love by which a man and a woman commit themselves totally to one another until death. The total physical self-giving would be a lie if it were not the sign and fruit of a total personal self-giving, in which the whole person, including the temporal dimension, is present: if the person were to withhold something or reserve the possibility of deciding otherwise in the future, by this very fact he or she would not be giving totally.

This totality which is required by conjugal love also corresponds to the demands of responsible fertility. This fertility is directed to the generation of a human being, and so by its nature it surpasses the purely biological order and involves a whole series of personal values. For the harmonious growth of these values, a persevering and unified contribution by both parents is necessary.

The only "place" in which this self-giving in its whole truth is made possible is marriage, the covenant of conjugal love freely and consciously chosen, whereby man and woman accept the intimate community of life and love willed by God Himself which only in this light manifests its true meaning. The institution of marriage is not an undue interference by society or authority, or the extrinsic imposition of a form. Rather it is an interior requirement of the covenant of conjugal love which is publicly affirmed as unique and exclusive, in order to live in complete fidelity to the plan of God, the Creator. A person's freedom, far from being restricted by this fidelity, is secured against every form of subjectivism or relativism and is made a sharer in creative Wisdom.

Marriage and Communion between God and People

12. The communion of love between God and people, a fundamental part of the Revelation and faith experience of Israel, finds a meaningful expression in the marriage covenant which is established between a man and a

woman. For this reason the central word of Revelation, "God loves His people," is likewise proclaimed through the living and concrete word whereby a man and a woman express their conjugal love. Their bond of love becomes the image and the symbol of the covenant which unites God and His people. The same sin which can harm the conjugal covenant becomes an image of the infidelity of the people to their God: idolatry is prostitution; infidelity is adultery; disobedience to the law is abandonment of the spousal love of the Lord, but the infidelity of Israel does not destroy the eternal fidelity of the Lord, and therefore the ever-faithful love of God is put forward as the model of the faithful love which should exist between spouses.

Jesus Christ, Bridegroom of the Church, and the Sacrament of Matrimony

13. The communion between God and His people finds its definitive fulfillment in Jesus Christ, the Bridegroom who loves and gives Himself as the Savior of humanity, uniting it to Himself as His body. He reveals the original truth of marriage, the truth of the "beginning," and, freeing man from his hardness of heart, He makes man capable of realizing this truth in its entirety.

This revelation reaches its definitive fullness in the gift of love which the Word of God makes to humanity in assuming a human nature, and in the sacrifice which Jesus Christ makes of Himself on the Cross for His bride, the Church. In this sacrifice there is entirely revealed that plan which God has imprinted on the humanity of man and woman since their creation; the marriage of baptized persons thus becomes a real symbol of that new and eternal covenant sanctioned in the blood of Christ. The Spirit which the Lord pours forth gives a new heart and renders man and woman capable of loving one another as Christ has loved us. Conjugal love reaches that fullness to which it is interiorly ordained, conjugal charity, which is the proper and specific way in which the spouses participate in and are called to live the very charity of Christ who gave Himself on the Cross.

In a deservedly famous page, Tertullian has well expressed the greatness of this conjugal life in Christ and its beauty: "How can I ever express the happiness of the marriage that is joined together by the Church strengthened by an offering, sealed by a blessing, announced by angels and ratified by the Father? ... How wonderful the bond between two believers with a single hope, a single desire, a single observance, a single service! They are both brethren and both fellow-servants; there is no separation between them in spirit or flesh; in fact they are truly two in one flesh and where the flesh is one, one is the spirit."

Receiving and meditating faithfully on the Word of God, the Church has solemnly taught and continues to teach that the marriage of the baptized is one of the seven sacraments of the New Covenant. Indeed, by means of baptism, man and woman are definitively placed within the new and eternal covenant, in the spousal covenant of Christ with the Church, and it is because of this indestructible insertion that the intimate community of conjugal life and love, founded by the Creator, is elevated and assumed into the spousal charity of Christ, sustained and enriched by His redeeming power.

By virtue of the sacramentality of their marriage, spouses are bound to one another in the most profoundly indissoluble manner. Their belonging to each other is the real representation, by means of the sacramental sign, of the very relationship of Christ with the Church.

Spouses are therefore the permanent reminder to the Church of what happened on the Cross; they are for one another and for the children witnesses to the salvation in which the sacrament makes them sharers. Of this salvation event, marriage, like every sacrament, is a memorial, actuation, and prophecy: "As a memorial, the sacrament gives them the grace and duty of commemorating the great works of God and of bearing witness to them before their children. As actuation, it gives them the grace and duty of putting into practice in the present, towards each other and their children, the demands of a love which forgives and redeems. As prophecy, it gives them the grace and duty of living and bearing witness to the hope of the future encounter with Christ."

Like each of the seven sacraments, so also marriage is a real symbol of the event of salvation, but in its own way.

The spouses participate in it as spouses, together, as a couple, so that the first and immediate effect of marriage (*res et sacramentum*) is not supernatural grace itself, but the Christian conjugal bond, a typically Christian communion of two persons because it represents the mystery of Christ's incarnation and the mystery of His covenant. The content of participation in Christ's life is also specific: conjugal love involves a totality, in which all the elements of the person enter—appeal of the body and instinct, power of feeling and affectivity, aspiration of the spirit and of will. It aims at a deeply personal unity, the unity that, beyond union in one flesh, leads to forming one heart and soul; it demands indissolubility and faithfulness in definitive mutual giving; and it is open to fertility (cf. *Humanae Vitae* 9). In a word it is a question of the normal characteristics of all natural conjugal love, but with a new significance which not only purifies and strengthens them, but raises them to the extent of making them the expression of specifically Christian values.

Children, the Precious Gift of Marriage

14. According to the plan of God, marriage is the foundation of the wider community of the family, since the very institution of marriage and conjugal love are ordained to the procreation and education of children, in whom they find their crowning. In its most profound reality, love is essentially a gift; and conjugal love, while leading the spouses to the reciprocal "knowledge" which makes them "one flesh," does not end with the couple because it makes them capable of the greatest possible gift, the gift by which they become cooperators with God for giving life to a new human person. The couple, while giving themselves to one another, give not just themselves but also the reality of children, who are a living reflection of their love, a permanent sign of conjugal unity and a living and inseparable synthesis of their being a father and a mother.

When they become parents, spouses receive from God the gift of a new responsibility. Their parental love is called to become for the children the visible sign of the very love of God, "from whom every family in heaven and on earth is named."

It must not be forgotten that, even when procreation is not possible, conjugal life does not for this reason lose its value. Physical sterility, in fact, can be for spouses the occasion for other important services to the life of the human person, for example, adoption, various forms of educational work, and assistance to other families and to poor or handicapped children.

The Family, a Communion of Persons

15. In matrimony and in the family, a complex of interpersonal relationships is set up—married life, fatherhood and motherhood, filiation and fraternity—through which each human person is introduced into the "human family" and into the "family of God," which is the Church. Christian

marriage and the Christian family build up the Church: for in the family the human person is not only brought into being and progressively introduced by means of education into the human community, but by means of the rebirth of baptism and education in the faith the child is also introduced into God's family, which is the Church.

The human family, disunited by sin, is reconstituted in its unity by the redemptive power of the death and Resurrection of Christ. Christian marriage, by participating in the salvific efficacy of this event, constitutes the natural setting in which the human person is introduced into the great family of the Church. The commandment to grow and multiply, given to man and woman in the beginning, in this way reaches its whole truth and full realization. The Church thus finds in the family, born from the sacrament, the cradle and the setting in which she can enter the human generations, and where these in their turn can enter the Church.

Marriage and Virginity or Celibacy

16. Virginity or celibacy for the sake of the Kingdom of God not only does not contradict the dignity of marriage but presupposes it and confirms it. Marriage and virginity or celibacy are two ways of expressing and living the one mystery of the covenant of God with His people. When marriage is not esteemed, neither can consecrated virginity or celibacy exist; when human sexuality is not regarded as a great value given by the Creator, the renunciation of it for the sake of the Kingdom of Heaven loses its meaning.

Rightly indeed does St. John Chrysostom say: "Whoever denigrates marriage also diminishes the glory of virginity. Whoever praises it makes virginity more admirable and resplendent. What appears good only in comparison with evil would not be particularly good. It is something better than what is admitted to be good that is the most excellent good."

In virginity or celibacy, the human being is awaiting, also in a bodily way, the eschatological marriage of Christ with the Church, giving himself or herself completely to the Church in the hope that Christ may give Himself to the Church in the full truth of eternal life. The celibate person thus anticipates in his or her flesh the new world of the future resurrection.

By virtue of this witness, virginity or celibacy keeps alive in the Church a consciousness of the mystery of marriage and defends it from any reduction and impoverishment. Virginity or celibacy, by liberating the human heart in a unique way, "so as to make it burn with greater love for God and all humanity," bears witness that the Kingdom of God and His justice is that pearl of great price which is preferred to every other value no matter how great, and hence must be sought as the only definitive value. It is for this reason that the Church, throughout her history, has always defended the superiority of this charism to that of marriage, by reason of the wholly singular link which it has with the Kingdom of God.

In spite of having renounced physical fecundity, the celibate person becomes spiritually fruitful, the father and mother of many, cooperating in the realization of the family according to God's plan. Christian couples, consequently, have the right to expect from celibate persons a good example and a witness of fidelity to their vocation until death. Just as fidelity at times becomes difficult for married people and requires sacrifice, mortification, and self-denial, the same can happen to celibate persons, and their fidelity, even in the trials that may occur, should strengthen the fidelity of married couples. These reflections on virginity or celibacy can enlighten and help those who, for reasons independent of their own will, have been unable to marry and have then accepted their situation in a spirit of service.

The Rights and Role of Women

22. In that it is, and ought always to become, a communion and community of persons, the family finds in love the source and the constant impetus for welcoming, respecting, and promoting each one of its members in his or her lofty dignity as a person, that is, as a living image of God. As the Synod Fathers rightly stated, the moral criterion for the authenticity of conjugal and family relationships consists in fostering the dignity and vocation of the individual persons, who achieve their fullness by sincere self-giving.

In this perspective the Synod devoted special attention to women, to their rights and role within the family and society. In the same perspective are also to be considered men as husbands and fathers, and likewise children and the elderly.

Above all, it is important to underline the equal dignity and responsibility of women with men. This equality is realized in a unique manner in that reciprocal self-giving by each one to the other and by both to the children which is proper to marriage and the family. What human reason intuitively perceives and acknowledges is fully revealed by the Word of God: the history of salvation, in fact, is a continuous and luminous testimony of the dignity of women.

In creating the human race "male and female," God gives man and woman an equal personal dignity, endowing them with the inalienable rights and responsibilities proper to the human person. God then manifests the dignity of women in the highest form possible, by assuming human flesh from the Virgin Mary, whom the Church honors as the Mother of God, calling her the new Eve and presenting her as the model of redeemed woman. The sensitive respect of Jesus towards the women that He called to His following and His friendship, His appearing on Easter morning to a woman before the other disciples, the mission entrusted to women to carry the good news of the Resurrection to the Apostles—these are all signs that confirm the special esteem of the Lord Jesus for women. The Apostle Paul will say: "In Christ Jesus you are all children of God through faith .... There is neither Jew nor Greek, there is neither slave nor free, there is neither male nor female; for you are all one in Christ Jesus."

Women and Society

23. Without intending to deal with all the various aspects of the vast and complex theme of the relationships between women and society, and limiting these remarks to a few essential points, one cannot but observe that in the specific area of family life a widespread social and cultural tradition has considered women's role to be exclusively that of wife and mother, without adequate access to public functions which have generally been reserved for men. There is no doubt that the equal dignity and responsibility of men and women fully justifies women's access to public functions. On the other hand, the true advancement of women requires that clear recognition be given to the value of their maternal and family role, by comparison with all other public roles and all other professions; furthermore, these roles and professions should be harmoniously combined, if we wish the evolution of society and culture to be truly and fully human.

This will come about more easily if, in accordance with the wishes expressed by the Synod, a renewed "theology of work" can shed light upon and study in depth the meaning of work in the Christian life and determine the fundamental bond between work and the family, and therefore the original and irreplaceable meaning of work in the home and in rearing children. The Church can and should help modern society by tirelessly insisting that the work of women in the home be recognized and respected by all in its irreplaceable value. This is of particular importance in education: for possible discrimination between the different types of work and professions is eliminated at its very root once it is clear that all people, in every area, are working with equal rights and equal responsibilities. The image of God in man and in woman will thus be seen with added luster.

While it must be recognized that women have the same right as men to perform various public functions, society must be structured in such a way that wives and mothers are not in practice compelled to work outside the home, and that their families can live and prosper in a dignified way even when they themselves devote their full time to their own family; furthermore, the mentality which honors women more for their work outside the home than for their work within the family must be overcome. This requires that men should truly esteem and love women with total respect for their personal dignity, and that society should create and develop conditions favoring work in the home.

With due respect to the different vocations of men and women, the Church must in her own life promote as far as possible their equality of rights and dignity: and this for the good of all, the family, the Church, and society, but clearly all of this does not mean for women a renunciation of their femininity or an imitation of the male role but the fullness of true feminine humanity which should be expressed in their activity, whether in the family or outside of it, without disregarding the differences of customs and cultures in this sphere.

Offenses Against Women's Dignity

24. Unfortunately, the Christian message about the dignity of women is contradicted by that persistent mentality which considers the human being not as a person but as a thing, as an object of trade, at the service of selfish interest and mere pleasure: the first victims of this mentality are women. This mentality produces very bitter fruits, such as contempt for men and

for women, slavery, oppression of the weak, pornography, prostitution—especially in an organized form—and all those various forms of discrimination that exist in the fields of education, employment, wages, etc. Besides, many forms of degrading discrimination still persist today in a great part of our society that affect and seriously harm particular categories of women, as for example childless wives, widows, separated or divorced women, and unmarried mothers. The Synod Fathers deplored these and other forms of discrimination as strongly as possible. I therefore ask that vigorous and incisive pastoral action be taken by all to overcome them definitively so that the image of God that shines in all human beings without exception may be fully respected.

Men as Husbands and Fathers

25. Within the conjugal and family communion-community, the man is called upon to live his gift and role as husband and father. In his wife he sees the fulfillment of God's intention: "It is not good that the man should be alone, I will make him a helper fit for him," and he makes his own the cry of Adam, the first husband: "This at last is bone of my bones and flesh of my flesh."

Authentic conjugal love presupposes and requires that a man have a profound respect for the equal dignity of his wife: "You are not her master," writes St. Ambrose, "but her husband; she was not given to you to be your slave, but your wife.... Reciprocate her attentiveness to you and be grateful to her for her love." With his wife a man should live "a very special form of personal friendship." As for the Christian, he is called upon to develop a new attitude of love, manifesting toward his wife a charity that is both gentle and strong like that which Christ has for the Church.

Love for his wife as mother of their children and love for the children themselves are for the man the natural way of understanding and fulfilling his own fatherhood. Above all, where social and cultural conditions so easily encourage a father to be less concerned with his family or at any rate less involved in the work of education, efforts must be made to restore socially the conviction that the place and task of the father in and for the family is of unique and irreplaceable importance. As experience teaches, the absence of a father causes psychological and moral imbalance and notable difficulties in family relationships, as does, in contrary circumstances, the oppressive presence of a father, especially where there still prevails the phenomenon of "machismo," or a wrong superiority of male prerogatives which humiliates women and inhibits the development of healthy family relationships.

In revealing and in reliving on earth the very fatherhood of God, a man is called upon to ensure the harmonious and united development of all the members of the family: he will perform this task by exercising generous responsibility for the life conceived under the heart of the mother, by a more solicitous commitment to education, a task he shares with his wife, by work which is never a cause of division in the family but promotes its unity and stability, and by means of the witness he gives of an adult Christian life which effectively introduces the children into the living experience of Christ and the Church.

The Rights of Children

26. In the family, which is a community of persons, special attention must be devoted to the children by developing a profound esteem for their personal dignity and a great respect and generous concern for their rights. This is true for every child, but it becomes all the more urgent the smaller the child is and the more it is in need of everything, when it is sick, suffering, or handicapped.

By fostering and exercising a tender and strong concern for every child that comes into this world, the Church fulfills a fundamental mission: for she is called upon to reveal and put forward anew in history the example and the commandment of Christ the Lord, who placed the child at the heart of the Kingdom of God: "Let the children come to me, and do not hinder them; for to such belongs the kingdom of heaven." I repeat once again what I said to the General Assembly of the United Nations on October 2, 1979: "I wish to express the joy that we all find in children, the springtime of life, the anticipation of the future history of each of our present earthly homelands. No country on earth, no political system can think of its own future otherwise than through the image of these new generations that will receive from their parents the manifold heritage of values, duties, and aspirations of the nation to which they belong and of the whole human family. Concern for the child, even before birth, from the first moment of conception and then throughout the years of infancy and youth, is the primary and fundamental test of the relationship of one human being to another. What better wish can I express for every nation and for the whole of mankind, and for all the children of the world, than a better future in which respect for human rights will become a complete reality throughout the third millennium, which is drawing near?"

Acceptance, love, esteem, many-sided and united material, emotional, educational, and spiritual concern for every child that comes into this world should always constitute a distinctive, essential characteristic of all Christians, in particular of the Christian family: thus children, while they are able to grow "in wisdom and in stature, and in favor with God and man," offer their own precious contribution to building up the family community and even to the sanctification of their parents.

The Elderly in the Family

27. There are cultures which manifest a unique veneration and great love for the elderly: far from being outcasts from the family or merely tolerated as a useless burden, they continue to be present and to take an active and responsible part in family life, though having to respect the autonomy of the new family; above all they carry out the important mission of being a witness to the past and a source of wisdom for the young and for the future. Other cultures, however, especially in the wake of disordered industrial and urban development, have both in the past and in the present set the elderly aside in unacceptable ways. This causes acute suffering to them and spiritually impoverishes many families.

The pastoral activity of the Church must help everyone to discover and to make good use of the role of the elderly within the civil and ecclesial community, in particular within the family. In fact, "the life of the aging helps to clarify a scale of human values; it shows the continuity of generations and marvelously demonstrates the interdependence of God's people. The elderly often have the charism to bridge generation gaps before they are made: how many children have found understanding and love in the eyes and words and caresses of the aging! And how many old people have willingly subscribed to the inspired word that the 'crown of the aged is their children's children!'" (Prv 17:6).

Society at the Service of the Family

45. Just as the intimate connection between the family and society demands that the family be open to and participate in society and its development, so also it requires that society should never fail in its fundamental task of respecting and fostering the family. The family and society have complementary functions in defending and fostering the good of each and every human being. Society—more specifically the State—must recognize that "the family is a society in its own original right" and so society is under a grave obligation in its relations with the family to adhere to the principle of subsidiarity.

By virtue of this principle, the State cannot and must not take away from families the functions that they can just as well perform on their own or in free associations; instead it must positively favor and encourage as far as possible responsible initiative by families. In the conviction that the good of the family is an indispensable and essential value of the civil community, the public authorities must do everything possible to ensure that families have all those aids—economic, social, educational, political, and cultural assistance—that they need in order to face all their responsibilities in a human way.

The Charter of Family Rights

46. The ideal of mutual support and development between the family and society is often very seriously in conflict with the reality of their separation and even opposition.

In fact, as was repeatedly denounced by the Synod, the situation experienced by many families in various countries is highly problematical, if not entirely negative: institutions and laws unjustly ignore the inviolable rights of the family and of the human person; and society, far from putting itself at the service of the family, attacks it violently in its values and fundamental requirements. The family, which in God's plan is the basic cell of society and a subject of rights and duties before the State or any other community, finds itself the victim of society, of the delays and slowness with which it acts, and even of its blatant injustice.

For this reason, the Church openly and strongly defends the rights of the family against the intolerable usurpations of society and the State.

In particular, the Synod Fathers mentioned the following rights of the family:

- the right to exist and progress as a family, that is to say, the right of every human being, even if he or she is poor, to found a family and to have adequate means to support it;
- the right to exercise its responsibility regarding the transmission of life and to educate children; family life;
- the right to the intimacy of conjugal and family life;
- the right to the stability of the bond and of the institution of marriage;
- the right to believe in and profess one's faith and to propagate it;
- the right to bring up children in accordance with the family's own traditions and religious and cultural values, with the necessary instruments, means, and institutions;
- the right, especially of the poor and the sick, to obtain physical, social, political, and economic security;
- the right to housing suitable for living family life in a proper way;
- the right to expression and to representation, either directly or through associations, before the economic, social, and cultural public authorities and lower authorities;
- the right to form associations with other families and institutions, in order to fulfill the family's role suitably and expeditiously;
- the right to protect minors by adequate institutions and legislation from harmful drugs, pornography, alcoholism, etc.;
- the right to wholesome recreation of a kind that also fosters family values;
- the right of the elderly to a worthy life and a worthy death;
- the right to emigrate as a family in search of a better life.

Acceding to the Synod's explicit request, the Holy See will give prompt attention to studying these suggestions in depth and to the preparation of a Charter of Rights of the Family, to be presented to the quarters and authorities concerned.

The Christian Family's Grace and Responsibility

47. The social role that belongs to every family pertains by a new and original right to the Christian family, which is based on the sacrament of marriage. By taking up the human reality of the love between husband and wife in all its implications, the sacrament gives to Christian couples and parents a power and a commitment to live their vocation as lay people and therefore to "seek the kingdom of God by engaging in temporal affairs and by ordering them according to the plan of God."

The social and political role is included in the kingly mission of service in which Christian couples share by virtue of the sacrament of marriage, and they receive both a command which they cannot ignore and a grace which sustains and stimulates them. The Christian family is thus called upon to offer everyone a witness of generous and disinterested dedication to social matters, through a "preferential option" for the poor and disadvantaged. Advancing in its following of the Lord by special love for all the poor, it must have special concern for the hungry, the poor, the old, the sick, drug victims, and those who have no family.

For a New International Order

48. In view of the worldwide dimension of various social questions nowadays, the family has seen its role with regard to the development of society extended in a completely new way: it now also involves cooperating for a new international order, since it is only in worldwide solidarity that the enormous and dramatic issues of world justice, the freedom of peoples, and the peace of humanity can be dealt with and solved.

The spiritual communion between Christian families, rooted in a common faith and hope and given life by love, constitutes an inner energy that generates, spreads, and develops justice, reconciliation, fraternity, and peace among human beings. Insofar as it is a "small-scale Church," the Christian family is called upon, like the "large-scale Church," to be a sign of unity for the world and in this way to exercise its prophetic role by bearing witness to the Kingdom and peace of Christ, toward which the whole world is journeying. Christian families can do this through their educational activity—that is to say by presenting to their children a model of life based on the values of truth, freedom, justice, and love—both through active and responsible involvement in the authentically human growth of society and its institutions, and by supporting in various ways the associations specifically devoted to international issues.

READING 7 (AUGUST 11, 1982): Reverence for Christ: The Basis of Relationship between Spouses[1]

1. Today we begin a more detailed analysis of the passage of the Letter to the Ephesians 5:21-33. Addressing husbands and wives, the author recommends them to be "subject to one another out of reverence for Christ" (5:21). Here it is a question of a relationship of a double dimension or degree: reciprocal and communitarian. One clarifies and characterizes the other. The mutual relations of husband and wife should flow from their common relationship with Christ. The author of the letter speaks of "reverence for Christ" in a sense analogous to that when he speaks of the "fear of God." In this case, it is not a question of fear which is a defensive attitude before the threat of evil, but it is above all a case of respect for holiness, for the *sacrum*. It is a question of *pietas*, which, in the language of the Old Testament, was expressed by the term "fear of God" (cf., e.g., Ps(s) 103:11; Prv 1:7; 23:17; Sir 1:11-16). Arising from a profound awareness of the mystery of Christ, this *pietas* should constitute the basis of the reciprocal relations between husbands and wives.

Moral Instruction

2. The text chosen by us, as likewise the immediate context, has a "parenetic" character, that is, of moral instruction. The author of the letter wishes to indicate to husbands and wives the basis of their mutual relationship and their entire conduct. He deduces the relative indications and directives from the mystery of Christ presented at the beginning of the letter. This mystery should be spiritually present in the mutual relationship of spouses. The mystery of Christ, penetrating their hearts, engendering in them that holy "reverence for Christ" (namely *pietas*), should lead them to "be subject to one another"—the mystery of Christ, that is, the mystery of the choice from eternity of each of them in Christ to be the adoptive sons of God.

Husband Not the "Lord"

3. The opening expression of our passage of Ephesians 5:21-33, which we have approached by an analysis of the remote and immediate context, has quite a special eloquence. The author speaks of the mutual subjection of the spouses, husband and wife, and in this way he explains the words which he will write afterward on the subjection of the wife to the husband. In fact, we read: "Wives, be subject to your husbands, as to the Lord" (5:22). In saying this, the author does not intend to say that the husband is the lord of the wife and that the interpersonal pact proper to marriage is a pact of domination of the husband over the wife. Instead, he expresses a different concept: that the wife can and should find in her relationship with Christ—who is the one Lord of both the spouses—the motivation of that relationship with her husband which flows from the very essence of marriage and of the family; however, such a relationship is not one of one-sided domination. According to the Letter to the Ephesians, marriage excludes that element of the pact which was a burden and, at times, does not cease to be a burden on this institution. The husband and the wife are in fact "subject to one another" and are mutually subordinated to one another. The source of this mutual subjection is to be found in Christian *pietas*, and its expression is love.

No One-Sided Domination

4. The author of the letter underlines this love in a special way, in addressing himself to husbands. He writes, "Husbands, love your wives...." By expressing himself in this way, he removes any fear that might have arisen (given the modern sensitivity) from the previous phrase: "Wives, be subject to your husbands." Love excludes every kind of subjection whereby the wife might become a servant or a slave of the husband, an object of unilateral domination. Love makes the husband simultaneously subject to the wife, and thereby subject to the Lord himself, just as the wife to the husband. The community or unity which they should establish through marriage is constituted by a reciprocal donation of self, which is also a mutual subjection. Christ is the source and at the same time the model of that subjection, which, being reciprocal "out of reverence for Christ," confers on the conjugal union a profound and mature character. In this source and

before this model many elements of a psychological or moral nature are so transformed as to give rise, I would say, to a new and precious fusion of the bilateral relations and conduct.

5. The author of the Letter to the Ephesians does not fear to accept those concepts which were characteristic of the mentality and customs of the times. He does not fear to speak of the subjection of the wife to the husband. He does not fear (also in the last verse of the text quoted by us) to recommend to the wife that "she respect her husband" (5:33). It is certain that when the husband and wife are subject to one another "out of reverence for Christ," a just balance will be established, such as to correspond to their Christian vocation in the mystery of Christ.

"Out of Reverence"

6. Nowadays, our contemporary sensitivity is certainly different. Our mentality and customs are quite different, too, as is the social position of women in regard to men. Nevertheless, the fundamental moral principle which we find in the Letter to the Ephesians remains the same and produces the same results. The mutual subjection "out of reverence for Christ"—a subjection arising from the basis of Christian *pietas*—always produces that profound and solid structure of the community of the spouses in which there is constituted the true "communion" of the person.

A Great Analogy

7. The author of the text to the Ephesians, who began his letter with a magnificent vision of God's eternal plan in regard to humanity, does not limit himself to emphasizing merely the traditional aspects of morality or the ethical aspects of marriage. He goes beyond the scope of teaching and writing on the reciprocal relationship of the spouses. He discovers therein the dimension of the mystery of Christ of which he is the herald and the Apostle: "Wives, be subject to your husbands as to the Lord. For the husband is the head of the wife as Christ is the head of the Church, his Body, and is himself its Savior. As the Church is subject to Christ, so let wives also be subject in everything to their husbands. Husbands, love your wives, as Christ loved the Church and gave himself up for her ..." (5:22-25). In this

way, the teaching of this parenetic part of the letter is inserted, in a certain sense, into the reality of the mystery hidden from eternity in God and revealed to mankind in Jesus Christ. In the Letter to the Ephesians, we are, I would say, witnesses of a particular meeting of that mystery with the essence of the vocation to marriage. How are we to understand this meeting? In the text of the Letter to the Ephesians it is presented above all as a great analogy. There we read: "Wives, be subject to your husbands as to the Lord...." Here we have the first component of the analogy. "For the husband is the head of the wife as Christ is the head of the Church...." Here we have the second component which clarifies and motivates the first. "As the Church is subject to Christ, so let wives also be subject to their husbands...." The relationship of Christ to the Church, presented previously, is now expressed as a relationship of the Church to Christ, and this contains the successive component of the analogy. Finally: "Husbands, love your wives, as Christ loved the Church and gave himself up for her...." This is the ultimate component of the analogy. The remainder of the text of the letter develops the fundamental thought contained in the passage just now quoted. The entire text of the Letter to the Ephesians in 5:21-33 is completely permeated with the same analogy. That is to say, the mutual relationship between the spouses, husband and wife, is to be understood by Christians in the light of the relationship between Christ and the Church.

READING 8 (DECEMBER 15, 1982): The Redemptive and Spousal Dimensions of Love[1]

1. The author of the Letter to the Ephesians, as we have already seen, speaks of a "great mystery," linked to the primordial sacrament through the continuity of God's saving plan. He also referred to the "beginning," as Christ did in his conversation with the Pharisees (cf. Mt 19:8), quoting the same words: "Therefore a man leaves his father and his mother and cleaves to his wife, and they become one flesh" (Gen 2:24). This "great mystery" is above all the mystery of the union of Christ with the Church, which the Apostle presents under the similitude of the unity of the spouses: "I mean it in reference to Christ and the Church" (Eph 5:32). We find ourselves in the domain of the great analogy in which marriage as a sacrament

is presupposed on the one hand, and on the other hand rediscovered. It is presupposed as the sacrament of the "beginning" of mankind united to the mystery of the creation; however, it is rediscovered as the fruit of the spousal love of Christ and of the Church linked with the mystery of the redemption.

Address to Spouses

2. The author of the Letter to the Ephesians, addressing spouses directly, exhorts them to mold their reciprocal relationship on the model of the spousal union of Christ and the Church. It can be said that—presupposing the sacramentality of marriage in its primordial significance—he orders them to learn anew this sacrament of the spousal unity of Christ and the Church: "Husbands, love your wives, as Christ loved the Church and gave himself up for her, that he might sanctify her ..." (cf. Eph 5:25-26). This invitation which the Apostle addressed to Christian spouses is fully motivated by the fact that through marriage as a sacrament, they participate in Christ's saving love, which is expressed at the same time as his spousal love for the Church. In the light of the Letter to the Ephesians—precisely through participation in this saving love of Christ—marriage as a sacrament of the human "beginning" is confirmed and at the same time renewed. It is the sacrament in which man and woman, called to become "one flesh," participate in God's own creative love. They participate in it both by the fact that, created in the image of God, they are called by reason of this image to a particular union (*communio personarum*) and because this same union has from the beginning been blessed with the blessing of fruitfulness (cf. Gen 1:28).

New Depths of Love

3. All this original and stable structure of marriage as a sacrament of the mystery of creation—according to the classic text of the Letter to the Ephesians (Eph 5:21-33)—is renewed in the mystery of the redemption, when that mystery assumes the aspect of the spousal love of the Church on the part of Christ. That original and stable form of marriage is renewed when the spouses receive it as a sacrament of the Church, drawing from the new depths of God's love for man. This love is revealed and opened with the

mystery of the redemption, "when Christ loved the Church and gave himself up for her to make her holy ..." (Eph 5:25-26). That original and stable image of marriage as a sacrament is renewed when Christian spouses, conscious of the authentic profundity of the redemption of the body, are united "out of reverence for Christ" (Eph 5:21).

Fusing the Dimensions

4. The Pauline image of marriage, inscribed in the "great mystery" of Christ and of the Church, brings together the redemptive dimension and the spousal dimension of love. In a certain sense it fuses these two dimensions into one. Christ has become the spouse of the Church. He has married the Church as a bride, because "He has given himself up for her" (Eph 5:25). Through marriage as a sacrament (as one of the sacraments of the Church), both these dimensions of love, the spousal and the redemptive, together with the grace of the sacrament, permeate the life of the spouses. The spousal significance of the body in its masculinity and femininity was manifested for the first time in the mystery of creation against the background of man's original innocence. This significance is linked in the image of the Letter to the Ephesians with the redemptive significance, and in this way it is confirmed and in a certain sense "newly created."

Understanding the Link

5. This is important in regard to marriage and to the Christian vocation of husbands and wives. The text of the Letter to the Ephesians (5:21-33) is directly addressed to them and speaks especially to them; however, that linking of the spousal significance of the body with its redemptive significance is equally essential and valid for the understanding of man in general, for the fundamental problem of understanding him and for the self-comprehension of his being in the world. It is obvious that we cannot exclude from this problem the question on the meaning of being a body, on the sense of being, as a body, man and woman. These questions were posed for the first time in relation to the analysis of the human beginning, in the context of Genesis. In a certain sense, that very context demanded that they should be posed. It is equally demanded by the classic text of the Letter to the Ephesians. The great mystery of the union of Christ to the Church

obliges us to link the spousal significance of the body with its redemptive significance. In this link the spouses find the answer to the question concerning the meaning of "being a body," and not only they, although this text of the Apostle's letter is addressed especially to them.

Explains by Analogy

6. The Pauline image of the great mystery of Christ and of the Church also spoke indirectly of celibacy for the sake of the kingdom of heaven. In this celibacy, both dimensions of love, the spousal and redemptive, are reciprocally united in a way different from that of marriage, according to diverse proportions. Is not perhaps that spousal love wherewith Christ "loved the Church"—his bride—"and gave himself up for her," at the same time the fullest incarnation of the ideal of celibacy for the kingdom of heaven (cf. Mt 19:12)? Is not support found precisely in this by all those—men and women—who, choosing the same ideal, desire to link the spousal dimension of love with the redemptive dimension according to the model of Christ himself? They wish to confirm with their life that the spousal significance of the body—of its masculinity and femininity—profoundly inscribed in the essential structure of the human person, has been opened in a new way on the part of Christ and with the example of his life, to the hope united to the redemption of the body. The grace of the mystery of the redemption bears fruit also—rather bears fruit in a special way—with the vocation to celibacy for the kingdom of heaven.

7. The text of the Letter to the Ephesians (5:21-33) does not speak of it explicitly. It is addressed to spouses and constructed according to the image of marriage, which by analogy explains the union of Christ with the Church—a union in both redemptive and spousal love together. Is it not perhaps precisely this love which, as the living and vivifying expression of the mystery of the redemption, goes beyond the circle of the recipients of the letter circumscribed by the analogy of marriage? Does it not embrace every man and, in a certain sense, the whole of creation as indicated by the Pauline text on the redemption of the body in Romans (cf. Rom 8:23)? The great sacrament in this sense is a new sacrament of man in Christ and in the Church. It is the sacrament "of man and of the world," just as the

creation of man, male and female, in the image of God, was the original sacrament of man and of the world. In this new sacrament of redemption marriage is organically inscribed, just as it was inscribed in the original sacrament of creation.

Fulfillment of the Kingdom

8. Man, who "from the beginning" is male and female, should seek the meaning of his existence and the meaning of his humanity by reaching out to the mystery of creation through the reality of redemption. There one finds also the essential answer to the question on the significance of the human body and the significance of the masculinity and femininity of the human person. The union of Christ with the Church permits us to understand in what way the spousal significance of the body is completed with the redemptive significance, and this in the diverse ways of life and in diverse situations. It is not only in marriage or in continency (that is, virginity and celibacy) but also, for example, in the many forms of human suffering, indeed, in the very birth and death of man. By means of the great mystery which the Letter to the Ephesians treats of, by means of the new covenant of Christ with the Church, marriage is again inscribed in that "sacrament of man" which embraces the universe, in the sacrament of man and of the world which, thanks to the forces of the redemption of the body, is modeled on the spousal love of Christ for the Church, to the measure of the definitive fulfillment of the kingdom of the Father. Marriage as a sacrament remains a living and vivifying part of this saving process.

MARCH 1987–MAY 1994

INTRODUCTION TO READING 9 BY VIRGINIA GALLOWAY

Twenty-first-century Catholic women, especially those who have long been embroiled in the cultural struggles that fall under the often-derided umbrella of "feminism," have—with some justification—been known to grumble that Pope John Paul II did not grasp the particular difficulties that women *who are not wives, not mothers, and not pledged to the religious life* face. Whether unmarried by choice or circumstance; whether childless through lack of opportunity, physical impediment, or disinclination; and lacking a vocation for religious life, women who do not fall into the wife/mother/professed categories can reasonably ask themselves "Did John Paul not understand that we, too, have a role to play, both in life and in the Church?"

To dismiss John Paul as a clueless member of the "old boys' club," as the hierarchy of the Church is lamentably often considered, is to ignore or elide the compelling arguments he made that women are fully participating members of the "royal priesthood" of believers described by St. Peter as "called out of the darkness into his wonderful light" (1 Pt 2:9). Beyond his calm inclusion of women into the great work of the Church, John Paul also recognized and honored the particular task of women who provide spiritual motherhood, a function that does not require biological motherhood as a qualification. In doing so, he recognized the special alliance with Mary, Mother of God, that such spiritual motherhood imparts.

In *Redemptoris Mater*, his encyclical letter of March 25, 1987, John Paul spoke of this alliance and this task:

[Subsect. 20] The Gospel of Luke records the moment when "a woman in the crowd raised her voice" and said to Jesus: "Blessed is the womb that bore you, and the breasts that you sucked!" (Lk 11:27) . . .

Jesus replies in a significant way: "Blessed rather are those who hear the word of God and keep it" (Lk 11:28). He wishes to divert attention from motherhood understood only as a fleshly bond, in order to direct it towards those mysterious bonds of the spirit which develop from hearing and keeping God's word . . . [adding] "My mother and my brothers are those who hear the word of God and do it" (cf. Lk 8:20-21) . . .

[Subsect. 23] And so this "new motherhood of Mary," generated by faith, is the fruit of the "new" love which came to definitive maturity in her at the foot of the Cross, through her sharing in the redemptive love of her Son.[1]

This "new kind of motherhood according to the spirit" is designed to aid in accomplishing the fulfillment of the Kingdom of God. While uniquely maternal, it is not necessarily limited to females; in fact, "Mary's solicitude for human beings, her coming to them in the wide variety of their wants and needs," offers a level of care and concern that should be emulated by all Christians.

Amplifying this charge to Christians to offer solicitude to others, John Paul spoke of the "fullness of life" in his encyclical letter of March 25, 1995, *Evangelium Vitae*,[2] asserting that achieving such fullness is "sharing the very life of God" and is a "supernatural vocation." Earthly life, he stipulated, "remains a sacred reality entrusted to us, to be preserved with a sense of responsibility and brought to perfection in love and in *the gift of ourselves to God and to our brothers and sisters*" [emphasis added]. He discussed "the natural law written in the heart (cf. Rom 2:14-15), the sacred value of human life from its very beginning until its end, and can affirm the right of every human being to have this primary good respected to the highest degree" and bluntly stated that "believers in Christ must defend and promote this right" (*Evangelium Vitae*, 1:2ff). What he did *not* say is "This is a job for men" or "This is a job for women"; instead, he was adamant that this is the work of all believers. Even so, the protective, even maternal, quality that he describes reminds the faithful of the steadfast, unwavering love of Mary for her Son and urges all Christians to emulate her example.

In urging all Christians to behave toward all people with loving concern and protective solicitude, does John Paul suggest that women have no unique role? Quite the contrary: While recognizing the work common to all, John Paul definitively recognizes the special character of women in his August 15, 1988, apostolic letter, *Mulieris Dignitatem*. Quoting the Fathers of the Second Vatican Council, he asserts that "[t]he hour is coming, in fact has come, when the vocation of women is being acknowledged in its fullness, the hour in which women acquire in the world an influence, an effect, and a power never hitherto achieved. That is why, at this moment when the human race is undergoing so deep a transformation, women imbued with a spirit of the Gospel can do so much to aid humanity in not falling." He develops this thought (*Mulieris Dignitatem*, Section IV, #10; emphasis original) by underscoring the

> dignity and vocation that result from the specific diversity and personal originality of man and woman. Consequently, even the rightful opposition of women to what is expressed in the biblical words "He shall rule over you" (Gen 3:16) must not under any condition lead to the "masculinization" of women. In the name of liberation from male "domination," women must not appropriate to themselves male characteristics contrary to their own feminine "originality." There is a well-founded fear that if they take this path, women will not "reach fulfilment," but instead will *deform and lose what constitutes their essential richness*.[3]

What is the "dignity and vocation" of women, and how does it differ from that of men? While John Paul prudently avoided attempting to stipulate those roles to be filled *only* by women, he offered a profound recognition of the "womanly" response to the Gospel by describing the interaction of Jesus with women and saying "Christ speaks to women about the things of God, and they understand them; there is a true resonance of mind and heart, a response of faith. Jesus expresses appreciation and admiration for this distinctly 'feminine' response, as in the case of the Canaanite woman (cf. Mt 15:28). Sometimes he presents this lively faith, filled with love, as an example. He teaches, therefore, taking as his starting point this feminine response of mind and heart" (*Mulieris Dignitatem*, IV, 15). This "lively faith, filled with love," is the foundation upon which spiritual motherhood rests, the openhearted embrace of others that particularly enables women, even those who are not biological mothers, to listen with fewer distractions and love without expectations, to be able to sigh and say "Oh, child, let me help you" when witnessing the anguish of one of the "little ones" of whom

Jesus spoke (Lk 17:2). That, finally, is the clearest sign of the spiritual motherhood as understood by John Paul II.

Virginia Galloway is a graduate of the Theology and Master in Liberal Arts programs at the University of St. Thomas.

READING 9 (MARCH 25, 1987): *Redemptoris Mater* (Mother of the Redeemer)[1]

Venerable Brothers and dear Sons and Daughters,
Health and the Apostolic Blessing

Introduction

The Mother of the Redeemer has a precise place in the plan of salvation, for "when the time had fully come, God sent forth his Son, born of woman, born under the law, to redeem those who were under the law, so that we might receive adoption as sons. And because you are sons, God has sent the Spirit of his Son into our hearts, crying, 'Abba! Father!'" (Gal 4:4-6).

With these words of the Apostle Paul, which the Second Vatican Council takes up at the beginning of its treatment of the Blessed Virgin Mary, I, too, wish to begin my reflection on the role of Mary in the mystery of Christ and on her active and exemplary presence in the life of the Church. For they are words which celebrate together the love of the Father, the mission of the Son, the gift of the Spirit, the role of the woman from whom the Redeemer was born, and our own divine filiation, in the mystery of the "fullness of time."

This "fullness" indicates the moment fixed from all eternity when the Father sent his Son "that whoever believes in him should not perish but have eternal life" (Jn 3:16). It denotes the blessed moment when the Word that "was with God ... became flesh and dwelt among us" (Jn 1:1, 14) and made himself our brother. It marks the moment when the Holy Spirit, who had already infused the fullness of grace into Mary of Nazareth, formed in her virginal womb the human nature of Christ. This "fullness" marks the moment when, with the entrance of the eternal into time, time itself is redeemed, and being filled with the mystery of Christ becomes definitively "salvation time." Finally, this "fullness" designates the hidden beginning of the Church's journey. In the liturgy the Church salutes Mary of Nazareth as the Church's own beginning, for in the event of the Immaculate Conception the Church sees projected, and anticipated in her most noble member, the saving grace of Easter. And above all, in the Incarnation she encounters Christ and Mary indissolubly joined: he who is the Church's Lord and Head and she who, uttering the first *fiat* of the New Covenant, prefigures the Church's condition as spouse and mother.

Strengthened by the presence of Christ (cf. Mt 28:20), the Church journeys through time toward the consummation of the ages and goes to meet the Lord who comes. On this journey—and I wish to make this point straightaway—she proceeds along the path already trodden by the Virgin Mary, who "advanced in her pilgrimage of faith, and loyally persevered in her union with her Son unto the cross."

I take these very rich and evocative words from the Constitution *Lumen Gentium,* which in its concluding part offers a clear summary of the Church's doctrine on the Mother of Christ, whom she venerates as her beloved Mother and as her model in faith, hope, and charity. Shortly after the Council, my great predecessor Paul VI decided to speak further of the Blessed Virgin. In the Encyclical Epistle *Christi Matri* and subsequently in the Apostolic Exhortations *Signum Magnum* and *Marialis Cultus* he expounded the foundations and criteria of the special veneration which the Mother of Christ receives in the Church, as well as the various forms of Marian devotion—liturgical, popular, and private—which respond to the spirit of faith.

The circumstance which now moves me to take up this subject once more is the prospect of the year 2000, now drawing near, in which the Bimillennial Jubilee of the birth of Jesus Christ at the same time directs our gaze toward his Mother. In recent years, various opinions have been voiced suggesting that it would be fitting to precede that anniversary by a similar Jubilee in celebration of the birth of Mary.

In fact, even though it is not possible to establish an exact chronological point for identifying the date of Mary's birth, the Church has constantly been aware that Mary appeared on the horizon of salvation history before Christ. It is a fact that when "the fullness of time" was definitively drawing near—the saving advent of Emmanuel—she who was from eternity destined to be his Mother already existed on earth. The fact that she "preceded" the coming of Christ is reflected every year in the liturgy of Advent. If to that ancient historical expectation of the Savior we compare these years which are bringing us closer to the end of the second Millennium after Christ and to the beginning of the third, it becomes fully comprehensible that in this present period we wish to turn in a special way to her, the one who in the "night" of the Advent expectation began to shine like a true "Morning Star" (*Stella Matutina*). Just as this star, together with the "dawn," precedes the rising of the sun, so Mary from the time of her Immaculate Conception preceded the coming of the Savior, the rising of the "Sun of Justice" in the history of the human race.

Her presence in the midst of Israel—a presence so discreet as to pass almost unnoticed by the eyes of her contemporaries—shone very clearly before the Eternal One, who had associated this hidden "daughter of Sion" (cf. Zep 3:14; Zep 2:10) with the plan of salvation embracing the whole history of humanity. With good reason, then, at the end of this Millennium, we Christians who know that the providential plan of the Most Holy Trinity is the central reality of Revelation and of faith feel the need to emphasize the unique presence of the Mother of Christ in history, especially during these last years leading up to the year 2000.

The Second Vatican Council prepares us for this by presenting in its teaching the Mother of God in the mystery of Christ and of the Church. If it is true, as the Council itself proclaims, that "only in the mystery of the Incarnate Word does the mystery of man take on light," then this principle must be applied in a very particular way to that exceptional "daughter of the human race," that extraordinary "woman" who became the Mother of Christ. Only in the mystery of Christ is her mystery fully made clear. The Church sought to interpret the mystery this way from the very beginning: the mystery of the Incarnation has enabled her to penetrate and to make ever clearer the mystery of the Mother of the Incarnate Word. The Council of Ephesus (431) was of decisive importance in clarifying this, for during that Council, to the great joy of Christians, the truth of the divine motherhood of Mary was solemnly confirmed as a truth of the Church's faith. Mary is the Mother of God (*Theotókos*), since by the power of the Holy Spirit she conceived in her virginal womb and brought into the world Jesus Christ, the Son of God, who is of one being with the Father. "The

Son of God … born of the Virgin Mary … has truly been made one of us," has been made man. Through the mystery of Christ, on the horizon of the Church's faith, there shines in its fullness the mystery of his Mother. In turn, the dogma of the divine motherhood of Mary was for the Council of Ephesus and is for the Church like a seal upon the dogma of the Incarnation, in which the Word truly assumes human nature into the unity of his person, without cancelling out that nature.

The Second Vatican Council, by presenting Mary in the mystery of Christ, also finds the path to a deeper understanding of the mystery of the Church. Mary, as the Mother of Christ, is in a particular way united with the Church, "which the Lord established as his own body." It is significant that the conciliar text places this truth about the Church as the Body of Christ (according to the teaching of the Pauline Letters) in close proximity to the truth that the Son of God "through the power of the Holy Spirit was born of the Virgin Mary." The reality of the Incarnation finds a sort of extension in the mystery of the Church—the Body of Christ, and one cannot think of the reality of the Incarnation without referring to Mary, the Mother of the Incarnate Word.

In these reflections, I wish to consider primarily that "pilgrimage of faith" in which "the Blessed Virgin advanced," faithfully preserving her union with Christ. In this way, the "twofold bond" which unites the Mother of God with Christ and with the Church takes on historical significance. This is not just a question of the Virgin Mother's life story, of her personal journey of faith and "the better part" which is hers in the mystery of salvation; it is also a question of the history of the whole People of God, of all those who take part in the same "pilgrimage of faith."

The Council expresses this when it states in another passage that Mary "has gone before," becoming "a model of the Church in the matter of faith, charity and perfect union with Christ." This "going before" as a figure or model is in reference to the intimate mystery of the Church, as she actuates and accomplishes her own saving mission by uniting in herself—as Mary did—the qualities of mother and virgin. She is a virgin who "keeps whole and pure the fidelity she has pledged to her Spouse" and "becomes herself a mother," for "she brings forth to a new and immortal life children who are conceived of the Holy Spirit and born of God."

All this is accomplished in a great historical process, comparable "to a journey." The pilgrimage of faith indicates the interior history, that is, the story of souls, but it is also the story of all human beings, subject here on earth to transitoriness and part of the historical dimension. In the following reflections, we wish to concentrate first of all on the present, which in itself is not yet history, but which nevertheless is constantly forming it, also in the sense of the history of salvation. Here there opens up a broad prospect, within which the Blessed Virgin Mary continues to "go before" the People of God. Her exceptional pilgrimage of faith represents a constant point of reference for the Church, for individuals and for communities, for peoples and nations, and, in a sense, for all humanity. It is indeed difficult to encompass and measure its range.

The Council emphasizes that the Mother of God is already the eschatological fulfillment of the Church: "In the most holy Virgin the Church has already reached that perfection whereby she exists without spot or wrinkle (cf. Eph 5:27)"; and at the same time the Council says that "the followers of Christ still strive to increase in holiness by conquering sin, and so they raise their eyes to Mary, who shines forth to the whole community of the elect as a model of the virtues." The pilgrimage of faith no longer belongs to the Mother of the Son of God: glorified at the side of her Son in heaven, Mary has already crossed the threshold between faith and that vision which is "face to face" (1 Cor 13:12). At the same time, however, in this eschatological fulfillment, Mary does not cease to be the "Star of the Sea" (*Maris Stella*) for all those who are still on the journey of faith. If they lift their eyes to her from their earthly existence, they do so because "the Son whom she brought forth is he whom God placed as the first-born among many brethren (Rom 8:29)," and also because "in the birth and development" of these brothers and sisters "she cooperates with a maternal love."

Full of Grace

"Blessed be the God and Father of our Lord Jesus Christ, who has blessed us in Christ with every spiritual blessing in the heavenly places" (Eph 1:3). These words of the Letter to the Ephesians reveal the eternal design of God the Father, his plan of man's salvation in Christ. It is a universal plan, which concerns all men and women created in the image and likeness of God (cf. Gen 1:26). Just as all are included in the creative work of God "in the beginning," so all are eternally included in the divine plan of salvation, which is to be completely revealed, in the "fullness of time," with the final coming of Christ. In fact, the God who is the "Father of our Lord Jesus Christ"—these are the next words of the same Letter—"chose us in him before the foundation of the world, that we should be holy and blameless before him. He destined us in love to be his sons through Jesus Christ, according to the purpose of his will, to the praise of his glorious grace, which he freely bestowed on us in the Beloved. In him we have redemption through his blood, the forgiveness of our trespasses, according to the riches of his grace" (Eph 1:4-7).

The divine plan of salvation—which was fully revealed to us with the coming of Christ—is eternal. And according to the teaching contained in the Letter just quoted and in other Pauline Letters (cf. Col 1:12-14; Rom 3:24; Gal 3:13; 2 Cor 5:18-29), it is also eternally linked to Christ. It includes everyone, but it reserves a special place for the "woman" who is the Mother of him to whom the Father has entrusted the work of salvation. As the Second Vatican Council says, "[S]he is already prophetically foreshadowed in that promise made to our first parents after their fall into sin"—according to the Book of Genesis (cf. 3:15). "Likewise she is the Virgin who is to conceive and bear a son, whose name will be called Emmanuel"—according to the words of Isaiah (cf. 7:14). In this way, the Old Testament prepares that "fullness of time" when God "sent forth his Son, born of woman ... so that we might receive adoption as sons." The coming into the world of the Son of God is an event recorded in the first chapters of the Gospels according to Luke and Matthew.

Mary is definitively introduced into the mystery of Christ through this event: the Annunciation by the angel. This takes place at Nazareth, within the concrete circumstances of the history of Israel, the people which first received God's promises. The divine messenger says to the Virgin: "Hail, full of grace, the Lord is with you" (Lk 1:28). Mary "was greatly troubled at the saying, and considered in her mind what sort of greeting this might be" (Lk 1:29): what could those extraordinary words mean, and in particular the expression "full of grace" (*kecharitoméne*)?

If we wish to meditate together with Mary on these words, and especially on the expression "full of grace," we can find a significant echo in the very passage from the Letter to the Ephesians quoted previously. If after the announcement of the heavenly messenger the Virgin of Nazareth is also called "blessed among women" (cf. Lk 1:42), it is because of that blessing with which "God the Father" has filled us "in the heavenly places, in Christ." It is a spiritual blessing which is meant for all people and which bears in itself fullness and universality ("every blessing"). It flows from that love which, in the Holy Spirit, unites the consubstantial Son to the Father. At the same time, it is a blessing poured out through Jesus Christ upon human history until the end: upon all people. This blessing, however, refers to Mary in a special and exceptional degree: for she was greeted by Elizabeth as "blessed among women."

The double greeting is due to the fact that in the soul of this "daughter of Sion" there is manifested, in a sense, all the "glory of grace," that grace which "the Father . . . has given us in his beloved Son." The messenger greets Mary as "full of grace"; he calls her thus as if it were her real name. He does not call her by her proper earthly name, *Miryam* (Mary), but by this new name, "full of grace." What does this name mean? Why does the archangel address the Virgin of Nazareth in this way?

In the language of the Bible "grace" means a special gift, which according to the New Testament has its source precisely in the Trinitarian life of God himself, God who is love (cf. 1 Jn 4:8). The fruit of this love is "the election" of which the Letter to the Ephesians speaks. On the part of God, this election is the eternal desire to save man through a sharing in his own life (cf. 2 Pt 1:4) in Christ: it is salvation through a sharing in supernatural life. The effect of this eternal gift, of this grace of man's election by God, is like a seed of holiness, or a spring which rises in the soul as a gift from God himself, who through grace gives life and holiness to those who are chosen. In this way, there is fulfilled, that is to say there comes about, that "blessing" of man "with every spiritual blessing," that "being his adopted sons and daughters . . . in Christ," in him who is eternally the "beloved Son" of the Father.

When we read that the messenger addresses Mary as "full of grace," the Gospel context, which mingles revelations and ancient promises, enables us to understand that among all the "spiritual blessings in Christ" this is a special "blessing." In the mystery of Christ she is present even "before the creation of the world," as the one whom the Father "has chosen" as Mother of his Son in the Incarnation and, what is more, together with the Father, the Son has chosen her, entrusting her eternally to the Spirit of holiness. In an entirely special and exceptional way, Mary is united to Christ, and similarly she is eternally loved in this "beloved Son," this Son who is of one being with the Father, in whom is concentrated all the "glory of grace." At the same time, she is and remains perfectly open to this "gift from above" (cf. Jas 1:17). As the Council teaches, Mary "stands out among the poor and humble of the Lord, who confidently await and receive salvation from him."

9. If the greeting and the name "full of grace" say all this, in the context of the angel's announcement they refer first of all to the election of Mary as Mother of the Son of God. At the same time the "fullness of grace" indicates all the supernatural munificence from which Mary benefits by being chosen and destined to be the Mother of Christ. If this election is fundamental for the accomplishment of God's salvific designs for humanity, and if the eternal choice in Christ and the vocation to the dignity of adopted children is the destiny of everyone, then the election of Mary is wholly exceptional and unique. Hence also the singularity and uniqueness of her place in the mystery of Christ.

The divine messenger says to her: "Do not be afraid, Mary, for you have found favor with God. And behold, you will conceive in your womb and bear a son, and you shall call his name Jesus. He will be great, and will be called the Son of the Most High" (Lk 1:30-32). When the Virgin, disturbed by that extraordinary greeting, asks: "How shall this be, since I have no husband?" she receives from the angel the confirmation and explanation of the preceding words. Gabriel says to her: "The Holy Spirit will come upon you, and the power of the Most High will overshadow you; therefore the child to be born will be called holy, the Son of God" (Lk 1:35).

The Annunciation, consequently, is the revelation of the mystery of the Incarnation at the very beginning of its fulfillment on earth. God's salvific giving of himself and his life, in some way to all creation but directly to man, reaches one of its high points in the mystery of the Incarnation. This is indeed a high point among all the gifts of grace conferred in the history of man and of the universe: Mary is "full of grace," because it is precisely in her that the Incarnation of the Word, the hypostatic union of the Son of God with human nature, is accomplished and fulfilled. As the Council says, Mary is "the Mother of the Son of God. As a result she is also the favorite daughter of the Father and the temple of the Holy Spirit. Because of this gift of sublime grace, she far surpasses all other creatures, both in heaven and on earth."

10. The Letter to the Ephesians, speaking of the "glory of grace" that "God, the Father ... has bestowed on us in his beloved Son," adds: "In him we have redemption through his blood" (Eph 1:7). According to the belief formulated in solemn documents of the Church, this "glory of grace" is manifested in the Mother of God through the fact that she has been "redeemed in a more sublime manner." By virtue of the richness of the grace of the beloved Son, by reason of the redemptive merits of him who willed to become her Son, Mary was preserved from the inheritance of original sin. In this way, from the first moment of her conception—which is to say of her existence—she belonged to Christ, sharing in the salvific and sanctifying grace and in that love which has its beginning in the "Beloved," the Son of the Eternal Father, who through the Incarnation became her own Son. Consequently, through the power of the Holy Spirit, in the order of grace, which is a participation in the divine nature, Mary receives life from him to whom she herself, in the order of earthly generation, gave life as a mother. The liturgy does not hesitate to call her "mother of her Creator" and to hail her with the words which Dante Alighieri places on the lips of St. Bernard: "daughter of your Son." Since Mary receives this "new life" with a fullness corresponding to the Son's love for the Mother, and thus corresponding to the dignity of the divine motherhood, the angel at the Annunciation calls her "full of grace."

11. In the salvific design of the Most Holy Trinity, the mystery of the Incarnation constitutes the superabundant fulfillment of the promise made by God to man after original sin, after that first sin whose effects oppress the whole earthly history of man (cf. Gen 3:15). And so, there comes into

the world a Son, "the seed of the woman" who will crush the evil of sin in its very origins: "he will crush the head of the serpent." As we see from the words of the *Proto-gospel*, the victory of the woman's Son will not take place without a hard struggle, a struggle that is to extend through the whole of human history. The "enmity," foretold at the beginning, is confirmed in the Apocalypse (the book of the final events of the Church and the world), in which there recurs the sign of the "woman," this time "clothed with the sun" (Rv 12:1).

Mary, Mother of the Incarnate Word, is placed at the very center of that enmity, that struggle which accompanies the history of humanity on earth and the history of salvation itself. In this central place, she who belongs to the "weak and poor of the Lord" bears in herself, like no other member of the human race, that "glory of grace" which the Father "has bestowed on us in his beloved Son," and this grace determines the extraordinary greatness and beauty of her whole being. Mary thus remains before God, and also before the whole of humanity, as the unchangeable and inviolable sign of God's election, spoken of in Paul's letter: "in Christ ... he chose us ... before the foundation of the world ... he destined us ... to be his sons" (Eph 1:4, 5). This election is more powerful than any experience of evil and sin, than all that "enmity" which marks the history of man. In this history Mary remains a sign of sure hope.

2. Blessed is She Who Believed

12. Immediately after the narration of the Annunciation, the evangelist Luke guides us in the footsteps of the Virgin of Nazareth toward "a city of Judah" (Lk 1:39). According to scholars this city would be the modern Ain Karim, situated in the mountains, not far from Jerusalem. Mary arrived there "in haste," to visit Elizabeth her kinswoman. The reason for her visit is also to be found in the fact that at the Annunciation Gabriel had made special mention of Elizabeth, who in her old age had conceived a son by her husband Zechariah, through the power of God: "your kinswoman Elizabeth in her old age has also conceived a Son; and this is the sixth month with her who was called barren. For with God nothing will be impossible" (Lk 1:36-37). The divine messenger had spoken of what had been accomplished in Elizabeth in order to answer Mary's question. "How shall this be,

since I have no husband?" (Lk 1:34) It is to come to pass precisely through the "power of the Most High," just as it happened in the case of Elizabeth, and even more so.

Moved by charity, Mary goes to the house of her kinswoman. When Mary enters, Elizabeth replies to her greeting and feels the child leap in her womb, and being "filled with the Holy Spirit" she greets Mary with a loud cry: "Blessed are you among women, and blessed is the fruit of your womb!" (cf. Lk 1:40-42). Elizabeth's exclamation or acclamation was subsequently to become part of the Hail Mary, as a continuation of the angel's greeting, thus becoming one of the Church's most frequently used prayers. Still more significant are the words of Elizabeth in the question which follows: "And why is this granted me, that the mother of my Lord should come to me?" (Lk 1:43) Elizabeth bears witness to Mary: she recognizes and proclaims that before her stands the Mother of the Lord, the Mother of the Messiah. The son whom Elizabeth is carrying in her womb also shares in this witness: "The babe in my womb leaped for joy" (Lk 1:44). This child is the future John the Baptist, who at the Jordan will point out Jesus as the Messiah.

While every word of Elizabeth's greeting is filled with meaning, her final words would seem to have fundamental importance: "And blessed is she who believed that there would be a fulfillment of what was spoken to her from the Lord" (Lk 1:45). These words can be linked with the title "full of grace" of the angel's greeting. Both of these texts reveal an essential Mariological content, namely the truth about Mary, who has become really present in the mystery of Christ precisely because she "has believed." The fullness of grace announced by the angel means the gift of God himself. Mary's faith, proclaimed by Elizabeth at the Visitation, indicates how the Virgin of Nazareth responded to this gift.

13. As the Council teaches, "'The obedience of faith' (Rom 16:26; cf. Rom 1:5; 2 Cor 10:5-6) must be given to God who reveals, an obedience by which man entrusts his whole self freely to God." This description of faith found perfect realization in Mary. The "decisive" moment was the Annunciation, and the very words of Elizabeth: "And blessed is she who believed" refer primarily to that very moment.

Indeed, at the Annunciation Mary entrusted herself to God completely, with the "full submission of intellect and will," manifesting "the obedience of faith" to him who spoke to her through his messenger. She responded with all her human and feminine "I," and this response of faith included both perfect cooperation with "the grace of God that precedes and assists" and perfect openness to the action of the Holy Spirit, who "constantly brings faith to completion by his gifts."

The word of the living God, announced to Mary by the angel, referred to her: "And behold, you will conceive in your womb and bear a son" (Lk 1:31). By accepting this announcement, Mary was to become the "Mother of the Lord," and the divine mystery of the Incarnation was to be accomplished in her: "The Father of mercies willed that the consent of the predestined Mother should precede the Incarnation." Mary gives this consent, after she has heard everything the messenger has to say. She says, "Behold, I am the handmaid of the Lord; let it be to me according to your word" (Lk 1:38). This *fiat* of Mary—"let it be to me"—was decisive, on the human level, for the accomplishment of the divine mystery. There is a complete harmony with the words of the Son, who, according to the Letter to the Hebrews, says to the Father as he comes into the world: "Sacrifices and offering you have not desired, but a body you have prepared for me .... Lo, I have come to do your will, O God" (Heb 10:5-7). The mystery of the Incarnation was accomplished when Mary uttered her *fiat*: "Let it be to me according to your word," which made possible, as far as it depended upon her in the divine plan, the granting of her Son's desire.

Mary uttered this *fiat* in faith. In faith she entrusted herself to God without reserve and "devoted herself totally as the handmaid of the Lord to the person and work of her Son." As the Fathers of the Church teach—she conceived this Son in her mind before she conceived him in her womb: precisely in faith! Rightly does Elizabeth praise Mary: "And blessed is she who believed that there would be a fulfillment of what was spoken to her from the Lord." These words have already been fulfilled: Mary of Nazareth presents herself at the threshold of Elizabeth and Zechariah's house as the Mother of the Son of God. This is Elizabeth's joyful discovery: "The mother of my Lord comes to me!"

14. Mary's faith can also be compared to that of Abraham, whom St. Paul calls "our father in faith" (cf. Rom 4:12). In the salvific economy of God's revelation, Abraham's faith constitutes the beginning of the Old Covenant; Mary's faith at the Annunciation inaugurates the New Covenant. Just as Abraham "in hope believed against hope, that he should become the father of many nations" (cf. Rom 4:18), so Mary, at the Annunciation, having professed her virginity ("How shall this be, since I have no husband?") believed that through the power of the Most High, by the power of the Holy Spirit, she would become the Mother of God's Son in accordance with the angel's revelation: "The child to be born will be called holy, the Son of God" (Lk 1:35).

Elizabeth's words "And blessed is she who believed" do not apply only to that particular moment of the Annunciation. Certainly the Annunciation is the culminating moment of Mary's faith in her awaiting of Christ, but it is also the point of departure from which her whole "journey towards God" begins, her whole pilgrimage of faith. And on this road, in an eminent and truly heroic manner—indeed with an ever greater heroism of faith—the "obedience" which she professes to the word of divine revelation will be fulfilled. Mary's "obedience of faith" during the whole of her pilgrimage will show surprising similarities to the faith of Abraham. Just like the Patriarch of the People of God, so too Mary, during the pilgrimage of her filial and maternal *fiat*, "in hope believed against hope." Especially during certain stages of this journey the blessing granted to her "who believed" will be revealed with particular vividness. To believe means "to abandon oneself" to the truth of the word of the living God, knowing and humbly recognizing "how unsearchable are his judgments and how inscrutable his ways" (Rom 11:33). Mary, who by the eternal will of the Most High stands, one may say, at the very center of those "inscrutable ways" and "unsearchable judgments" of God, conforms herself to them in the dim light of faith, accepting fully and with a ready heart everything that is decreed in the divine plan.

15. When at the Annunciation Mary hears of the Son whose Mother she is to become and to whom "she will give the name Jesus" (Savior), she also learns that "the Lord God will give to him the throne of his father David,"

and that "he will reign over the house of Jacob forever and of his kingdom there will be no end" (Lk 1:32-33). The hope of the whole of Israel was directed toward this. The promised Messiah is to be "great," and the heavenly messenger also announces that "he will be great"—great both by bearing the name of Son of the Most High and by the fact that he is to assume the inheritance of David. He is to be a king; he is to reign "over the house of Jacob." Mary had grown up in the midst of these expectations of her people: could she guess, at the moment of the Annunciation, the vital significance of the angel's words? How is one to understand that "kingdom" which "will have no end"?

Although through faith she might have perceived in that instant she was the mother of the "Messiah King," nevertheless she replied: "Behold, I am the handmaid of the Lord; let it be to me according to your word" (Lk 1:38). From the first moment Mary professed above all the "obedience of faith," abandoning herself to the meaning which was given to the words of the Annunciation by him from whom they proceeded: God himself.

16. Later, a little further along this way of the "obedience of faith," Mary hears other words: those uttered by Simeon in the Temple of Jerusalem. It was now forty days after the birth of Jesus when, in accordance with the precepts of the Law of Moses, Mary and Joseph "brought him up to Jerusalem to present him to the Lord" (Lk 2:22). The birth had taken place in conditions of extreme poverty. We know from Luke that when, on the occasion of the census ordered by the Roman authorities, Mary went with Joseph to Bethlehem, having found "no place in the inn," she gave birth to her Son in a stable and "laid him in a manger" (cf. Lk 2:7).

A just and God-fearing man called Simeon appears at this beginning of Mary's "journey" of faith. His words, suggested by the Holy Spirit (cf. Lk 2:25-27), confirm the truth of the Annunciation. We read that he took up in his arms the child to whom—in accordance with the angel's command—the name Jesus was given (cf. Lk 2:21). Simeon's words match the meaning of this name, which is Savior: "God is salvation." Turning to the Lord, he says: "For my eyes have seen your salvation which you have prepared in the presence of all peoples, a light for revelation to the Gentiles, and for glory to your people Israel" (Lk 2:30-32). At the same time, Simeon addresses Mary with the following words: "Behold, this child is set for the fall and rising of many in Israel, and for a sign that is spoken against, that thoughts out of many hearts may be revealed"; and he adds with direct reference to her: "and a sword will pierce through your own soul also" (cf. Lk 2:34-35). Simeon's words cast new light on the announcement which Mary had heard from the angel: Jesus is the Savior; he is "a light for revelation" to mankind.

Is not this what was manifested in a way on Christmas night, when the shepherds come to the stable (cf. Lk 2:8-20)? Is not this what was to be manifested even more clearly in the coming of the Magi from the East (cf. Mt 2:1-12)? At the same time, at the very beginning of his life, the Son of Mary, and his Mother with him, will experience in themselves the truth of those other words of Simeon: "a sign that is spoken against" (Lk 2:34). Simeon's words seem like a second Annunciation to Mary, for they tell her of the actual historical situation in which the Son is to accomplish his mission, namely, in misunderstanding and sorrow. While this announcement on the one hand confirms her faith in the accomplishment of the divine promises of salvation, on the other hand it also reveals to her that she will have to live her obedience of faith in suffering, at the side of the suffering Savior, and that her motherhood will be mysterious and sorrowful; thus, after the visit of the Magi who came from the East, after their homage ("they fell down and worshipped him"), and after they had offered gifts (cf. Mt 2:11), Mary together with the child has to flee into Egypt in the protective care of Joseph, for "Herod is about to search for the child, to destroy him" (cf. Mt 2:13). Until the death of Herod they will have to remain in Egypt (cf. Mt 2:15).

17. When the Holy Family returns to Nazareth after Herod's death, there begins the long period of the hidden life. She "who believed that there would be a fulfillment of what was spoken to her from the Lord" (Lk 1:45) lives the reality of these words day by day. Daily at her side is the Son to whom "she gave the name Jesus"; therefore, in contact with him she certainly uses this name, a fact which would have surprised no one, since the name had long been in use in Israel. Mary knows that he who bears the name Jesus has been called by the angel "the Son of the Most High" (cf.

Lk 1:32). Mary knows she has conceived and given birth to him "without having a husband," by the power of the Holy Spirit, by the power of the Most High who overshadowed her (cf. Lk 1:35), just as at the time of Moses and the Patriarchs the cloud covered the presence of God (cf. Ex 24:16; 40:34-35; 1 Kgs 8:10-12). Mary knows that the Son to whom she gave birth in a virginal manner is precisely that "Holy One," the Son of God, of whom the angel spoke to her.

During the years of Jesus' hidden life in the house at Nazareth, Mary's life too is "hid with Christ in God" (cf. Col 3:3) through faith. Faith is contact with the mystery of God. Every day Mary is in constant contact with the ineffable mystery of God made man, a mystery that surpasses everything revealed in the Old Covenant. From the moment of the Annunciation, the mind of the Virgin-Mother has been initiated into the radical "newness" of God's self-revelation and has been made aware of the mystery. She is the first of those "little ones" of whom Jesus will say one day: "Father, … you have hidden these things from the wise and understanding and revealed them to babes" (Mt 11:25). "No one knows the Son except the Father" (Mt 11:27). If this is the case, how can Mary "know the Son"? Of course she does not know him as the Father does; yet she is the first of those to whom the Father "has chosen to reveal him" (cf. Mt 11:26-27; 1 Cor 2:11). If though, from the moment of the Annunciation, the Son—whom only the Father knows completely, as the one who begets him in the eternal "today" (cf. Ps(s) 2:7)—was revealed to Mary, she, his Mother, is in contact with the truth about her Son only in faith and through faith! She is specifically blessed because "she has believed," and she continues to believe day after day amidst all the trials and the adversities of Jesus' infancy and then during the years of the hidden life at Nazareth, where he "was obedient to them" (Lk 2:51). He was obedient both to Mary and also to Joseph, since Joseph took the place of his father in people's eyes; for this reason, the Son of Mary was regarded by the people as "the carpenter's son" (Mt 13:55).

The Mother of that Son, mindful of what has been told her at the Annunciation and in subsequent events, bears within herself the radical "newness" of faith: the beginning of the New Covenant. This is the beginning of the Gospel, the joyful Good News; however, it is not difficult to see in that beginning a particular heaviness of heart, linked with a sort of "night of faith"—to use the words of St. John of the Cross—a kind of "veil" through which one has to draw near to the Invisible One and to live in intimacy with the mystery. This is the way that Mary, for many years, lived in intimacy with the mystery of her Son, and went forward in her "pilgrimage of faith," while Jesus "increased in wisdom … and in favor with God and man" (Lk 2:52). God's predilection for him was manifested ever more clearly in people's eyes. The first human creature thus permitted to discover Christ was Mary, who lived with Joseph in the same house at Nazareth.

When he had been found in the Temple, and his Mother asked him, "Son, why have you treated us so?" the twelve-year-old Jesus answered: "Did you not know that I must be in my Father's house?" The Evangelist adds: "And they (Joseph and Mary) did not understand the saying which he spoke to them" (Lk 2:48-50). Jesus was aware that "no one knows the Son except the Father" (cf. Mt 11:27); thus even his Mother, to whom had been revealed most completely the mystery of his divine sonship, lived in intimacy with this mystery only through faith! Living side by side with her Son under the same roof, and faithfully persevering "in her union with her Son," she "advanced in her pilgrimage of faith," as the Council emphasizes. It was during Christ's public life, too (cf. Mk 3:21-35), that day by day there was fulfilled in her the blessing uttered by Elizabeth at the Visitation: "Blessed is she who believed."

18. This blessing reaches its full meaning when Mary stands beneath the Cross of her Son (cf. Jn 19:25). The Council says that this happened "not without a divine plan": by "suffering deeply with her only-begotten Son and joining herself with her maternal spirit to his sacrifice, lovingly consenting to the immolation of the victim to whom she had given birth," in this way Mary "faithfully preserved her union with her Son even to the Cross." It is a union through faith—the same faith with which she had received the angel's revelation at the Annunciation. At that moment she had also heard the words: "He will be great … and the Lord God will give to him the throne of his father David, and he will reign over the house of Jacob forever; and of his kingdom there will be no end" (Lk 1:32-33).

Now, standing at the foot of the Cross, Mary is the witness, humanly speaking, of the complete negation of these words. On that wood of the

Cross her Son hangs in agony as one condemned. "He was despised and rejected by men; a man of sorrows ... he was despised, and we esteemed him not": as one destroyed (cf. Is 53:3-5). How great, how heroic then is the obedience of faith shown by Mary in the face of God's "unsearchable judgments"! How completely she "abandons herself to God" without reserve, offering the "full assent of the intellect and the will" to him whose "ways are inscrutable" (cf. Rom 11:33)! How powerful, too, is the action of grace in her soul, how all-pervading is the influence of the Holy Spirit and of his light and power!

Through this faith Mary is perfectly united with Christ in his self-emptying. "Christ Jesus, who, though he was in the form of God, did not count equality with God a thing to be grasped, but emptied himself, taking the form of a servant, being born in the likeness of men": precisely on Golgotha "humbled himself and became obedient unto death, even death on a cross" (cf. Phil 2:5-8). At the foot of the Cross, Mary shares through faith in the shocking mystery of this self-emptying. This is perhaps the deepest "kenosis" of faith in human history. Through faith the Mother shares in the death of her Son, in his redeeming death; but in contrast with the faith of the disciples who fled, hers was far more enlightened. On Golgotha, Jesus through the Cross definitively confirmed that he was the "sign of contradiction" foretold by Simeon. At the same time, there were also fulfilled on Golgotha the words which Simeon had addressed to Mary: "and a sword will pierce through your own soul also."

19. Yes, truly "blessed is she who believed"! These words, spoken by Elizabeth after the Annunciation, here at the foot of the Cross seem to re-echo with supreme eloquence, and the power contained within them becomes something penetrating. From the Cross, that is to say from the very heart of the mystery of Redemption, there radiates and spreads out the prospect of that blessing of faith. It goes right back to "the beginning," and, as a sharing in the sacrifice of Christ—the new Adam—it becomes in a certain sense the counterpoise to the disobedience and disbelief embodied in the sin of our first parents. As the Fathers of the Church—and especially St. Irenaeus—teach, quoted by the Constitution *Lumen Gentium*: "The knot of Eve's disobedience was untied by Mary's obedience; what the virgin

Eve bound through her unbelief, the Virgin Mary loosened by her faith." In the light of this comparison with Eve, the Fathers of the Church—as the Council also says—call Mary the "mother of the living" and often speak of "death through Eve, life through Mary."

In the expression "Blessed is she who believed," we can rightly find a kind of "key" which unlocks for us the innermost reality of Mary, whom the angel hailed as "full of grace." If, as "full of grace," she has been eternally present in the mystery of Christ, through faith she became a sharer in that mystery in every extension of her earthly journey. She "advanced in her pilgrimage of faith" and at the same time, in a discreet yet direct and effective way, she made present to humanity the mystery of Christ, and she still continues to do so. Through the mystery of Christ, she too is present within mankind; thus through the mystery of the Son the mystery of the Mother is also made clear.

3. Behold Your Mother

20. The Gospel of Luke records the moment when "a woman in the crowd raised her voice" and said to Jesus: "Blessed is the womb that bore you, and the breasts that you sucked!" (Lk 11:27). These words were an expression of praise of Mary as Jesus' mother according to the flesh. Probably the Mother of Jesus was not personally known to this woman; in fact, when Jesus began his messianic activity Mary did not accompany him but continued to remain at Nazareth. One could say that the words of that unknown woman in a way brought Mary out of her hiddenness.

Through these words, there flashed out in the midst of the crowd, at least for an instant, the gospel of Jesus' infancy. This is the gospel in which Mary is present as the mother who conceives Jesus in her womb, gives him birth, and nurses him: the nursing mother referred to by the woman in the crowd. Thanks to this motherhood, Jesus, the Son of the Most High (cf. Lk 1:32), is a true son of man. He is "flesh," like every other man: he is "the Word (who) became flesh" (cf. Jn 1:14). He is of the flesh and blood of Mary!

To the blessing uttered by that woman upon her who was his mother according to the flesh, Jesus replies in a significant way: "Blessed rather are those who hear the word of God and keep it" (Lk 11:28). He wishes to divert attention from motherhood understood only as a fleshly bond, in order to direct it toward those mysterious bonds of the spirit which develop from hearing and keeping God's word.

This same shift into the sphere of spiritual values is seen even more clearly in another response of Jesus reported by all the Synoptics. When Jesus is told that "his mother and brothers are standing outside and wish to see him," he replies: "My mother and my brothers are those who hear the word of God and do it" (cf. Lk 8:20-21). This he said "looking around on those who sat about him," as we read in Mark (3:34) or, according to Matthew (12:49), "stretching out his hand towards his disciples." These statements seem to fit in with the reply which the twelve-year-old Jesus gave to Mary and Joseph when he was found after three days in the Temple at Jerusalem.

Now, when Jesus left Nazareth and began his public life throughout Palestine, he was completely and exclusively "concerned with his Father's business" (cf. Lk 2:49). He announced the Kingdom: the "Kingdom of God" and "his Father's business," which add a new dimension and meaning to everything human, and therefore to every human bond, insofar as these things relate to the goals and tasks assigned to every human being. Within this new dimension, also a bond such as that of "brotherhood" means something different from "brotherhood according to the flesh" deriving from a common origin from the same set of parents. "Motherhood," too, in the dimension of the Kingdom of God and in the radius of the fatherhood of God himself, takes on another meaning. In the words reported by Luke, Jesus teaches precisely this new meaning of motherhood.

Is Jesus thereby distancing himself from his mother according to the flesh? Does he perhaps wish to leave her in the hidden obscurity which she herself has chosen? If this seems to be the case from the tone of those words, one must nevertheless note that the new and different motherhood which Jesus speaks of to his disciples refers precisely to Mary in a very special way. Is not Mary the first of "those who hear the word of God and do it"? Does not the blessing uttered by Jesus in response to the woman in the crowd refer primarily to Mary? Without any doubt, Mary is worthy of blessing by the very fact that she became the mother of Jesus according to the flesh ("Blessed is the womb that bore you, and the breasts that you sucked"), but also and especially because already at the Annunciation she accepted the word of God, because she believed it, because she was obedient to God, and because she "kept" the word and "pondered it in her heart" (cf. Lk 1:38, 45; 2:19, 51) and by means of her whole life accomplished it. We can say that the blessing proclaimed by Jesus is not in opposition, despite appearances, to the blessing uttered by the unknown woman, but rather coincides with that blessing in the person of this Virgin Mother, who called herself only "the handmaid of the Lord" (Lk 1:38). If it is true that "all generations will call her blessed" (cf. Lk 1:48), then it can be said that the unnamed woman was the first to confirm unwittingly that prophetic phrase of Mary's *Magnificat* and to begin the *Magnificat* of the ages.

If through faith Mary became the bearer of the Son given to her by the Father through the power of the Holy Spirit, while preserving her virginity intact, in that same faith she discovered and accepted the other dimension of motherhood revealed by Jesus during his messianic mission. One can say that this dimension of motherhood belonged to Mary from the beginning, that is to say from the moment of the conception and birth of her Son. From that time she was "the one who believed." As the messianic mission of her Son grew clearer to her eyes and spirit, she herself as a mother became ever more open to that new dimension of motherhood which was to constitute her "part" beside her Son. Had she not said from the very beginning: "Behold, I am the handmaid of the Lord; let it be to me according to your word" (Lk 1:38)? Through faith Mary continued to hear and to ponder that word, in which there became ever clearer, in a way "which surpasses knowledge" (Eph 3:19), the self-revelation of the living God. In a sense, Mary as Mother became the first "disciple" of her Son, the first to whom he seemed to say: "Follow me," even before he addressed this call to the Apostles or to anyone else (cf. Jn 1:43).

21. From this point of view, particularly eloquent is the passage in the Gospel of John which presents Mary at the wedding feast of Cana. She appears there as the Mother of Jesus at the beginning of his public life: "There was a marriage at Cana in Galilee, and the mother of Jesus was there; Jesus also was invited to the marriage, with his disciples" (Jn 2:1-2). From the text it appears that Jesus and his disciples were invited together with Mary, as if by reason of her presence at the celebration: the Son seems to have

been invited because of his mother. We are familiar with the sequence of events which resulted from that invitation, that "beginning of the signs" wrought by Jesus—the water changed into wine—which prompts the Evangelist to say that Jesus "manifested his glory; and his disciples believed in him" (Jn 2:11).

Mary is present at Cana in Galilee as the Mother of Jesus, and in a significant way she contributes to that "beginning of the signs" which reveal the messianic power of her Son. We read: "When the wine gave out, the mother of Jesus said to him, 'They have no wine.' And Jesus said to her, 'O woman, what have you to do with me? My hour has not yet come'" (Jn 2:3-4). In John's Gospel that "hour" means the time appointed by the Father when the Son accomplishes his task and is to be glorified (cf. Jn 7:30; 8:20; 12:23, 27; 13:1; 17:1; 19:27). Even though Jesus' reply to his mother sounds like a refusal (especially if we consider the blunt statement "My hour has not yet come" rather than the question), Mary nevertheless turns to the servants and says to them: "Do whatever he tells you" (Jn 2:5). Then Jesus orders the servants to fill the stone jars with water, and the water becomes wine, better than the wine which has previously been served to the wedding guests.

What deep understanding existed between Jesus and his mother? How can we probe the mystery of their intimate spiritual union? The fact speaks for itself: It is certain that that event already quite clearly outlines the new dimension, the new meaning of Mary's motherhood. Her motherhood has a significance which is not exclusively contained in the words of Jesus and in the various episodes reported by the Synoptics (Lk 11:27-28 and Lk 8:19-21; Mt 12:46-50; Mk 3:31-35). In these texts Jesus means above all to contrast the motherhood resulting from the fact of birth with what this "motherhood" (and also "brotherhood") is to be in the dimension of the Kingdom of God, in the salvific radius of God's fatherhood. In John's text, on the other hand, the description of the Cana event outlines what is actually manifested as a new kind of motherhood according to the spirit and not just according to the flesh, that is to say Mary's solicitude for human beings, her coming to them in the wide variety of their wants and needs. At Cana in Galilee there is shown only one concrete aspect of human need, apparently a small one of little importance ("They have no wine"), but it has a symbolic value: this coming to the aid of human needs means, at the same time, bringing those needs within the radius of Christ's messianic mission and salvific power. There is a mediation: Mary places herself between her Son and mankind in the reality of their wants, needs, and sufferings. She puts herself "in the middle," that is to say she acts as a mediatrix, not as an outsider but in her position as mother. She knows that as such she can point out to her Son the needs of mankind; in fact, she "has the right" to do so. Her mediation is thus in the nature of intercession: Mary "intercedes" for mankind. That is not all: As a mother she also wishes the messianic power of her Son to be manifested, that salvific power of his which is meant to help man in his misfortunes, to free him from the evil which in various forms and degrees weighs heavily upon his life. Precisely as the Prophet Isaiah had foretold about the Messiah in the famous passage which Jesus quoted before his fellow townsfolk in Nazareth: "To preach good news to the poor ... to proclaim release to the captives and recovering of sight to the blind ..." (cf. Lk 4:18).

Another essential element of Mary's maternal task is found in her words to the servants: "Do whatever he tells you." The Mother of Christ presents herself as the spokeswoman of her Son's will, pointing out those things which must be done so that the salvific power of the Messiah may be manifested. At Cana, thanks to the intercession of Mary and the obedience of the servants, Jesus begins "his hour." At Cana Mary appears as believing in Jesus. Her faith evokes his first "sign" and helps to kindle the faith of the disciples.

22. We can therefore say that in this passage of John's Gospel we find as it were a first manifestation of the truth concerning Mary's maternal care. This truth has also found expression in the teaching of the Second Vatican Council. It is important to note how the Council illustrates Mary's maternal role as it relates to the mediation of Christ: "Mary's maternal function towards mankind in no way obscures or diminishes the unique mediation of Christ, but rather shows its efficacy," because "there is one mediator between God and men, the man Christ Jesus" (1 Tm 2:5). This maternal role of Mary flows, according to God's good pleasure, "from the superabundance of the merits of Christ; it is founded on his mediation, absolutely depends on it, and draws all its efficacy from it." It is precisely in this sense

that the episode at Cana in Galilee offers us a sort of first announcement of Mary's mediation, wholly oriented toward Christ and tending to the revelation of his salvific power.

From the text of John it is evident that it is a mediation which is maternal. As the Council proclaims, Mary became "a mother to us in the order of grace." This motherhood in the order of grace flows from her divine motherhood. Because she was, by the design of divine Providence, the mother who nourished the divine Redeemer, Mary became "an associate of unique nobility, and the Lord's humble handmaid," who "cooperated by her obedience, faith, hope and burning charity in the Savior's work of restoring supernatural life to souls," and "this maternity of Mary in the order of grace... will last without interruption until the eternal fulfillment of all the elect."

23. If John's description of the event at Cana presents Mary's caring motherhood at the beginning of Christ's messianic activity, another passage from the same Gospel confirms this motherhood in the salvific economy of grace at its crowning moment, namely when Christ's sacrifice on the Cross, his Paschal Mystery, is accomplished. John's description is concise: "Standing by the cross of Jesus were his mother, and his mother's sister, Mary the wife of Clopas, and Mary Magdalene. When Jesus saw his mother, and the disciple whom he loved standing near, he said to his mother: 'Woman, behold your son!' Then he said to the disciple, 'Behold, your mother!' And from that hour the disciple took her to his own home" (Jn 19:25-27).

Undoubtedly, we find here an expression of the Son's particular solicitude for his Mother, whom he is leaving in such great sorrow, yet the "testament of Christ's Cross" says more. Jesus highlights a new relationship between Mother and Son, the whole truth and reality of which he solemnly confirms. One can say that if Mary's motherhood of the human race had already been outlined, now it is clearly stated and established. It emerges from the definitive accomplishment of the Redeemer's Paschal Mystery. The Mother of Christ, who stands at the very center of this mystery—a mystery which embraces each individual and all humanity—is given as mother to every single individual and all mankind. The man at the foot of the Cross is John, "the disciple whom he loved," but it is not he alone. Following tradition, the Council does not hesitate to call Mary "the Mother of Christ and mother of mankind": since she "belongs to the offspring of Adam she is one with all human beings.... Indeed she is 'clearly the mother of the members of Christ ... since she cooperated out of love so that there might be born in the Church the faithful.'"

This "new motherhood of Mary," generated by faith, is the fruit of the "new" love which came to definitive maturity in her at the foot of the Cross, through her sharing in the redemptive love of her Son.

24. We find ourselves at the very center of the fulfillment of the promise contained in the *Proto-gospel*: the "seed of the woman ... will crush the head of the serpent" (cf. Gen 3:15). By his redemptive death Jesus Christ conquers the evil of sin and death at its very roots. It is significant that, as he speaks to his mother from the Cross, he calls her "woman" and says to her: "Woman, behold your son!" He had addressed her by the same term at Cana, too (cf. Jn 2:4). How can one doubt that especially now, on Golgotha, this expression goes to the very heart of the mystery of Mary and indicates the unique place which she occupies in the whole economy of salvation? As the Council teaches, in Mary "the exalted Daughter of Sion, and after a long expectation of the promise, the times were at length fulfilled and the new dispensation established. All this occurred when the Son of God took a human nature from her, that he might in the mysteries of his flesh free man from sin."

The words uttered by Jesus from the Cross signify that the motherhood of her who bore Christ finds a "new" continuation in the Church and through the Church, symbolized and represented by John. In this way, she who as the one "full of grace" was brought into the mystery of Christ in order to be his Mother and thus the Holy Mother of God, through the Church remains in that mystery as "the woman" spoken of by the Book of Genesis (3:15) at the beginning and by the Apocalypse (12:1) at the end of the history of salvation. In accordance with the eternal plan of Providence, Mary's divine motherhood is to be poured out upon the Church, as indicated by statements of Tradition, according to which Mary's "motherhood" of the Church is the reflection and extension of her motherhood of the Son of God.

According to the Council the very moment of the Church's birth and full manifestation to the world enables us to glimpse this continuity of Mary's motherhood: "Since it pleased God not to manifest solemnly the mystery of the salvation of the human race until he poured forth the Spirit promised by Christ, we see the Apostles before the day of Pentecost 'continuing with one mind in prayer with the women and Mary the mother of Jesus, and with his brethren' (Acts 1:14). We see Mary prayerfully imploring the gift of the Spirit, who had already overshadowed her in the Annunciation."

In the redemptive economy of grace, brought about through the action of the Holy Spirit, there is a unique correspondence between the moment of the Incarnation of the Word and the moment of the birth of the Church. The person who links these two moments is Mary: Mary at Nazareth and Mary in the Upper Room at Jerusalem. In both cases her discreet yet essential presence indicates the path of "birth from the Holy Spirit"; thus she who is present in the mystery of Christ as Mother becomes—by the will of the Son and the power of the Holy Spirit—present in the mystery of the Church. In the Church, too, she continues to be a maternal presence, as is shown by the words spoken from the Cross: "Woman, behold your son!"; "Behold, your mother!"

The Church, the People of God Present in All the Nations of the Earth

25. "The Church, 'like a pilgrim in a foreign land, presses forward amid the persecutions of the world and the consolations of God,' announcing the Cross and Death of the Lord until he comes (cf. 1 Cor 11:26)." Israel according to the flesh, which wandered as an exile in the desert, was already called the Church of God (cf. 2 Esd 13:1; Nm 20:4; Dt 23:1ff.); likewise, the new Israel ... is also called the Church of Christ (cf. Mt 16:18). He has bought it for himself with his blood (Acts 20:28), has filled it with his Spirit, and provided it with those means which befit it as a visible and social unity. God has gathered together as one all those who in faith look upon Jesus as the author of salvation and the source of unity and peace, and has established them as Church, that for each and all she may be the "visible sacrament of this saving unity."

The Second Vatican Council speaks of the pilgrim Church, establishing an analogy with the Israel of the Old Covenant journeying through the desert. The journey also has an external character, visible in the time and space in which it historically takes place. The Church "is destined to extend to all regions of the earth and so to enter into the history of mankind," but at the same time "she transcends all limits of time and of space," yet the essential character of her pilgrimage is interior: it is a question of a pilgrimage through faith, by "the power of the Risen Lord," a pilgrimage in the Holy Spirit, given to the Church as the invisible Comforter (*parakletos*) (cf. Jn 14:26; 15:26; 16:7): "Moving forward through trial and tribulation, the Church is strengthened by the power of God's grace promised to her by the Lord, so that ... moved by the Holy Spirit, she may never cease to renew herself, until through the Cross she arrives at the light which knows no setting."

It is precisely in this ecclesial journey or pilgrimage through space and time, and even more through the history of souls, that Mary is present, as the one who is "blessed because she believed," as the one who advanced on the pilgrimage of faith, sharing unlike any other creature in the mystery of Christ. The Council further says that "Mary figured profoundly in the history of salvation and in a certain way unites and mirrors within herself the central truths of the faith." Among all believers she is like a "mirror" in which are reflected in the most profound and limpid way "the mighty works of God" (Acts 2:11).

26. Built by Christ upon the Apostles, the Church became fully aware of these mighty works of God on the day of Pentecost, when those gathered together in the Upper Room "were all filled with the Holy Spirit and began to speak in other tongues, as the Spirit gave them utterance" (Acts 2:4). From that moment there also begins that journey of faith, the Church's pilgrimage through the history of individuals and peoples. We know that at the beginning of this journey Mary is present. We see her in the midst of the Apostles in the Upper Room, "prayerfully imploring the gift of the Spirit."

In a sense her journey of faith is longer. The Holy Spirit had already come down upon her, and she became his faithful spouse at the Annunciation, welcoming the Word of the true God, offering "the full submission of intellect and will ... and freely assenting to the truth revealed by him," indeed abandoning herself totally to God through "the obedience of faith," whereby she replied to the angel: "Behold, I am the handmaid of the Lord; let it be to me according to your word." The journey of faith made by Mary, whom we see praying in the Upper Room, is thus longer than that of the others gathered there: Mary "goes before them," "leads the way" for them. The moment of Pentecost in Jerusalem had been prepared for by the moment of the Annunciation in Nazareth, as well as by the Cross. In the Upper Room, Mary's journey meets the Church's journey of faith. In what way?

Among those who devoted themselves to prayer in the Upper Room, preparing to go "into the whole world" after receiving the Spirit, some had been called by Jesus gradually from the beginning of his mission in Israel. Eleven of them had been made Apostles, and to them Jesus had passed on the mission which he himself had received from the Father. "As the Father has sent me, even so I send you" (Jn 20:21), he had said to the Apostles after the Resurrection. Forty days later, before returning to the Father, he had added: "[W]hen the Holy Spirit has come upon you … you shall be my witnesses … to the end of the earth" (cf. Acts 1:8). This mission of the Apostles began the moment they left the Upper Room in Jerusalem. The Church is born and then grows through the testimony that Peter and the Apostles bear to the Crucified and Risen Christ (cf. Acts 2:31-34; 3:15-18; 4:10-12; 5:30-32).

Mary did not directly receive this apostolic mission. She was not among those whom Jesus sent "to the whole world to teach all nations" (cf. Mt 28:19) when he conferred this mission on them, but she was in the Upper Room, where the Apostles were preparing to take up this mission with the coming of the Spirit of Truth: she was present with them. In their midst Mary was "devoted to prayer" as the "mother of Jesus" (cf. Acts 1:13-14), of the Crucified and Risen Christ. That first group of those who in faith looked "upon Jesus as the author of salvation" knew that Jesus was the Son of Mary, and that she was his Mother, and that as such she was from the moment of his conception and birth a unique witness to the mystery of Jesus, that mystery which before their eyes had been disclosed and confirmed in the Cross and Resurrection. From the very first moment, the Church "looked at" Mary through Jesus, just as she "looked at" Jesus through Mary.

For the Church of that time and of every time, Mary is a singular witness to the years of Jesus' infancy and hidden life at Nazareth, when she "kept all these things, pondering them in her heart" (Lk 2:19; cf. Lk 2:51).

Above all, in the Church of that time and of every time Mary was and is the one who is "blessed because she believed"; she was the first to believe. From the moment of the Annunciation and conception, from the moment of his birth in the stable at Bethlehem, Mary followed Jesus step by step in her maternal pilgrimage of faith. She followed him during the years of his hidden life at Nazareth; she followed him also during the time after he left home, when he began "to do and to teach" (cf. Acts 1:1) in the midst of Israel. Above all she followed him in the tragic experience of Golgotha. Now, while Mary was with the Apostles in the Upper Room in Jerusalem at the dawn of the Church, her faith, born from the words of the Annunciation, found confirmation. The angel had said to her then: "You will conceive in your womb and bear a son, and you shall call his name Jesus. He will be great ... and he will reign over the house of Jacob forever; and of his kingdom there will be no end." The recent events on Calvary had shrouded that promise in darkness, yet not even beneath the Cross did Mary's faith fail. She had still remained the one who, like Abraham, "in hope believed against hope" (Rom 4:18). But it is only after the Resurrection that hope had shown its true face and the promise had begun to be transformed into reality. For Jesus, before returning to the Father, had said to the Apostles: "Go therefore and make disciples of all nations.... Lo, I am with you always, to the close of the age" (cf. Mt 28:19-20). Thus had spoken the one who by his Resurrection had revealed himself as the conqueror of death, as the one who possessed the kingdom of which, as the angel said, "there will be no end."

27. Now, at the first dawn of the Church, at the beginning of the long journey through faith which began at Pentecost in Jerusalem, Mary was with all those who were the seed of the "new Israel." She was present among them as an exceptional witness to the mystery of Christ. The Church was assiduous in prayer together with her, and at the same time "contemplated her in the light of the Word made man." It was always to be so. When the Church "enters more intimately into the supreme mystery of the In-

carnation," she thinks of the Mother of Christ with profound reverence and devotion. Mary belongs indissolubly to the mystery of Christ, and she belongs also to the mystery of the Church from the beginning, from the day of the Church's birth. At the basis of what the Church has been from the beginning, and of what she must continually become from generation to generation, in the midst of all the nations of the earth, we find the one "who believed that there would be a fulfillment of what was spoken to her from the Lord" (Lk 1:45). It is precisely Mary's faith which marks the beginning of the new and eternal Covenant of God with man in Jesus Christ; this heroic faith of hers "precedes" the apostolic witness of the Church and ever remains in the Church's heart hidden like a special heritage of God's revelation. All those who from generation to generation accept the apostolic witness of the Church share in that mysterious inheritance, and in a sense share in Mary's faith.

Elizabeth's words "Blessed is she who believed" continue to accompany the Virgin also at Pentecost; they accompany her from age to age, wherever knowledge of Christ's salvific mystery spreads, through the Church's apostolic witness and service. The words of Elizabeth fulfill the prophecy of the *Magnificat*: "All generations will call me blessed; for he who is mighty has done great things for me, and holy is his name" (Lk 1:48-49). Knowledge of the mystery of Christ leads us to bless his Mother, in the form of special veneration for the *Theotókos*, but this veneration always includes a blessing of her faith, for the Virgin of Nazareth became blessed above all through this faith, in accordance with Elizabeth's words. Those who from generation to generation among the different peoples and nations of the earth accept with faith the mystery of Christ, the Incarnate Word and Redeemer of the world, not only turn with veneration to Mary and confidently have recourse to her as his Mother but also seek in her faith support for their own. It is precisely this lively sharing in Mary's faith that determines her special place in the Church's pilgrimage as the new People of God throughout the earth.

28. As the Council says, "Mary figured profoundly in the history of salvation ... ; hence when she is being preached and venerated, she summons the faithful to her Son and his sacrifice, and to love for the Father." For this

reason, Mary's faith, according to the Church's apostolic witness, in some way continues to become the faith of the pilgrim People of God: the faith of individuals and communities, of places and gatherings, and of the various groups existing in the Church. It is a faith that is passed on simultaneously through both the mind and the heart. It is gained or regained continually through prayer; therefore, "the Church in her apostolic work also rightly looks to her who brought forth Christ, conceived by the Holy Spirit and born of the Virgin, so that through the Church Christ may be born and increase in the hearts of the faithful also."

Today, as on this pilgrimage of faith we draw near to the end of the second Christian Millennium, the Church, through the teaching of the Second Vatican Council, calls our attention to her vision of herself, as the "one People of God ... among all the nations of the earth." She reminds us of that truth according to which all the faithful, though "scattered throughout the world, are in communion with each other in the Holy Spirit." We can, as a result, say that in this union the mystery of Pentecost is continually being accomplished. At the same time, the Lord's Apostles and disciples, in all the nations of the earth, "devote themselves to prayer together with Mary, the mother of Jesus" (Acts 1:14). As they constitute from generation to generation the "sign of the Kingdom" which is not of his world, they are also aware that in the midst of this world they must gather around that King to whom the nations have been given in heritage (cf. Ps(s) 2:8), to whom the Father has given "the throne of David his father," so that he "will reign over the house of Jacob forever, and of his kingdom there will be no end."

During this time of vigil, Mary, through the same faith which made her blessed, especially from the moment of the Annunciation, is present in the Church's mission, present in the Church's work of introducing into the world the Kingdom of her Son. This presence of Mary finds many different expressions in our day, just as it did throughout the Church's history. It also has a wide field of action. Through the faith and piety of individual believers; through the traditions of Christian families or "domestic churches," of parish and missionary communities, religious institutes and dioceses; through the radiance and attraction of the great shrines where not only individuals or local groups but sometimes whole nations and societies, even whole continents, seek to meet the Mother of the Lord, the one who is blessed because she believed is the first among believers and therefore became the Mother of Emmanuel. This is the message of the Land of Palestine, the spiritual homeland of all Christians because it was the homeland of the Savior of the world and of his Mother. This is the message of the many churches in Rome and throughout the world which have been raised up during the course of the centuries by the faith of Christians. This is the message of centers like Guadalupe, Lourdes, Fatima, and the others situated in the various countries. Among them how could I fail to mention the one in my own native land, Jasna Gora? One could perhaps speak of a specific "geography" of faith and Marian devotion, which includes all these special places of pilgrimage where the People of God seek to meet the Mother of God in order to find, within the radius of the maternal presence of her "who believed," a strengthening of their own faith. For in Mary's faith, first at the Annunciation and then fully at the foot of the Cross, an interior space was reopened within humanity which the eternal Father can fill "with every spiritual blessing." It is the space "of the new and eternal Covenant," and it continues to exist in the Church, which in Christ is "a kind of sacrament or sign of intimate union with God, and of the unity of all mankind."

In the faith which Mary professed at the Annunciation as the "handmaid of the Lord" and in which she constantly "precedes" the pilgrim People of God throughout the earth, the Church "strives energetically and constantly to bring all humanity ... back to Christ its Head in the unity of his Spirit."

The Church's Journey and the Unity of All Christians

29. "In all of Christ's disciples the Spirit arouses the desire to be peacefully united, in the manner determined by Christ, as one flock under one shepherd." The journey of the Church, especially in our own time, is marked by the sign of ecumenism: Christians are seeking ways to restore that unity which Christ implored from the Father for his disciples on the day before his Passion: "That they may all be one; even as you, Father, are in me, and I in you that they also may be in us, so that the world may believe that you have sent me" (Jn 17:21); therefore, the unity of Christ's disciples

is a great sign given in order to kindle faith in the world while their division constitutes a scandal.

The ecumenical movement, on the basis of a clearer and more widespread awareness of the urgent need to achieve the unity of all Christians, has found on the part of the Catholic Church its culminating expression in the work of the Second Vatican Council: Christians must deepen in themselves and each of their communities that "obedience of faith" of which Mary is the first and brightest example. Since she "shines forth on earth, . . . as a sign of sure hope and solace for the pilgrim People of God," "it gives great joy and comfort to this most holy Synod that among the divided brethren, too, there are those who give due honor to the Mother of our Lord and Savior. This is especially so among the Easterners."

30. Christians know that their unity will be truly rediscovered only if it is based on the unity of their faith. They must resolve considerable discrepancies of doctrine concerning the mystery and ministry of the Church, and sometimes also concerning the role of Mary in the work of salvation. The dialogues begun by the Catholic Church with the Churches and Ecclesial Communities of the West are steadily converging upon these two inseparable aspects of the same mystery of salvation. If the mystery of the Word made flesh enables us to glimpse the mystery of the divine motherhood and, in turn, contemplation of the Mother of God brings us to a more profound understanding of the mystery of the Incarnation, then the same must be said for the mystery of the Church and Mary's role in the work of salvation. By a more profound study of both Mary and the Church, clarifying each by the light of the other, Christians who are eager to do what Jesus tells them—as their Mother recommends (cf. Jn 2:5)—will be able to go forward together on this "pilgrimage of faith." Mary, who is still the model of this pilgrimage, is to lead them to the unity which is willed by their one Lord and so much desired by those who are attentively listening to what "the Spirit is saying to the Churches" today (Rv 2:7, 11, 17).

Meanwhile, it is a hopeful sign that these Churches and Ecclesial Communities are finding agreement with the Catholic Church on fundamental points of Christian belief, including matters relating to the Virgin Mary. They recognize her as the Mother of the Lord and hold that this forms part of our faith in Christ, true God and true man. They look to her who at the foot of the Cross accepts as her son the beloved disciple, the one who in his turn accepts her as his mother.

Why should we not all together look to her as our common Mother, who prays for the unity of God's family and who "precedes" us all at the head of the long line of witnesses of faith in the one Lord, the Son of God, who was conceived in her virginal womb by the power of the Holy Spirit?

31. On the other hand, I wish to emphasize how profoundly the Catholic Church, the Orthodox Church, and the ancient Churches of the East feel united by love and praise of the *Theotókos*. Not only "basic dogmas of the Christian faith concerning the Trinity and God's Word made flesh of the Virgin Mary were defined in Ecumenical Councils held in the East" but also in their liturgical worship "the Orientals pay high tribute, in very beautiful hymns, to Mary ever Virgin ... God's Most Holy Mother."

The brethren of these Churches have experienced a complex history, but it is one that has always been marked by an intense desire for Christian commitment and apostolic activity, despite frequent persecution, even to the point of bloodshed. It is a history of fidelity to the Lord, an authentic "pilgrimage of faith" in space and time, during which Eastern Christians have always looked with boundless trust to the Mother of the Lord, celebrated her with praise, and invoked her with unceasing prayer. In the difficult moments of their troubled Christian existence, "they have taken refuge under her protection," conscious of having in her a powerful aid. The Churches which profess the doctrine of Ephesus proclaim the Virgin as "true Mother of God," since "our Lord Jesus Christ, born of the Father before time began according to his divinity, in the last days, for our sake and for our salvation, was himself begotten of Mary, the Virgin Mother of God according to his humanity." The Greek Fathers and the Byzantine tradition contemplating the Virgin in the light of the Word made flesh have sought to penetrate the depth of that bond which unites Mary, as the Mother of God, to Christ and the Church: the Virgin is a permanent presence in the whole reality of the salvific mystery.

The Coptic and Ethiopian traditions were introduced to this contemplation of the mystery of Mary by St. Cyril of Alexandria, and in their turn they have celebrated it with a profuse poetic blossoming. The poetic genius of St. Ephrem the Syrian, called "the lyre of the Holy Spirit," tirelessly sang of Mary, leaving a still-living mark on the whole tradition of the Syriac Church. In his panegyric of the *Theotókos*, St. Gregory of Narek, one of the outstanding glories of Armenia, with powerful poetic inspiration ponders the different aspects of the mystery of the Incarnation, and each of them is for him an occasion to sing and extol the extraordinary dignity and magnificent beauty of the Virgin Mary, Mother of the Word made flesh. It does not surprise us that Mary occupies a privileged place in the worship of the ancient Oriental Churches with an incomparable abundance of feasts and hymns.

32. In the Byzantine liturgy, in all the hours of the Divine Office, praise of the Mother is linked with praise of her Son and with the praise which, through the Son, is offered up to the Father in the Holy Spirit. In the *Anaphora* or Eucharistic Prayer of St. John Chrysostom, immediately after the *epiclesis*, the assembled community sings in honor of the Mother of God: "It is truly just to proclaim you blessed, O Mother of God, who are most blessed, all pure and Mother of our God. We magnify you who are more honorable than the Cherubim and incomparably more glorious than the Seraphim. You who, without losing your virginity, gave birth to the Word of God. You who are truly the Mother of God."

These praises, which in every celebration of the Eucharistic Liturgy are offered to Mary, have molded the faith, piety, and prayer of the faithful. In the course of the centuries, they have permeated their whole spiritual outlook, fostering in them a profound devotion to the "All Holy Mother of God."

33. This year there occurs the twelfth centenary of the Second Ecumenical Council of Nicaea (787). Putting an end to the well-known controversy about the cult of sacred images, this Council defined that, according to the teaching of the holy Fathers and the universal tradition of the Church, there could be exposed for the veneration of the faithful, together with the Cross, also images of the Mother of God, of the angels, and of the saints, in churches and houses and at the roadside. This custom has been main-

tained in the whole of the East and also in the West. Images of the Virgin have a place of honor in churches and houses. In them Mary is represented in a number of ways: as the throne of God carrying the Lord and giving him to humanity (*Theotókos*), as the way that leads to Christ and manifests him (*Hodegetria*), as a praying figure in an attitude of intercession and as a sign of the divine presence on the journey of the faithful until the day of the Lord (*Deesis*), as the protectress who stretches out her mantle over the peoples (*Pokrov*), or as the merciful Virgin of tenderness (*Eleousa*). She is usually represented with her Son, the child Jesus, in her arms: it is the relationship with the Son which glorifies the Mother. Sometimes she embraces him with tenderness (*Glykophilousa*); at other times she is a hieratic figure, apparently rapt in contemplation of him who is the Lord of history (cf. Rv 5:9-14).

It is also appropriate to mention the icon of Our Lady of Vladimir, which continually accompanied the pilgrimage of faith of the peoples of ancient Rus'. The first Millennium of the conversion of those noble lands to Christianity is approaching: lands of humble folk, of thinkers, and of saints. The Icons are still venerated in the Ukraine, in Byelorussia, and in Russia under various titles. They are images which witness to the faith and spirit of prayer of that people, who sense the presence and protection of the Mother of God. In these Icons the Virgin shines as the image of divine beauty, the abode of Eternal Wisdom, the figure of the one who prays, the prototype of contemplation, the image of glory: she who even in her earthly life possessed the spiritual knowledge inaccessible to human reasoning and who attained through faith the most sublime knowledge. I also recall the Icon of the Virgin of the Cenacle, praying with the Apostles as they awaited the Holy Spirit: could she not become the sign of hope for all those who, in fraternal dialogue, wish to deepen their obedience of faith?

34. Such a wealth of praise, built up by the different forms of the Church's great tradition, could help us to hasten the day when the Church can begin once more to breathe fully with her "two lungs," the East and the West. As I have often said, this is more than ever necessary today. It would be an effective aid in furthering the progress of the dialogue already taking place between the Catholic Church and the Churches and Ecclesial Com-

munities of the West. It would also be the way for the pilgrim Church to sing and to live more perfectly her "*Magnificat*."

The "*Magnificat*" of the Pilgrim Church

35. At the present stage of her journey, therefore, the Church seeks to rediscover the unity of all who profess their faith in Christ, in order to show obedience to her Lord, who prayed for this unity before his Passion. "Like a pilgrim in a foreign land, the Church presses forward amid the persecutions of the world and the consolations of God, announcing the Cross and Death of the Lord until he comes." "Moving forward through trial and tribulation, the Church is strengthened by the power of God's grace promised to her by the Lord, so that in the weakness of the flesh she may not waver from perfect fidelity, but remain a bride worthy of her Lord; that moved by the Holy Spirit she may never cease to renew herself, until through the Cross she arrives at the light which knows no setting."

The Virgin Mother is constantly present on this journey of faith of the People of God toward the light. This is shown in a special way by the canticle of the "*Magnificat*," which, having welled up from the depths of Mary's faith at the Visitation, ceaselessly re-echoes in the heart of the Church down the centuries. This is proved by its daily recitation in the liturgy of Vespers and at many other moments of both personal and communal devotion.

My soul magnifies the Lord,
and my spirit rejoices in God my Savior,
for he has looked on his servant in her lowliness.
For behold, henceforth all generations
will call me blessed;
for he who is mighty has done great things for me,
and holy is his name:
and his mercy is from age to age
on those who fear him.
He has shown strength with his arm,
he has scattered the proud-hearted,
he has cast down the mighty from their thrones,
and lifted up the lowly;

he has filled the hungry with good things,
sent the rich away empty.
He has helped his servant Israel,
remembering his mercy,
as he spoke to our fathers,
to Abraham and to his posterity forever. (Lk 1:46-55)

⇝

36. When Elizabeth greeted her young kinswoman coming from Nazareth, Mary replied with the *Magnificat*. In her greeting, Elizabeth first called Mary "blessed" because of "the fruit of her womb," and then she called her "blessed" because of her faith (cf. Lk 1:42, 45). These two blessings referred directly to the Annunciation. Now, at the Visitation, when Elizabeth's greeting bears witness to that culminating moment, Mary's faith acquires a new consciousness and a new expression. That which remained hidden in the depths of the "obedience of faith" at the Annunciation can now be said to spring forth like a clear and life-giving flame of the spirit. The words used by Mary on the threshold of Elizabeth's house are an inspired profession of her faith, in which her response to the revealed word is expressed with the religious and poetical exultation of her whole being towards God. In these sublime words, which are simultaneously very simple and wholly inspired by the sacred texts of the people of Israel, Mary's personal experience, the ecstasy of her heart, shines forth. In them shines a ray of the mystery of God, the glory of his ineffable holiness, the eternal love which, as an irrevocable gift, enters into human history.

Mary is the first to share in this new revelation of God and, within the same, in this new "self-giving" of God; therefore she proclaims, "For he who is mighty has done great things for me, and holy is his name." Her words reflect a joy of spirit which is difficult to express: "My spirit rejoices in God my Savior." Indeed, "the deepest truth about God and the salvation of man is made clear to us in Christ, who is at the same time the mediator and the fullness of all revelation." In her exultation Mary confesses that she finds herself in the very heart of this fullness of Christ. She is conscious that the promise made to the fathers, first of all "to Abraham and to his posterity forever," is being fulfilled in herself. She is thus aware that concentrated within herself as the mother of Christ is the whole salvific economy, in which "from age to age" is manifested he who as the God of the Covenant, "remembers his mercy."

37. The Church, which from the beginning has modeled her earthly journey on that of the Mother of God, constantly repeats after her the words of the *Magnificat*. From the depths of the Virgin's faith at the Annunciation and the Visitation, the Church derives the truth about the God of the Covenant: the God who is Almighty and does "great things" for man: "holy is his name." In the *Magnificat* the Church sees uprooted that sin which is found at the outset of the earthly history of man and woman, the sin of disbelief and of "little faith" in God. In contrast with the "suspicion" which the "father of lies" sowed in the heart of Eve, the first woman, Mary, whom tradition is wont to call the "new Eve" and the true "Mother of the living," boldly proclaims the undimmed truth about God: the holy and almighty God, who from the beginning is the source of all gifts, he who "has done great things" in her, as well as in the whole universe. In the act of creation God gives existence to all that is. In creating man, God gives him the dignity of the image and likeness of himself in a special way as compared with all earthly creatures. Moreover, in his desire to give God gives himself in the Son, notwithstanding man's sin: "He so loved the world that he gave his only Son" (Jn 3:16). Mary is the first witness of this marvelous truth, which will be fully accomplished through "the works and words" (cf. Acts 1:1) of her Son and definitively through his Cross and Resurrection.

The Church, which even "amid trials and tribulations" does not cease repeating with Mary the words of the *Magnificat*, is sustained by the power of God's truth, proclaimed on that occasion with such extraordinary simplicity. At the same time, by means of this truth about God, the Church desires to shed light upon the difficult and sometimes-tangled paths of man's earthly existence. The Church's journey, therefore, near the end of the second Christian Millennium, involves a renewed commitment to her mission. Following him who said of himself: "(God) has anointed me to preach good news to the poor" (cf. Lk 4:18), the Church has sought from generation to generation and still seeks today to accomplish that same mission.

The Church's love of preference for the poor is wonderfully inscribed in Mary's *Magnificat*. The God of the Covenant, celebrated in the exultation of her spirit by the Virgin of Nazareth, is also he who "has cast down the mighty from their thrones, and lifted up the lowly, … filled the hungry with good things, sent the rich away empty, … scattered the proud-hearted … and his mercy is from age to age on those who fear him." Mary is deeply imbued with the spirit of the "poor of Yahweh," who in the prayer of the Psalms awaited from God their salvation, placing all their trust in him (cf. Ps(s) 25; 31; 35; 55). Mary truly proclaims the coming of the "Messiah of the poor" (cf. Is 11:4; 61:1). Drawing from Mary's heart, from the depth of her faith expressed in the words of the *Magnificat*, the Church renews ever more effectively in herself the awareness that the truth about God who saves, the truth about God who is the source of every gift, cannot be separated from the manifestation of his love of preference for the poor and humble, that love which, celebrated in the *Magnificat*, is later expressed in the words and works of Jesus.

The Church is thus aware—and at the present time this awareness is particularly vivid—not only that these two elements of the message contained in the *Magnificat* cannot be separated but also that there is a duty to safeguard carefully the importance of "the poor" and of "the option in favor of the poor" in the word of the living God. These are matters and questions intimately connected with the Christian meaning of freedom and liberation. "Mary is totally dependent upon God and completely directed towards him, and at the side of her Son, she is the most perfect image of freedom and of the liberation of humanity and of the universe. It is to her as Mother and Model that the Church must look in order to understand in its completeness the meaning of her own mission."

Mary, the Handmaid of the Lord

38. The Church knows and teaches with Saint Paul that there is only one mediator: "For there is one God, and there is one mediator between God and men, the man Christ Jesus, who gave himself as a ransom for all" (1 Tm 2:5-6). "The maternal role of Mary towards people in no way obscures or diminishes the unique mediation of Christ, but rather shows its power": it is mediation in Christ.

The Church knows and teaches that "all the saving influences of the Blessed Virgin on mankind originate … from the divine pleasure. They flow forth from the superabundance of the merits of Christ, rest on his mediation, depend entirely on it, and draw all their power from it. In no way do they impede the immediate union of the faithful with Christ. Rather, they foster this union." This saving influence is sustained by the Holy Spirit, who, just as he overshadowed the Virgin Mary when he began in her the divine motherhood, in a similar way constantly sustains her solicitude for the brothers and sisters of her Son.

In effect, Mary's mediation is intimately linked with her motherhood. It possesses a specifically maternal character, which distinguishes it from the mediation of the other creatures who in various and always subordinate ways share in the one mediation of Christ, although her own mediation is also a shared mediation. In fact, while it is true that "no creature could ever be classed with the Incarnate Word and Redeemer," at the same time "the unique mediation of the Redeemer does not exclude but rather gives rise among creatures to a manifold cooperation which is but a sharing in this unique source"; thus "the one goodness of God is in reality communicated diversely to his creatures."

The teaching of the Second Vatican Council presents the truth of Mary's mediation as "a sharing in the one unique source that is the mediation of Christ himself." We read: "The Church does not hesitate to profess this subordinate role of Mary. She experiences it continuously and commends it to the hearts of the faithful, so that, encouraged by this maternal help, they may more closely adhere to the Mediator and Redeemer." This role is at the same time special and extraordinary. It flows from her divine motherhood and can be understood and lived in faith only on the basis of the full truth of this motherhood. Since by virtue of divine election Mary is the earthly Mother of the Father's consubstantial Son and his "generous companion" in the work of redemption, "she is a mother to us in the order of grace." This role constitutes a real dimension of her presence in the saving mystery of Christ and the Church.

39. From this point of view we must consider once more the fundamental event in the economy of salvation, namely the Incarnation of the Word at the moment of the Annunciation. It is significant that Mary, recognizing in the words of the divine messenger the will of the Most High and sub-

mitting to his power, says: "Behold, I am the handmaid of the Lord; let it be done to me according to your word" (Lk 1:38). The first moment of submission to the one mediation "between God and men"—the mediation of Jesus Christ—is the Virgin of Nazareth's acceptance of motherhood. Mary consents to God's choice, in order to become through the power of the Holy Spirit the Mother of the Son of God. It can be said that a consent to motherhood is above all a result of her total self-giving to God in virginity. Mary accepted her election as Mother of the Son of God, guided by spousal love, the love which totally "consecrates" a human being to God. By virtue of this love, Mary wished to be always and in all things "given to God," living in virginity. The words "Behold, I am the handmaid of the Lord" express the fact that from the outset she accepted and understood her own motherhood as a total gift of self, a gift of her person to the service of the saving plans of the Most High. To the very end she lived her entire maternal sharing in the life of Jesus Christ, her Son, in a way that matched her vocation to virginity.

Mary's motherhood, completely pervaded by her spousal attitude as the "handmaid of the Lord," constitutes the first and fundamental dimension of that mediation which the Church confesses and proclaims in her regard and continually "commends to the hearts of the faithful," since the Church has great trust in her. For it must be recognized that before anyone else it was God himself, the Eternal Father, who entrusted himself to the Virgin of Nazareth, giving her his own Son in the mystery of the Incarnation. Her election to the supreme office and dignity of Mother of the Son of God refers, on the ontological level, to the very reality of the union of the two natures in the person of the Word (hypostatic union). This basic fact of being the Mother of the Son of God is from the very beginning a complete openness to the person of Christ, to his whole work, to his whole mission. The words "Behold, I am the handmaid of the Lord" testify to Mary's openness of spirit: she perfectly unites in herself the love proper to virginity and the love characteristic of motherhood, which are joined and, as it were, fused together.

For this reason Mary became not only the "nursing mother" of the Son of Man but also the "associate of unique nobility" of the Messiah and Redeemer. As I have already said, she advanced in her pilgrimage of faith, and in this pilgrimage to the foot of the Cross there was simultaneously accomplished her maternal cooperation with the Savior's whole mission through her actions and sufferings. Along the path of this collaboration with the work of her Son, the Redeemer, Mary's motherhood itself underwent a singular transformation, becoming ever more imbued with "burning charity" toward all those to whom Christ's mission was directed. Through this "burning charity," which sought to achieve, in union with Christ, the restoration of "supernatural life to souls," Mary entered, in a way all her own, into the one mediation "between God and men," which is the mediation of the man Christ Jesus. If she was the first to experience within herself the supernatural consequences of this one mediation—in the Annunciation she had been greeted as "full of grace"—then we must say that through this fullness of grace and supernatural life she was especially predisposed to cooperation with Christ, the one Mediator of human salvation. Such cooperation is precisely this mediation subordinated to the mediation of Christ.

In Mary's case we have a special and exceptional mediation, based upon her "fullness of grace," which was expressed in the complete willingness of the "handmaid of the Lord." In response to this interior willingness of his Mother, Jesus Christ prepared her ever more completely to become for all people their "mother in the order of grace." This is indicated, at least indirectly, by certain details noted by the Synoptics (cf. Lk 11:28; 8:20-21; Mk 3:32-35; Mt 12:47-50) and still more so by the Gospel of John (cf. 2:1-12; 19:25-27), which I have already mentioned. Particularly eloquent in this regard are the words spoken by Jesus on the Cross to Mary and John.

40. After the events of the Resurrection and Ascension, Mary entered the Upper Room together with the Apostles to await Pentecost and was present there as the Mother of the glorified Lord. She was not only the one who "advanced in her pilgrimage of faith" and loyally persevered in her union with her Son "unto the Cross," but she was also the "handmaid of the Lord," left by her Son as Mother in the midst of the infant Church: "Behold your mother." Through her perseverance there began to develop a special bond between this Mother and the Church. The infant Church was the fruit of the Cross and Resurrection of her Son. Mary, who from the beginning had given herself without reserve to the person and work of

her Son, could not but pour out upon the Church, from the very beginning, her maternal self-giving. After her Son's departure, her motherhood remains in the Church as maternal mediation: interceding for all her children, the Mother cooperates in the saving work of her Son, the Redeemer of the world. In fact, the Council teaches that the "motherhood of Mary in the order of grace ... will last without interruption until the eternal fulfillment of all the elect." With the redeeming death of her Son, the maternal mediation of the handmaid of the Lord took on a universal dimension, for the work of redemption embraces the whole of humanity. Through Mary's mediation is manifested in a singular way the efficacy of the one and universal mediation of Christ "between God and men." Mary's cooperation shares, in its subordinate character, in the universality of the mediation of the Redeemer, the one Mediator. This is clearly indicated by the Council in the words quoted previously.

"For," the text goes on, "taken up to heaven, she did not lay aside this saving role, but by her manifold acts of intercession continues to win for us gifts of eternal salvation." With this character of "intercession," first manifested at Cana in Galilee, Mary's mediation continues in the history of the Church and the world. We read that Mary, "by her maternal charity, cares for the brethren of her Son who still journey on earth surrounded by dangers and difficulties, until they are led to their happy homeland." In this way, Mary's motherhood continues unceasingly in the Church as the mediation which intercedes, and the Church expresses her faith in this truth by invoking Mary "under the titles of *Advocate*, *Auxiliatrix*, *Adjutrix*, and *Mediatrix*."

41. Through her mediation, subordinate to that of the Redeemer, Mary contributes in a special way to the union of the pilgrim Church on earth with the eschatological and heavenly reality of the Communion of Saints, since she has already been "assumed into heaven." The truth of the Assumption, defined by Pius XII, is reaffirmed by the Second Vatican Council, which thus expresses the Church's faith: "Preserved free from all guilt of original sin, the Immaculate Virgin was taken up body and soul into heavenly glory upon the completion of her earthly sojourn. She was exalted by the Lord as Queen of the Universe, in order that she might be the more

thoroughly conformed to her Son, the Lord of lords (cf. Rv 19:16) and the conqueror of sin and death." In this teaching Pius XII was in continuity with Tradition, which has found many different expressions in the history of the Church, both in the East and in the West.

By the mystery of the Assumption into heaven there were definitively accomplished in Mary all the effects of the one mediation of Christ the Redeemer of the world and Risen Lord: "In Christ shall all be made alive. But each in his own order: Christ the first fruits, then at his coming those who belong to Christ" (1 Cor 15:22-23). In the mystery of the Assumption is expressed the faith of the Church, according to which Mary is "united by a close and indissoluble bond" to Christ, for, if as Virgin and Mother she was singularly united with him in his first coming, so through her continued collaboration with him she will also be united with him in expectation of the second; "redeemed in an especially sublime manner by reason of the merits of her Son," she also has that specifically maternal role of *mediatrix* of mercy at his final coming, when all those who belong to Christ "shall be made alive," when "the last enemy to be destroyed is death" (1 Cor 15:26).

Connected with this exaltation of the noble "Daughter of Sion" through her Assumption into heaven is the mystery of her eternal glory. The Mother of Christ is glorified as "Queen of the Universe." She who at the Annunciation called herself the "handmaid of the Lord" remained throughout her earthly life faithful to what this name expresses. In this she confirmed that she was a true "disciple" of Christ, who strongly emphasized that his mission was one of service: "the Son of Man came not to be served but to serve, and to give his life as a ransom for many" (*Mt* 20:28). In this way, Mary became the first of those who, "serving Christ also in others, with humility and patience lead their brothers and sisters to that King whom to serve is to reign," and she fully obtained that "state of royal freedom" proper to Christ's disciples: to serve means to reign!

"Christ obeyed even at the cost of death, and was therefore raised up by the Father (cf. Phil 2:8-9). Thus he entered into the glory of his kingdom. To him all things are made subject until he subjects himself and all created things to the Father, that God may be all in all" (cf. 1 Cor 15:27-28). Mary, the handmaid of the Lord, has a share in this Kingdom of the Son. The glory of serving does not cease to be her royal exaltation: assumed into heaven, she does not cease her saving service, which expresses her maternal mediation "until the eternal fulfillment of all the elect"; thus she who here on earth "loyally preserved in her union with her Son unto the Cross" continues to remain united with him, while now "all things are subjected to him, until he subjects to the Father himself and all things." In her Assumption into heaven, Mary is, as it were, clothed by the whole reality of the Communion of Saints, and her very union with the Son in glory is wholly oriented toward the definitive fullness of the Kingdom, when "God will be all in all."

In this phase, too, Mary's maternal mediation does not cease to be subordinate to him who is the one Mediator, until the final realization of "the fullness of time," that is to say until "all things are united in Christ" (cf. Eph 1:10).

Mary in the Life of the Church and of Every Christian

42. Linking itself with Tradition, the Second Vatican Council brought new light to bear on the role of the Mother of Christ in the life of the Church. "Through the gift ... of divine motherhood, Mary is united with her Son, the Redeemer, and with his singular graces and offices. By these, the Blessed Virgin is also intimately united with the Church: the Mother of God is a figure of the Church in the matter of faith, charity and perfect union with Christ." We have already noted how, from the beginning, Mary remains with the Apostles in expectation of Pentecost and how, as "the blessed one who believed," she is present in the midst of the pilgrim Church from generation to generation through faith and as the model of the hope which does not disappoint (cf. Rom 5:5).

Mary believed in the fulfillment of what had been said to her by the Lord. As Virgin, she believed that she would conceive and bear a son: the "Holy One," who bears the name of "Son of God," the name "Jesus" (*God who saves*). As handmaid of the Lord, she remained in perfect fidelity to the person and mission of this Son. As Mother, "believing and obeying ... she brought forth on earth the Father's Son. This she did, knowing not man but overshadowed by the Holy Spirit."

For these reasons Mary is honored in the Church "with special reverence. Indeed, from most ancient times the Blessed Virgin Mary has been venerated under the title of 'God-bearer.' In all perils and needs, the faithful have fled prayerfully to her protection." This cult is altogether special: it bears in itself and expresses the profound link which exists between the Mother of Christ and the Church. As Virgin and Mother, Mary remains for the Church a "permanent model." It can therefore be said that especially under this aspect, namely as a model, or rather as a "figure," Mary, present in the mystery of Christ, remains constantly present also in the mystery of the Church. The Church, too, is "called mother and virgin," and these names have a profound biblical and theological justification.

43. The Church "becomes herself a mother by accepting God's word with fidelity." Like Mary, who first believed by accepting the word of God revealed to her at the Annunciation and by remaining faithful to that word in all her trials even unto the Cross, so, too, the Church becomes a mother when, accepting with fidelity the word of God, "by her preaching and by baptism she brings forth to a new and immortal life children who are conceived of the Holy Spirit and born of God." This "maternal" characteristic of the Church was expressed in a particularly vivid way by the Apostle to the Gentiles when he wrote: "My little children, with whom I am again in travail until Christ be formed in you!" (Gal 4:19). These words of Saint Paul contain an interesting sign of the early Church's awareness of her own motherhood, linked to her apostolic service to mankind. This awareness enabled and still enables the Church to see the mystery of her life and mission modeled upon the example of the Mother of the Son, who is "the firstborn among many brethren" (Rom 8:29).

It can be said that from Mary the Church also learns her own motherhood: she recognizes the maternal dimension of her vocation, which is essentially bound to her sacramental nature, in "contemplating Mary's mysterious sanctity, imitating her charity and faithfully fulfilling the Father's will." If the Church is the sign and instrument of intimate union with God, she is so by reason of her motherhood, because, receiving life from the Spirit, she "generates" sons and daughters of the human race to a new life in Christ. Just as Mary is at the service of the mystery of the Incarnation, so the Church is always at the service of the mystery of adoption to sonship through grace.

Following the example of Mary, the Church remains the virgin faithful to her spouse: The Church herself is a virgin who keeps whole and pure the fidelity she has pledged to her Spouse. For the Church is the spouse of Christ, as is clear from the Pauline Letters (cf. Eph 5:21-33; 2 Cor 11:2) and from the title found in John: "bride of the Lamb" (Rv 21:9). If the Church as spouse "keeps the fidelity she has pledged to Christ," this fidelity, even though in the Apostle's teaching it has become an image of marriage (cf. Eph 5:23-33), also has value as a model of total self-giving to God in celibacy "for the kingdom of heaven," in virginity consecrated to God (cf. Mt 19:11-12; 2 Cor 11:2). Precisely such virginity, after the example of the Virgin of Nazareth, is the source of a special spiritual fruitfulness: it is the source of motherhood in the Holy Spirit.

The Church also preserves the faith received from Christ. Following the example of Mary, who kept and pondered in her heart everything relating to her divine Son (cf. Lk 2:19, 51), the Church is committed to preserving the word of God and investigating its riches with discernment and prudence, in order to bear faithful witness to it before all mankind in every age.

44. Given Mary's relationship to the Church as an exemplar, the Church is close to her and seeks to become like her: "Imitating the Mother of her Lord, and by the power of the Holy Spirit, she preserves with virginal purity an integral faith, a firm hope, and a sincere charity." Mary is thus present in the mystery of the Church as a model, but the Church's mystery also consists in generating people to a new and immortal life: this is her motherhood in the Holy Spirit. Here Mary is not only the model and figure of the Church; she is much more. "[W]ith maternal love she cooperates in the birth and development" of the sons and daughters of Mother Church. The Church's motherhood is accomplished not only according to the model and figure of the Mother of God but also with her "cooperation." The Church draws abundantly from this cooperation, that is to say from the maternal mediation which is characteristic of Mary, insofar as already on earth she cooperated in the rebirth and development of the Church's sons and daughters, as the Mother of that Son whom the Father "placed as the first-born among many brethren."

She cooperated, as the Second Vatican Council teaches, with a maternal love. Here we perceive the real value of the words spoken by Jesus to his Mother at the hour of the Cross: "Woman, behold your son" and to the disciple: "Behold your mother" (Jn 19:26-27). They are words which determine Mary's place in the life of Christ's disciples and they express—as I have already said—the new motherhood of the Mother of the Redeemer: a spiritual motherhood, born from the heart of the Paschal Mystery of the Redeemer of the world. It is a motherhood in the order of grace, for it implores the gift of the Spirit, who raises up the new children of God, redeems through the sacrifice of Christ that Spirit whom Mary, too, together with the Church, received on the day of Pentecost. Her motherhood is particularly noted and experienced by the Christian people at the Sacred Banquet—the liturgical celebration of the mystery of the Redemption—at which Christ, his true body born of the Virgin Mary, becomes present.

The piety of the Christian people has always very rightly sensed a profound link between devotion to the Blessed Virgin and worship of the Eucharist: this is a fact that can be seen in the liturgy of both the West and the East, in the traditions of the Religious Families, in the modern movements of spirituality, including those for youth, and in the pastoral practice of the Marian Shrines. Mary guides the faithful to the Eucharist.

45. Of the essence of motherhood is the fact that it concerns the person. Motherhood always establishes a unique and unrepeatable relationship between two people: between mother and child and between child and mother. Even when the same woman is the mother of many children, her personal relationship with each one of them is of the very essence of motherhood. Each child is generated in a unique and unrepeatable way, and this is true both for the mother and for the child. Each child is surrounded in the same way by that maternal love on which are based the child's development and coming to maturity as a human being.

It can be said that motherhood "in the order of grace" preserves the analogy with what "in the order of nature" characterizes the union between mother and child. In the light of this fact it becomes easier to understand why in Christ's testament on Golgotha his Mother's new motherhood is expressed in the singular, in reference to one man: "Behold your son."

It can also be said that these same words fully show the reason for the Marian dimension of the life of Christ's disciples. This is true not only of John, who at that hour stood at the foot of the Cross together with his Master's Mother, but it is also true of every disciple of Christ, of every Christian. The Redeemer entrusts his mother to the disciple, and at the same time he gives her to him as his mother. Mary's motherhood, which becomes man's inheritance, is a gift: a gift which Christ himself makes personally to every individual. The Redeemer entrusts Mary to John because he entrusts John to Mary. At the foot of the Cross there begins that special entrusting of humanity to the Mother of Christ, which in the history of the Church has been practiced and expressed in different ways. The same Apostle and Evangelist, after reporting the words addressed by Jesus on the Cross to his Mother and to himself, adds: "And from that hour the disciple took her to his own home" (Jn 19:27). This statement certainly means that the role of son was attributed to the disciple and that he assumed responsibility for the Mother of his beloved Master. Since Mary was given as a mother to him personally, the statement indicates, even though indirectly, everything expressed by the intimate relationship of a child with its mother. And all of this can be included in the word "entrusting." Such entrusting is the response to a person's love and, in particular, to the love of a mother.

The Marian dimension of the life of a disciple of Christ is expressed in a special way precisely through this filial entrusting to the Mother of Christ, which began with the testament of the Redeemer on Golgotha. Entrusting himself to Mary in a filial manner, the Christian, like the Apostle John, "welcomes" the Mother of Christ "into his own home" and brings her into everything that makes up his inner life, that is to say into his human and Christian "I": he "took her to his own home." The Christian seeks to be taken into that "maternal charity" with which the Redeemer's Mother "cares for the brethren of her Son," "in whose birth and development she cooperates" in the measure of the gift proper to each one through the power of Christ's spirit. In this way also is exercised that motherhood in the Spirit which became Mary's role at the foot of the Cross and in the Upper Room.

46. This filial relationship, this self-entrusting of a child to its mother, not only has its beginning in Christ but can also be said to be definitive-

ly directed toward him. Mary can be said to continue to say to each individual the words which she spoke at Cana in Galilee: "Do whatever he tells you." He, Christ, is the one Mediator between God and mankind; he is "the way, and the truth, and the life" (Jn 14:6); it is he whom the Father has given to the world, so that man "should not perish but have eternal life" (Jn 3:16). The Virgin of Nazareth became the first "witness" of this saving love of the Father, and she also wishes to remain its humble handmaid always and everywhere. For every Christian, for every human being, Mary is the one who first "believed," and precisely with her faith as Spouse and Mother she wishes to act upon all those who entrust themselves to her as her children. It is well known that the more her children persevere and progress in this attitude, the nearer Mary leads them to the "unsearchable riches of Christ" (Eph 3:8). To the same degree they recognize more and more clearly the dignity of man in all its fullness and the definitive meaning of his vocation, for "Christ ... fully reveals man to man himself."

This Marian dimension of Christian life takes on special importance in relation to women and their status. In fact, femininity has a unique relationship with the Mother of the Redeemer, a subject which can be studied in greater depth elsewhere. Here I simply wish to note that the figure of Mary of Nazareth sheds light on womanhood as such by the very fact that God, in the sublime event of the Incarnation of his Son, entrusted himself to the ministry, the free and active ministry of a woman. It can thus be said that women, by looking to Mary, find in her the secret of living their femininity with dignity and of achieving their own true advancement. In the light of Mary, the Church sees in the face of women the reflection of a beauty which mirrors the loftiest sentiments of which the human heart is capable: the self-offering totality of love; the strength that is capable of bearing the greatest sorrows; limitless fidelity and tireless devotion to work; the ability to combine penetrating intuition with words of support and encouragement.

47. At the Council Paul VI solemnly proclaimed that Mary is the Mother of the Church, "that is, Mother of the entire Christian people, both faithful and pastors." Later, in 1968, in the Profession of faith known as the "Credo of the People of God," he restated this truth in an even more force-

ful way in these words: “We believe that the Most Holy Mother of God, the new Eve, the Mother of the Church, carries on in heaven her maternal role with regard to the members of Christ, cooperating in the birth and development of divine life in the souls of the redeemed.”

The Council's teaching emphasized that the truth concerning the Blessed Virgin, Mother of Christ, is an effective aid in exploring more deeply the truth concerning the Church. When speaking of the Constitution *Lumen Gentium*, which had just been approved by the Council, Paul VI said: “Knowledge of the true Catholic doctrine regarding the Blessed Virgin Mary will always be a key to the exact understanding of the mystery of Christ and of the Church.” Mary is present in the Church as the Mother of Christ, and at the same time as that Mother whom Christ, in the mystery of the Redemption, gave to humanity in the person of the Apostle John. Thus, in her new motherhood in the Spirit, Mary embraces each and every one in the Church, and embraces each and every one through the Church. In this sense Mary, Mother of the Church, is also the Church's model. Indeed, as Paul VI hopes and asks, the Church must draw “from the Virgin Mother of God the most authentic form of perfect imitation of Christ.”

Thanks to this special bond linking the Mother of Christ with the Church, there is further clarified the mystery of that “woman” who, from the first chapters of the Book of Genesis until the Book of Revelation, accompanies the revelation of God's salvific plan for humanity. For Mary, present in the Church as the Mother of the Redeemer, takes part, as a mother, in that monumental struggle against “the powers of darkness” which continues throughout human history. By her ecclesial identification as the “woman clothed with the sun” (Rv 12:1), it can be said that “in the Most Holy Virgin the Church has already reached that perfection whereby she exists without spot or wrinkle.” As Christians raise their eyes with faith to Mary in the course of their earthly pilgrimage, they “strive to increase in holiness.” Mary, the exalted Daughter of Sion, helps all her children, wherever they may be and whatever their condition, to find in Christ the path to the Father's house.

Throughout her life, the Church maintains with the Mother of God a link which embraces, in the saving mystery, the past, the present, and the future and venerates her as the spiritual mother of humanity and the advocate of grace.

The Meaning of the Marian Year

48. It is precisely the special bond between humanity and this Mother which has led me to proclaim a Marian Year in the Church. In this period before the end of the second Millennium since Christ's birth, a similar initiative was taken in the past when Pius XII proclaimed 1954 as a Marian Year, in order to highlight the exceptional holiness of the Mother of Christ as expressed in the mysteries of her Immaculate Conception (defined exactly a century before) and of her Assumption into heaven.

Now, following the line of the Second Vatican Council, I wish to emphasize the special presence of the Mother of God in the mystery of Christ and his Church. For this is a fundamental dimension emerging from the Mariology of the Council, the end of which is now more than twenty years behind us. The Extraordinary Synod of Bishops held in 1985 exhorted everyone to follow faithfully the teaching and guidelines of the Council. We can say that these two events—the Council and the synod—embody what the Holy Spirit himself wishes "to say to the Church" in the present phase of history.

In this context, the Marian Year is meant to promote a new and more careful reading of what the Council said about the Blessed Virgin Mary, Mother of God, in the mystery of Christ and of the Church, the topic to which the contents of this Encyclical are devoted. Here we speak not only of the doctrine of faith but also of the life of faith, and thus of authentic "Marian spirituality," seen in the light of Tradition, and especially the spirituality to which the Council exhorts us. Marian spirituality, like its corresponding devotion, finds a very rich source in the historical experience of individuals and of the various Christian communities present among the different peoples and nations of the world. In this regard, I would like to recall, among the many witnesses and teachers of this spirituality, the figure of Saint Louis Marie Grignion de Montfort, who proposes consecration to Christ through the hands of Mary as an effective means for Christians to live faithfully their baptismal commitments. I am pleased to note that in our own time, too, new manifestations of this spirituality and devotion are not lacking. There thus exist solid points of reference to look to and follow in the context of this Marian Year.

49. This Marian Year will begin on the Solemnity of Pentecost, on June 7 next, for it is a question not only of recalling that Mary "preceded" the entry of Christ the Lord into the history of the human family but also of emphasizing, in the light of Mary, that from the moment when the mystery of the Incarnation was accomplished, human history entered "the fullness of time," and that the Church is the sign of this fullness. As the People of God, the Church makes her pilgrim way toward eternity through faith, in the midst of all the peoples and nations, beginning from the day of Pentecost. Christ's Mother—who was present at the beginning of "the time of the Church," when in expectation of the coming of the Holy Spirit she devoted herself to prayer in the midst of the Apostles and her Son's disciples—constantly "precedes" the Church in her journey through human history. She is also the one who, precisely as the "handmaid of the Lord," cooperates unceasingly with the work of salvation accomplished by Christ, her Son.

By means of this Marian Year the Church is called not only to remember everything in her past that testifies to the special maternal cooperation of the Mother of God in the work of salvation in Christ the Lord, but also, on her own part, to prepare for the future the paths of this cooperation. For the end of the second Christian Millennium opens up as a new prospect.

50. As has already been mentioned, also among our divided brethren many honor and celebrate the Mother of the Lord, especially among the Orientals. It is a Marian light cast upon ecumenism. In particular, I wish to mention once more that during the Marian Year there will occur the Millennium of the Baptism of Saint Vladimir, Grand Duke of Kiev [988]. This marked the beginning of Christianity in the territories of what was then called Rus', and subsequently in other territories of Eastern Europe. In this way, through the work of evangelization, Christianity spread beyond Europe, as far as the northern territories of the Asian continent. We would therefore like, especially during this Year, to join in prayer with all those who are celebrating the Millennium of this Baptism, both Orthodox and Catholics, repeating and confirming with the Council those sentiments of joy and comfort that "the Easterners ... with ardent emotion and devout mind concur in reverencing the Mother of God, ever Virgin." Even

though we are still experiencing the painful effects of the separation which took place some decades later [1054], we can say that in the presence of the Mother of Christ we feel that we are true brothers and sisters within that messianic People, which is called to be the one family of God on earth. As I announced at the beginning of the New Year, "We desire to reconfirm this universal inheritance of all the Sons and daughters of this earth."

In announcing the Year of Mary, I also indicated that it will end next year on the Solemnity of the Assumption of the Blessed Virgin into heaven, in order to emphasize the "great sign in heaven" spoken of by the Apocalypse. In this way, we also wish to respond to the exhortation of the Council, which looks to Mary as "a sign of sure hope and solace for the pilgrim People of God." The Council expresses this exhortation in the following words: "Let the entire body of the faithful pour forth persevering prayer to the Mother of God and Mother of mankind. Let them implore that she who aided the beginning of the Church by her prayers may now, exalted as she is in heaven above all the saints and angels, intercede with her Son in the fellowship of all the saints. May she do so until all the peoples of the human family, whether they are honored with the name of Christian or whether they still do not know their Savior, are happily gathered together in peace and harmony into the one People of God, for the glory of the Most Holy and Undivided Trinity."

Conclusion

51. At the end of the daily Liturgy of the Hours, among the invocations addressed to Mary by the Church, is the following:

> Loving Mother of the Redeemer, gate of heaven, star of the sea,
> assist your people who have fallen yet strive to rise again.
> To the wonderment of nature you bore your Creator!

"To the wonderment of nature"! These words of the antiphon express that wonderment of faith which accompanies the mystery of Mary's divine motherhood. In a sense, it does so in the heart of the whole of creation, and, directly, in the heart of the whole People of God, in the heart of the Church. How wonderfully far God has gone, the Creator and Lord of all things, in the "revelation of himself" to man! How clearly he has bridged all the spaces of that infinite "distance" which separates the Creator from the creature! If in himself he remains ineffable and unsearchable, still more ineffable and unsearchable is he in the reality of the Incarnation of the Word, who became man through the Virgin of Nazareth.

If he has eternally willed to call man to share in the divine nature (cf. 2 Pt 1:4), it can be said that he has matched the "divinization" of man to humanity's historical conditions, so that even after sin he is ready to restore at a great price the eternal plan of his love through the "humanization" of his Son, who is of the same being as himself. The whole of creation, and more directly man himself, cannot fail to be amazed at this gift in which he has become a sharer, in the Holy Spirit: "God so loved the world that he gave his only Son" (Jn 3:16).

At the center of this mystery, in the midst of this wonderment of faith, stands Mary. As the loving Mother of the Redeemer, she was the first to experience it: "To the wonderment of nature you bore your Creator!"

52. The words of this liturgical antiphon also express the truth of the "great transformation" which the mystery of the Incarnation establishes for man. It is a transformation which belongs to his entire history, from that beginning which is revealed to us in the first chapters of Genesis until the final end, in the perspective of the end of the world, of which Jesus has revealed to us "neither the day nor the hour" (Mt 25:13). It is an unending and continuous transformation between falling and rising again, between the man of sin and the man of grace and justice. The Advent liturgy in particular is at the very heart of this transformation and captures its unceasing "here and now" when it exclaims: "Assist your people who have fallen yet strive to rise again!"

These words apply to every individual, every community, to nations and peoples, and to the generations and epochs of human history, to our own epoch, to these years of the Millennium which is drawing to a close: "Assist, yes assist, your people who have fallen!"

This is the invocation addressed to Mary, the "loving Mother of the Redeemer," the invocation addressed to Christ, who through Mary entered human history. Year after year the antiphon rises to Mary, evoking that moment which saw the accomplishment of this essential historical transformation, which irreversibly continues: the transformation from "falling" to "rising."

Mankind has made wonderful discoveries and achieved extraordinary results in the fields of science and technology. It has made great advances along the path of progress and civilization, and in recent times one could say that it has succeeded in speeding up the pace of history. The fundamental transformation, the one which can be called "original," constantly accompanies man's journey and, through all the events of history, accompanies each and every individual. It is the transformation from "falling" to "rising," from death to life. It is also a constant challenge to people's consciences, a challenge to man's whole historical awareness: the challenge to follow the path of "not falling" in ways that are ever old and ever new, and of "rising again" if a fall has occurred.

As she goes forward with the whole of humanity toward the frontier between the two millennia, the Church, for her part, with the whole community of believers and in union with all men and women of good will, takes up the great challenge contained in these words of the Marian antiphon: "[T]he people who have fallen yet strive to rise again," and she addresses both the Redeemer and his Mother with the plea: "Assist us." As this prayer attests, the Church sees the Blessed Mother of God in the saving mystery of Christ and in her own mystery. She sees Mary deeply rooted in humanity's history, in man's eternal vocation according to the providential plan which God has made for him from eternity. She sees Mary maternally present and sharing in the many complicated problems which today beset the lives of individuals, families, and nations; she sees her helping the Christian people in the constant struggle between good and evil, to ensure that it "does not fall," or, if it has fallen, that it "rises again."

I hope with all my heart that the reflections contained in the present Encyclical will also serve to renew this vision in the hearts of all believers. As bishop of Rome, I send to all those to whom these thoughts are addressed the kiss of peace, my greeting, and my blessing in our Lord Jesus Christ. Amen.

Given in Rome, at Saint Peter's, on March 25, the Solemnity of the Annunciation of the Lord, in the year 1987, the ninth of my Pontificate.

INTRODUCTION TO READING 10 BY BROOKE WILLIAMS DEELY

In this Apostolic Letter on the dignity of women, John Paul II ventures forth in a strikingly original way. In keeping with unchanging principles in the Catholic tradition, he yet achieves in his application of these principles a truly transformational development of the living tradition by achieving the widened horizon of a non-domination paradigm inspired by the gospel. His method is contemplatively to meditate on a "sign" of the times, the historical coming of age of women in all spheres of influence.

Pope John Paul offers an historic point of departure from any justification of the domination of woman by man by identifying that domination as a moral failure resulting from original sin. The traditional imposition of "male rule," he clarifies, needs to be redressed precisely as a bad effect of original sin, as something to be overcome. What he calls for is the restoring of the *original unity* of man and woman, both created equally as human subjects, in their solitude, each as complete beings who then freely come into *reciprocal relation*, each equally as *gift* to the other. As man and as woman they both equally reflect the image of God, while in their embodied differences they complement each other.

This Letter evidences, as elucidated in the general introduction to this volume, that this pope's teaching remarkably bears no resemblance to Western historically dominant discourse on the nature of woman (accruing from a mistaken biology of Aristotle and, as a result, transmitted through St. Thomas Aquinas) that would render woman, precisely in her embodiment as *woman*, as less rational in general and therefore less perfect than man. Nor does this Pope directly engage such discourse either to defend it or to disentangle it from its presuppositions, as did the Dominican Vincent Guagliardo in his posthumously published and pioneering article on the question.[1] John Paul II simply moves *beyond* such binary logic of past or present that misrepresents either sex as more perfect than the other.

John Paul II further clarifies that God communicates to humans through the "anthropomorphic" mediation of human language, wherein the needed use of human concepts and images is nonetheless limited in signifying divine transcendence, since "God is spirit." Hence the mystery of the inner life of the Trinity, in its eternal "*generating*," has neither masculine nor feminine qualities characteristic of the body, including speaking of God as a Father.

In so deepening understanding, Pope John Paul draws on the Catholic contemplative experience embracing Gospel values. These authentically *human* values transcend diverse cultures. This human experience of transcendent human values is exemplified by the Virgin Mary as a "*sign*," he emphasizes, of such values as are in themselves irreducible to gender. In her consent Mary embodied both receptivity (as female-identified) and activity (as male-identified) as a complete, integrated human person, speaking for herself in relation to God—and thereby as a woman engendering social relations that no longer reduce woman simply to her relation to a man. She exemplifies, *for all humans*, the integration of contemplation and action in transforming culture.

Pope John Paul II draws inspiration from the unique teaching of Jesus in relation to women. The pope evidences that he has deeply pondered—indeed, contemplated—in dialogue with the world, the modern and postmodern feminist critique of patriarchal attitudes. He meditates on how Jesus, in every encounter with women, countered and transcended such attitudes, both in his counter-cultural actions and in principle. Nowhere in the world, before or since, has there been a religious leader who so challenged the patriarchal culture of a given time and place.

This encyclical thereby definitively puts an end to any justification for male domination or exploitation of women, while opening the way to an ethos of love wherein women and men each contribute the personal resources of femininity and masculinity in collaborative *relation* as gift that overflows toward the common good, whatever be one's state of life. John Paul II thus responds, with an ear to heartfelt truth—not simply to the errors but at the same time to the truths—of "feminist" thinkers in their formidable and sometimes-ferocious critique of patriarchal cultures, including Catholic tradition.

Paradoxically, both modern and postmodern forms of secular feminist thought have, until recently, by and large dismissed, or editorially screened out, the Catholic *contemplative* tradition as having nothing to do with changing women's condition in the temporal order. We see from this encyclical, quite to the contrary, that the pope moves in the direction of *trans-*

forming the temporal order as a final end in the order of nature. He upholds the *equal* dignity of women because the time has come in history to humanize social relations in both private and public spheres. He grounds such a cultural transformation in the efficacy of mystical contemplation, which is, as Aquinas himself taught, the ultimate end of the person in the order of grace, the highest level of knowledge—knowledge by way of love. Mary is the best exemplar of humanity, according to Aquinas, of such knowledge in relation to the Word of God.

READING 10 (AUGUST 15, 1988): *Mulieris Dignitatem* (On the Dignity and Vocation of Women)[1]

Venerable Brothers and dear Sons and Daughters,
Health and the Apostolic Blessing

Introduction

A Sign of the Times

1. The dignity and the vocation of women—subjects of constant human and Christian reflection—have gained exceptional prominence in recent years. This can be seen, for example, *in the statements of the Church's Magisterium* present in various documents *of the Second Vatican Council,* which declares in its Closing Message: "The hour is coming, in fact has come, when the vocation of women is being acknowledged in its fullness, the hour in which women acquire in the world an influence, an effect and a power never hitherto achieved. That is why, at his moment when the human race is undergoing so deep a transformation, women imbued with a spirit of the Gospel can do so much to aid humanity in not falling." *This Message* sums up what had already been expressed in the Council's teaching, specifically in the Pastoral Constitution *Gaudium et Spes* and in the Decree on the Apostolate of the Laity *Apostolicam Actuositatem.* Similar thinking had already been put forth in the period before the Council, as can be seen in a number of Pope Pius XII's Discourses and in the Encyclical *Pacem in Terris* of *Pope John XXIII.*

After the Second Vatican Council, my predecessor *Paul VI* showed the relevance of this "sign of the times" when he conferred the title "Doctor of the Church" upon Saint Teresa of Jesus and Saint Catherine of Siena, and likewise when, at the request of the 1971 Assembly of the Synod of Bishops, he set up *a special Commission* for the study of contemporary problems concerning the "*effective promotion of the dignity and the responsibility of women.*" In one of his Discourses Paul VI said: "Within Christianity, more than in any other religion, and since its very beginning, women have had a special dignity, of which the New Testament shows us many important aspects . . .; it is evident that women are meant to form part of the living and working structure of Christianity in so prominent a manner that perhaps not all their potentialities have yet been made clear."

The Fathers of the recent Assembly of the Synod of Bishops (October 1987), which was devoted to "The Vocation and Mission of the Laity in the Church and in the World Twenty Years after the Second Vatican Council," once more dealt with the dignity and vocation of women. One of their recommendations was for a further study of the anthropological and theological bases that are needed in order to solve the problems connected with the meaning and dignity of being a woman and being a man. It is a question of understanding the reason for and the consequences of the Creator's decision that the human being should always and only exist as a woman or a man. It is only by beginning from these bases, which make it possible to understand the greatness of the dignity and vocation of women, that one is able to speak of their active presence in the Church and in society.

This is what I intend to deal with in this document. The Post-Synodal Exhortation, which will be published later, will present proposals of a pastoral nature on the place of women in the Church and in society. On this subject the Fathers offered some important reflections, after they had taken into consideration the testimonies of the lay Auditors—both women and men—from the particular Churches throughout the world.

The Marian Year

2. The last Synod took place *within the Marian Year*, which gives special thrust to the consideration of this theme, as the Encyclical *Redemptoris Mater* points out. This Encyclical develops and updates the Second Vatican Council's teaching contained in chapter VIII of the Dogmatic Constitution on the Church *Lumen Gentium*. The title of this chapter is signifi-

cant: "*The Blessed Virgin Mary, the Mother of God, in the Mystery of Christ and of the Church.*" Mary—the "woman" of the Bible (cf. Gen 3:15; Jn 2:4; 19:16)—intimately belongs to the salvific mystery of Christ and is therefore also present in a special way in the mystery of the Church. Since "the Church is in Christ as a sacrament ... of intimate union with God and of the unity of the whole human race," the special presence of the Mother of God in the mystery of the Church makes us think of *the exceptional link between this "woman" and the whole human family*. It is a question here of every man and woman, all the sons and daughters of the human race, in whom from generation to generation a *fundamental inheritance* is realized, the inheritance that belongs to all humanity and that is linked with the mystery of the biblical "beginning": "God created man in his own image, in the image of God he created him; male and female he created them" (Gen 1: 27).

This eternal *truth about the human being*, man and woman—a truth which is immutably fixed in human experience—*at the same time constitutes the mystery which only in "the Incarnate Word takes on light* ... [since] Christ fully reveals man to himself and makes his supreme calling clear," as the Council teaches. In this "revealing of man to himself," do we not need to find a special place for that "woman" who was the Mother of Christ? Cannot the "*message*" *of Christ*, contained in the Gospel, which has as its background the whole of Scripture, both the Old and the New Testament, say much to the Church and to humanity about the dignity of women and their vocation?

This is precisely what is meant to be the common thread running throughout the present document, which fits into the broader context of the Marian Year, as we approach the end of the Second Millennium after Christ's birth and the beginning of the third, and it seems to me that the best thing is to *give this text the style and character of a meditation*.

Woman-Mother of God (*Theotókos*)

Union with God

3. "When the time had fully come, *God sent forth his son, born of woman*." With these words of his Letter to the Galatians (4:4), the Apostle Paul links together the principal moments which essentially determine the ful-

fillment of the mystery "pre-determined in God" (cf. Eph 1:9). The Son, the Word one in substance with the Father, becomes man, born of a woman, at "the fullness of time." This event leads *to the turning point* of man's history on earth, understood as salvation history. It is significant that Saint Paul does not call the Mother of Christ by her own name "Mary," but calls her "woman": this coincides with the words of the *Proto-evangelium* in the Book of Genesis (cf. 3:15). She is that "woman" who is present in the central salvific event which marks the "fullness of time": this event is realized in her and through her.

In this there begins *the central event, the key event in the history of salvation*: the Lord's Paschal Mystery. Perhaps it would be worthwhile to reconsider it from the point of view of man's spiritual history, understood in the widest possible sense, and as this history is expressed through the different world religions. Let us recall at this point the words of the Second Vatican Council: "People *look to the various religions for answers* to those profound mysteries of the human condition which, today, even as in olden times, deeply stir the human heart: What is a human being? What is the meaning and purpose of our life? What is goodness and what is sin? What gives rise to our sorrows, and to what intent? Where lies the path to true happiness? What is the truth about death, judgment and retribution beyond the grave? What, finally, is *that ultimate and unutterable mystery which engulfs our being*, and from which we take our origin and towards which we move?" "From ancient times down to the present, there has existed among different peoples a certain perception of that hidden power which is present in the course of things and in the events of human life; at times, indeed, recognition can be found of a Supreme Divinity or even a Supreme Father."

Against the background of this broad panorama, which testifies to the aspirations of the human spirit in search of God—at times as it were "groping its way" (cf. Acts 17: 27)—the "fullness of time" spoken of in Paul's Letter emphasizes *the response of God himself, "in whom we live and move and have our being"* (cf. Acts 17:28). This is the God who "in many and various ways spoke of old to our fathers by the prophets, but in these last days has spoken to us by a Son" (Heb 1:1-2). The sending of this Son, one in substance with the Father, as a man "born of woman," constitutes the culminating and *definitive point of God's self-revelation to humanity*. This self-revelation is *salvific in character*, as the Second Vatican Council teaches in another passage: "In his goodness and wisdom, God chose to reveal himself and to make known to us the hidden purpose of his will (cf. Eph 1: 9) by which through Christ, the Word made flesh, man has access to the Father in the Holy Spirit and comes to share in the divine nature" (cf. Eph 2:18; 2 Pt 1:4).

A woman is to be found *at the center of this salvific event*. The self-revelation of God, who is the inscrutable unity of the Trinity, is outlined *in the Annunciation at Nazareth*. "Behold, you will conceive in your womb and bear a son, and you shall call his name Jesus. He will be great, and will be called the Son of the Most High"—"How shall this be, since I have no husband?"—"The Holy Spirit will come upon you, and the power of the Most High will overshadow you; therefore the child to be born will be called holy, the Son of God.... For with God nothing will be impossible" (cf. Lk 1:31-37).

It might be easy to think of this event *in the setting of the history of Israel*, the Chosen People of which Mary is a daughter, but it is also easy to think of it in the context of all the different ways in which humanity has always sought to answer the fundamental and definitive questions which most beset it. Do we not find in the Annunciation at Nazareth the beginning of that definitive answer by which *God himself "attempts to calm people's hearts"*? It is not just a matter here of God's words revealed through the Prophets; rather with this response "the Word is truly made flesh" (cf. Jn 1:14); hence Mary attains *a union with God that exceeds* all the expectations of the human spirit. It even exceeds the expectations of all Israel, in particular the daughters of this Chosen People, who, on the basis of the promise, could hope that one of their number would one day become the mother of the Messiah. Who among them, however, could have imagined that the promised Messiah would be "the Son of the Most High"? On the basis of the Old Testament's monotheistic faith, such a thing was difficult to imagine. Only by the power of the Holy Spirit, who "overshadowed" her, was Mary able to accept what is "impossible with men, but not with God" (cf. Mk 10:27).

Theotókos

4. The "fullness of time" manifests the extraordinary dignity of the "woman." On the one hand, this dignity consists in *the supernatural elevation to union with God* in Jesus Christ, which determines the ultimate finality of the existence of every person both on earth and in eternity. From this point of view, the "woman" is the representative and the archetype of the whole human race: she *represents the humanity* which belongs to all human beings, both men and women. On the other hand, however, the event at Nazareth highlights a form of union with the living God which can *only belong to the "woman,"* Mary: *the union between mother and son*. The Virgin of Nazareth truly becomes the Mother of God.

This truth, which Christian faith has accepted from the beginning, was solemnly defined at the Council of Ephesus (431 C.E.). In opposition to the opinion of Nestorius, who held that Mary was only the mother of the man Jesus, this Council emphasized the essential meaning of the motherhood of the Virgin Mary. At the moment of the Annunciation, by responding with her "*fiat*," Mary conceived a man who was the Son of God, of one substance with the Father; therefore *she is truly the Mother of God, because motherhood concerns the whole person*, not just the body, nor even just human "nature." In this way, the name "*Theotókos*"—Mother of God—became the name proper to the union with God granted to the Virgin Mary.

The particular union of the "*Theotókos*" with God—which fulfils in the most eminent manner the supernatural predestination to union with the Father which is granted to every human being (*filii in Filio*)—is a pure grace and, as such, *a gift of the Spirit*. At the same time, through her response of faith Mary exercises her free will and thus fully shares with her personal and feminine "I" in the event of the Incarnation. With her "*fiat*," *Mary becomes the authentic subject* of that union with God which was realized in the mystery of the Incarnation of the Word, who is of one substance with the Father. All of God's action in human history at all times respects the free will of the human "I." Such was the case with the Annunciation at Nazareth.

"To Serve Means to Reign"

5. This event is clearly *interpersonal in character*: it is a dialogue. We only understand it fully if we place the whole conversation between the Angel and Mary in the context of the words: "full of grace." The whole Annunciation dialogue reveals the essential dimension of the event, namely, its *supernatural* dimension. Grace never casts nature aside or cancels it out, but rather perfects it and ennobles it; therefore the "*fullness of grace*" that was granted to the Virgin of Nazareth, with a view to the fact that she would become "*Theotókos," also signifies the fullness of the perfection of "what is characteristic of woman,"* of "*what is feminine.*" Here we find ourselves, in a sense, at the culminating point, the archetype, of the personal dignity of women.

When Mary responds to the words of the heavenly messenger with her "*fiat*," she who is "full of grace" feels the need to express her personal relationship to the gift that has been revealed to her, saying: "*Behold, I am the handmaid of the Lord*" (Lk 1:38). This statement should not be deprived of its profound meaning, nor should it be diminished by artificially removing it from the overall context of the event and from the full content of the truth revealed about God and man. In the expression "handmaid of the Lord," one senses Mary's complete awareness of being a creature of God. The word "handmaid," near the end of the Annunciation dialogue, is inscribed throughout the whole history of the Mother and the Son. In fact, this *Son*, who is the true and consubstantial "Son of the Most High," will often say of himself, especially at the culminating moment of his mission: "The Son of Man came not to be served but to serve" (Mk 10:45).

At all times Christ is aware of being "the servant of the Lord" according to the prophecy of *Isaiah* (cf. Is 42:1; 49:3, 6; 52:13) which includes the essential content of his messianic mission, namely, his awareness of being the Redeemer of the world. From the first moment of her divine motherhood, of her union with the Son whom "the Father sent into the world, that the world might be saved through him" (cf. Jn 3:17), *Mary takes her place within Christ's messianic service.* It is precisely this service which constitutes the very foundation of that kingdom in which "to serve ... means to reign."

Christ, the "Servant of the Lord," will show all people the royal dignity of service, the dignity which is joined in the closest possible way to the vocation of every person.

By considering the reality "Woman–Mother of God," we enter in a very appropriate way into this Marian Year meditation. *This reality* also *determines the essential horizon of reflection on the dignity and the vocation of women*. In anything we think, say, or do concerning the dignity and the vocation of women, our thoughts, hearts, and actions must not become detached from this horizon. The dignity of every human being and the vocation corresponding to that dignity find their definitive measure *in union with God*. Mary, the woman of the Bible, is the most complete expression of this dignity and vocation. No human being, male or female, created in the image and likeness of God, can in any way attain fulfillment apart from this image and likeness.

The Image and Likeness of God

The Book of Genesis

6. Let us enter into the setting of the biblical "beginning." In it, the revealed truth concerning man as "the image and likeness" of God constitutes the immutable *basis of all Christian anthropology*. "God created man in his own image, in the image of God he created him; male and female he created them" (Gen 1:27). This concise passage contains the fundamental anthropological truths: man is the high point of the whole order of creation in the visible world; the human race, which takes its origin from the calling into existence of man and woman, crowns the whole work of creation; *both man and woman are human beings to an equal degree*, both are created *in God's image*. This image and likeness of God, which is essential for the human being, is passed on by the man and woman, as spouses and parents, to their descendants: "Be fruitful and multiply, and fill the earth and subdue it" (Gen 1:28). The Creator entrusts dominion over the earth to the human race, to all persons, to all men and women, who derive their dignity and vocation from the common "beginning."

In the Book of Genesis we find another description of the creation of man—man and woman (cf. 2:18-25)—to which we shall refer shortly. At this point we can say that the biblical account puts forth the truth about the personal character of the human being. *Man is a person, man and woman equally so*, since both were created in the image and likeness of the personal God. What makes man like God is the fact that—unlike the whole world of other living creatures, including those endowed with senses (*animalia*)—man is also a rational being (*animal rationale*). Thanks to this property, man and woman are able to "dominate" the other creatures of the visible world (cf. Gen 1:28).

The second description of the creation of man (cf. Gen 2:18-25) makes use of different language to express the truth about the creation of man, and especially of woman. In a sense the language is less precise, and, one might say, more descriptive and metaphorical, closer to the language of the myths known at the time; nevertheless, we find no essential contradiction between the two texts. The text of Genesis 2:18-25 helps us to understand better what we find in the concise passage of Genesis 1:27-28. At the same time, if it is read together with the latter, it *helps us to understand even more profoundly* the fundamental *truth* which it contains *concerning man* created as man and woman in the image and likeness of God.

In the description found in Genesis 2:18-25, the woman is created by God "from the rib" of the man and is placed at his side as another "I," as the companion of the man, who is alone in the surrounding world of living creatures and who finds in none of them a "helper" suitable for himself. Called into existence in this way, the woman is immediately recognized by the man as "flesh of his flesh and bone of his bones" (cf. Gen 2:23), and for this very reason she is called "woman." In biblical language, this name indicates her essential identity with regard to man—*'is-'issah*—something which unfortunately modern languages in general are unable to express: "She shall be called woman (*'issah*) because she was taken out of man (*'is*)": (Gen 2:23).

The biblical text provides sufficient bases for recognizing the essential equality of man and woman from the point of view of their humanity. From the very beginning, both are persons, unlike the other living beings in the world around them. *The woman is another "I" in a common humanity*. From the very beginning they appear as a "unity of the two," and this signifies that the original solitude is overcome, the solitude in which man does not find "a helper fit for him" (Gen 2:20). Is it only a question here of a "helper" in activity, in "subduing the earth" (cf. Gen 1: 28)? Certainly it is a matter of a life's companion, with whom, as a wife, the man can unite himself, becoming with her "one flesh" and for this reason leaving "his father and his mother" (cf. Gen 2: 24). In the same context as the creation of man and woman, the biblical account speaks of God's *instituting marriage* as an indispensable condition for the transmission of life to new generations, the transmission of life to which marriage and conjugal love are by their nature ordered: "Be fruitful and multiply, and fill the earth and subdue it" (Gen 1:28).

Person, Communion, Gift

7. By reflecting on the whole account found in Genesis 2:18-25, and by interpreting it in light of the truth about the image and likeness of God (cf. Gen 1:26-27), we can *understand* even *more fully what constitutes the personal character* of the human being, thanks to which both man and woman are like God. For every individual is made in the image of God, insofar as he or she is a rational and free creature capable of knowing God and loving him. We also read that man cannot exist "alone" (cf. Gen 2:18); he can exist only as a "unity of the two," and therefore *in relation to another human person.* It is a question here of a mutual relationship: man to woman and woman to man. Being a person in the image and likeness of God thus also involves existing in a relationship, in relation to the other "I." This is a prelude to the definitive self-revelation of the Triune God: a living unity in the communion of the Father, Son, and Holy Spirit.

At the beginning of the Bible this is not yet stated directly. The whole Old Testament is mainly concerned with revealing the truth about the oneness and unity of God. Within this fundamental truth about God the New Testament will reveal the inscrutable mystery of God's inner life. *God*, who allows himself to be known by human beings through Christ, is the *unity of the Trinity*: unity in communion. In this way, new light is also thrown upon man's image and likeness to God, spoken of in the Book of Genesis. The fact that man "created as man and woman" is the image of God means not only that each of them individually is like God, as a rational and free being. It also means that man and woman, created as a "unity of the two" in their common humanity, are called to live in a communion of love, and in this way to mirror in the world the communion of love that is in God, through which the Three Persons love each other in the intimate mystery of the one divine life. The Father, Son, and Holy Spirit, one God through the unity of the divinity, exist as persons through the inscrutable divine relationship. Only in this way can we understand the truth that God in himself is love (cf. 1 Jn 4:16).

The image and likeness of God in man, created as man and woman (in the analogy that can be presumed between Creator and creature), thus also expresses the "unity of the two" in a common humanity. This "unity of the two," which is a sign of interpersonal communion, *shows that the creation of man* is also marked by a certain likeness to the divine communion ("*communio*"). This likeness is a quality of the personal being of both man and woman and is also a call and a task. The foundation of the whole *human* "*ethos*" is rooted in the image and likeness of God, which the human being bears within himself from the beginning. Both the Old and New Testament will develop that "*ethos*," which reaches its apex in the *commandment of love.*

In the "unity of the two," man and woman are called from the beginning not only to exist "side by side" or "together," but they are also called *to exist mutually "one for the other."* This also explains the meaning of the "help" spoken of in Genesis 2:18-25: "I will make him *a helper fit for him.*" The biblical context enables us to understand this in the sense that the woman must "help" the man—and in his turn he must help her—first of all by the very fact of their "being human persons." In a certain sense this enables man and woman to discover their humanity ever anew and to confirm its whole meaning. We can easily understand that—on this fundamental level—it is a question of a *"help" on the part of both, and at the same time a mutual "help."* To be human means to be called to interpersonal communion. The text of Genesis 2:18-25 shows that marriage is the first and, in a sense, the fundamental dimension of this call. But it is not the only one. The whole of human history unfolds within the context of this call. In this history, on the basis of the principle of mutually being "for" the other, in interpersonal "communion," there develops in humanity itself, in accordance with God's will, the integration of *what is "masculine" and what is "feminine."* The biblical texts, from Genesis onward, constantly enable us to discover the ground in which the truth about man is rooted, the solid and inviolable ground amid the many changes of human existence.

This truth also has to do with *the history of salvation*. In this regard, a statement of the Second Vatican Council is especially significant. In the chapter on "The Community of Mankind" in the Pastoral Constitution *Gaudium et Spes*, we read: "The Lord Jesus, when he prayed to the Father 'that all may be one ... as we are one' (Jn 17: 21-22), opened up vistas closed to human reason. For he implied *a certain likeness* between the union of the divine Persons and the union of God's children in truth and charity. This likeness reveals that man, who is the only creature on earth which God willed for its own sake, cannot fully find himself except through a sincere gift of self."

With these words, the Council text presents a summary of the whole truth about man and woman—a truth which is already outlined in the first chapters of the Book of Genesis, and which is the structural basis of biblical and Christian anthropology. *Man*—whether man or woman—is *the only being among the creatures* of the visible world *that God the Creator "has willed for its own sake"*; that creature is thus a person. Being a person means striving toward self-realization (the Council text speaks of self-discovery), which can only be achieved *"through a sincere gift of self."* The model for this interpretation of the person is God himself as Trinity, as a communion of Persons. To say that man is created in the image and likeness of God means that man is called to exist "for" others, to become a gift.

This applies to every human being, whether woman or man, who live it out in accordance with the special qualities proper to each. Within the framework of the present meditation on the dignity and vocation of women, this truth about being human constitutes the *indispensable point of departure*. Already in the Book of Genesis we can discern, in preliminary outline, the spousal character of the relationship between persons, which will serve as the basis for the subsequent development of the truth about motherhood, and about virginity, as two particular dimensions of the vocation of women in the light of divine Revelation. These two dimensions will find their loftiest expression at the "fullness of time" (cf. Gal 4:4) in the "woman" of Nazareth: the Virgin-Mother.

The Anthropomorphism of Biblical Language

8. The presentation of man as "the image and likeness of God" at the very beginning of Sacred Scripture has *another significance, too*. It is the key

for understanding biblical Revelation as God's word about himself. Speaking about himself, whether through the prophets, or through the Son "who became man" (cf. Heb 1:1, 2), *God speaks in human language*, using human concepts and images. If this manner of expressing himself is characterized by a certain anthropomorphism, the reason is that man is "like" God: created in his image and likeness. *God, too,* is in some measure "like man," and precisely because of this likeness, he can be humanly known. At the same time, the language of the Bible is sufficiently precise to indicate the limits of the "likeness," the limits of the "analogy." For biblical Revelation says that, while man's "likeness" to God is true, the "*non-likeness*" which separates the whole of creation from the Creator is *still more essentially true*. Although man is created in God's likeness, God does not cease to be for him the one "who dwells in unapproachable light" (1 Tm 6:16): he is the "Different One," by essence the "totally Other."

This observation on the limits of the analogy—the limits of man's likeness to God in biblical language—must also be kept in mind when, in different passages of Sacred Scripture (especially in the Old Testament), we find *comparisons that attribute to God "masculine" or "feminine"* qualities. We find in these passages an indirect confirmation of the truth that both man and woman were created in the image and likeness of God. If there is a likeness between Creator and creatures, it is understandable that the Bible would refer to God using expressions that attribute to him both "masculine" and "feminine" qualities.

We may quote here some characteristic passages from the prophet *Isaiah*: "But Zion said, 'The Lord has forsaken me, my Lord has forgotten me'. '*Can a woman forget* her sucking child, that she should have no compassion on the son of her womb? Even these may forget, yet I will *not* forget you.'" (49:14-15). Elsewhere: "As one whom his *mother* comforts, so will I comfort you; you shall be comforted in Jerusalem" (66:13). In the Psalms, too, God is compared to a caring mother: "Like a child quieted at its mother's breast; like a child that is quieted is my soul. O Israel, hope in the Lord." (Ps(s) 131:2-3). In various passages the love of God who cares for his people is shown to be like that of a mother: thus, *like a mother God* "has carried" humanity, and in particular his Chosen People, within his own womb; he has given birth to it in travail, has nourished and comforted it (cf. Is 42:14;

46:3-4). In many passages God's love is presented as the "masculine" love of the bridegroom and father (cf. Hos 11:1-4; Jer 3:4-19), but also sometimes as the "feminine" love of a mother.

This characteristic of biblical language—its anthropomorphic way of speaking about God *—points* indirectly *to the mystery of the eternal "generating"* which belongs to the inner life of God. Nevertheless, in itself this "generating" has neither "masculine" nor "feminine" qualities. It is by nature totally divine. It is spiritual in the most perfect way, since "God is spirit" (Jn 4:24) and possesses no property typical of the body, neither "feminine" nor "masculine." Even *"fatherhood" in God is completely divine* and free of the "masculine" bodily characteristics proper to human fatherhood. In this sense the Old Testament spoke of God as a Father and turned to him as a Father. Jesus Christ—who called God "Abba Father" (Mk 14: 36), and who as the only-begotten and consubstantial Son placed this truth at the very center of his Gospel, thus establishing the norm of Christian prayer—referred to fatherhood in this ultra-corporeal, superhuman, and completely divine sense. He spoke as the Son, joined to the Father by the eternal mystery of divine generation, and he did so while being at the same time the truly human Son of his Virgin Mother.

Although it is not possible to attribute human qualities to the eternal generation of the Word of God, and although the divine fatherhood does not possess "masculine" characteristics in a physical sense, we must nevertheless seek in God the absolute *model* of all *"generation"* among human beings. This would seem to be the sense of the Letter to the Ephesians: "I bow my knees before the Father, from whom every family in heaven and on earth is named" (3:14-15). All "generating" among creatures finds its primary model in that generating which in God is completely divine, that is, spiritual. All "generating" in the created world is to be likened to this absolute and uncreated model; thus every element of human generation which is proper to man, and every element which is proper to woman, namely human *"fatherhood"* and *"motherhood,"* bears within itself a likeness to, or analogy with, the divine "generating" and with that "fatherhood" which in God is "totally different," that is, completely spiritual and divine in essence; whereas in the human order, generation is proper to the "unity of the two": both are "parents," the man and the woman alike.

Eve-Mary

The "Beginning" and the Sin

9. "Although he was made by God in a state of justice, from the very dawn of history man abused his liberty, at the urging of the Evil One. Man set himself against God and sought to find fulfillment apart from God." With these words the teaching of the last Council recalls the revealed doctrine about sin and in particular about that first sin, which is the "original" one. The biblical "beginning"—the creation of the world and of man in the world—*contains* in itself the *truth* about *this sin*, which can also be called the sin of man's "beginning" on the earth. Even though what is written in the Book of Genesis is expressed in the form of a symbolic narrative, as is the case in the description of the creation of man as male and female (cf. Gen 2:18-25), at the same time it reveals what should be called "the mystery of sin" and, even more fully, "the mystery of evil" which exists in the world created by God.

It is not possible to read "the mystery of sin" without making reference to the whole truth about the "image and likeness" to God, which is the basis of biblical anthropology. This truth presents the creation of man as a special gift from the Creator, containing not only the foundation and source of the essential dignity of the human being—man and woman—in the created world but also *the beginning of the call to both of them to share in the intimate life of God himself.* In the light of Revelation, *creation likewise means the beginning of salvation history*. It is precisely in this beginning that sin is situated and manifests itself as opposition and negation.

It can be said, paradoxically, that the sin presented in the third chapter of Genesis confirms the truth about the image and likeness of God in man, since this truth means freedom, that is, man's use of free will by choosing good or his abuse of it by choosing evil, against the will of God. In its essence, however, sin is a negation of God as Creator in his relationship to man, and of what God wills for man, from the beginning and forever. Creating man and woman in his own image and likeness, God wills for them the fullness of good, or supernatural happiness, which flows from sharing in his own life. *By committing sin, man rejects this gift* and at the same time wills to become "as God, knowing good and evil" (Gen 3:5), that is to say, deciding what is good and what is evil independently of God, his Creator.

The sin of the first parents has its own human "measure": an interior standard of its own in man's free will, and it also has within itself a certain "diabolic" characteristic, which is clearly shown in the Book of Genesis (3:15). Sin brings about a break in the original unity which man enjoyed in the state of original justice: union with God as the source of the unity within his own "I," in the mutual relationship between man and woman ("*communio personarum*") as well as in regard to the external world, to nature.

The biblical description of original sin in the third chapter of Genesis in a certain way "distinguishes the roles" which the woman and the man had in it. This is also referred to later in certain passages of the Bible, for example, Paul's Letter to Timothy: "For Adam was formed first, then Eve; and Adam was not deceived, but the woman was deceived and became a transgressor" (1 Tm 2:13-14). There is no doubt that, independent of this "distinction of roles" in the biblical description, *that first sin is the sin of man*, created by God as male and female. It is also *the sin of the "first parents,"* to which is connected its hereditary character. In this sense we call it "original sin."

This sin, as already said, *cannot be properly understood without reference to the mystery of the creation* of the human being—man and woman—*in the image and likeness of God*. By means of this reference one can also understand the mystery of that "non-likeness" to God in which sin consists, and which manifests itself in the evil present in the history of the world. Similarly, one can understand the mystery of that "non-likeness" to God, who "alone is good" (cf. Mt 19:17) and the fullness of good. If sin's "non-likeness" to God, who is Holiness itself, presupposes "likeness" in the sphere of freedom and free will, it can then be said that for this very reason *the "non-likeness" contained in sin* is all the more tragic and sad. It must be admitted that God, as Creator and Father, is here wounded, "offended"—obviously offended—in the very heart of that gift which belongs to God's eternal plan for man.

At the same time, as the author of the evil of sin, *the human being—man and woman—is affected by it*. The third chapter of Genesis shows this with the words which clearly describe the new situation of man in the created world. It shows the perspective of "toil," by which man will earn his living (cf. Gen 3:17-19) and likewise the great "pain" with which the woman will give birth to her children (cf. Gen 3:16). All this is marked by the necessity of death, which is the end of human life on earth. In this way, man, as dust, will "return to the ground, for out of it he was taken"; "you are dust, and to dust you shall return" (cf. Gen 3:19).

These words are confirmed generation after generation. They do not mean that *the image and the likeness of God in the human being*, whether woman or man, has been destroyed by sin; they mean rather that it has been "*obscured*" and in a sense "diminished." Sin, in fact, "diminishes" man, as the Second Vatican Council also recalls. If man is the image and likeness of God by his very nature as a person, then his greatness and his dignity are achieved in the covenant with God, in union with him, in striving toward that fundamental unity which belongs to the internal "logic" of the very mystery of creation. This unity corresponds to the profound truth concerning all intelligent creatures and in particular concerning man, who among all the creatures of the visible world was *elevated* from the beginning through the eternal choice of God in Jesus: "He chose us in (Christ) before the foundation of the world.... He destined us in love to be his sons through Jesus Christ, according to the purpose of his will" (Eph 1:4-6). The biblical teaching taken as a whole enables us to say that predestination concerns all human persons, men and women, each and every one without exception.

"He shall rule over you"

10. The biblical description in the Book of Genesis outlines the truth about the consequences of man's sin, as it is shown by *the disturbance* of that original *relationship between man and woman* which corresponds to their individual dignity as persons. A human being, whether male or female, is a person and therefore "the only creature on earth which God willed for its own sake"; and at the same time this unique and unrepeatable creature "cannot fully find himself except through a sincere gift of self." Here begins the relationship of "communion" in which the "unity of the two" and the personal dignity of both man and woman find expression. When we read in the biblical description the words addressed to the woman: "*Your desire shall be for your husband, and he shall rule over you*" (Gen 3:16), we discover a break and a constant threat precisely in regard to this "unity of the two"

which corresponds to the dignity of the image and likeness of God in both of them. This threat is more serious for the woman, since domination takes the place of "being a sincere gift" and living "for" the other: "he shall rule over you." This "domination" indicates the disturbance and *loss of the stability* of that *fundamental equality* which the man and the woman possess in the "unity of the two"; this is especially to the disadvantage of the woman, whereas only the equality resulting from their dignity as persons can give to their mutual relationship the character of an authentic "*communio personarum.*" While the violation of this equality, which is both a gift and a right deriving from God the Creator, involves an element to the disadvantage of the woman, at the same time it also diminishes the true dignity of the man. Here we touch upon *an extremely sensitive point in the dimension of that "ethos"* which was originally inscribed by the Creator in the very creation of both of them in his own image and likeness.

This statement in Genesis 3:16 is of great significance. It implies a reference to the mutual relationship of man and woman *in marriage*. It refers to the desire born in the atmosphere of spousal love whereby the woman's "sincere gift of self" is responded to and matched by a corresponding "gift" on the part of the husband. Only on the basis of this principle can both of them, and in particular the woman, "discover themselves" as a true "unity of the two" according to the dignity of the person. The matrimonial union requires respect for and a perfecting of the true personal subjectivity of both of them. *The woman cannot become the "object" of "domination" and male "possession."* The words of the biblical text directly concern original sin and its lasting consequences in man and woman. Burdened by hereditary sinfulness, they bear within themselves the constant *"inclination to sin,"* the tendency to go against the moral order which corresponds to the rational nature and dignity of man and woman as persons. This tendency is expressed in *a threefold concupiscence*, which Saint John defines as the lust of the eyes, the lust of the flesh, and the pride of life (cf. 1 Jn 2:16). The words of the Book of Genesis quoted previously (3:16) show how this threefold concupiscence, the "inclination to sin," will burden the mutual relationship of man and woman.

These words of Genesis refer directly to marriage, but indirectly they *concern the different spheres of social life*: the situations in which the woman remains disadvantaged or discriminated against by the fact of being a woman. The revealed truth concerning the creation of the human being as male and female constitutes the principal argument against all the objectively injurious and unjust situations which contain and express the inheritance of the sin which all human beings bear within themselves. The books of Sacred Scripture confirm in various places *the actual existence of such situations* and at the same time proclaim the need for conversion, that is to say, for purification from evil and liberation from sin: from what offends neighbor, what "diminishes" man, not only the one who is offended but also the one who causes the offence. This is the unchangeable message of the Word revealed by God. In it is expressed the biblical "*ethos*" until the end of time.

In our times the question of "women's rights" has taken on new significance in the broad context of the rights of the human person. *The biblical and evangelical message* sheds light on this cause, which is the object of much attention today, *by safeguarding the truth about the "unity" of the "two,"* that is to say the truth about that dignity and vocation that result from the specific diversity and personal originality of man and woman. Even the rightful opposition of women to what is expressed in the biblical words "He shall rule over you" (Gen 3:16) must not under any condition lead to the "masculinization" of women. In the name of liberation from male "domination," women must not appropriate to themselves male characteristics contrary to their own feminine "originality." There is a well-founded fear that if they take this path, women will not "reach fulfillment" but instead will *deform and lose what constitutes their essential richness*. It is indeed an enormous richness. In the biblical description, the words of the first man at the sight of the woman who had been created are words of admiration and enchantment, words which fill the whole history of man on earth.

The personal resources of femininity are certainly no less than the resources of masculinity: they are merely different. A woman, as well as a man, must understand her "fulfillment" as a person, her dignity and vocation, on the basis of these resources, according to the richness of the femininity which she received on the day of creation and which she inherits as an expression of the "image and likeness of God" that is specifically hers.

The inheritance of sin suggested by the words of the Bible—"Your desire shall be for your husband, and he shall rule over you"—*can be conquered* only by following this path. The overcoming of this evil inheritance is, generation after generation, the task of every human being, whether woman or man. Whenever man is responsible for offending a woman's personal dignity and vocation, he acts contrary to his own personal dignity and his own vocation.

Proto-evangelium

11. The Book of Genesis attests to the fact that sin is the evil at man's "beginning" and that since then its consequences weigh upon the whole human race. At the same time, it contains the *first foretelling of victory* over evil, over sin. This is proved by the words which we read in Genesis 3:15, usually called the "*Proto-evangelium*": "I will put enmity between you and the woman, and between your seed and her seed; he shall bruise your head, and you shall bruise his heel." It is significant that the foretelling of the Redeemer contained in these words refers to "the woman." She is assigned the first place in the *Proto-evangelium* as the *progenitrix* of him who will be the Redeemer of man, and since the redemption is to be accomplished through a struggle against evil—through the "enmity" between the offspring of the woman and the offspring of him who, as "the father of lies" (Jn 8:44), is the first author of sin in human history—it is also *an enmity between him and the woman.*

These words give us a comprehensive view of the whole of Revelation, first as a preparation for the Gospel and later as the Gospel itself. From this vantage point the two female figures, *Eve* and *Mary*, are joined under the *name of woman*. The words of the *Proto-evangelium*, re-read in the light of the New Testament, express well the mission of woman in the Redeemer's salvific struggle against the author of evil in human history.

The comparison of Eve and Mary constantly recurs in the course of reflection on the deposit of faith received from divine Revelation. It is one of the themes frequently taken up by the Fathers, ecclesiastical writers, and theologians. As a rule, from this comparison there emerges at first sight a difference, a contrast. *Eve*, as "the mother of all the living" (Gen 3: 20), is *the witness to the biblical "beginning,"* which contains the truth about the creation of man made in the image and likeness of God and the truth about original sin. *Mary is the witness to the new "beginning"* and the "new creation" (cf. 2 Cor 5:17), since she herself, as the first of the redeemed in salvation history, is "a new creation": she is "full of grace." It is difficult to grasp why the words of the *Proto-evangelium* place such strong emphasis on the "woman," if it is not admitted that *in her the new and definitive Covenant* of God with humanity *has its beginning*, the Covenant in the redeeming blood of Christ. The Covenant begins with a woman, the "woman" of the Annunciation at Nazareth. Herein lies the absolute originality of the Gospel: many times in the Old Testament, in order to intervene in the history of his people, God addressed himself to women, as in the case of the mothers of Samuel and Samson. To make his Covenant with humanity, he addressed himself only to men: *Noah, Abraham, and Moses*. At the beginning of the New Covenant, which is to be eternal and irrevocable, there is a woman: the Virgin of Nazareth. It is a sign that points to the fact that "in Jesus Christ" "*there is neither male nor female*" (Gal 3:28). In Christ the mutual opposition between man and woman—which is the inheritance of original sin—is essentially overcome. "For you are all one in Jesus Christ," Saint Paul will write (ibid.).

These words concern that original "unity of the two" which is linked with the creation of the human being as male and female, made in the image and likeness of God, and based on the model of that most perfect communion of Persons which is God himself. Saint Paul states that the mystery of man's redemption in Jesus Christ, the son of Mary, resumes and renews that which in the mystery of creation corresponded to the eternal design of God the Creator. Precisely for this reason, on the day of the creation of the human being as male and female "God saw everything that he had made, and behold, it was very good" (Gen 1:31). *The Redemption restores*, in a sense, at its very root, the good that was essentially "diminished" by sin and its heritage in human history.

The "woman" of the *Proto-evangelium* fits into the perspective of the Redemption. The comparison Eve-Mary can be understood also in the sense that *Mary assumes* in herself and embraces the *mystery of the "woman"* whose beginning is Eve, "the mother of all the living" (Gen 3:20). First of all she assumes and embraces it within the mystery of Christ, "the new and the last Adam" (cf. 1 Cor 15:45), who assumed in his own person the nature of the first Adam. The essence of the New Covenant consists in the fact that the Son of God, who is of one substance with the eternal Father, becomes man: he takes humanity into the unity of the divine Person of the Word. The one who accomplishes the Redemption is also a true man. The mystery of the world's Redemption presupposes that *God the Son assumed humanity as the inheritance of Adam,* becoming like him and like every man in all things, "yet without sinning" (Heb 4:15). In this way, he "fully reveals man to himself and makes man's supreme calling clear," as the Second Vatican Council teaches. In a certain sense, he has helped man to discover "who he is" (cf. Ps(s) 8:5).

In the tradition of faith and of Christian reflection throughout the ages, *the coupling of Adam and Christ* is often linked with that of *Eve and Mary.* If Mary is described also as the "new Eve," what are the meanings of this analogy? Certainly there are many. Particularly noteworthy is the meaning which sees Mary as the full revelation of all that is included in the biblical word "woman": a revelation commensurate with the mystery of the Redemption. *Mary* means, in a sense, a going beyond the limit spoken of in the Book of Genesis (3:16) and a return to that "beginning" in which one finds the "woman" as she was intended to be in *creation,* and therefore in the eternal mind of God: in the bosom of the Most Holy Trinity. Mary is "the new beginning" of the *dignity and vocation of women,* of each and every woman.

A particular key for understanding this can be found in the words which the Evangelist puts on Mary's lips after the Annunciation, during her visit to Elizabeth: "He who is mighty has done great things for me" (Lk 1:49). These words certainly refer to the conception of her Son, who is the "Son of the Most High" (Lk 1:32), the "holy one" of God; but they can also signify *the discovery of her own feminine humanity. He "has done great things for me": this is the discovery of all the richness and personal resources of femininity,* all the eternal originality of the "woman," just as God wanted her to be, a person for her own sake, who discovers herself "by means of a sincere gift of self."

This discovery is connected with a clear awareness of God's gift, of his generosity. From the very "beginning," sin had obscured this awareness, in a sense had stifled it, as is shown in the words of the first temptation by the "father of lies" (cf. Gen 3:1-5). At the advent of the "fullness of time" (cf. Gal 4:4), when the mystery of Redemption begins to be fulfilled in the history of humanity, this awareness bursts forth in all its power in the words of the biblical "woman" of Nazareth. *In Mary, Eve discovers* the nature of the true dignity of woman, of feminine humanity. This discovery must continually reach the heart of every woman and shape her vocation and her life.

Jesus Christ

"They Marveled that He was Talking with a Woman"

12. The words of the *Proto-evangelium* in the Book of Genesis enable us to move into the context of the Gospel. Man's Redemption, foretold in Genesis, now becomes a reality in the person and mission of Jesus Christ, in which we also recognize *what the reality of the Redemption means* for the dignity and the vocation *of women*. This meaning becomes clearer for us from Christ's words and from his whole attitude toward women, an attitude which is extremely simple, and for this very reason extraordinary, if seen against the background of his time. It is an attitude marked by great clarity and depth. Various women appear along the path of the mission of Jesus of Nazareth, and his meeting with each of them is a confirmation of the already-spoken evangelical "newness of life."

It is universally admitted—even by people with a critical attitude toward the Christian message—that *in the eyes of his contemporaries Christ became a promoter of women's true dignity* and of the *vocation* corresponding to this dignity. At times this caused wonder, surprise, often to the point of scandal: "They marveled that he was talking with a woman" (Jn 4:27), because this behavior differed from that of his contemporaries. Even Christ's own disciples "marveled." The Pharisee to whose house the sinful woman went to anoint Jesus' feet with perfumed oil "said to himself, 'If this man were a prophet, *he would have known who* and what sort of woman this is who is touching him, for she is a sinner'" (Lk 7:39). Even greater dismay, or even "holy indignation," must have filled the self-satisfied hearers of Christ's words: "the tax collectors and the harlots go into the Kingdom of God before you" (Mt 21:31).

By speaking and acting in this way, Jesus made it clear that "the mysteries of the Kingdom" were known to him in every detail. He also "knew what was in man" (Jn 2:25), in his innermost being, in his "heart." He was a witness of God's eternal plan for the human being, created in his own image and likeness as man and woman. He was also perfectly aware of the consequences of sin, of that "mystery of iniquity" working in human hearts as the bitter fruit of the obscuring of the divine image. It is truly significant that in his important discussion about marriage and its indissolubility, in the presence of "the Scribes," who by profession were experts in the Law, *Jesus makes reference to the "beginning."* The question asked concerns a man's right "to divorce one's wife for any cause" (Mt 19:3) and therefore also concerns the woman's right, her rightful position in marriage, her dignity. The questioners think they have on their side the Mosaic legislation then followed in Israel: "Why then did Moses command one to give a certificate of divorce, and to put her away?" (Mt 19:7). Jesus answers: "For your hardness of heart Moses allowed you to divorce your wives, but from the beginning it was not so" (Mt 19:8). Jesus appeals to the "beginning," to the creation of man as male and female and their ordering by God himself, which is based upon the fact that *both were created "in his image and likeness."* When "a man shall leave his father and mother and is joined to his wife, so that the two become one flesh," there remains in force the law which comes from God himself: "What therefore God has joined together, let no man put asunder" (Mt 19:6).

The principle of this "*ethos*," which from the beginning marks the reality of creation, is now confirmed by Christ in opposition to that tradition which discriminated against women. In this tradition the male "dominated," without having proper regard for woman and for her dignity, which the "*ethos*" of creation made the basis of the mutual relationships of two people united in marriage. This "*ethos*" is *recalled and confirmed by Christ's words*; it is the "*ethos*" of the Gospel and of Redemption.

Women in the Gospel

13. As we scan the pages of the Gospel, *many women, of different ages and conditions*, pass before our eyes. We meet women with illnesses or physical sufferings, such as the one who had "a spirit of infirmity for eighteen years; she was bent over and could not fully straighten herself" (Lk 13:11); or Si-

mon's mother-in-law, who "lay sick with a fever" (Mk 1:30); or the woman "who had a flow of blood" (cf. Mk 5:25-34), who could not touch anyone because it was believed that her touch would make a person "impure." Each of them was healed, and the last-mentioned—the one with a flow of blood, who touched Jesus' garment "in the crowd" (Mk 5:27)—was praised by him for her great faith: "Your faith has made you well" (Mk 5:34). Then there is *the daughter of Jairus*, whom Jesus brings back to life, saying to her tenderly: "Little girl, I say to you, arise" (Mk 5:41). There also is *the widow of Nain*, whose only son Jesus brings back to life, accompanying his action by an expression of affectionate mercy: "He had compassion on her and said to her, 'Do not weep!'"(Lk 7:13). Finally there is *the Canaanite woman*, whom Christ extols for her faith, her humility, and for that greatness of spirit of which only a mother's heart is capable. "O woman, great is your faith! Be it done for you as you desire" (Mt 15:28). The Canaanite woman was asking for the healing of her daughter.

Sometimes the women whom Jesus met, and who received so many graces from him, also accompanied him as he journeyed with the Apostles through the towns and villages, proclaiming the Good News of the Kingdom of God; and they "provided for them out of their means." The Gospel names Joanna, who was the wife of Herod's steward, Susanna, and "many others" (cf. Lk 8:1-3).

Sometimes women appear *in the parables* which Jesus of Nazareth used to illustrate for his listeners the truth about the Kingdom of God. This is the case in the parables of the lost coin (cf. Lk 15:8-10), the leaven (cf. Mt 13:33), and the wise and foolish virgins (cf. Mt 25:1-13). Particularly eloquent is the story of the widow's mite. While "the rich were putting their gifts into the treasury ... a poor widow put in two copper coins." Then Jesus said: "This poor widow *has put in more than all of them* ... she out of her poverty put in all the living that she had" (Lk 21:1-4). In this way, Jesus presents her as a model for everyone and defends her, for in the sociojuridical system of the time widows were totally defenseless people (cf. also Lk 18:1-7).

In all of Jesus' teaching, as well as in his behavior, one can find nothing which reflects the discrimination against women prevalent in his day. On the contrary, *his words and works always express the respect and honor due to women.* The woman with a stoop is called a "daughter of Abraham" (Lk 13:16), while in the whole Bible the title "son of Abraham" is used only of men. Walking the *Via Dolorosa* to Golgotha, Jesus will say to the women: "Daughters of Jerusalem, do not weep for me" (Lk 23:28). This way of speaking to and about women, as well as his manner of treating them, clearly constitutes an "innovation" with respect to the prevailing custom at that time.

This becomes even more explicit in regard to women whom popular opinion contemptuously labeled sinners, public sinners, and adulteresses. There is the Samaritan woman, to whom Jesus himself says: "For you have had five husbands, and he whom you now have is not your husband." She, realizing that he knows the secrets of her life, recognizes him as the Messiah and runs to tell her neighbors. The conversation leading up to this realization is one of the most beautiful in the Gospel (cf. Jn 4:7-27).

Then there is the public sinner who, in spite of her condemnation by common opinion, enters into the house of the Pharisee to anoint the feet of Jesus with perfumed oil. To his host, who is scandalized by this, he will say: "Her sins, which are many, are forgiven, for she loved much" (cf. Lk 7:37-47).

Finally, there is a situation which is perhaps the most eloquent: *a woman caught in adultery* is brought to Jesus. To the leading question "In the law Moses commanded us to stone such. What do you say about her?" Jesus replies, "Let him who is without sin among you be the first to throw a stone at her." The power of truth contained in this answer is so great that "they went away, one by one, beginning with the eldest." Only Jesus and the woman remain. "Woman, where are they? Has no one condemned you?" "No one, Lord." "Neither do I condemn you; go, and do not sin again" (cf. Jn 8:3-11).

These episodes provide a very clear picture. Christ is the one who "knows what is in man" (cf. Jn 2:25)—in man and woman. He knows *the dignity of man*, his *worth in God's eyes*. He himself, the Christ, is the definitive confirmation of this worth. Everything he says and does is definitively fulfilled in the Paschal Mystery of the Redemption. Jesus' attitude to the women whom he meets in the course of his Messianic service reflects the eternal plan of God, who, in creating each one of them, chooses her and loves her in Christ (cf. Eph 1:1-5). Each woman therefore is "the only creature on earth which God willed for its own sake." *Each of them from the "beginning" inherits as a woman the dignity of personhood.* Jesus of Nazareth confirms this dignity, recalls it, renews it, and makes it a part of the Gospel and of the Redemption for which he is sent into the world. Every word and gesture of Christ about women must therefore be brought into the dimension of the Paschal Mystery. In this way, everything is completely explained.

The Woman Caught in Adultery

14. Jesus enters *into the concrete and historical situation of women*, a situation which is *weighed down by the inheritance of sin*. One of the ways in which this inheritance is expressed is habitual discrimination against women in favor of men. This inheritance is rooted within women, too. From this point of view the episode of the woman "caught in adultery" (cf. Jn 8:3-11) is particularly eloquent. In the end Jesus says to her: "*Do not sin again*," but first he *evokes an awareness of sin* in the men who accuse her in order to stone her, thereby revealing his profound capacity to see human consciences and actions in their true light. Jesus seems to say to the accusers: Is not this woman, for all her sin, above all a confirmation of your own transgressions, of your "male" injustice, your misdeeds?

This truth is *valid for the whole human race*. The episode recorded in the Gospel of John is repeated in countless similar situations in every period of history. A woman is left alone, exposed to public opinion with "her sin," while behind "her" sin there lurks a man—a sinner, guilty "of the other's sin," indeed equally responsible for it, yet his sin escapes notice and is passed over in silence: he does not appear to be responsible for "the other's sin"! Sometimes, forgetting his own sin, he even makes himself the accuser, as in the case described. How often, in a similar way, *the woman pays* for her own sin (maybe it is she, in some cases, who is guilty of the "other's sin"—the sin of the man), but she alone pays and she pays *all alone*! How often is she abandoned with her pregnancy, when the man, the child's father, is unwilling to accept responsibility for it? Besides the many "unwed mothers" in our society, we also must consider all those who, as a result of various pressures, even on the part of the guilty man, very often "get rid of" the child before it is born. "They get rid of it": but at what price? Public opinion today tries in various ways to "abolish" the evil of this sin. Normally a *woman's conscience does not let her forget* that she has taken the life of her own child, for she cannot destroy that readiness to accept life which marks her "*ethos*" from the "beginning."

The attitude of Jesus in the episode described in John 8:3-11 is significant. This is one of the few instances in which his power—the power of truth—is so clearly manifested with regard to human consciences. Jesus is calm, collected, and thoughtful. As in the conversation with the Pharisees (cf. Mt 19:3-9), is Jesus not aware of being in contact with the mystery of the "beginning," when man was created male and female, and the woman was entrusted to the man with her feminine distinctiveness, and with her potential for motherhood? The man was also entrusted by the Creator to the woman—they were *entrusted to each other as persons* made in the image and likeness of God himself. This entrusting is the test of love, spousal love. In order to become "a sincere gift" to each other, each person has to feel responsible for the gift. This test is meant for both of them—man and woman—from the "beginning." After original sin, contrary forces are at work in man and woman as a result of the threefold concupiscence, the "stimulus of sin." They act from deep within the human being; thus Jesus will say in the Sermon on the Mount: *"Everyone who looks at a woman lustfully has already committed adultery with her in his heart"* (Mt 5:28). These words, addressed directly to man, show the fundamental truth of his responsibility vis-a-vis woman: her dignity, her motherhood, her vocation; indirectly, these words concern the woman. Christ did everything possible to ensure that—in the context of the customs and social relationships of that time—women would find in his teaching and actions their own subjectivity and dignity. On the basis of the eternal "unity of the two," *this dignity directly depends on woman herself, as a subject responsible for herself, and at the same time it is "given as a task" to man.* Christ logically appeals to man's responsibility. In the present meditation on women's dignity and vocation, it is necessary that we refer to the context which we find in the Gospel. The dignity and the vocation of women—as well as those of men—find their eternal source in the heart of God. In the temporal conditions of human existence, they are closely connected with the "unity of the two." Consequently, each man must look within himself to see whether she who was entrusted to him as a sister in humanity, as a spouse, has not become in his heart an object of adultery; to see whether she who, in different ways, is the co-subject of his existence in the world, has not become for him an "object": an object of pleasure, of exploitation.

Guardians of the Gospel Message

15. *Christ's way of acting, the Gospel of his words and deeds,* is a consistent *protest* against whatever offends the dignity of women. Consequently, the women who are close to Christ discover themselves in the truth which he "teaches" and "does," even when this truth concerns their "sinfulness." They feel *"liberated" by this truth,* restored to themselves: they feel loved with "eternal love," with a love which finds direct expression in Christ himself.

In Christ's sphere of action their position is transformed. They feel that Jesus is speaking to them about matters which in those times one did not discuss with a woman. Perhaps the most significant example of this is the *Samaritan woman* at the well of Sychar. Jesus—who knows that she is a sinner and speaks to her about this—*discusses the most profound mysteries of God with her.* He speaks to her of God's infinite gift of love, which is like a "spring of water welling up to eternal life" (Jn 4:14). He speaks to her about God who is Spirit, and about the true adoration which the Father has a right to receive in spirit and truth (cf. Jn 4:24). Finally, he reveals to her that he is the Messiah promised to Israel (cf. Jn 4:26).

This is an event without precedent: that a *woman,* and what is more a "sinful woman," becomes a "disciple" of Christ. Indeed, once taught, she proclaims Christ to the inhabitants of Samaria, so that they, too, receive him with faith (cf. Jn 4:39-42). This is an unprecedented event, if one remembers the usual way women were treated by those who were teachers in Israel, whereas in Jesus of Nazareth's way of acting such an event becomes normal. In this regard, the sisters of Lazarus also deserve special mention: "Jesus loved Martha and her sister (Mary) and Lazarus" (cf. Jn 11:5). Mary "listened to the teaching" of Jesus: when he pays them a visit, he calls Mary's behavior "the good portion" in contrast to Martha's preoccupation with domestic matters (cf. Lk 10:38-42). On another occasion—*after the death of Lazarus*—Martha is the one who talks to Christ, and the conversation concerns the most profound truths of revelation and faith: "Lord, if you had been here, my brother would not have died." "Your brother will rise again." "I know that he will rise again in the resurrection at the last day." Jesus said to her: "I am the resurrection and the life; he who believes in me, though he die, yet shall he live, and whoever lives and believes in me shall never die. Do you believe this?" "Yes, Lord; I believe that you are the Christ, the Son of God, he who is coming into the world" (Jn 11:21-27). After this profession of faith Jesus raises Lazarus. *This conversation with Martha is one of the most important in the Gospel.*

Christ speaks to women about the things of God, and they understand them; there is a true resonance of mind and heart, a response of faith. Jesus expresses appreciation and admiration for this distinctly "feminine" response, as in the case of the Canaanite woman (cf. Mt 15:28). Sometimes he presents this lively faith, filled with love, as an example. *He teaches, taking as his starting point this feminine response of mind and heart.* This is the case with the "sinful" woman in the Pharisee's house, whose way of acting is taken by Jesus as the starting point for explaining the truth about the forgiveness of sins: "Her sins, which are many, are forgiven, for she loved much; but he who is forgiven little, loves little" (Lk 7:47). On the occasion of another anointing, Jesus defends the woman and her action before the disciples, Judas in particular: "Why do you trouble this woman? *For she has done a beautiful thing to me....* In pouring this ointment on my body she has done it to prepare me for burial. Truly, I say to you, wherever this gospel is preached in the whole world, what she has done will be told in memory of her" (Mt 26:6-13).

Indeed, the Gospels not only describe what that woman did at Bethany in the house of Simon the Leper; they also highlight the fact that *women were in the forefront at the foot of the Cross*, at the decisive moment in Jesus of Nazareth's whole messianic mission. John was the only Apostle who remained faithful, but there were many faithful women. Not only the Mother of Christ and "his mother's sister, Mary the wife of Clopas and Mary Magdalene" (Jn 19:25) were present but "there were also many women there, looking on from afar, who had followed Jesus from Galilee, ministering to him" (Mt 27: 55). As we see, in this most arduous test of faith and fidelity the women proved stronger than the Apostles. In this moment of danger, those who love much succeed in overcoming their fear. Before this there were the *women on the Via Dolorosa, "who bewailed and lamented him"* (Lk 23:27). Earlier still, there was *Pilate's wife*, who had warned her husband: "Have nothing to do with that righteous man, for I have suffered much over him today in a dream" (Mt 27:19).

First Witnesses of the Resurrection

16. From the beginning of Christ's mission, women show to him and to his mystery a special *sensitivity which is characteristic* of their *femininity*. It must also be said that this is especially confirmed in the Paschal Mystery, not only at the Cross but also at the dawn of the Resurrection. The women *are the first at the tomb*. They are the first to find it empty. They are the first to hear: "He is not here. *He has risen*, as he said" (Mt 28:6). They are the first to embrace his feet (cf. Mt 28:9). They are also the first to be called to announce this truth to the Apostles (cf. Mt 28:1-10; Lk 24:8-11). The Gospel of John (cf. also Mk 16: 9) emphasizes *the special role of Mary Magdalene*. She is the first to meet the Risen Christ. At first she thinks he is the gardener; she recognizes him only when he calls her by name: "Jesus said to her, 'Mary'. She turned and said to him in Hebrew, '*Rabbuni*' (which means Teacher). Jesus said to her, 'Do not hold me, for I have not yet ascended to the Father, but go to my brethren and say to them, I am ascending to my Father and to your Father, to my God and your God'. Mary Magdalene went and said to the disciples, 'I have seen the Lord'; and she told them that he had said these things to her" (Jn 20:16-18).

Because of what she had seen, Mary Magdalene came to be called "the apostle of the Apostles." She was the first eyewitness of the Risen Christ, and for this reason she was also *the first to bear witness to him before the Apostles*. This event, in a sense, crowns all that has been said previously about Christ entrusting divine truths to women as well as men. One can say that this fulfilled the words of the Prophet: "*I will pour out my spirit* on all flesh; your sons and *your daughters shall prophesy*" (Jl 3:1). On the fiftieth day after Christ's Resurrection, these words are confirmed once more in the Upper Room in Jerusalem, at the descent of the Holy Spirit, the Paraclete (cf. Acts 2:17).

Everything that has been said so far about Christ's attitude toward women confirms and clarifies, in the Holy Spirit, the truth about the equality of man and woman. One must speak of an essential "equality," since both of them—the woman as much as the man—are created in the image and likeness of God. Both of them are equally capable of receiving the outpouring of divine truth and love in the Holy Spirit. Both receive his salvific and sanctifying "visits."

The fact of being a man or a woman involves no limitation here, just as the salvific and sanctifying action of the Spirit in man is in no way limited by the fact that one is a Jew or a Greek, slave or free, according to the well-known words of Saint Paul: "For you are all one in Christ Jesus" (Gal 3:28). *This unity does not cancel out diversity*. The Holy Spirit, who brings about this unity in the supernatural order of sanctifying grace, contributes in equal measure to the fact that "your sons will prophesy" and that "your daughters will prophesy." "To prophesy" means to express by one's words and one's life "the mighty works of God" (Acts 2: 11), preserving the truth and originality of each person, whether woman or man. Gospel "equality," the "equality" of women and men in regard to the *"mighty works of God"*—manifested so clearly in the words and deeds of Jesus of Nazareth—constitutes the most obvious basis for the dignity and vocation of women in the Church and in the world. *Every vocation* has a profoundly *personal and prophetic meaning*. In "vocation" understood in this way, what is personally feminine reaches a new dimension: the dimension of the "mighty works of God," of which the woman becomes the living subject and an irreplaceable witness.

Motherhood, Virginity

Two Dimensions of Women's Vocation

17. We must now focus our meditation on virginity and motherhood as two particular dimensions of the fulfillment of the female personality. In the light of the Gospel, they acquire their full meaning and value in Mary, who as a Virgin became the Mother of the Son of God. These *two dimensions of the female vocation* were united in her in an exceptional manner, in such a way that one did not exclude the other but wonderfully complemented it. The description of the Annunciation in the Gospel of Luke clearly shows that this seemed impossible to the Virgin of Nazareth. When

she hears the words: "You will conceive in your womb and bear a son, and you shall call his name Jesus," she immediately asks "How can this be, since I have no husband?" (Lk 1: 31, 34). In the usual order of things motherhood is the result of mutual "knowledge" between a man and woman in the marriage union. Mary, firm in her resolve to preserve her virginity, puts this question to the divine messenger and obtains from him the explanation: *"The Holy Spirit will come upon you"*—your motherhood will not be the consequence of matrimonial "knowledge" but will be the work of the Holy Spirit; the "power of the Most High" will "overshadow" the mystery of the Son's conception and birth; as the Son of the Most High, he is given to you exclusively by God, in a manner known to God. Mary, therefore, maintained her virginal "I have no husband" (cf. Lk 1: 34) and at the same time became a Mother. *Virginity and motherhood coexist in her*: they do not mutually exclude each other or place limits on each other. Indeed, the person of the Mother of God helps everyone—especially women—to see how these two dimensions, these two paths in the vocation of women as persons, explain and complete each other.

Motherhood

18. In order to share in this "vision," we must once *again seek a deeper understanding of the truth about the human person* recalled by the Second Vatican Council. The human being—both male and female—is the only being in the world which God willed for its own sake. The human being is a person, a subject who decides for himself. At the same time, man "cannot fully find himself except through a sincere gift of self." It has already been said that this description, indeed this definition of the person, corresponds to the fundamental biblical truth about the creation of the human being—man and woman—in the image and likeness of God. This is not a purely theoretical interpretation, nor an abstract definition, for *it gives an essential indication of what it means to be human, while emphasizing the value of the gift of self, the gift of the person*. In this vision of the person we also find the essence of that "*ethos*" which, together with the truth of creation, will be fully developed by the books of Revelation, particularly the Gospels.

This truth about the person also opens up *the path to a full understanding of women's motherhood*. Motherhood is the fruit of the marriage union of a man and woman, of that biblical "knowledge" which corresponds to the "union of the two in one flesh" (cf. Gen 2:24). This brings about—on the woman's part—a special "gift of self," as an expression of that spousal love whereby the two are united to each other so closely that they become "one flesh." Biblical "knowledge" is achieved in accordance with the truth of the person only when the mutual self-giving is not distorted either by the desire of the man to become the "master" of his wife ("he shall rule over you") or by the woman remaining closed within her own instincts ("your desire shall be for your husband": Gen 3:16).

This mutual gift of the person in marriage opens to the gift of a new life, *a new human being*, who is also a person in the likeness of his parents. Motherhood implies from the beginning a special openness to the new person: and this is precisely the woman's "part." In this openness, in conceiving and giving birth to a child, the woman "discovers herself through a sincere gift of self." The gift of interior readiness to accept the child and bring it into the world is linked to the marriage union, which—as mentioned earlier—should constitute a special moment in the mutual self-giving both by the woman and the man. According to the Bible, the conception and birth of a new human being are accompanied by the following words of the woman: *"I have brought a man into being with the help of the Lord"* (Gen 4:1). This exclamation of Eve, the "mother of all the living," is repeated every time a new human being comes into the world. It expresses the woman's joy and awareness that she is sharing in the great mystery of eternal generation. The spouses share in the creative power of God!

The woman's motherhood in the period between the baby's conception and birth is a bio-physiological and psychological process which is better understood in our days than in the past, and is the subject of many detailed studies. Scientific analysis fully confirms that the very physical constitution of women is naturally disposed to motherhood—conception, pregnancy, and giving birth—which is a consequence of the marriage union with the man. At the same time, this also corresponds to the psycho-physical structure of women. What the different branches of science have to say on this subject is important and useful, provided that it is not limited to an exclusively bio-physiological interpretation of women and of motherhood. Such a *"restricted" picture* would go hand in hand with a materialistic concept of the human being and of the world. In such a case, what is truly essential would unfortunately be lost. Motherhood as a *human* fact and phenomenon is fully explained on the basis of the truth about the person. Motherhood *is linked to the personal structure of the woman and to the personal dimension of the gift*: "I have brought a man into being with the help of the Lord" (Gen 4:1). The Creator grants the parents the gift of a child. On the woman's part, this fact is linked in a special way to "a sincere gift of self." Mary's words at the Annunciation—"Let it be to me according to your word"—signify the woman's readiness for the gift of self and her readiness to accept a new life.

The eternal mystery of generation, which is in God himself, the one and Triune God (cf. Eph 3:14-15), is reflected in the woman's motherhood and in the man's fatherhood. Human parenthood is something shared by both the man and the woman. Even if the woman, out of love for her husband, says: "I have given you a child," her words also mean: "This is our child." Although both of them together are parents of their child, *the woman's motherhood constitutes a special* "part" *in this shared parenthood*, and the most demanding part. Parenthood—even though it belongs to both—is realized much more fully in the woman, especially in the prenatal period. It is the woman who "pays" directly for this shared generation, which literally absorbs the energies of her body and soul. It is therefore necessary that *the man* be fully aware that in their shared parenthood he owes *a special debt to the woman*. No program of "equal rights" between women and men is valid unless it takes this fact fully into account.

Motherhood involves a special communion with the mystery of life, as it develops in the woman's womb. The mother is filled with wonder at this mystery of life and "understands" with unique intuition what is happening inside her. In the light of the "beginning," the mother accepts and loves as a person the child she is carrying in her womb. This unique contact with the new human being developing within her gives rise to an attitude toward human beings—not only toward her own child but every human being—which profoundly marks the woman's personality. It is commonly thought that women are more capable than men of paying attention *to another person*, and that motherhood develops this predisposition even more. The man—even with all his sharing in parenthood—always remains "outside" the process of pregnancy and the baby's birth; in many ways he has to *learn* his own *"fatherhood" from the mother*. One can say that this is part of the normal human dimension of parenthood, including the stages that follow the birth of the baby, especially the initial period. The child's upbringing, taken as a whole, should include the contribution of both parents: the maternal and paternal contribution. In any event, the mother's contribution is decisive in laying the foundation for a new human personality.

Motherhood in Relation to the Covenant

19. Our reflection returns to *the biblical exemplar of the "woman"* in the *Proto-evangelium*. The "woman," as mother and first teacher of the human being (education being the spiritual dimension of parenthood), has a specific precedence over the man. Although motherhood, especially *in the bio-physical sense*, depends upon the man, it places an essential "mark" on the whole personal growth process of new children. Motherhood *in the bio-physical sense* appears to be passive: the formation process of a new life "takes place" in her, in her body, which is nevertheless profoundly involved in that process. At the same time, motherhood *in its personal-ethical sense* expresses a very important creativity on the part of the woman, upon whom the very humanity of the new human being mainly depends. In this sense, too, the woman's motherhood presents a special call and a special challenge to the man and to his fatherhood.

The biblical exemplar of the "woman" finds its culmination *in the motherhood of the Mother of God*. The words of the *Proto-evangelium*—"I will put enmity between you and the woman"—find here a fresh confirmation. We see that through Mary—through her maternal "*fiat*," ("Let it be done to me")—God *begins a New Covenant with humanity*. This is the eternal and definitive Covenant in Christ, in his body and blood, in his Cross and Resurrection. Precisely because this Covenant is to be fulfilled "in flesh and blood" its beginning is in the Mother. Thanks solely to her and to her virginal and maternal "*fiat*," the "Son of the Most High" can say to the Father: "A body you have prepared for me. Lo, I have come to do your will, O God" (cf. Heb 10:5, 7).

Motherhood has been introduced into the order of the Covenant that God made with humanity in Jesus Christ. Each and every time that *moth-*

erhood is repeated in human history, it is always *related to the Covenant* which God established with the human race through the motherhood of the Mother of God.

Does not Jesus bear witness to this reality when he answers the exclamation of that woman in the crowd who blessed him for Mary's motherhood: "Blessed is the womb that bore you, and the breasts that you sucked!"? Jesus replies, "Blessed rather are those who hear the word of God and keep it" (Lk 11:27-28). Jesus confirms the meaning of motherhood in reference to the body, but at the same time he indicates an even deeper meaning, which is connected with the order of the spirit: it is a sign of the Covenant with God who "is spirit" (Jn 4: 24). This is true above all for the motherhood of the Mother of God. *The motherhood* of every woman, understood in the light of the Gospel, is similarly not only "of flesh and blood": it expresses a profound *"listening to the word of the living God"* and a readiness to "safeguard" this Word, which is "the word of eternal life" (cf. Jn 6:68). For it is precisely those born of earthly mothers, the sons and daughters of the human race, who receive from the Son of God the power to become "children of God" (Jn 1:12). A dimension of the New Covenant in Christ's blood enters into human parenthood, making it a reality and a task for "new creatures" (cf. 2 Cor 5: 17). The history of every human being passes through the threshold of a woman's motherhood; crossing it conditions "the revelation of the children of God" (cf. Rom 8: 19).

"*When a woman is in travail she has sorrow*, because her hour has come; but when she is delivered of the child, *she no longer remembers the anguish*, for joy that a child is born into the world" (Jn 16: 21). The first part of Christ's words refers to the "pangs of childbirth" which belong to the heritage of original sin; at the same time, these words indicate *the link that exists between the woman's motherhood and the Paschal Mystery*. For this mystery also includes the Mother's sorrow at the foot of the Cross—the Mother who through faith shares in the amazing mystery of her Son's "self-emptying": "This is perhaps the deepest *'kenosis'* of faith in human history."

As we contemplate this Mother, whose heart "a sword has pierced" (cf. Lk 2: 35), our thoughts go to *all the suffering women in the world*, suffering either physically or morally. In this suffering a woman's sensitivity plays a role, even though she often succeeds in resisting suffering better than a man. It is difficult to enumerate these sufferings; it is difficult to call them all by name. We may recall her maternal care for her children, especially when they fall sick or fall into bad ways; the death of those most dear to her; the loneliness of mothers forgotten by their grown up children; the loneliness of widows; the sufferings of women who struggle alone to make a living; and women who have been wronged or exploited. Then there are the sufferings of consciences as a result of sin, which has wounded the woman's human or maternal dignity: the wounds of consciences which do not heal easily. With these sufferings, too, we must place ourselves at the foot of the Cross.

The words of the Gospel about the woman who suffers when the time comes for her to give birth to her child, immediately afterward, express joy: it is *"the joy that a child is born into the world."* This joy, too, is referred to the Paschal Mystery, to the joy which is communicated to the Apostles on *the day of Christ's Resurrection*: "So you have sorrow now" (these words were said the day before the Passion); "but I will see you again and your hearts will rejoice, and no one will take your joy from you" (Jn 16: 22-23).

Virginity for the Sake of the Kingdom

20. In the teaching of Christ, *motherhood is connected with virginity* but also *distinct from it*. Fundamental to this is Jesus' statement in the conversation on the indissolubility of marriage. Having heard the answer given to the Pharisees, the disciples say to Christ: "If such is the case of a man with his wife, it is not expedient to marry" (Mt 19:10). Independently of the meaning which "it is not expedient" had at that time in the mind of the disciples, *Christ* takes their mistaken opinion as a starting point for instructing them *on the value of celibacy*. He distinguishes celibacy which results from natural defects—even though they may have been caused by man—from *"celibacy for the sake of the Kingdom of heaven."* Christ says, "[A]nd there are eunuchs who have made themselves eunuchs for the sake of the Kingdom of heaven" (Mt 19:12). It is, then, a voluntary celibacy, chosen for the sake of the Kingdom of heaven, in view of man's eschatological vocation to union with God. He then adds, "He who is able to receive this, let him receive it." These words repeat what he had said at the beginning of the discourse on celibacy (cf. Mt 19:11). Consequently, *celibacy for the kingdom of heaven results not*

only from a free choice on the part of man but also from a special *grace* on the part of God, who calls a particular person to live celibacy. While this is a special sign of the Kingdom of God to come, it also serves as a way to devote all the energies of soul and body during one's earthly life exclusively for the sake of the eschatological kingdom.

Jesus' words are the answer to the disciples' question. They are addressed directly to those who put the question: in this case they were men. Nevertheless, Christ's answer, in itself, has *a value both for men and for women.* In this context it indicates the evangelical ideal of virginity, an ideal which constitutes a clear "innovation" with respect to the tradition of the Old Testament. Certainly that tradition was connected in some way with Israel's expectation of the Messiah's coming, especially among the women of Israel from whom he was to be born. In fact, the ideal of celibacy and virginity for the sake of greater closeness to God was not entirely foreign to certain Jewish circles, especially in the period immediately preceding the coming of Jesus; nevertheless, celibacy for the sake of the Kingdom, or rather virginity, is undeniably an innovation connected with the incarnation of God.

From the moment of Christ's coming, the expectation of the People of God has to be directed to the eschatological Kingdom which is coming and to which he must lead "the new Israel." A new awareness of faith is essential for such a turn-about and change of values. Christ emphasizes this twice: "He who is able to receive this, let him receive it." Only "those to whom it is given" understand it (Mt 19:11). *Mary* is the first person in whom this *new awareness* is manifested, for she asks the Angel: "How can this be, since I have no husband?" (Lk 1:34). Even though she is "betrothed to a man whose name was Joseph" (cf. Lk 1:27), she is firm in her resolve to remain a virgin. The motherhood which is accomplished in her comes exclusively from the "power of the Most High" and is the result of the Holy Spirit's coming down upon her (cf. Lk 1:35). This divine motherhood, therefore, is an altogether unforeseen response to the human expectation of women in Israel: it comes to Mary as a gift from God himself. This gift is the beginning and the prototype of a new expectation on the part of all. It measures up to the Eternal Covenant, to God's new and definitive promise: it is *a sign of eschatological hope.*

On the basis of the Gospel, the meaning of virginity was developed and better understood as a vocation for women, too, one in which their dignity, like that of the Virgin of Nazareth, finds confirmation. The Gospel puts forward *the ideal of the consecration of the person*, that is, the person's exclusive dedication to God by virtue of the evangelical counsels: in particular, chastity, poverty, and obedience. Their perfect incarnation is Jesus Christ himself. Whoever wishes to follow him in a radical way chooses to live according to these counsels. They are distinct from the commandments and show the Christian the radical way of the Gospel. From the very beginning of Christianity, men and women have set out on this path, since the evangelical ideal is addressed to human beings without any distinction of sex.

In this wider context, *virginity* has to be considered *also as a path for women*, a path on which they realize their womanhood in a way different from marriage. In order to understand this path, it is necessary to refer once more to the fundamental idea of Christian anthropology. By freely choosing virginity, women confirm themselves as persons, as beings whom the Creator from the beginning has willed for their own sake. At the same time, they realize the personal value of their own femininity by becoming "a sincere gift" for God who has revealed himself in Christ, a gift for Christ, the Redeemer of humanity and the Spouse of souls: a "spousal" gift. *One cannot correctly understand virginity*—a woman's consecration in virginity—*without referring to spousal love*. It is through this kind of love that a person becomes a gift for the other.

A man's consecration in priestly celibacy or in the religious state is to be understood analogously. The naturally spousal predisposition of the feminine personality finds a response in virginity understood in this way. Women, called from the very "beginning" to be loved and to love, in a vocation to virginity *find Christ* first of all as the Redeemer who "loved until the end" through his total gift of self; *and they respond to this gift with a "sincere gift"* of their whole lives. They thus give themselves to the divine Spouse, and this personal gift creates the union, which is properly spiritual in character. Through the Holy Spirit's action a woman becomes "one spirit" with Christ the Spouse (cf. 1 Cor 6:17).

This is the evangelical ideal of virginity, in which both the dignity and the vocation of women are realized in a special way. In virginity thus understood, the so-called *radicalism of the Gospel* finds expression: "Leave everything and follow Christ" (cf. Mt 19:27). This cannot be compared to remaining simply unmarried or single, because virginity is not restricted to a mere "no," but contains a profound "yes" in the spousal order: the gift of self for love in a total and undivided manner.

Motherhood According to the Spirit

21. Virginity according to the Gospel means *renouncing marriage and thus physical motherhood.* Nevertheless, the renunciation of this kind of motherhood, a renunciation that can involve great sacrifice for a woman, makes possible a different kind of motherhood: motherhood *"according to the Spirit"* (cf. Rom 8:4). For virginity does not deprive a woman of her prerogatives. Spiritual motherhood takes on many different forms. In the life of consecrated women, for example, who live according to the charism and the rules of the various apostolic institutes, it can express itself as concern for people, especially the most needy: the sick, the handicapped, the abandoned, orphans, the elderly, children, young people, the imprisoned, and, in general, people on the edges of society. *In this way, a consecrated woman finds her Spouse,* different and the same in each and every person, according to his very words: "As you did it to one of the least of these my brethren, you did it to me" (Mt 25:40). Spousal love always involves a special readiness to be poured out for the sake of those who come within one's range of activity. In marriage this readiness, even though open to all, consists mainly in the love that parents give to their children. In virginity this readiness is open *to all people who are embraced by the love of Christ the Spouse.*

Spousal love—with its maternal potential hidden in the heart of the woman as a virginal bride—when joined to Christ, the Redeemer of each and every person, is also predisposed to being open to each and every person. This is confirmed in the religious communities of apostolic life, and in a different way in communities of contemplative life, or the cloister. There exist still other forms of a vocation to virginity for the sake of the Kingdom; for example, the Secular Institutes, or the communities of consecrated persons which flourish within Movements, Groups, and Associations. In all of these, *the same truth about the spiritual motherhood* of virgins is confirmed in various ways; however, it is not only a matter of communal forms but also of noncommunal forms. In brief, virginity as a woman's vocation is always the vocation of a person—of a unique, individual person. The spiritual motherhood which makes itself felt in this vocation is also profoundly personal.

This is also the basis of a specific *convergence between the virginity* of the unmarried woman and *the motherhood* of the married woman. This convergence moves not only from motherhood toward virginity, as emphasized previously, it also moves from virginity toward marriage, the form of woman's vocation in which she becomes a mother by giving birth to her children. The starting point of this second analogy is *the meaning of marriage*. A woman is "married" either through the sacrament of marriage or spiritually through marriage to Christ. *In both cases marriage* signifies the "sincere gift of the person" of the bride to the groom. In this way, one can say that the profile of marriage is found spiritually in virginity. Does not physical motherhood also have to be a spiritual motherhood, in order to respond to the whole truth about the human being who is a unity of body and spirit? There exist many reasons for discerning in these two different paths—the two different vocations of women—a profound complementarity, and even a profound union within a person's being.

"My Little Children with Whom I Am Again in Travail"

22. The Gospel reveals and enables us to understand precisely *this mode of being of the human person*. The Gospel helps every woman and every man to live it and thus attain fulfillment. There exists a total equality with respect to the gifts of the Holy Spirit, with respect to the "mighty works of God" (Acts 2:11); moreover, it is precisely in the face of the "mighty works of God" that Saint Paul, as a man, feels the need to refer to what is essentially feminine in order to express the truth about his own apostolic service. This is exactly what Paul of Tarsus does when he addresses the Galatians with the words: *"My little children, with whom I am again in travail"* (Gal 4:19). In the First Letter to the Corinthians (7:38) Saint Paul proclaims the superiority of virginity over marriage, which is a constant teaching of the Church in accordance with the spirit of Christ's words recorded in the Gospel of Matthew (19:10-12); he does so without in any way obscur-

ing the importance of physical and spiritual motherhood. Indeed, in order to illustrate the Church's fundamental mission, he finds nothing better than the reference to motherhood.

The same analogy—and the same truth—are present in the Dogmatic Constitution on the Church. *Mary is the "figure" of the Church*: "For in the mystery of the Church, herself rightly called mother and virgin, the Blessed Virgin came first as an eminent and singular exemplar of both virginity and motherhood ... The Son whom she brought forth is He whom God placed as the first-born among many brethren (cf. Rom 8: 29), namely, among the faithful. In their birth and development she cooperates with a maternal love." "Moreover, contemplating Mary's mysterious sanctity, imitating her charity, and faithfully fulfilling the Father's will, the Church *herself becomes a mother* by accepting God's word in faith. For by her preaching and by baptism she brings forth to a new and immortal life children who are conceived by the Holy Spirit and born of God." This is motherhood "according to the Spirit" with regard to the sons and daughters of the human race. This motherhood—as already mentioned—becomes the woman's "role" also in virginity. "The Church *herself is a virgin*, who keeps whole and pure the fidelity she has pledged to her Spouse."

This is most perfectly fulfilled in Mary. The Church, therefore, "imitating the Mother of her Lord, and by the power of the Holy Spirit ... preserves with virginal purity an integral faith, a firm hope, and a sincere charity."

The Council has confirmed that, unless one looks to the Mother of God, it is impossible to understand the mystery of the Church, her reality, her essential vitality. Indirectly we find here a *reference to the biblical exemplar of the "woman"* which is already clearly outlined in the description of the "beginning" (cf. Gen 3:15) and which proceeds from creation, through sin to the Redemption. In this way, there is a confirmation of the profound union between what is human and what constitutes the divine economy of salvation in human history. The Bible convinces us of the fact that one can have no adequate hermeneutic of man, or of what is "human," without appropriate reference to what is "feminine." There is an analogy in God's salvific economy: if we wish to understand it fully in relation to the whole of human history, we cannot omit, in the perspective of our faith, the mystery of "woman": virgin-mother-spouse.

The Church, the Bride of Christ

The "Great Mystery"

23. Of fundamental importance here are the words of the Letter to the Ephesians: "Husbands, love your wives, as Christ loved the Church and gave himself up for her, that he might sanctify her, having cleansed her by the washing of water with the word, that he might present the Church to himself in splendor, without spot or wrinkle or any such thing, that she might be holy and without blemish. Even so husbands should love their wives as their own bodies. He who loves his wife loves himself. For no man ever hates his own flesh, but nourishes and cherishes it, as Christ does the Church, because we are members of his body. 'For this reason a man shall leave his father and mother and be joined to his wife, and the two shall become one flesh'. *This mystery is a profound one*, and I am saying that *it refers to Christ and the Church*" (5:25-32).

In this Letter, the author expresses the truth about the Church as the bride of Christ and also indicates how this truth is *rooted in the biblical reality of the creation of the human being as male and female.* Created in the image and likeness of God as a "unity of the two," both have been called to a spousal love. Following the description of creation in the Book of Genesis (2:18-25), one can also say that this fundamental call appears in the creation of woman and is inscribed by the Creator in the institution of marriage, which, according to Genesis 2:24, has the character of a union of persons ("*communio personarum*") from the very beginning. Although not directly, the very description of the "beginning" (cf. Gen 1:27; 2:24) shows that the whole "*ethos*" of mutual relations between men and women has to correspond to the personal truth of their being.

All this has already been considered. The Letter to the Ephesians once again confirms this truth, while at the same time comparing the spousal character of the love between man and woman to the mystery of Christ and of the Church. *Christ is the Bridegroom of the Church—the Church is the Bride of Christ.* This analogy is not without precedent; it transfers to the New Testament what was already contained *in the Old Testament*, especially in the prophets Hosea, Jeremiah, Ezekiel, and Isaiah. The respective passages deserve a separate analysis. Here we will cite only one text. This is how God speaks to his Chosen People through the Prophet: "Fear not, for you will not be ashamed; be not confounded, for you will not be put to shame; for you will forget the shame of your youth, and the reproach of your widowhood you will remember no more. *For your Maker is your husband,* the Lord of hosts is his name; and the Holy One of Israel is *your Redeemer,* the God of the whole earth he is called. For the Lord has called you like a wife forsaken and grieved in spirit, like a wife of youth when she is cast off, says your God. For a brief moment I forsook you, but with great compassion I will gather you. In overflowing wrath for a moment I hid my face from you, but with everlasting love I will have compassion on you, says the Lord, your Redeemer.... For the mountains may depart and the hills be removed, *but my steadfast love shall not depart from you,* and my covenant of peace shall not be removed, says the Lord, who has compassion on you" (Is 54:4-8, 10).

Since the human being—man and woman—has been created in God's image and likeness, God can speak about himself through the lips of the Prophet using language which is essentially human. In the text of Isaiah quoted previously, the expression of God's love is "*human,*" but the *love* itself is *divine.* Since it is God's love, its spousal character is properly divine, even though it is expressed by the analogy of a man's love for a woman. The woman-bride is Israel, God's Chosen People, and this choice originates exclusively in God's gratuitous love. It is precisely this love which explains the Covenant, a Covenant often presented as a marriage covenant which God always renews with his Chosen People. On the part of God the Covenant is a lasting "commitment"; he remains faithful to his spousal love even if the bride often shows herself to be unfaithful.

This *image of spousal love,* together with the figure of the divine Bridegroom—a very clear image in the texts of the Prophets—finds crowning confirmation in the Letter to the Ephesians (5:23-32). *Christ* is greeted as the bridegroom by John the Baptist (cf. Jn 3:27-29). Indeed Christ applies to himself this comparison drawn from the Prophets (cf. Mk 2:19-20). The Apostle Paul, who is a bearer of the Old Testament heritage, writes to the Corinthians: "I feel a divine jealousy for you, for I betrothed you to Christ to present you as a pure bride to her one husband" (2 Cor 11:2). The fullest expression of the truth about Christ the Redeemer's love, according to the analogy of spousal love in marriage, is found in the Letter to the Ephesians:

"*Christ loved the Church and gave himself up for her*" (5:25), thereby fully confirming the fact that the Church is the bride of Christ: "The Holy One of Israel is your Redeemer" (Is 54:5). In Saint Paul's text the analogy of the spousal relationship moves simultaneously in two directions which make up the whole of the "great mystery" ("*sacramentum magnum*").

The covenant proper to spouses "explains" the spousal character of the union of Christ with the Church, and in its turn this union, as a "great sacrament," determines the sacramentality of marriage as a holy covenant between the two spouses, man and woman. Reading this rich and complex passage, which *taken as a whole is a great analogy*, we must *distinguish* that element which expresses the human reality of interpersonal relations from that which expresses in symbolic language the "great mystery" which is divine.

The Gospel "Innovation"

24. The text is addressed to the spouses as real women and men. It reminds them of the "*ethos*" of spousal love which goes back to the divine institution of marriage from the "beginning." Corresponding to the truth of this institution is the exhortation: "*Husbands, love your wives*," love them because of that special and unique bond whereby in marriage a man and a woman become "one flesh" (Gen 2:24; Eph 5:31). In this love there is a fundamental *affirmation of the woman* as a person. This affirmation makes it possible for the female personality to develop fully and be enriched. This is precisely the way Christ acts as the bridegroom of the Church; he desires that she be "in splendor, without spot or wrinkle" (Eph 5:27). One can say that this fully captures the whole "style" of Christ in dealing with women. Husbands should make their own the elements of this style in regard to their wives; analogously, all men should do the same in regard to women in every situation. In this way, both men and women bring about "the sincere gift of self."

The author of the Letter to the Ephesians sees no contradiction between an exhortation formulated in this way and the words: "Wives, be subject to your husbands, as to the Lord. For the husband is the head of the wife" (5:22-23). The author knows that this way of speaking, so profoundly rooted in the customs and religious tradition of the time, is to be understood and carried out in a new way: as a "*mutual subjection out of reverence for Christ*" (cf. Eph 5:21). This is especially true because the husband is called the "head" of the wife as Christ is the head of the Church; he is so in order to give "himself up for her" (Eph 5:25), and giving himself up for her means giving up even his own life. However, whereas in the relationship between Christ and the Church the subjection is only on the part of the Church, in the relationship between husband and wife the "subjection" is not one-sided but mutual.

In relation to the "old" this is evidently something "new": it is an innovation of the Gospel. We find various passages in which the apostolic writings express this innovation, even though they also communicate what is "old": what is rooted in the religious tradition of Israel, in its way of understanding and explaining the sacred texts, as for example the second chapter of the Book of Genesis.

The apostolic letters are addressed to people living in an environment marked by that same traditional way of thinking and acting. The "innovation" of Christ is a fact: it constitutes the unambiguous content of the evangelical message and is the result of the Redemption; however, the awareness that in marriage there is mutual "subjection of the spouses out of reverence for Christ," and not just that of the wife to the husband, must gradually establish itself in hearts, consciences, behavior, and customs. This is a call which from that time onward does not cease to challenge succeeding generations; it is a call which people have to accept ever anew. Saint Paul not only wrote: "In Christ Jesus … there is no more man or woman," but also wrote: "There is no more slave or freeman." How many generations were needed for such a principle to be realized in the history of humanity through the abolition of slavery! What is one to say of the many forms of slavery to which individuals and peoples are subjected, which have not yet disappeared from history?

The challenge presented by the "ethos" of the Redemption is clear and definitive. All the reasons in favor of the "subjection" of woman to man in marriage must be understood in the sense of a "mutual subjection" of both "out of reverence for Christ." The measure of true spousal love finds its deepest source in Christ, who is the Bridegroom of the Church, his Bride.

The Symbolic Dimension of the "Great Mystery"

25. In the Letter to the Ephesians we encounter a *second dimension* of the analogy which, taken as a whole, serves to reveal the "great mystery." This is a *symbolic dimension*. If God's love for the human person, for the Chosen People of Israel, is presented by the Prophets as the love of the bridegroom for the bride, such an analogy expresses the "spousal" quality and the divine and nonhuman character of God's love: "For your Maker is your husband ... the God of the whole earth he is called" (Is 54:5). The same can also be said of the spousal love of Christ the Redeemer: "For God so loved the world that he gave his only Son" (Jn 3:16). It is a matter, therefore, of God's love expressed by means of the Redemption accomplished by Christ. According to Saint Paul's Letter, this love is "like" the spousal love of human spouses, but naturally it is not "the same." For the analogy implies a likeness, while at the same time leaving ample room for non-likeness.

This is easily seen in regard to the person of the "bride." According to the Letter to the Ephesians, the bride *is the Church*, just as for the Prophets the bride was Israel. She is therefore *a collective subject* and not *an individual person*. This collective subject is the People of God, a community made up of many persons, both women and men. "Christ has loved the Church" precisely as a community, as the People of God. At the same time, in this Church, which in the same passage is also called his "body" (cf. Eph 5:23), he has loved every individual person. For Christ has redeemed all without exception, every man and woman. It is precisely this love of God which is expressed in the Redemption; the spousal character of this love reaches completion in the history of humanity and of the world.

Christ has entered this history and remains in it as the Bridegroom who "has given himself." "To give" means "to become a sincere gift" in the most complete and radical way: "Greater love has no man than this" (Jn 15:13). According to this conception, *all human beings—both women and men—are called* through the Church *to be the "Bride" of Christ, the Redeemer of the world*. In this way, "being the bride," and thus the "feminine" element, becomes a symbol of all that is "human." According to the words of Paul: "There is neither male nor female; for you are all one in Christ Jesus" (Gal 3:28).

From a linguistic viewpoint we can say that the analogy of spousal love found in the Letter to the Ephesians links what is "masculine" to what is "feminine," since, as members of the Church, men, too, are included in the concept of "Bride." This should not surprise us, for Saint Paul, in order to express his mission in Christ and in the Church, speaks of the "little children with whom he is again in travail" (cf. Gal 4:19). In the sphere of what is "human"—of what is humanly personal—"*masculinity*" and "*femininity*" *are distinct*, yet at the same time they *complete and explain each other*. This is also present in the great analogy of the "Bride" in the Letter to the Ephesians. In the Church every human being—male and female—is the "Bride," in that he or she accepts the gift of the love of Christ the Redeemer and seeks to respond to it with the gift of his or her own person.

Christ is the Bridegroom. This expresses the truth about the love of God who "first loved us" (cf. 1 Jn 4:19) and who, with the gift generated by this spousal love for man, has exceeded all human expectations: "He loved them to the end" (Jn 13:1). The Bridegroom—the Son consubstantial with the Father as God—became the son of Mary; he became the "son of man," true man, a male. *The symbol of the Bridegroom is masculine*. This masculine symbol represents the human aspect of the divine love which God has for Israel, for the Church, and for all people. Meditating on what the Gospels say about Christ's attitude toward women, we can conclude that *as a man*, a son of Israel, he *revealed* the dignity of the "daughters of Abraham" (cf. Lk 13:16), *the dignity belonging to women* from the very "beginning" on an equal footing with men. At the same time, Christ emphasized the originality which distinguishes women from men, all the richness lavished upon women in the mystery of creation. Christ's attitude toward women serves as a model of what the Letter to the Ephesians expresses with the concept of "bridegroom." Precisely because Christ's divine love is the love of a Bridegroom, it is the model and pattern of all human love, men's love in particular.

The Eucharist

26. Against the broad background of the "great mystery" expressed in the spousal relationship between Christ and the Church, it is possible to understand adequately the calling of the "Twelve." *In calling only men as his Apostles*, Christ acted *in a completely free and sovereign manner*. In doing so,

he exercised the same freedom with which, in all his behavior, he emphasized the dignity and the vocation of women, without conforming to the prevailing customs and to the traditions sanctioned by the legislation of the time. Consequently, the assumption that he called men to be Apostles in order to conform with the widespread mentality of his times does not at all correspond to Christ's way of acting. "Teacher, we know that you are true, and teach the way of God truthfully, and care for no man; for you *do not regard the position of men*" (Mt 22:16). These words fully characterize *Jesus of Nazareth's behavior*. Here one also finds an explanation for the calling of the "Twelve." They are with Christ at the Last Supper. They alone receive the sacramental charge, "Do this in remembrance of me" (Lk 22:19; 1 Cor 11:24), which is joined to the institution of the Eucharist. On Easter Sunday night they receive the Holy Spirit for the forgiveness of sins: "Whose sins you forgive are forgiven them, and whose sins you retain are retained" (Jn 20:23).

We find ourselves at the very heart of the Paschal Mystery, which completely reveals the spousal love of God. Christ is the Bridegroom because "he has given himself": his body has been "given," his blood has been "poured out" (cf. Lk 22:19-20). In this way, "he loved them to the end" (Jn 13:1). The "sincere gift" contained in the Sacrifice of the Cross gives definitive prominence to the spousal meaning of God's love. As the Redeemer of the world, Christ is the Bridegroom of the Church. *The Eucharist is the Sacrament of our Redemption. It is the Sacrament of the Bridegroom and of the Bride.* The Eucharist makes present and realizes anew in a sacramental manner the redemptive act of Christ, who "creates" the Church, his body. Christ is united with this "body" as the bridegroom with the bride. All this is contained in the Letter to the Ephesians. The perennial "unity of the two" that exists between man and woman from the very "beginning" is introduced into this "great mystery" of Christ and of the Church.

Since Christ, in instituting the Eucharist, linked it in such an explicit way to the priestly service of the Apostles, it is legitimate to conclude that he thereby wished to express the relationship between man and woman, between what is "feminine" and what is "masculine." It is a relationship willed by God both in the mystery of creation and in the mystery of Redemption. It is *the Eucharist* above all that expresses *the redemptive act of*

Christ the Bridegroom toward the Church the Bride. This is clear and unambiguous when the sacramental ministry of the Eucharist, in which the priest acts "*in persona Christi*," is performed by a man. This explanation confirms the teaching of the Declaration *Inter Insigniores*, published at the behest of Paul VI in response to the question concerning the admission of women to the ministerial priesthood.

The Gift of the Bride

27. The Second Vatican Council renewed the Church's awareness of the universality of the priesthood. In the New Covenant there is only one sacrifice and only one priest: Christ. *All the baptized share in the one priesthood of Christ*, both men and women, inasmuch as they must "present their bodies as a living sacrifice, holy and acceptable to God (cf. Rom 12:1), give witness to Christ in every place, and give an explanation to anyone who asks the reason for the hope in eternal life that is in them" (cf. 1 Pt 3:15). Universal participation in Christ's sacrifice, in which the Redeemer has offered to the Father the whole world and humanity in particular, brings it about that all in the Church are "a kingdom of priests" (Rv 5:10; cf. 1 Pt 2:9), who not only share in the priestly mission but also in the prophetic and kingly mission of Christ the Messiah; furthermore, this participation determines the organic unity of the Church, the People of God, with Christ. It expresses at the same time the "great mystery" described in the Letter to the Ephesians: *the bride united to her Bridegroom*; united because she lives his life; united because she shares in his threefold mission (*tria munera Christi*); united *in such a manner as to respond* with a "sincere gift" of self *to the inexpressible gift of the love of the Bridegroom,* the Redeemer of the world. This concerns everyone in the Church, women as well as men. It obviously concerns those who share in the ministerial priesthood, which is characterized by service. In the context of the "great mystery" of Christ and of the Church, all are called to respond—as a bride—with the gift of their lives to the inexpressible gift of the love of Christ, who alone, as the Redeemer of the world, is the Church's Bridegroom. The "royal priesthood," which is universal, at the same time expresses the gift of the Bride.

This is of fundamental importance for understanding the Church in her own essence, so as to avoid applying to the Church—even in her dimension as an "institution" made up of human beings and forming part of history—criteria of understanding and judgment which do not pertain to her nature. Although the Church possesses a "hierarchical" structure, nevertheless this structure is totally ordered to the holiness of Christ's members. Holiness is measured according to the "great mystery" in which the Bride responds with the gift of love to the gift of the Bridegroom. She does this "in the Holy Spirit," since "God's love has been poured into our hearts through the Holy Spirit who has been given to us" (Rom 5:5). The Second Vatican Council, confirming the teaching of the whole of tradition, recalled that in the hierarchy of holiness it is *precisely the "woman,"* Mary of Nazareth, who is the "figure" of the Church. She "precedes" everyone on the path to holiness; in her person "the Church has already reached that perfection whereby she exists without spot or wrinkle (cf. Eph 5:27)." In this sense, one can say that the Church is *both* "Marian" and "Apostolic-Petrine."

In the history of the Church, even from earliest times, there were side-by-side with men *a number of women*, for whom the response of the Bride to the Bridegroom's redemptive love acquired full expressive force. First we see those women who had personally encountered Christ and followed him. After his departure, together with the Apostles, they "devoted themselves to prayer" in the Upper Room in Jerusalem until the day of Pentecost. On that day, the Holy Spirit spoke through "the sons and daughters" of the People of God, thus fulfilling the words of the prophet Joel (cf. Acts 2:17). These women, and others afterward, played *an active and important role in the life of the early Church*, in building up from its foundations the first Christian community—and subsequent communities—*through their own charisms and their varied service*. The apostolic writings note their names, such as Phoebe, "a deaconess of the Church at Cenchreae" (cf. Rom 16:1); Prisca with her husband Aquila (cf. 2 Tm 4:19); Euodia and Syntyche (cf. Phil 4:2); and Mary, Tryphaena, Persis, and Tryphosa (cf. Rom 16:6, 12). Saint Paul speaks of their "hard work" for Christ, and this hard work indicates the various fields of the Church's apostolic service, beginning with the "domestic Church." For in the latter, "sincere faith" passes from the mother to her children and grandchildren, as was the case in the house of Timothy (cf. 2 Tm 1:5).

The same thing is repeated down the centuries, from one generation to the next, as *the history of the Church* demonstrates. By defending the dignity of women and their vocation, the Church has shown honor and gratitude for those women who—faithful to the Gospel—have shared in every age in the apostolic mission of the whole People of God. They are the holy martyrs, virgins, and mothers of families who bravely bore witness to their faith and passed on the Church's faith and tradition by bringing up their children in the spirit of the Gospel.

In every age and in every country we find many "perfect" women (cf. Prv 31:10) who, despite persecution, difficulties, and discrimination, have shared in the Church's mission. It suffices to mention: Monica, the mother of Augustine; Macrina; Olga of Kiev; Matilda of Tuscany; Hedwig of Silesia; Jadwiga of Cracow; Elizabeth of Thuringi; Birgitta of Sweden; Joan of Arc; Rose of Lima; Elizabeth Ann Seton; and Mary Ward.

The witness and the achievements of Christian women have had a significant impact on the life of the Church as well as of society. Even in the face of serious social discrimination, holy women have acted "freely," strengthened by their union with Christ. Such union and freedom rooted in God explain, for example, the great work of Saint Catherine of Siena in the life of the Church, and the work of Saint Teresa of Jesus in the monastic life.

In our own days, too, the Church is constantly enriched by the witness of the many women who fulfill their vocation to holiness. Holy women are an incarnation of the feminine ideal; they are also a model for all Christians, a model of the "*sequela Christi*," an example of how the Bride must respond with love to the love of the Bridegroom.

"The Greatest of These is Love"

In the Face of Changes

28. "The Church believes that Christ, who died and was raised up for all, can through his Spirit offer man the light and the strength to respond to his supreme destiny." We can apply these words of the Conciliar Constitution *Gaudium et Spes* to the present reflections. The particular reference to the dignity of women and their vocation, precisely in our time, can and must be received in the "light and power" which the Spirit grants to human beings, including the people of our own age, which is marked by so many different transformations. The Church "holds that in her Lord and Master

can be found the key, the focal point, and the goal" of man and "of all human history," and she "maintains that beneath all changes there are many realities which do not change and which have their ultimate foundation in Christ, who is the same yesterday and today, yes and forever."

These words of the Constitution on the Church in the Modern World show the path to be followed in undertaking the tasks connected with the dignity and vocation of women, against the background of the significant changes of our times. We can face these changes correctly and adequately only if we go back to the foundations which are to be found in Christ, to those "immutable" truths and values of which he himself remains the "faithful witness" (cf. Rv 1:5) and Teacher. A different way of acting would lead to doubtful, if not actually erroneous and deceptive, results.

The Dignity of Women and the Order of Love

29. The passage from the Letter to the Ephesians already quoted (5:21-33), in which the relationship between Christ and the Church is presented as the link between the Bridegroom and the Bride, also makes reference to the institution of marriage as recorded in the Book of Genesis (cf. 2:24). This passage connects the truth about marriage as a primordial sacrament with the creation of man and woman in the image and likeness of God (cf. Gen 1:27; 5:1). The significant comparison in the Letter to the Ephesians gives perfect clarity to *what is decisive for the dignity of women both in the eyes of God*—the Creator and Redeemer—*and in the eyes of human beings*—men and women. In God's eternal plan, woman is the one in whom the order of love in the created world of persons takes first root. The order of love belongs to the intimate life of God himself, the life of the Trinity. In the intimate life of God, the Holy Spirit is the personal hypostasis of love. Through the Spirit, Uncreated Gift, love becomes a gift for created persons. *Love, which is of God, communicates itself to creatures*: "God's love has been poured into our hearts through the Holy Spirit who has been given to us" (Rom 5:5).

The calling of woman into existence at man's side as "a helper fit for him" (Gen 2:18) in the "unity of the two" provides the visible world of creatures with particular conditions so that "the love of God may be poured into the hearts" of the beings created in his image. When the author of the Letter to the Ephesians calls Christ "the Bridegroom" and the Church "the Bride," he indirectly confirms through this analogy *the truth about woman as bride.* The Bridegroom is the one who loves. The Bride is loved: *it is she who receives love in order to love in return.*

Rereading Genesis in light of the spousal symbol in the Letter to the Ephesians enables us to grasp a truth which seems to determine in an essential manner the question of women's dignity and, subsequently, also the question of their vocation: *the dignity of women is measured by the order of love,* which is essentially the order of justice and charity.

Only a person can love and only a person can be loved. This statement is primarily ontological in nature, and it gives rise to an ethical affirmation. Love is an ontological and ethical requirement of the person. The person must be loved, since love alone corresponds to what the person is. This explains *the commandment of love,* known already in the Old Testament (cf. Dt 6:5; Lv 19:18) and placed by Christ at the very center of the Gospel "*ethos*" (cf. Mt 22:36-40; Mk 12:28-34). This also explains the *primacy of love* expressed by Saint Paul in the First Letter to the Corinthians: "the greatest of these is love" (cf. 13:13).

Unless we refer to this order and primacy we cannot give a complete and adequate answer to the question about women's dignity and vocation. When we say that the woman is the one who receives love in order to love in return, this refers not only or above all to the specific spousal relationship of marriage. It means something more universal, based on the very fact of her being a woman within all the interpersonal relationships which, in the most varied ways, shape society and structure the interaction between all persons—men and women. In this broad and diversified context, *a woman represents a particular value by the fact that she is a human person,* and, at the same time, this particular person, *by the fact of her femininity.* This concerns each and every woman, independently of the cultural context in which she lives, and independently of her spiritual, psychological, and physical characteristics, for example, age, education, health, work, and whether she is married or single.

The passage from the Letter to the Ephesians which we have been considering enables us to think of a special kind of "prophetism" that belongs to women in their femininity. The analogy of the Bridegroom and the Bride speaks of the love with which every human being—man and woman—is loved by God in Christ. In the context of the biblical analogy and the text's interior logic, it is precisely the woman—the bride—who manifests this truth to everyone. This "*prophetic*" *character of women in their femininity* finds its highest expression in the Virgin Mother of God. She emphasizes, in the fullest and most direct way, the intimate linking of the order of love—which enters the world of human persons through a Woman—with the Holy Spirit. At the Annunciation Mary hears the words: "The Holy Spirit will come upon you" (Lk 1:35).

Awareness of a Mission

30. A woman's dignity is closely connected with the love which she receives by the very reason of her femininity; it is likewise connected *with the love which she gives in return*. The truth about the person and about love is thus confirmed. In examining the truth about the person, we must turn again to the Second Vatican Council: "Man, who is the only creature on earth that God willed for its own sake, cannot fully find himself except through a sincere gift of self." This applies to every human being, as a person created in God's image, whether man or woman. This ontological affirmation also indicates the ethical dimension of a person's vocation. *Woman can only find herself by giving love to others.*

From the "beginning," woman—like man—was created and "placed" by God in this order of love. The sin of the first parents did not destroy this order, nor irreversibly cancel it out. This is proved by the words of the *Proto-evangelium* (cf. Gen 3:15). Our reflections have focused *on the particular place occupied by the* "*woman*" in this key text of revelation. It is also to be noted how the same Woman, who attains the position of a biblical "exemplar," also appears within the eschatological perspective of the world and of humanity given in the Book of Revelation. She is "*a woman clothed with the sun,*" with the moon under her feet, and on her head a crown of stars (cf. Rv 12:1). One can say she is a Woman of cosmic scale, on a scale with the whole work of creation. At the same time, she is "suffering the pangs and anguish of childbirth" (Rv 12:2) like Eve, "the mother of all the living" (Gen 3:20). She also suffers because "before the woman who is about to give birth" (cf. Rv 12:4) there stands "the great dragon … that ancient serpent" (Rv 12:9), already known from the *Proto-evangelium*: the Evil One, the "father of lies" and of sin (cf. Jn 8:44). The "ancient serpent" wishes to devour "the child." While we see in this text an echo of the Infancy Narrative (cf. Mt 2:13,16), we can also see that the struggle with evil, and the Evil One marks the biblical exemplar of the "woman" from the beginning to the end of history. It is also *a struggle for man, for his true good*, for his salvation. Is not the Bible trying to tell us that it is precisely in the "woman"—Eve-Mary—that history witnesses a dramatic struggle for every human being, the struggle for his or her fundamental "yes" or "no" to God and God's eternal plan for humanity?

While the dignity of woman witnesses to the love which she receives in order to love in return, the biblical "exemplar" of the Woman also seems to reveal *the true order of love which constitutes woman's own vocation*. Vocation is meant here in its fundamental, and one may say universal, significance, a significance which is then actualized and expressed in women's many different "vocations" in the Church and the world.

The moral and spiritual strength of a woman is joined to her awareness that *God entrusts the human being to her in a special way*. Of course, God entrusts every human being to each and every other human being, but this entrusting concerns women in a special way—precisely by reason of their femininity—and this in a particular way determines their vocation.

The moral force of women, which draws strength from this awareness and this entrusting, expresses itself in a great number of figures of the Old Testament, of the time of Christ, and of later ages right up to our own day. *A woman is strong because of her awareness of this entrusting*, strong because of the fact that God "entrusts the human being to her," always and in every way, even in the situations of social discrimination in which she may find herself. This awareness and this fundamental vocation speak to women of the dignity which they receive from God himself, and this makes them "strong" and strengthens their vocation.

The "perfect woman" (cf. Prv 31:10) becomes an irreplaceable support and source of spiritual strength for other people who perceive the great energies of her spirit. These "perfect women" are owed much by their families, and sometimes by whole nations.

In our own time, the successes of science and technology make it possible to attain material well-being to a degree hitherto unknown. While this favors some, it pushes others to the edges of society. In this way, unilateral progress can also lead to a gradual *loss of sensitivity for man, that is, for what is essentially human*. In this sense, our time in particular *awaits the manifestation* of that "genius" which belongs to women, and which can ensure sensitivity for human beings in every circumstance: because they are human!—and because "the greatest of these is love" (cf. 1 Cor 13:13).

A careful reading of the biblical exemplar of the Woman—from the Book of Genesis to the Book of Revelation—confirms that which constitutes women's dignity and vocation, as well as that which is unchangeable and ever relevant in them, because it has its "ultimate foundation in Christ, who is the same yesterday and today, yes and forever." If the human being is entrusted by God to women in a particular way, does not this mean that *Christ looks to them for the accomplishment of the "royal priesthood"* (1 Pt 2:9), which is the treasure he has given to every individual? Christ, as the supreme and only priest of the New and Eternal Covenant, and as the Bridegroom of the Church, does not cease to submit this same inheritance to the Father through the Spirit, so that God may be "everything to everyone" (1 Cor 15:28). Then the truth that "the greatest of these is love" (cf. 1 Cor 13:13) will have its definitive fulfillment.

Conclusion

"If You Knew the Gift of God"

31. "If you knew the gift of God" (Jn 4:10), Jesus says to the Samaritan woman during one of those remarkable conversations which show his great esteem for the dignity of women and for the vocation which enables them to share in his messianic mission.

The present reflections, now at an end, have sought to recognize, within the "gift of God," what he, as Creator and Redeemer, entrusts to women, to every woman. In the Spirit of Christ, in fact, women can discover the entire meaning of their femininity and thus be disposed to making a "sincere gift of self" to others, thereby finding themselves.

During the Marian Year, *the Church desires to give thanks to the Most Holy Trinity* for the "mystery of woman" and for every woman—for that which constitutes the eternal measure of her feminine dignity, for the "great works of God," which throughout human history have been accomplished in and through her. After all, was it not in and through her that the greatest event in human history—the incarnation of God himself—was accomplished?

The Church gives thanks for each and every woman: for mothers, for sisters, for wives; for women consecrated to God in virginity; for women dedicated to the many human beings who await the gratuitous love of another person; for women who watch over the human persons in the family, which is the fundamental sign of the human community; for women who work professionally, and who at times are burdened by a great social responsibility; for "*perfect*" women and for "weak" women—for all women as they have come forth from the heart of God in all the beauty and richness of their femininity; as they have been embraced by his eternal love; as, together with men, they are pilgrims on this earth, which is the temporal "homeland" of all people and is transformed sometimes into a "valley of tears"; as they assume, together with men, *a common responsibility for the destiny of humanity* according to daily necessities and according to that definitive destiny which the human family has in God himself, in the bosom of the ineffable Trinity.

The Church gives thanks for all the manifestations of the feminine "genius" which have appeared in the course of history, in the midst of all peoples and nations; she gives thanks for all the charisms which the Holy Spirit distributes to women in the history of the People of God, for all the victories which she owes to their faith, hope, and charity: she gives thanks for *all the fruits of feminine holiness*.

The Church asks at the same time that these invaluable "manifestations of the Spirit" (cf. 1 Cor 12:4ff.), which with great generosity are poured forth upon the "daughters" of the eternal Jerusalem, may be attentively recognized and appreciated so that they may return for the common good of the Church and of humanity, especially in our times. Meditating on the biblical mystery of the "woman," the Church prays that in this mystery all women may discover themselves and their "supreme vocation."

May *Mary*, who "is a model of the Church in the matter of faith, charity, and perfect union with Christ," obtain for all of us *this same "grace"* in the Year which we have dedicated to her as we approach the Third Millennium from the coming of Christ. With these sentiments, I impart the Apostolic Blessing to all the faithful, and in a special way to women, my sisters in Christ.

READING 11 (SEPTEMBER 4, 1988)

Discovery of a New Feminine Identity[1]

Address to Women Religious (Turin, Italy)

Dearest Sisters,

I am happy to meet you on the occasion of these celebrations in honor of St. John Bosco on the centenary of his death. Your very presence here, in the town of Valdocco, is itself an eloquent discourse!

In the variety of your charisms and vocations you are a splendid image of the Church, enriched by the Spirit of the Lord with so many gifts and ministries to serve humanity evangelically.

"The Church expresses to you her gratitude for your consecration and for your profession of the evangelical counsels, which are a particular testimony of love."

Indeed, throughout the centuries, this testimony is uninterrupted, and it has grown ever more luminous.

Don Bosco, that man who was gifted with a keen sense of spiritual discernment, was deeply aware of it; he always valued the contribution of women, and in particular that of consecrated women, in the building up of a more human and more Christian society. It was no accident that from the very beginning of his work as an educator he was joined by his mother Margherita, and he later involved an ever-growing number of women from every social class in his intense apostolate. He founded a women's congregation, accepting the original and creative contribution of those women, especially that of St. Maria Domenica Mazzarello.

⋘

2. Don Bosco, disciple of Christ, gave witness throughout his life to the primacy of the interior life. He marvelously combined this primacy with intense activity for others, a generous and joyous service, both tireless and radical, which allowed his communion with the Lord to shine through. Religious life always maintains this primacy, and you, dear Sisters, can offer a precious contribution along these lines, in seeking and offering a new feminine identity with your being, which in turn shines forth in your work.

"With your being," because by the profession of the evangelical counsels, all too often presented solely as renunciation, you positively and happily bear witness wherein lies the absolute of the human person and you give the lie to the idolatry of society of possessions, of the empirical and the contingent.

By your profession of the evangelical counsels you prophetically anticipate the future good, that is, you indicate the origin, the meaning, and the definitive goal of human destiny. From the viewpoint of this eschatological horizon you have much to say, particularly to the women of today, as a response to the emerging situations of the present sociocultural context.

A Love That Does Not Disappoint

3. The first response concerns the many and complex questions about the meaning of religious life today, from the secularized society which without reference to the transcendent can no longer value the richness of a life lived within the walls of a convent, does not understand the renunciation of the joy of one's own family for a deeper and broader motherhood, the choice of a love that does not disappoint, the meaning of femininity that is authentic in virginity seen as a way to a loftier realization.

In this society in which there is "an invading theoretical and pragmatic materialism which closes the horizons of the spirit and of the transcendent . . . you are called to sustain the civilization of love and of life, to be the soul of the Christian leaven, the guides within the horizons of the faith. . . . In the Church you incarnate the task of Mary Most Holy. You have an irreplaceable role, especially in the areas that typically correspond to your charisms and your sensitivities" (Discourse in Florence, October 18, 1985, *L'Osservatore Romano*, English language edition, November 17, 1986, 4).

In the contemporary world you are called to show forth with crystal clarity invisible values that are real and can be lived by all.

You have inherited a rich tradition: frequently in the past, in particular from consecrated women, has come a prophetic proposal of a new feminine identity, which met entreaties and appeals of the surrounding world.

Turin and this diocese have always been a fertile source of generous and creative women from all social classes. They served and still serve with evangelical spirit those who are in need, as well as those who are sometimes forgotten and despised.

The response, then, comes from you, from your being, from your profession of the evangelical counsels, from your apostolic activity. "The world needs the authentic 'contradiction' provided by religious consecration as an unceasing stimulus of salvific renewal" (*Redemptionis Donum* 14). Experience also teaches that no movement of the religious life has any value if it is not simultaneously a movement toward the interior, toward the depth of being, where Christ has his dwelling.

4. In the course of history so many ideological proposals which regard progress and personal fulfillment as sexual license, elimination of moral laws, emancipation from religion, have not been verified. The identity crisis of persons and institutions is a sad sign of this and is a pressing cry for help. Christian Revelation offers the salvific response that is born of the truth about humanity, from an anthropology that is linked to the divine.

Indeed, in proclaiming the truth about the human person, it makes its specific contribution in confirming the perfect equality of man and woman as the image of God and his interlocutors. Man and woman, in that they are the image of God, make visible in the universe the unity of God who lives not in solitude but in communion: the One and Triune God. In establishing the Kingdom of God, Jesus goes back to this original communion so that "there is neither Jew nor Greek, there is neither slave nor free person, there is not male and female; for you are all one in Christ Jesus" (Gal 3:28).

Particularly in regard to woman, Jesus showed himself as Liberator and Savior. He frees her from the desire for possession and the dominion of man (Mt 5:28) and overturns the mentality of the age which also affects his disciples, a mentality that seeks to perpetuate overbearing relationships (cf. Mt 19:3-10). He declares her exempt from legal impurity precisely by his behavior. He refuses to identify her role with biological motherhood and reveals her dignity in the faith in a new type of relationship. He proposes her as the model of faith and love. It is by means of the woman whose sins had been pardoned that he announces the specific nature of the Gospel message: love without limits (cf. Lk 7:47, 50); he points out the generous gift of the widow who, in offering her mite for the Temple, was giving all that she had (cf. Lk 21:14). On the lips of a woman John places one of the most beautiful professions of faith (cf. Jn 11:27).

The women followed Jesus spontaneously and they became heralds of the messianic announcement (cf. Jn 4:28, 30; Mt 28:14).

Among all of them a singular and unique place belongs to Mary, the

Mother of Jesus, who synthesizes the Israel of God through her unreserved "yes," her charity without limits, through her maternity in relationship to the disciples of Jesus for all times.

The Church Overcomes All Dialectical Argument

5. The Church, fruit of Christ's salvific work and the place in which he continues to save every person, is presented as overcoming all dialectical argument when she is understood in her profound constitutive mystery. Indeed, she was described by the Council as "a kind of sacrament or sign of intimate union with God, and of the unity of all mankind. She is also an instrument for the achievement of such union and unity" (*Lumen Gentium* 1).

Let you, dearest Sisters, be witnesses to this Church, to this mystery in life and word, as was Blessed Anna Michelotto, who was a tireless promoter of the Gospel message here in Turin, in every social class, but most of all among the poor and the infirm.

Like her, you also give your precious testimony announcing the primacy of the Absolute, of the One and Triune God who makes us his interlocutors, showing that for the believer, communion with the Transcendent, also expressed in the solitude of prayer, cannot be an escape or withdrawal from the company of one's brothers and sisters. As in Mary and in the Church, so also in you, the women of today should be able to see a down-to-earth and unique life, lived not individualistically in a self-centered way but in solidarity with the whole of human history and all of creation.

This is the message which you can proclaim today in the Church and in society. The message is a timely one, an urgent one, and is meant to emphasize that the solution of problems must be sought in a wider and therefore more human framework of values, which gives the primacy to the person as the subject of communion, overcoming claims, the absolutization of roles, the opposition of rights, all expressions which are still a sign of sin and not of freedom.

The Gospel marks the road of liberation that is beyond the expectation of our human capabilities: Jesus proposes a new type of relationship that is not under the hegemony of sin, of "hardness of heart," but in God's merciful and paternal lordship which celebrates the victory of charity without limits. Through this proposal is born a new bond of relationship, not founded on flesh and blood but on faith, which is expressed in fruitful and profound communion, which transcends biological and earthly dimensions.

Mary, the Mother of Jesus and of the Church, is the prototype of it; your consecration is a prophecy of it extended in time.

6. Now, here is a task for you: be signs of this new type of relations, of this new bond of relationship, not in an abstract manner but in the concrete fabric of your existence, as a progressive rediscovery of the way of being disciples of Jesus in every moment and condition of life.

May the Spirit of the Lord and Mary's motherly protection guide you in this marvelous adventure to bring about the civilization of love and of life. With your Gospel witness you should be like leaven on this human and Christian journey.

Your being becomes a mission, and it could not be otherwise, because this is the structure of the believer according to the Gospel.

Your coming here to the sanctuary of Mary Help of Christians, in memory of Don Bosco, is an invitation to reflect profoundly on your reality in order to draw courageously from it effective results.

In the letter addressed to the Rector Major of the Salesian Society I treated some of these results which are an appeal especially to you, called to fulfill many apostolic works: the Church "in this period so close to the year 2000, … feels invited by her Lord to look upon (youth) with a special love and hope, and to consider their education as one of her primary pastoral responsibilities" (*Iuvenum Patris* 1).

I would therefore like to call your attention to your responsibility particularly for the young generations, according to your particular charism, in the educational task.

Your prophecy, your evangelical life, the expression of the new bond of relationship, is most of all an announcement for those who are the future of society and of the Church.

Today still, or rather more than yesterday, you can and should let the beauty of a life spent entirely for the Lord in service of one's brothers and sisters shine before youth.

7. With your chastity you announce to young people the beauty of love in the human heart made faithful by the Gospel; you announce the future resurrection and eternal life, that life in union with God, that love which contains in itself and completely pervades all the other loves of the human heart, that liberation brought by Jesus for all (cf. *Redemptionis Donum* 11).

In her Magnificat, which has become the Canticle of the Church and of humanity which yearns for salvation, Mary has proclaimed this human and feminine liberation: she "is the most perfect image of freedom and of the liberation of humanity and of the universe" (*Redemptoris Mater* 37).

May she, who in her own life gave us an "example of that maternal love by which all should be fittingly animated who cooperate in the apostolic mission of the Church on behalf of the rebirth of humanity" (*Lumen Gentium* 65), teach you and guide you in the Gospel of motherhood typical of your vocation.

"She continues through the centuries to be a maternal presence as is shown by Christ's words, 'Woman, behold your Son'; 'Behold your Mother' (cf. Jn 16:26 f) (*Redemptoris Mater* 24). "Never take your gaze off Mary; listen to her when she says: 'Do what Jesus tells you'" (Jn 2:5).

Pray to her, too, with daily solicitude, that the Lord may continue to raise up generous souls who can say "yes" to his vocational call.

"To her I entrust you, and with you the whole world of youth, that being attracted, animated and guided by her, they may be able to attain through the mediation of your educative work the stature of 'new men' for a new world: the world of Christ, Master and Lord" (*Iuvenum Patris* 20).

To her I entrust you that the New Woman, Mother of the Church and of the New Humanity, may be the inspiration in your discovery of a new feminine identity in the Gospel perspective.

By her powerful intercession may she make fruitful all of your initiatives and assist you with her maternal protection.

With this wish I bless you with all my heart.

INTRODUCTION TO READING 12
BY DEBORAH SAVAGE

Pope John Paul II's Apostolic Exhortation *Christifideles Laici* (On the Vocation and Mission of the Lay Faithful in the Church and in the World, December 1988) was written and promulgated in response to a request for instruction on the matter from the Synod of Bishops on the Laity, held the previous year. Though the Second Vatican Council had clarified and highlighted this theme more than twenty-two years before, and the role of the laity had garnered significant magisterial reflection in the intervening years, *Christifideles Laici* is a document completely unprecedented in the history of papal writings. Never before had a pope issued such a comprehensive and definitive teaching on the role of the laity in building up the Body of Christ. Over two hundred pages long, the document incorporates most of the fifty-four recommendations advanced by the Synod, proposals shaped and affirmed not only by the bishops but also by the fifty-four lay persons (twenty-four women and thirty men) who participated in the deliberations. It is a profoundly meaningful document on the place the laity occupies in the New Evangelization and the transformation of our culture.

The passages from the document included in the following selection are aptly chosen. They include what is arguably the late Holy Father's most explicit and dramatic statements concerning the significance of pursuing an investigation of the "anthropological foundation for masculinity and femininity" (50). Such a consideration, he states unequivocally, is the fundamental "condition that will assure the rightful presence of woman in the Church and in society," a result that can only be achieved by "clarifying woman's personal identity in relation to man"; however, he is emphatic that this investigation must go beyond the question of what her roles or functions might be; it must involve a deep and penetrating grasp of her very nature and the meaning of her personhood as a creature made, alongside man, in the image of God. In these passages, Pope John Paul II commits the Church herself to the pursuit of the requisite grasp of the anthropological and theological basis of femininity, a reflection of his profound respect for woman and of the Church's own thrust toward a more complete understanding of her contribution to the creation of human history.

The collaborators for this collection also have chosen to include in the selection several passages that illuminate the context within which the personhood of women finds its fullest significance and greatest freedom of expression. It is noteworthy that we find the importance of woman affirmed so vigorously in a document whose primary purpose is to articulate the vocation of the laity which, in virtue of their baptism, is grounded in their participation in the three-fold office of Christ as priest, prophet, and king. The task of the laity is to transform the secular order; it is the place in which they receive their call from God. Along with the ministerial priesthood, they are instructed to maintain constantly an active "*ecclesial consciousness*" (64; italics in original) that reveals that they share in this three-fold office through their daily sacrifices, their public witness, the ordering of all their activity to "the authentic well-being of humanity" (14). The dignity and vocation of woman is to be seen in light of a sacramental reality in which the laity as a whole fully participates. John Paul II's respect for woman is articulated, not in isolation from its ecclesial meaning but in light of her baptism. As we learn from the lives of the great woman saints, ultimately, the "feminine genius" is to be understood as a supernatural reality given to woman at her creation but only fully realized through a life of prayer and worship—and the action of grace.

The Holy Father makes it categorically clear that the "task of advancing the dignity of women in the Church and in society" belongs to women themselves. It is up to women to take full responsibility for realizing that they are, along with men, "leading characters" in the unfolding drama of human history (49). Unrecognized for the most part in contemporary culture, but nonetheless profoundly true, it was Jesus Christ himself who called women to this role. He did not act under the shadow of the cultural norms of his age in his relationships with women but instead elevated and honored them. Scripture also documents that the early Church "detached herself from the culture of the time, calling women to the task of spreading the gospel" (49). From the beginning, both women and men were active and essential branches of the one true vine.

Woman, John Paul II tells us, has her own gifts and her own specific vocation (49). She is entrusted with two great tasks. First is that of "bringing full dignity to the conjugal life and to motherhood" (51). Through her "intelligent, loving and decisive intervention," woman is to assist man—as husband and father—to enter into a deeper interpersonal communion and lead him to the discovery of the joy found in the act of self-gift. Second, it is woman who is responsible for "assuring the moral dimension of culture ... of a culture worthy of the person" (51). Here we see an unstated but unmistakable reference to the role woman plays in the pursuit of the Church's social vision. Though from the beginning, the Creator willed that man and woman as "the prime community of persons" would collaborate as full partners in the rich and harmonious pursuit if the Church's salvific mission (52), in this passage we learn that the crux of the Church's social teaching—to make life more human for all—is laid before woman. By entrusting Adam to Eve in the Garden, in a special way he also entrusted all human beings for all time to woman. She fulfills her vocation by recognizing and fully appropriating the knowledge that she possesses a "specific sensitivity towards the human person and all that constitutes the individual's true welfare, beginning with the fundamental value of life" (51). Both her possibilities and her responsibilities will be realized when she recognizes this and takes up this vocation with dignity and courage.

Finally, this introduction to the selection would not be complete without mention of the beautiful prayer to the Most Blessed Virgin Mary found at the end of the document, an appeal to our Blessed Mother to come to the aid of all those who would accomplish the mission given to us by her Son—and a plea that she instill a renewed sense of purpose and hope on the part of the laity whose vocation and mission it is, indeed, to return all things to Christ.

In *Christifideles Laici*, John Paul II makes clear that it is the entire Church that calls woman to a fuller participation in her mission by taking up those tasks that only woman can accomplish. The very future of humanity relies on woman accepting this *fiat*. Lest there be any doubt, consider these words from the closing address to women at the end of the Second Vatican Council; perhaps they serve to illuminate the great import of this profound document:

> But the hour is coming, in fact has come, when the vocation of woman is being achieved in its fullness, the hour in which woman acquires in the world an influence, an effect and a power never hitherto achieved. That is why, at this moment when the human race is under-going so deep a transformation, women impregnated with the spirit of the Gospel can do so much to aid mankind in not falling.

Deborah Savage teaches philosophy and theology in the pre-theology and master's in pastoral ministry programs in the St. Paul Seminary School of Divinity at the University of St. Thomas in St. Paul, Minn. She is also program director for the master of arts in pastoral ministry program.

READING 12 (DECEMBER 30, 1988): *Christifideles Laici* (The Lay Members of Christ's Faithful People)[1]

To Bishops
To Priests and Deacons
To Women and Men Religious and to All the Lay Faithful

Introduction

Who are the Lay Faithful?

9. The Synod Fathers have rightly pointed to the need for a definition of the lay faithful's vocation and mission in *positive terms*, through an in-depth study of the teachings of the Second Vatican Council in light of both recent documentation from the Magisterium and the lived experience of the Church, guided as she is by the Holy Spirit.

In giving a response to the question "Who are the lay faithful," the Council went beyond previous interpretations which were predominantly negative. Instead, it opened itself to a decidedly positive vision and displayed a basic intention of asserting *the full belonging of the lay faithful to the Church and to its mystery*.

At the same time, it insisted on the unique character of their vocation, which is in a special way to "seek the Kingdom of God by engaging in temporal affairs and ordering them according to the plan of God." "The term 'lay faithful'"—we read in the Constitution on the Church, *Lumen Gentium*—"is here understood to mean all the faithful except those in Holy Orders and those who belong to a religious state sanctioned by the Church. Through Baptism the lay faithful are made one body with Christ and are established among the People of God. They are in their own way made sharers in the priestly, prophetic, and kingly office of Christ. They carry out their own part in the mission of the whole Christian people with respect to the Church and the world."

Pius XII once stated: "The Faithful, more precisely the lay faithful, find themselves on the front lines of the Church's life; for them the Church is the animating principle for human society. Therefore, they in particular ought to have an ever-clearer consciousness *not only of belonging to the Church but of being the Church*, that is to say, the community of the faithful on earth under the leadership of the Pope, the head of all, and of the Bishops in communion with him. *These are the Church* ..." According to the Biblical image of the vineyard, the lay faithful, together with all the other members of the Church, are branches engrafted to Christ the true vine, and from him derive their life and fruitfulness.

Incorporation into Christ through faith and Baptism is the source of being a Christian in the mystery of the Church. This mystery constitutes the Christian's most basic "features" and serves as the basis for all the vocations and dynamism of the Christian life of the lay faithful (cf. Jn 3:5). In Christ who died and rose from the dead, the baptized become a "new creation" (Gal 6:15; 2 Cor 5:17), washed clean from sin and brought to life through grace. Only through accepting the richness in mystery that God gives to the Christian in Baptism is it possible to come to a basic description of the lay faithful.

Chapter 1: I Am the Vine and You Are the Branches

The Dignity of the Lay Faithful in the Church as Mystery Sharers in the Priestly, Prophetic, and Kingly Mission of Jesus Christ

14. Referring to the baptized as "newborn babes," the Apostle Peter writes: "Come to him, to that living stone, rejected by men but in God's sight chosen and precious; and like living stones be yourselves built into a spiritual house, to be a holy priesthood to offer spiritual sacrifices acceptable to God through Jesus Christ ... you are a chosen race, a royal priesthood, a holy nation, God's own people, that you may declare the wonderful deeds of him who called you out of darkness into his marvelous light" (1 Pt 2:4-5, 9).

A new aspect to the grace and dignity coming from Baptism is here introduced: the lay faithful participate, for their part, in the threefold mission of Christ as Priest, Prophet, and King. This aspect has never been forgotten in the living tradition of the Church, as exemplified in the explanation which St. Augustine offers for Psalm 26: "David was anointed king. In those days only a king and a priest were anointed. These two persons prefigured the one and only priest and king who was to come, Christ (the name 'Christ' means 'anointed'). Not only has our head been anointed but we, his body, have also been anointed ... therefore *anointing* comes to all Christians, even though in Old Testament times it belonged only to two persons. Clearly we are the Body of Christ because we are all 'anointed' and in him are 'christs,' that is, 'anointed ones,' as well as Christ himself, 'The Anointed One.' In a certain way, then, it thus happens that with head and body the whole Christ is formed."

In the wake of the Second Vatican Council, at the beginning of my pastoral ministry, my aim was to emphasize forcefully the priestly, prophetic, and kingly dignity of the entire People of God in the following words: "He who was born of the Virgin Mary, the carpenter's Son—as he was thought to be—Son of the living God (confessed by Peter), has come to make us 'a kingdom of priests.' The Second Vatican Council has reminded us of the mystery of this power and of the fact that the mission of Christ—Priest, Prophet-Teacher, King—continues in the Church. Everyone, the whole People of God, shares in this threefold mission."

With this Exhortation the lay faithful are invited to take up again and reread, meditate on, and assimilate with renewed understanding and love the rich and fruitful teaching of the Council which speaks of their participation in the threefold mission of Christ. Here in summary form are the essential elements of this teaching.

The lay faithful are sharers in the *priestly mission*, for which Jesus offered himself on the cross and continues to be offered in the celebration of the Eucharist for the glory of God and the salvation of humanity. Incorporated in Jesus Christ, the baptized are united to him and to his sacrifice in the offering they make of themselves and their daily activities (cf. Rom 12:1, 2). Speaking of the lay faithful the Council says: "For their work, prayers and apostolic endeavors, their ordinary married and family life, their daily labor, their mental and physical relaxation, if carried out in the Spirit, and even the hardships of life if patiently borne—all of these become spiritual sacrifices acceptable to God through Jesus Christ (cf. 1 Pt 2:5). During the celebration of the Eucharist these sacrifices are most lovingly offered to the Father along with the Lord's body. Thus as worshipers whose every deed is holy, the lay faithful consecrate the world itself to God."

Through their participation in the *prophetic mission* of Christ, "who proclaimed the kingdom of his Father by the testimony of his life and by the power of his world," the lay faithful are given the ability and responsibility to accept the gospel in faith and to proclaim it in word and deed, without hesitating to identify and denounce evil courageously. United to Christ, the "great prophet" (Lk 7:16), and in the Spirit-made "witnesses" of the Risen Christ, the lay faithful are made sharers in the appreciation of the Church's supernatural faith, that "cannot err in matters of belief" and sharers as well in the grace of the word (cf. Acts 2:17-18; Rv 19:10). They are also called to allow the newness and the power of the gospel to shine out every day in their family and social life, as well as to express patiently and courageously in the contradictions of the present age their hope of future glory even "through the framework of their secular life."

Because the lay faithful belong to Christ, Lord and King of the Universe, they share in his *kingly mission* and are called by him to spread that Kingdom in history. They exercise their kingship as Christians, above all in the spiritual combat in which they seek to overcome in themselves the kingdom of sin (cf. Rom 6:12), and then to make a gift of themselves so as to serve, in justice and in charity, Jesus who is himself present in all his brothers and sisters, above all in the very least (cf. Mt 25:40).

In particular the lay faithful are called to restore to creation all its original value. In ordering creation to the authentic well-being of humanity in an activity governed by the life of grace, they share in the exercise of the power with which the Risen Christ draws all things to himself and subjects them along with himself to the Father, so that God might be everything to everyone (cf. 1 Cor 15:28; Jn 12:32).

The participation of the lay faithful in the threefold mission of Christ as Priest, Prophet, and King finds its source in the anointing of Baptism, its further development in Confirmation and its realization and dynamic sustenance in the Holy Eucharist. It is a participation given to each member of the lay faithful *individually*, in as much as each is one of the *many* who form the *one Body* of the Lord: in fact, Jesus showers his gifts upon the Church which is his Body and his Spouse. In such a way, individuals are sharers in the threefold mission of Christ in virtue of their being members of the Church, as St. Peter clearly teaches when he defines the baptized as "a chosen race, a royal priesthood, a holy nation, God's own people" (1 Pt 2:9). Precisely because it derives *from* Church *communion*, the sharing of the lay faithful in the threefold mission of Christ requires that it be lived and realized *in communion* and *for the increase of communion itself*. Saint Augustine writes, "As we call everyone 'Christians' in virtue of a mystical anointing, so we call everyone 'priests' because all are members of only one priesthood."

The Lay Faithful and Their Secular Character

15. The newness of the Christian life is the foundation and title for equality among all the baptized in Christ, for all the members of the People of God: "As members, they share a common dignity from their rebirth in Christ; they have the same filial grace and the same vocation to perfection. They possess in common one salvation, one hope and one undivided charity." Because of the one dignity flowing from Baptism, each member of the lay faithful, together with ordained ministers and men and women religious, shares a responsibility for the Church's mission.

Among the lay faithful, this one baptismal dignity takes on *a manner of life which sets a person apart, without, however, bringing about a separation* from the ministerial priesthood or from men and women religious. The Second Vatican Council has described this manner of life as the "secular character": "The secular character is properly and particularly that of the lay faithful."

To understand properly the lay faithful's position in the Church in a complete, adequate, and specific manner, it is necessary to come to a deeper theological understanding of their secular character in light of God's plan of salvation and in the context of the mystery of the Church.

Pope Paul VI said the Church "has an authentic secular dimension, inherent to her inner nature and mission, which is deeply rooted in the mystery of the Word Incarnate, and which is realized in different forms through her members."

The Church, in fact, lives in the world, even if she is not of the world (cf. Jn 17:16). She is sent to continue the redemptive work of Jesus Christ, which "by its very nature concerns the salvation of humanity, and also involves the renewal of the whole temporal order." Certainly *all the members* of the Church are sharers in this secular dimension but *in different ways*. In particular, the sharing of the *lay faithful* has its own manner of realization and function, which, according to the Council, is "properly and particularly" theirs. Such a manner is designated with the expression "secular character."

In fact the Council, in describing the lay faithful's situation in the secular world, points to it above all as the place in which they receive their call from God: "There they are called by God." This "place" is treated and presented in dynamic terms: the lay faithful "live in the world, that is, in every one of the secular professions and occupations. They live in the ordinary circumstances of family and social life, from which the very fabric of their existence is woven." They are persons who live an ordinary life in the world: they study, they work, and they form relationships as friends, professionals, members of society, cultures, etc. The Council considers their condition not simply an external and environmental framework but as a reality *destined to find in Jesus Christ the fullness of its meaning*. Indeed it leads to the affirmation that "the Word made flesh willed to share in human fellowship.... He sanctified those human ties, especially family ones, from which social relationships arise, willingly submitting himself to the laws of his country. He chose to lead the life of an ordinary craftsman of his own time and place."

The "world" thus becomes the place and the means for the lay faithful to fulfill their Christian vocation, because the world itself is destined to glorify God the Father in Christ. The Council is able then to indicate the proper and special sense of the divine vocation which is directed to the lay faithful. They are not called to abandon the position that they have in the world. Baptism does not take them from the world at all, as the Apostle Paul points out: "So, brethren, in whatever state each was called, there let him remain with God" (1 Cor 7:24). On the contrary, he entrusts a vocation to them that properly concerns their situation in the world. The lay faithful, in fact, "are called by God so that they, led by the spirit of the Gospel, might contribute to the sanctification of the world, as from within like leaven, by fulfilling their own particular duties. Thus, especially in this way of life, resplendent in faith, hope and charity they manifest Christ to others." For the lay faithful to be present and active in the world is not only an anthropological and sociological reality but, in a specific way, a theological and ecclesiological reality as well. In fact, in their situation in the world God manifests his plan and communicates to them their particular vocation of "seeking the Kingdom of God by engaging in temporal affairs and by ordering them according to the plan of God."

Precisely with this in mind the Synod Fathers said: "The secular character of the lay faithful is not therefore to be defined only in a sociological sense, but most especially in a theological sense. The term secular must be understood in light of the act of God the creator and redeemer, who has handed over the world to women and men, so that they may participate in the work of creation, free creation from the influence of sin and sanctify themselves in marriage or the celibate life, in a family, in a profession and in the various activities of society."

The lay faithful's *position in the Church*, then, comes to be fundamentally defined by their *newness in Christian life* and distinguished by their *secular character*.

The images taken from the gospel of salt, light, and leaven, although indiscriminately applicable to all Jesus' disciples, are specifically applied to the lay faithful. They are particularly meaningful images because they speak not only of the deep involvement and the full participation of the lay faithful in the affairs of the earth, the world, and the human community, but also and above all they tell of the radical newness and unique character of an involvement and participation which has as its purpose the spreading of the Gospel that brings salvation.

Called to Holiness

16. We come to a full sense of the dignity of the lay faithful if we consider *the prime and fundamental vocation* that the Father assigns to each of them in Jesus Christ through the Holy Spirit: the vocation to holiness, that is, the perfection of charity. Holiness is the greatest testimony of the dignity conferred on a disciple of Christ.

The Second Vatican Council has significantly spoken on the universal call to holiness. It is possible to say that this call to holiness is precisely the basic charge entrusted to all the sons and daughters of the Church by a Council which intended to bring a renewal of Christian life based on the gospel. This charge is not a simple moral exhortation but an *undeniable requirement arising from the mystery of the Church: she is the choice vine*, whose branches live and grow with the same holy and life-giving energies that come from Christ; she is the Mystical Body, whose members share in the same life of holiness of the Head who is Christ; she is the Beloved Spouse of the Lord Jesus, who delivered himself up for her sanctification (cf. Eph 5:25 ff.). The Spirit that sanctified the human nature of Jesus in Mary's virginal womb (cf. Lk 1:35) is the same Spirit that is abiding and working in the Church to communicate to her the holiness of the Son of God made man.

It is ever more urgent that today all Christians take up again the way of gospel renewal, welcoming in a spirit of generosity the invitation expressed by the Apostle Peter "to be holy in all conduct" (1 Pt 1:15). The 1985 Extraordinary Synod, twenty years after the Council, opportunely insisted on this urgency: "Since the Church in Christ is a mystery, she ought to be considered the sign and instrument of holiness ... Men and women saints have always been the source and origin of renewal in the most difficult circumstances in the Church's history. Today we have the greatest need of saints whom we must assiduously beg God to raise up."

Everyone in the Church, precisely because they are members, receive and thereby share in the common vocation to holiness. In the fullness of this title and on equal par with all other members of the Church, the lay faithful are called to holiness: "All the faithful of Christ of whatever rank or status are called to the fullness of Christian life and to the perfection of charity." "All of Christ's followers are invited and bound to pursue holiness and the perfect fulfillment of their own state of life."

The call to holiness is *rooted in Baptism* and proposed anew in the other Sacraments, principally in the *Eucharist*. Since Christians are re-clothed in Christ Jesus and refreshed by his Spirit, they are "holy." They therefore have the ability to manifest this holiness and the responsibility to bear witness to it in all that they do. The Apostle Paul never tires of admonishing all Christians to live "as is fitting among saints" (Eph 5:3).

Life according to the Spirit, whose fruit is holiness (cf. Rom 6:22; Gal 5:22), stirs up every baptized person and requires each to *follow and imitate Jesus Christ*, in embracing the Beatitudes, in listening and meditating on the Word of God, in conscious and active participation in the liturgical and sacramental life of the Church, in personal prayer, in family or in community, in the hunger and thirst for justice, in the practice of the commandment of love in all circumstances of life and service to the brethren, especially the least, the poor and the suffering.

The Life of Holiness in the World

17. The vocation of the lay faithful to holiness implies that life according to the Spirit expresses itself in a particular way in *their involvement in temporal affairs* and in *their participation in earthly activities*. Once again the Apostle admonishes us: "Whatever you do, in word or deed, do everything in the name of the Lord Jesus, giving thanks to God the Father through him" (Col 3:17). Applying the Apostle's words to the lay faithful, the Council categorically affirms: "Neither family concerns nor other secular affairs should be excluded from their religious program of life." Likewise, the Synod Fathers have said: "The unity of life of the lay faithful is of the greatest importance: indeed they must be sanctified in everyday professional and social life. To respond to their vocation, the lay faithful must see their daily activities as an occasion to join themselves to God, fulfill his will, serve other people and lead them to communion with God in Christ."

The vocation to holiness must be recognized and lived by the lay faithful, first of all as an undeniable and demanding obligation and as a shining example of the infinite love of the Father that has regenerated them in his own life of holiness. Such a vocation, then, ought to be called an *essential and inseparable element of the new life of Baptism*, and therefore an element which determines their dignity. At the same time, the vocation to holiness is *intimately connected to the mission* and to the responsibility entrusted to the lay faithful in the Church and in the world. In fact, that same holiness which is derived simply from their participation in the Church's holiness represents their first and fundamental contribution to the building of the Church herself, who is the "Communion of Saints." The eyes of faith behold a wonderful scene: that of a countless number of lay people, both women and men, busy at work in their daily lives and activities, oftentimes far from view and quite unacclaimed by the world, unknown to the world's great personages but nonetheless looked upon in love by the Father, untiring laborers who work in the Lord's vineyard. Confident and steadfast through the power of God's grace, these are the humble yet great builders of the Kingdom of God in history.

Holiness, then, must be called a fundamental presupposition and an irreplaceable condition for everyone in fulfilling the mission of salvation within the Church. The Church's holiness is the hidden source and the infallible measure of the works of the apostolate and of the missionary effort. Only in the measure that the Church, Christ's Spouse, is loved by him and she, in turn, loves him does she become a mother fruitful in the Spirit.

Again we take up the image from the gospel: the fruitfulness and the growth of the branches depends on their remaining united to the vine. "As the branch cannot bear fruit by itself, unless it abides in the vine, neither can you, unless you abide in me. I am the vine, you are the branches. He who abides in me, and I in him, he it is that bears much fruit, for apart from me you can do nothing" (Jn 15:4-5).

It is appropriate to recall here the solemn proclamation of beatification and canonization of lay men and women which took place during the month of the Synod. The entire People of God, and the lay faithful in particular, can find at this moment new models of holiness and new witnesses of heroic virtue lived in the ordinary everyday circumstances of human existence. The Synod Fathers have said: "Particular Churches especially should be attentive to recognizing among their members the younger men and women of those Churches who have given witness to holiness in such conditions (everyday secular conditions and the conjugal state) and who can be an example for others, so that, if the case calls for it, they (the Churches) might propose them to be beatified and canonized."

At the end of these reflections intended to define the lay faithful's position in the Church, the celebrated admonition of Saint Leo the Great comes to mind: "Acknowledge, O Christian, your dignity!" Saint Maximus, Bishop of Turin, in addressing those who had received the holy anointing of Baptism, repeats the same sentiments: "Ponder the honor that has made you sharers in this mystery!" All the baptized are invited to hear once again the words of Saint Augustine: "Let us rejoice and give thanks: we have not only become Christians, but Christ himself.... Stand in awe and rejoice: We have become Christ."

The dignity as a Christian, the source of equality for all members of the Church, guarantees and fosters the spirit of *communion* and fellowship, and, at the same time, becomes the hidden dynamic force in the lay faithful's apostolate and mission. It is a dignity, however, *which brings demands*, the dignity of laborers called by the Lord to work in his vineyard: "Upon all the lay faithful, then, rests the exalted duty of working to assure that each day the divine plan of salvation is further extended to every person, of every era, in every part of the earth."

Chapter IV: Laborers in the Lord's Vineyard: Good Stewards of God's Varied Grace

Women and Men

49. The Synod Fathers gave special attention to the status and role of women, with two purposes in mind: to themselves acknowledge and to invite all others to once again acknowledge the indispensable contribution of women to the building up of the Church and the development of society. They wished as well to work on a more specific analysis of women's participation in the life and mission of the Church.

Making reference to Pope John XXIII, who saw women's greater consciousness of their proper dignity and their entrance into public life as signs of our times, the Synod Fathers, when confronted with the various forms of discrimination and marginalization to which women are subjected simply because they are women, time and time again strongly affirmed the urgency to defend and to promote *the personal dignity of woman* and, consequently, her equality with man.

If anyone has this task of advancing the dignity of women in the Church and society, it is women themselves, who must recognize their responsibility as leading characters. There is still much effort to be done, in many parts of the world and in various surroundings, to destroy that unjust and deleterious mentality which considers the human being as a thing, as an object to buy and sell, as an instrument for selfish interests or for pleasure only. Women themselves, for the most part, are the prime victims of such a mentality. Only through openly acknowledging the personal dignity of women is the first step taken to promote the full participation of women in Church life as well as in social and public life. A more extensive and decisive response must be given to the demands made in the Exhortation *Familiaris Consortio*, concerning the many discriminations of which women are the victims: "Vigorous and incisive pastoral action must be taken by all to overcome completely these forms of discrimination so that the image of God that shines in all human beings without exception may be fully respected." Along the same lines, the Synod Fathers stated: "As an expression of her mission the Church must stand firmly against all forms of discrimination and abuse of women." Again, "The dignity of women, gravely wounded in public esteem, must be restored through effective respect for the rights of the human person and by putting the teaching of the Church into practice."

In particular when speaking of *active and responsible participation in the life and mission of the Church*, emphasis should be placed on what has already been stated and clearly urged by the Second Vatican Council: "Since in our days women are taking an increasingly active share in the whole life of society, it is very important that they participate more widely also in the various fields of the Church's apostolate."

The awareness that women with their own gifts and tasks have *their own specific vocation* has increased and been deepened in the years following the Council and has found its fundamental inspiration in the Gospel and the Church's history. In fact, for the believer the Gospel, namely, the word and example of Jesus Christ, remains the necessary and decisive point of reference. In no other moment in history is this fact more fruitful and innovative.

Though not called to the apostolate of the Twelve, and thereby to the ministerial priesthood, many women, nevertheless, accompanied Jesus in his ministry and assisted the group of Apostles (cf. Lk 8:2-3), were present at the foot of the Cross (cf. Lk 23:49), assisted at the burial of Christ (cf. Lk 23:55) received and transmitted the message of resurrection on Easter morn (cf. Lk 24:1-10), and prayed with the Apostles in the Cenacle awaiting Pentecost (cf. Acts 1:14).

From the evidence of the Gospel, the Church at its origin detached herself from the culture of the time and called women to tasks connected with spreading the gospel. In his letters, the Apostle Paul even cites by name a great number of women for their various functions in service of the primitive Christian community (cf. Rom 16:1-15; Phil 4:2-3; Col 4:15; 1 Cor 11:5;

1 Tm 5:16). "If the witness of the Apostles founds the Church," stated Paul VI, "the witness of women contributes greatly towards nourishing the faith of Christian communities."

Both in her earliest days and in her successive development, the Church, albeit in different ways and with diverse emphases, has always known women who have exercised an oftentimes decisive role in the Church herself and accomplished tasks of considerable value on her behalf. History is marked by grand works, quite often lowly and hidden, but not for this reason any less decisive to the growth and the holiness of the Church. It is necessary that this history continue, indeed that it be expanded and intensified in the face of the growing and widespread awareness of the personal dignity of woman and her vocation, particularly in light of the urgency of a "re-evangelization" and a major effort toward "humanizing" social relations.

Gathering together the pronouncements of the Second Vatican Council, which reflect the Gospel's message and the Church's history, the Synod Fathers formulated, among others, this precise "recommendation": "It is necessary that the Church recognize all the gifts of men and women for her life and mission, and put them into practice." Again, "This Synod proclaims that the Church seeks the recognition and use of all the gifts, experiences and talents of men and women to make her mission effective" (cf. Congregation for the Doctrine of the Faith, Instruction on Christian Freedom and Liberation, 72).

Anthropological and Theological Foundations

50. The condition that will assure the rightful presence of woman in the Church and in society is a more penetrating and accurate consideration of the *anthropological foundation for masculinity and femininity* with the intent of clarifying woman's personal identity in relation to man, that is, a diversity yet mutual complementarity not only as it concerns roles to be held and functions to be performed but also, and more deeply, as it concerns her makeup and meaning as a person. The Synod Fathers have deeply felt this requirement, maintaining that "the anthropological and theological foundations for resolving questions about the true significance and dignity of each sex require deeper study."

Through committing herself to a reflection on the anthropological and theological basis of femininity, the Church enters the historic process of the various movements for the promotion of woman and, in going to the very basic aspect of woman as a personal being, provides her most precious contribution. Even before this the Church intends, in such a way, to obey God, who created the individual "in his image," "male and female he created them" (Gen 1:27) and who intended that they would accept the call of God to come to know, reverence, and live his plan. It is a plan that "from the beginning" has been indelibly imprinted in the very being of the human person—men and women—and, therefore, in the makeup, meaning, and deepest workings of the individual. This most wise and loving plan must be explored to discover all its richness of content—a richness that "from the beginning" came to be progressively manifested and realized in the whole history of salvation and was brought to completion in "the fullness of time" when "God sent his Son, born of a woman" (Gal 4:4). That "fullness" continues in history: God's plan for woman is read and is to be read within the context of the faith of the Church and also in the lives lived by so many Christian women today. Without forgetting the help that can come from different human sciences and cultures, researchers, because of an informed discernment, will be able to help gather and clarify the values and requirements that belong to the enduring essential aspects of women and those bound to evolve in history. The Second Vatican Council reminds us: "The Church maintains that beneath all changes there are many realities which do not change; these find their ultimate foundation in Christ, who is the same yesterday, and today, and forever" (cf. Heb 13:8). The Apostolic Letter *on the Dignity and Vocation of Woman* gives much attention to the anthropological and theological foundation of woman's dignity as a person. The document seeks to again treat and develop the catechetical reflections of the Wednesday General Audiences devoted over a long period of time to the "theology of the body," while at the same time fulfilling a promise made in the Encyclical *Redemptoris Mater* and serving as a response to the request of the Synod Fathers.

May the reading of the Apostolic Letter *Mulieris Dignitatem*, in particular, as a biblical theological meditation, be an incentive for everyone, both women and men, and especially for those who devote their lives to the human sciences and theological disciplines, to pursue on the basis of the personal dignity of man and woman and their mutual relationship, a critical study to *better and more deeply* understand the values and specific gifts of femininity and masculinity, not only in the surroundings of social living but also and above all in living as Christians and as members of the Church. This meditation on the anthropological and theological foundations of women ought to enlighten and guide the Christian response to the most frequently asked questions, oftentimes so crucial, on the *"place" that women can have and ought to have in the Church and in society.*

It is quite clear from the words and attitude of Christ, which are normative for the Church, that no discrimination exists on the level of an individual's relation to Christ, in which "there is neither male nor female; for you are all one in Christ Jesus" (Gal 3:28) and on the level of participation in the Church's life of grace and holiness, as Joel's prophecy fulfilled at Pentecost wonderfully attests: "I will pour out my spirit on all flesh; your sons and daughters shall prophecy" (Jl 3:1; cf. Acts 2:17 ff). As the Apostolic Letter *on the Dignity and Vocation of Woman* reads: "Both women and men ... are equally capable of receiving the outpouring of divine truth and love in the Holy Spirit. Both receive his salvific and sanctifying visits."

Mission in the Church and in the World

51. In speaking about participation in the apostolic mission of the Church, there is no doubt that in virtue of Baptism and Confirmation, a woman—as well as a man—is made a sharer in the threefold mission of Jesus Christ, Priest, Prophet, and King, and is thereby charged and given the ability to fulfill the fundamental apostolate of the Church: *evangelization.* A woman is called to put to work in this apostolate the "gifts" which are properly hers: first of all, the gift that is her very dignity as a person exercised in word and testimony of life, gifts therefore connected with her vocation as a woman.

In her participation in the life and mission of the Church, a woman cannot receive the *Sacrament of Orders* and therefore cannot fulfill the proper function of the ministerial priesthood. This is a practice that the Church has always found in the expressed will of Christ, totally free and sovereign, who called only men to be his Apostles; a practice that can be understood from the rapport between Christ, the Spouse, and his Bride, the Church.

Here we are in the area of *function*, not of *dignity* and *holiness*. In fact, it must be maintained: "Although the Church possesses a 'hierarchical' structure, nevertheless this structure is totally ordered to the holiness of Christ's members." As Paul VI has already said, "We cannot change what our Lord did, nor his call to women; but we can recognize and promote the role of women in the mission of evangelization and in the life of the Christian community."

Above all, the *acknowledgment in theory* of the active and responsible presence of women in the Church must be *realized in practice*. With this in mind, this Exhortation addressed to the lay faithful with its deliberate and repeated use of the terms "women and men" must be read. Furthermore, the revised Code of Canon Law contains many provisions on the participation of women in the life and mission of the Church: they are provisions that must be more commonly known and, according to the diverse sensibilities of culture and opportuneness in a pastoral situation, be realized with greater timeliness and determination.

An example comes to mind in the participation of women on diocesan and parochial Pastoral Councils as well as Diocesan Synods and particular Councils. In this regard, the Synod Fathers have written: "Without discrimination women should be participants in the life of the Church, and also in consultation and the process of coming to decisions." Again, "Women, who already hold places of great importance in transmitting the faith and offering every kind of service in the life of the Church, ought to be associated in the preparation of pastoral and missionary documents and ought to be recognized as cooperators in the mission of the church in the family, in professional life and in the civil community."

In the more specific area of evangelization and catechesis, the particular work that women have in the transmission of the faith, not only in the family but also in the various educational environments, is to be more strongly fostered. In broader terms, this should be applied in all that regard embracing the Word of God, its understanding, and its communication, as well as its study, research, and theological teaching.

While she is to fulfill her duty to evangelize, woman is to feel more acutely her need to be evangelized. With her vision illumined by faith (cf. Eph 1:18), woman is to be able to distinguish what truly responds to her dignity as a person and to her vocation from all that, under the pretext of this "dignity" and in the name of "freedom" and "progress," militates against true values. On the contrary, these false values become responsible for the moral degradation of the person, the environment, and society. This same "discernment," made possible and demanded from Christian women's participation in the prophetic mission of Christ and his Church, recurs with continued urgency throughout history. This "discernment," often mentioned by the Apostle Paul, is not only a matter of evaluating reality and events in the light of faith but also involves a real decision and obligation to employ it, not only in Church life but also in human society.

It can be said that the problems of today's world already cited in the second part of the Council's Constitution *Gaudium et Spes*, which remain unresolved and not at all affected by the passage of time, must witness the presence and commitment of women with their irreplaceable and customary contributions. In particular, two great tasks entrusted to women merit the attention of everyone: first of all, the task of bringing full dignity to the conjugal life and to motherhood. Today, new possibilities are opened to women for a deeper understanding and a richer realization of human and Christian values implied in the conjugal life and the experience of motherhood. Man himself—husband and father—can be helped to overcome forms of absenteeism and of periodic presence as well as a partial fulfillment of parental responsibilities—indeed he can be involved in new and significant relations of interpersonal communion—precisely as a result of the intelligent, loving, and decisive intervention of woman.

Secondly, women have the task of *assuring the moral dimension of culture*, the dimension, namely of *a culture worthy of the person*, of an individual yet social life. The Second Vatican Council seems to connect the moral dimension of culture with the participation of the lay faithful in the kingly mission of Christ: "Let the lay faithful by their combined efforts remedy the institutions and conditions of the world when the latter are an inducement to sin, that all such things may be conformed to the norms of justice, and may favor the practice of virtue rather than hindering it. By so doing, they will infuse culture and human works with a moral value."

As women increasingly participate more fully and responsibly in the activities of institutions which are associated with safeguarding the basic duty to human values in various communities, the words of the Council just quoted point to an important field in the apostolate of women: in all aspects of the life of such communities, from the socioeconomic to the sociopolitical dimension, the personal dignity of woman and her specific vocation ought to be respected and promoted. Likewise, this should be the case in living situations not only affecting the individual but also communities, not only in forms left to personal freedom and responsibility but even in those guaranteed by just civil laws.

"It is not good for man to be alone: let us make him a helper fit for him" (Gen 2:18). *God entrusted the human being to woman.* Certainly, every human being is entrusted to each and every other human being, but in a special way the human being is entrusted to woman, precisely because the woman in virtue of her special experience of motherhood is seen to have a *specific sensitivity* toward the human person and all that constitutes the individual's true welfare, beginning with the fundamental value of life. How great are the possibilities and responsibilities of woman in this area, at a time when the development of science and technology is not always inspired and measured by true wisdom, with the inevitable risk of "dehumanizing" human life, above all when it would demand a more intense love and a more generous acceptance.

The participation of women in the life of the Church and society in the sharing of her gifts is likewise the path necessary of her personal fulfillment—on which so many justly insist today—and the basic contribution of woman to the enrichment of Church communion and the dynamism in the apostolate of the People of God. From this perspective the presence also of men, together with women, ought to be considered.

The Presence and Collaboration of Men Together with Women

52. Many voices were raised in the Synod Hall expressing the fear that excessive insistence given to the status and role of women would lead to an unacceptable omission, that, in point, regarding men. In reality, various sectors in the Church must lament the absence or the scarcity of the presence of men, some of whom abdicate their proper Church responsibilities, allowing them to be fulfilled only by women. Such instances are participation in the liturgical prayer of the Church, education and, in particular,

catechesis of their own sons and daughters and other children, presence at religious and cultural meetings, and collaboration in charitable and missionary initiatives. The coordinated presence of both men and women is to be pastorally urged so that the participation of the lay faithful in the salvific mission of the Church might be rendered more rich, complete, and harmonious.

The fundamental reason that requires and explains the presence and the collaboration of both men and women is not only, as it was just emphasized, the major source of meaning and efficacy in the pastoral action of the Church, nor even less is it the simple sociological fact of sharing a life together as human beings, which is natural for man and woman. It is, rather, the original plan of the Creator who from the "beginning" willed the human being to be a "unity of the two" and willed man and woman to be the prime community of persons, source of every other community, and, at the same time, to be a "sign" of that interpersonal communion of love which constitutes the mystical, intimate life of God, One in Three.

Precisely for this reason, the most common and widespread way, and at the same time, fundamental way, to assure this coordinated and harmonious presence of men and women in the life and mission of the Church is the fulfillment of the tasks and responsibilities of the couple and the Christian family, in which the variety of diverse forms of life and love is seen and communicated: conjugal, paternal and maternal, filial and familial. We read in the Exhortation *Familiaris Consortio*: "Since the Christian family is a community in which the relationships are renewed by Christ through faith and the sacraments, the family's sharing in the Church's mission should follow a *community pattern*: the spouses together *as a couple*, the parents and children *as a family*, must live their service to the Church and to the world.... The Christian family also builds up the Kingdom of God in history through the everyday realities that concern and distinguish its *state of life*: it is thus in the *love between husband and wife and between members of the family*—a love lived out in all its extraordinary richness of values and demands: totality, oneness, fidelity and fruitfulness—that the Christian family's participation in the prophetic, priestly and kingly mission of Jesus Christ and of his Church finds expression and realization."

From this perspective, the Synod Fathers have recalled the meaning that the Sacrament of Matrimony ought to assume in the Church and society in order to illuminate and inspire all the relations between men and women. In this regard they have emphasized an "urgent need for every Christian to live and proclaim the message of hope contained in the relation between man and woman. The Sacrament of Matrimony, which consecrates this relation in its conjugal form and reveals it as a sign of the relation of Christ with his Church, contains a teaching of great importance for the Church's life—a teaching that ought to reach today's world through the Church; all those relations between man and woman must be imbued by this spirit. The Church should even more fully rely on the riches found here." These same Fathers have rightly emphasized that "the esteem for virginity and reverence for motherhood must be respectively restored," and still again they have called for the development of diverse and complementary vocations in the living context of Church communion and in the service of its continued growth.

The States of Life and Vocations

55. All the members of the People of God—clergy, men and women religious, the lay faithful—are laborers in the vineyard. At one and the same time they all are the goal and subjects of Church communion as well as of participation in the mission of salvation. Every one of us possessing charisms and ministries, diverse yet complementary, works in the one and the same vineyard of the Lord. Simply in *being* Christians, even before actually doing the works of a Christian, all are branches of the one fruitful vine which is Christ.

All are living members of the one Body of the Lord built up through the power of the Spirit. The significance of "being" a Christian does not come about simply from the life of grace and holiness which is the primary and more productive source of the apostolic and missionary fruitfulness of Holy Mother Church. Its meaning also arises from the state of life that characterizes the clergy, men and women religious, members of secular institutes, and the lay faithful.

In Church communion, the states of life by being ordered one to the other are thus bound together among themselves. They all share in a deeply basic meaning: that of being *the manner of living out the commonly shared Christian dignity and the universal call to holiness in the perfection of love.*

They are *different yet complementary* in the sense that each of them has a basic and unmistakable character which sets each apart, while at the same time each of them is seen in relation to the other and placed at each other's service.

The *lay* state of life has its distinctive feature in its secular character. It fulfills an ecclesial service in bearing witness and, in its own way, recalling for priests, women and men religious the significance of the earthly and temporal realities in the salvific plan of God. In turn, the ministerial priesthood represents in different times and places the permanent guarantee of the sacramental presence of Christ, the Redeemer. The religious state bears witness to the eschatological character of the Church, that is, the straining toward the Kingdom of God that is prefigured and in some way anticipated and experienced even now through the vows of chastity, poverty, and obedience.

All the states of life, whether taken collectively or individually in relation to the others, are at the service of the Church's growth. While different in expression they are deeply united in the Church's "mystery of communion" and are dynamically coordinated in its unique mission.

In the diversity of the states of life and the variety of vocations this same, unique mystery of the Church reveals and experiences anew *the infinite richness of the mystery of Jesus Christ*. The Fathers were fond of referring to the Church as a field of a pleasing and wonderful variety of herbs, plants, flowers and, fruits. Saint Ambrose writes, "A field produces many fruits, but the one which has an abundance of both fruits and flowers is far better. The field of holy Church is fruitful in both one and the other. In this field there are the priceless buds of virginity blossoming forth, widowhood stands out boldly as the forest in the plain; elsewhere the rich harvest of weddings blessed by the Church fills the great granary of the world with abundant produce, and the wine-presses of the Lord Jesus overflow with the grapes of a productive vine, enriching Christian marriages."

Chapter V: That You Bear Much Fruit: The Formation of the Lay Faithful in the Lay State

An Appeal and a Prayer

64. At the conclusion of this post-Synodal document, I once again put forward the invitation of "the householder," proposed in the gospel: *You go*

into my vineyard, too. It can be said that the significance of the Synod on the vocation and mission of the lay faithful might very well consist in this *call of the Lord which he addresses to everyone*, yet, in a particular way to the lay faithful, both women and men.

The happenings at the Synod have been a great spiritual experience for all the participants. The experience has been that of a Church under the light and the power of the Spirit, intent on discerning and embracing the renewed call of her Lord so that she can again propose to today's world the mystery of her communion and the dynamism of her mission of salvation, especially by centering on the specific place and role of the lay faithful. This Exhortation, then, intends to urge the most abundant possible fruitfulness from this Synod in every part of the Church worldwide. This will come about as a result of an effective hearkening to the Lord's call by the entire People of God, in particular, by the lay faithful. I make a strong appeal to one and all, pastors and faithful, never to become tired of maintaining—indeed always taking an active part to fix deeply in one's mind, heart, and life—an *ecclesial consciousness*, which is ever mindful of what it means to be members of the Church of Jesus Christ, participants in her mystery of communion and in her dynamism in mission and the apostolate.

It is of particular importance that all Christians be aware that through Baptism they have received an *extraordinary dignity*: through grace we are called to be children loved by the Father, members incorporated in Christ and his Church, living and holy temples of the Spirit. With deep emotion and gratitude we again hear the words of John the Evangelist: "See what love the Father has given us, that we should be called children of God; and so we are" (1 Jn 3:1).

While this "Christian *newness of life*" given to the members of the Church constitutes for all the basis of their participation in the priestly, prophetic, and kingly mission of Christ and of their vocation to holiness in love, it receives expression and is fulfilled in the lay faithful through the "secular character" which is "uniquely and properly" theirs.

Besides imparting an awareness of a commonly shared Christian dignity, an ecclesial consciousness brings a sense of belonging to *the mystery of the Church as Communion*. This is a basic and undeniable aspect of the life and mission of the Church. For one and all the earnest prayer of Jesus at the Last Supper, "*That all may be one*" (Jn 17-21), ought to become a daily required and undeniable program of life and action.

A real sense of Church communion, the gift of the Spirit that urges our free and generous response, will bring forth as its precious fruit, in the "one and catholic" Church, the continuing value of the rich variety of vocations and conditions of life, charisms, ministries, works, and responsibilities, as well as a more demonstrable and decisive collaboration of groups, associations, and movements of the lay faithful in keeping with the accomplishment of the commonly shared salvific mission of the Church herself. This communion is already in itself the first great sign in the world of the presence of Christ, the Savior. At the same time, it promotes and stimulates the proper apostolic and missionary action of the Church.

The whole Church, pastors and lay faithful alike, standing on the threshold of the Third Millennium, ought to feel more strongly the Church's responsibility to obey the command of Christ, "Go into all the world and preach the gospel to the whole creation" (Mk 16:15), and take up anew the missionary endeavor. A great venture, both challenging and wonderful, is entrusted to the Church—that of a *re-evangelization*, which is so much needed by the present world. The lay faithful ought to regard themselves as an active and responsible part of this venture, called as they are to proclaim and to live the gospel in service to the person and to society while respecting the totality of the values and needs of both.

Since the Synod of Bishops was celebrated last October during the Marian Year, its work was entrusted in a very special way to the intercession of the Most Blessed Virgin Mary, Mother of the Redeemer. I, too, entrust the spiritual fruitfulness of the Synod to her prayerful intercession. Along with the Synod Fathers, the lay faithful present at the Synod, and all the other members of the People of God, I have recourse at the end of this post-Synodal document to the Virgin Mary. At this moment this appeal becomes a prayer:

O Most Blessed Virgin Mary,
Mother of Christ and Mother of the Church,
With joy and wonder we seek to make our own your *Magnificat*,
joining you in your hymn of thankfulness and love.
With you we give thanks to God,

"whose mercy is from generation to generation,"
for the exalted vocation
and the many forms of mission entrusted to the lay faithful.

God has called each of them by name to live his own communion of love and holiness
and to be one in the great family of God's children.
He has sent them forth to shine with the light of Christ
and to communicate the fire of the Spirit in every part of society
through their life inspired by the gospel.

O Virgin of the *Magnificat*,
fill their hearts
with a gratitude and enthusiasm for this vocation and mission.

With humility and magnanimity
you were the "handmaid of the Lord";
give us your unreserved willingness for service to God
and the salvation of the world.
Open our hearts
to the great anticipation of the Kingdom of God
and of the proclamation of the Gospel
to the whole of creation. Your mother's heart
is ever mindful of the many dangers and evils which threaten
to overpower men and women in our time.

At the same time your heart also takes notice of the many initiatives undertaken for good,
the great yearning for values, and the progress achieved
in bringing forth
the abundant fruits of salvation.

O Virgin full of courage, may your spiritual strength and trust in God inspire us,
so that we might know how to overcome all the obstacles

that we encounter in accomplishing our mission.
Teach us to treat the affairs of the world
with a real sense of Christian responsibility and a joyful hope
of the coming of God's Kingdom, and of a "new heaven and a new earth."

⇝

You who were gathered in prayer with the Apostles in the Cenacle,
awaiting the coming of the Spirit at Pentecost, implore his renewed outpouring
on all the faithful, men and women alike, so that they might more fully respond
to their vocation and mission,
as branches engrafted to the true vine, called to bear much fruit
for the life of the world.

⇝

O Virgin Mother, guide and sustain us
so that we might always live
as true sons and daughters of the Church of your Son. Enable us to do our part
in helping to establish on earth
the civilization of truth and love, as God wills it,
for his glory. Amen

Given in Rome, at St. Peter's, on December 30, the Feast of the Holy Family of Jesus, Mary, and Joseph, in the year 1988, the eleventh of my Pontificate.

READING 13 (SEPTEMBER 25, 1993): True Human Love Reflects the Divine[1]

Given in Asti, Italy

Dear Married Couples,

1. It gives me great joy to meet you in this cathedral, where you frequently gather with your Bishop and priests for the Married Couples' Mission in which you are involved, and which will end at Pentecost next year. I am even more delighted to be doing so in the company of Cardinal Angelo Sodano, an illustrious son of your land.

I greet dear Bishop Severino Poletto, your dynamic Pastor, and I thank him for the words he has addressed to me. I also greet the married couples who, on your behalf, have expressed sentiments of devoted affection to me, explaining the interesting pastoral enterprise in which you are involved. You are aiming at strengthening your links with Christ, deepening his message by paying special attention to "the Gospel of marriage."

Your experience is very timely. The Church and the world today more than ever need married couples and families who generously let themselves be schooled by Christ.

The many sad aspects of our time and the unprecedented forms of violence that unfortunately mark it are ultimately explained by the closure of hearts to God's love. How urgent then is the task of believers, above all of Christian families, to restore to today's society the necessary anchoring of faith and love in the safe haven of God's word.

The love experienced within the family offers a favorable climate where that personal relationship with God which is the source of authentic individual and community renewal can take root and develop. Obviously this implies that it is genuine love. Often, unfortunately, in the hedonistic culture we experience today, it is rather its caricature and even its betrayal that are labeled with the name of love. Appropriately, the biblical passage just proclaimed is, in two instances, concerned with clarifying the true meaning of love.

⋘

2. "In this way the love of God was revealed to us: God sent his only Son into the world so that we might have life through him" (1 Jn 4:9). Here is love at its source. Love is the gift of self. It means emptying oneself to reach out to others. In a certain sense, it means forgetting oneself for the good of others. Authentic human love reflects within itself the logic of the divine. In this perspective, the duty of conjugal fidelity can be fully grasped. "You are everything to me, I give myself totally to you, forever": this is the commitment that springs from the heart of every person who is sincerely in love.

Fidelity! Next to this comes fruitfulness, another typical aspect of the relationship between spouses. Is there not a link between the demographic decline and the alarming phenomenon of a considerable number of couples between whom love so easily withers and dies?

Dear married couples, do not be afraid! You are living the greatness of love animated by the generous desire to see it spread and virtually incarnated in the faces of your children. When a couple refuses to collaborate with God to transmit the gift of life, they have great difficulty in finding in themselves the resources to sustain mutual understanding.

⋙

3. The biblical text continues: "In this is love: not that we have loved God, but that he loved us" (1 Jn 4:10). God's love is totally gratuitous. Such therefore should be the love of a couple and the relationship between the members of a family. By virtue of love the parents will be able to devote their best energies to the work of bringing up their children, assuring them of consistent guidance and surrounding them with caring and respectful affection. In turn, the children will find in love the deepest motivation for a responsible, docile, and grateful attitude toward their parents. Love drawn from God's heart spurs the whole family to find the time to attend to the elderly, to devote themselves to the sick, to be involved in the difficult situations around them, including regional problems and the more general problems of the nation. The family does not live its vocation to the full if it is not open to the needs of the community. When its members seal themselves off in a sort of group selfishness, they automatically deprive themselves of the opportunity to grow in love and thus to experience true joy.

⋙

4. Dear married couples, the presence of so many of you and your children fills my heart with emotion. Allow me to embrace you with affection. At the end of our meeting I should like to leave you two "assignments" in the Lord's name.

I draw one from the recommendation contained in the First Letter of Peter: "Come to him, [Christ] a living stone" (1 Pt 2:4). Yes, dear brothers and sisters, make sure that Christ the Lord is your teacher and also your children's.

It is from him that you should draw the right criteria for direction and discernment in every situation. Forcefully resist the divorce mentality that disrupts God's plan for marriage as an indissoluble covenant of love. Do not let into your homes that permissive culture which allows everything, even the suppression of life before it blossoms or before it declines and comes to an end naturally.

5. The other assignment concerns your responsibility to proclaim the Gospel. Be evangelizing communities, able to transmit and radiate the Gospel! Is not this the goal of the Married Couples' Mission in which you are involved? Have the courage of the Gospel!

I bless you, dear friends, and I encourage you to continue in your providential initiative, hoping that the missionary concern that motivates you will continue to shape the entire pastoral activity of the diocese.

Dear brothers and sisters! I entrust each one of you, your children, your families, your projects, to the love of the Father, and I invoke the protection of your patron saints and the motherly intercession of our Lady on your homes.

My blessing to all of you! I must say that the expression "Married Couples' Mission" is very thought-provoking because usually when we think of mission and missionaries we are referring to those who go to distant lands. Sometimes married couples do, too.

Instead today, after the Second Vatican Council, we are very aware of the mission that involves all Christians. We are all missionaries and the family's mission is irreplaceable. It is irreplaceable if we consider it as the fundamental cell of that larger society, for the Church, for evangelization, and for the new evangelization.

We also know from experience and from tradition how much all of us, Bishops, Cardinals, and the Pope himself, owe to our family, to our parents, our teachers in the faith, in human and Christian nobility and in the virtues. We are indebted to them, and first and foremost to God, but we are also indebted to our many brothers and sisters and above all to our parents who gave us life and raised us. Human life must be reared not only in the physical and biological dimension but also in the spiritual.

This is the irreplaceable evangelization that takes place in the family and to which you are called. This is why, although you do not travel to distant lands, you are the Apostles, evangelizers, and missionaries of your own families.

For this, the missionary spirit is necessary, the very spirit of the Apostles but also of our parents and grandparents, who knew how to make the family a domestic Church. This is a lovely expression that we have inherited from the Fathers of the Church. We have the universal Church, the diocesan, and the parish Church, but the domestic Church is irreplaceable.

I hope that all of you, fathers, mothers, and all your children, will form this domestic Church to be a community mission. It happens through this communion of individuals which is specific to the family, between the couple and then between the generations.

I thank you for this meeting. I entrust you to the protection of the Holy Family, a family in which the Son of God was born and brought up as a man, as a human child. This is a wonderful reality. Be devoted to the Holy Family, Jesus, Mary, and Joseph. I entrust all those present and all the families of your city and your diocese to them.

READING 14 (MARCH 18, 1994): Population Conference Draft Document Criticized[1]

1. I greet you, Madam Secretary General, at a time when you are closely involved in preparing the 1994 International Conference on Population and Development to be held in Cairo in September.

Your visit provides an occasion for me to share with you some thoughts on a topic which, we all agree, is of vital importance for the well-being and progress of the human family. The theme of the Cairo conference takes on a heightened significance in light of the fact that the gap between the rich and the poor of the world continues to widen, a situation which poses an ever-increasing threat to the peace for which mankind longs.

The global population situation is very complex: There are variations not simply from continent to continent but even from one region to another. U.N. studies tell us that a rapid decrease in the global rate of population growth is expected to begin during the 1990s and carry on into the new century. At the same time, growth rates remain high in some of the least-developed nations of the world, while population growth has declined appreciably in the industrialized developed nations.

2. The Holy See has carefully followed these matters, with a special concern to make accurate and objective assessments of population issues and to urge global solidarity in regard to development strategies, especially as they

affect the developing nations of the world. In this we have derived benefit from participation in the meetings of the U.N. Population Commission and from the studies of the U.N. Population Division.

The Holy See has also participated in all the regional preparatory meetings of the Cairo conference, gaining a better understanding of regional differences and contributing to the discussion on each occasion. In accordance with its specific competence and mission, the Holy See is concerned that proper attention should be given to the ethical principles determining actions taken in response to the demographic, sociological, and public policy analyses of the data on population trends. Consequently, the Holy See seeks to focus attention on certain basic truths: that each and every person—regardless of age, sex, religion, or national background—has a dignity and worth that is unconditional and inalienable; that human life itself from conception to natural death is sacred; that human rights are innate and transcend any constitutional order; and that the fundamental unity of the human race demands that everyone be committed to building a community which is free from injustice and which strives to promote and protect the common good. These truths about the human person are the measure of any response to the findings which emerge from the consideration of demographic data. It is in light of authentic human values—recognized by peoples of diverse cultures, religious and national backgrounds across the globe—that all policy choices must be evaluated. No goal or policy will bring positive results for people if it does not respect the unique dignity and objective needs of those same people.

3. There is widespread agreement that a population policy is only one part of an overall development strategy. Accordingly, it is important that any discussion of population policies should keep in mind the actual and projected development of nations and regions. At the same time, it is impossible to leave out of account the very nature of what is meant by the term "development." All development worthy of the name must be integral, that is, it must be directed to the true good of every person and of the whole person. True development cannot consist in the simple accumulation of wealth and in the greater availability of goods and services but must be pursued with due consideration for the social, cultural, and spiritual dimensions of the human being.

Development programs must be built on justice and equality, enabling people to live in dignity, harmony, and peace. They must respect the cultural heritage of peoples and nations, and those social qualities and virtues that reflect the God-given dignity of each and every person and the divine plan which calls all persons to unity. Importantly, men and women must be active agents of their own development, for to treat them as mere objects in some scheme or plan would be to stifle that capacity for freedom and responsibility which is fundamental to the good of the human person.

⪢

4. Development has been and remains the proper context for the international community's consideration of population issues. Within such discussions there naturally arise questions relating to the transmission and nurturing of human life. To formulate population issues in terms of individual "sexual and reproductive rights" or even in terms of "women's rights" is to change the focus which should be the proper concern of governments and international agencies. I say this without in any way wishing to reduce the importance of securing justice and equity for women.

Further, questions involving the transmission of life and its subsequent nurturing cannot be adequately dealt with except in relation to the good of the family: that communion of persons established by the marriage of husband and wife, which is, as the Universal Declaration of Human Rights affirms, "the natural and fundamental group unit of society" (Art. 16.3). The family is an institution founded upon the very nature of the human person, and it is the proper setting for the conception, birth, and upbringing of children. At this moment in history, when so many powerful forces are arrayed against the family, it is more important than ever that the Conference on Population and Development should respond to the challenge implicit in the United Nations' designation of 1994 as the International Year of the Family by doing everything within its power to ensure that that family receives from "society and the state" that protection to which the same universal declaration says it is "entitled" (ibid.). Anything less would be a betrayal of the noblest ideals of the United Nations.

⪢

5. Today the duty to safeguard the family demands that particular attention be given to securing for husband and wife the liberty to decide respon-

sibly, free from all social or legal coercion, the number of children they will have and the spacing of their births. It should not be the intent of governments or other agencies to decide for couples, but rather to create the social conditions which will enable them to make appropriate decisions in the light of their responsibilities to God, to themselves, to the society of which they are a part, and to the objective moral order. What the church calls "responsible parenthood" is not a question of unlimited procreation or lack of awareness of what is involved in rearing children, but rather the empowerment of couples to use their inviolable liberty wisely and responsibly, taking into account social and demographic realities as well as their moral criteria. All propaganda and misinformation directed at persuading couples that they must limit their family to one or two children should be steadfastly avoided, and couples that generously choose to have large families are to be supported.

In defense of the human person, the church stands opposed to the imposition of limits on family size and to the promotion of methods of limiting births which separate the unitive and procreative dimensions of marital intercourse, which are contrary to the moral law inscribed on the human heart or which constitute an assault on the sacredness of life. As a result, sterilization, which is more and more promoted as a method of family planning, because of its finality and its potential for the violation of human rights, especially of women, is clearly unacceptable; it poses a most grave threat to human dignity and liberty when promoted as part of a population policy. Abortion, which destroys existing human life, is a heinous evil, and it is never an acceptable method of family planning, as was recognized by consensus at the Mexico City U.N. International Conference on Population (1984).

6. To summarize, I wish to emphasize once again what I have written in the encyclical *Centesimus Annus*: "It is necessary to go back to seeing the family as the sanctuary of life. The family is indeed sacred: It is the place in which life—the gift of God—can be properly welcomed and protected against the many attacks to which it is exposed and can develop in accordance with what constitutes authentic human growth. In the face of the so-called culture of death, the family is the heart of the culture of life. Human

ingenuity seems to be directed more toward limiting, suppressing, or destroying the sources of life—including recourse to abortion, which unfortunately is so widespread in the world—than toward defending and opening up the possibility of life" (no. 39).

↠

7. As well as reaffirming the fundamental role of the family in society, I wish to draw special attention to the status of children and women who all too often find themselves the most vulnerable members of our communities. Children must not be treated as a burden or inconvenience but should be cherished as bearers of hope and signs of promise for the future. The care which is essential for their growth and nurture comes primarily from their parents, but society must help by sustaining the family in its needs and in its efforts to maintain the caring environment in which children can develop. Society ought to promote "social policies which have the family as their principal object, policies which assist the family by providing adequate resources and efficient means of support, both for bringing up children and for looking after the elderly, so as to avoid distancing the latter from the family unit and in order to strengthen relations between generations" (*Centesimus Annus* 49). A society cannot say that it is treating children justly or protecting their interests if its laws do not safeguard their rights and respect the responsibility of parents for their well-being.

↠

8. It is a sad reflection on the human condition that still today, at the end of the twentieth century, it is necessary to affirm that every woman is equal in dignity to man and a full member of the human family, within which she has a distinctive place and vocation that is complementary to but in no way less valuable than man's. In much of the world much still has to be done to meet the educational and health needs of girls and young women so that they may achieve their full potential in society.

In the family which a woman establishes with her husband she enjoys the unique role and privilege of motherhood. In a special way it belongs to her to nurture the new life of the child from the moment of conception. The mother in particular enwraps the newborn child in love and security and creates the environment for its growth and development. Society should not allow woman's maternal role to be demeaned or count it as of little value in comparison with other possibilities. Greater consideration should be given to the social role of mothers, and support should be given to programs which aim at decreasing maternal mortality, providing prenatal and perinatal care, meeting the nutritional needs of pregnant women and nursing mothers, and helping mothers themselves to provide preventive health care for their infants. In this regard, attention should be given to the positive benefits of breastfeeding for nourishment and disease prevention in infants as well as for maternal bonding and birth spacing.

9. The study of population and development inevitably poses the question of the environmental implications of population growth. The ecological issue, too, is fundamentally a moral one. While population growth is often blamed for environmental problems, we know that the matter is more complex. Patterns of consumption and waste, especially in developed nations, depletion of natural resources, the absence of restrictions or safeguards in some industrial or production processes, all endanger the natural environment.

The Cairo conference will also want to give due attention to morbidity and mortality, and to the need to eliminate life-threatening diseases of every sort. While advances have been made that have resulted in an increased life span, policies must also provide for the elderly and for the contribution that they make to society in their retirement years. Society should develop policies to meet their needs for social security, health care, and active participation in the life of their community.

Migration is likewise a major concern in examining demographic data, and the international community needs to ensure that the rights of migrants are recognized and protected. In this regard, I draw special attention to the situation of migrant families. The state's task is to ensure that immigrant families do not lack what it ordinarily guarantees its own citizens as well as to protect them from any attempt at marginalization, intolerance, or racism, and to promote an attitude of convinced and active solidarity in their regard (cf. Message for World Migration Day, 1993–1994, no. 1).

10. As the preparations for the Cairo conference proceed, I wish to assure you, Madam Secretary General, that the Holy See is fully aware of the

complexity of the issues involved. This very complexity requires that we carefully weigh the consequences for the present and future generations of the strategies and recommendations to be proposed. In this context, the draft final document of the Cairo conference, which is already being circulated, is a cause of grave concern to me. Many of the principles which I have just mentioned find no place in its pages or are totally marginalized. Indeed, certain basic ethical principles are contradicted by its proposals. Political or ideological considerations cannot be, by themselves, the basis on which essential decisions for the future of our society are founded. What is at stake here is the very future of humanity. Fundamental questions like the transmission of life, the family, and the material and moral development of society need very serious consideration.

For example, the international consensus of the 1984 Mexico City International Conference on Population that "in no case should abortion be promoted as a method of family planning" is completely ignored in the draft document. Indeed, there is a tendency to promote an internationally recognized right to access to abortion on demand without any restriction, with no regard to the rights of the unborn, in a manner which goes beyond what even now is unfortunately accepted by the laws of some nations. The vision of sexuality which inspires the document is individualistic. Marriage is ignored as if it were something of the past. An institution as natural, universal, and fundamental as the family cannot be manipulated without causing serious damage to the fabric and stability of society.

The seriousness of the challenges that governments and, above all, parents must face in the education of the younger generation means that we cannot abdicate our responsibility of leading young people to a deeper understanding of their own dignity and potentiality as persons. What future do we propose to adolescents if we leave them, in their immaturity, to follow their instincts without taking into consideration the interpersonal and moral implications of their sexual behavior? Do we not have an obligation to open their eyes to the damage and suffering to which morally irresponsible sexual behavior can lead them? Is it not our task to challenge them with a demanding ethic which fully respects their dignity and which leads them to that self-control which is needed in order to face the many demands of life?

I am sure, Madam Secretary General, that in the remaining period of preparation for the Cairo conference you and your collaborators, as well as the nations which will take part in the conference itself, will devote adequate attention to deeper questions. None of the issues to be discussed is simply an economic or demographic concern, but at root each is a matter of profound moral significance with far-reaching implications. Accordingly, the Holy See's contribution will consist in providing an ethical perspective on the issues to be considered, always with the conviction that mankind's efforts to respect and conform to God's providential plan is the only way to succeed in building a world of genuine equality, unity, and peace.

May Almighty God enlighten all those taking part in the conference.

Talk given during a March 18 meeting at the Vatican with Nafis Sadik, executive director of the U.N. Fund for Population Activities. The pope criticizes a final draft document prepared for the September U.N. International Conference on Population and Development in Cairo, Egypt.

READING 15 (MAY 22, 1994): *Ordinatio Sacerdotalis* (On Ordination to the Priesthood)[1]

Venerable Brothers in the Episcopate,

1. Priestly ordination, which hands on the office entrusted by Christ to his Apostles of teaching, sanctifying and governing the faithful, has in the Catholic Church from the beginning always been reserved to men alone. This tradition has also been faithfully maintained by the Oriental Churches.

When the question of the ordination of women arose in the Anglican Communion, Pope Paul VI, out of fidelity to his office of safeguarding the Apostolic Tradition, and also with a view to removing a new obstacle placed in the way of Christian unity, reminded Anglicans of the position of the Catholic Church: "She holds that it is not admissible to ordain women to the priesthood, for very fundamental reasons. These reasons include: the example recorded in the Sacred Scriptures of Christ choosing his Apostles only from among men; the constant practice of the Church, which has imitated Christ in choosing only men; and her living teaching authority which has consistently held that the exclusion of women from the priesthood is in accordance with God's plan for his Church."

Since the question had also become the subject of debate among theologians and in certain Catholic circles, Paul VI directed the Congregation for the Doctrine of the Faith to set forth and expound the teaching of the Church on this matter. This was done through the Declaration *Inter Insigniores*, which the Supreme Pontiff approved and ordered to be published.

⇾

2. The Declaration recalls and explains the fundamental reasons for this teaching, reasons expounded by Paul VI, and concludes that the Church "does not consider herself authorized to admit women to priestly ordination." To these fundamental reasons the document adds other theological reasons which illustrate the appropriateness of the divine provision, and it also shows clearly that Christ's way of acting did not proceed from sociological or cultural motives peculiar to his time. As Paul VI later explained: "The real reason is that, in giving the Church her fundamental constitution, her theological anthropology—thereafter always followed by the Church's Tradition—Christ established things in this way."

In the Apostolic Letter *Mulieris Dignitatem*, I myself wrote in this regard: "In calling only men as his Apostles, Christ acted in a completely free and sovereign manner. In doing so, he exercised the same freedom with which, in all his behavior, he emphasized the dignity and the vocation of women, without conforming to the prevailing customs and to the traditions sanctioned by the legislation of the time."

In fact, the Gospels and the Acts of the Apostles attest that this call was made in accordance with God's eternal plan; Christ chose those whom he willed (cf. Mk 3:13-14; Jn 6:70), and he did so in union with the Father, "through the Holy Spirit" (Acts 1:2), after having spent the night in prayer (cf. Lk 6:12). Therefore, in granting admission to the ministerial priesthood, the Church has always acknowledged as a perennial norm her Lord's way of acting in choosing the twelve men whom he made the foundation of his Church (cf. Rv 21:14). These men did not in fact receive only a function which could thereafter be exercised by any member of the Church; rather they were specifically and intimately associated in the mission of the Incarnate Word himself (cf. Mt 10:1, 7-8; 28:16-20; Mk 3:13-16; 16:14-15). The Apostles did the same when they chose fellow workers who would succeed them in their ministry. Also included in this choice were those who, throughout the time of the Church, would carry on the Apostles' mission of representing Christ the Lord and Redeemer.

3. The fact that the Blessed Virgin Mary, Mother of God and Mother of the Church, received neither the mission proper to the Apostles nor the ministerial priesthood clearly shows that the non-admission of women to priestly ordination cannot mean that women are of lesser dignity, nor can it be construed as discrimination against them. Rather, it is to be seen as the faithful observance of a plan to be ascribed to the wisdom of the Lord of the universe.

The presence and the role of women in the life and mission of the Church, although not linked to the ministerial priesthood, remain absolutely necessary and irreplaceable. As the Declaration *Inter Insigniores* points out, "[T]he Church desires that Christian women should become fully aware of the greatness of their mission: today their role is of capital importance both for the renewal and humanization of society and for the rediscovery by believers of the true face of the Church."

The New Testament and the whole history of the Church give ample evidence of the presence in the Church of women, true disciples, witnesses to Christ in the family and in society, as well as in total consecration to the service of God and of the Gospel. "By defending the dignity of women and their vocation, the Church has shown honor and gratitude for those women who—faithful to the Gospel—have shared in every age in the apostolic mission of the whole People of God. They are the holy martyrs, virgins and mothers of families, who bravely bore witness to their faith and passed on the Church's faith and tradition by bringing up their children in the spirit of the Gospel."

It is to the holiness of the faithful that the hierarchical structure of the Church is totally ordered. For this reason, the Declaration *Inter Insigniores* recalls: "[T]he only better gift, which can and must be desired, is love (cf. 1 Cor 12 and 13). The greatest in the Kingdom of Heaven are not the ministers but the saints."

4. Although the teaching that priestly ordination is to be reserved to men alone has been preserved by the constant and universal Tradition of the Church and firmly taught by the Magisterium in its more recent documents, at the present time in some places it is nonetheless considered still open to debate, or the Church's judgment that women are not to be admitted to ordination is considered to have a merely disciplinary force.

Wherefore, in order that all doubt may be removed regarding a matter of great importance, a matter which pertains to the Church's divine constitution itself, in virtue of my ministry of confirming the brethren (cf. Lk 22:32) I declare that the Church has no authority whatsoever to confer priestly ordination on women and that this judgment is to be definitively held by all the Church's faithful. Invoking an abundance of divine assistance upon you, venerable brothers, and upon all the faithful, I impart my apostolic blessing.

From the Vatican, on May 22, the Solemnity of Pentecost, in the year 1994, the sixteenth of my Pontificate.

JANUARY 1995–JUNE 1995

READING 16 (JANUARY 1, 1995): Women: Teachers of Peace[1]

1. At the beginning of 1995, with my gaze fixed on the new millennium now fast approaching, I once again address to you, men and women of goodwill, a pressing appeal for peace in the world. The violence which so many individuals and peoples continue to experience, the wars which still cause bloodshed in many areas of the world, and the injustice which burdens the life of whole continents can no longer be tolerated.

The time has come to move from words to deeds: May individual citizens and families, believers and Churches, States, and International Organizations all recognize that they are called to renew their commitment to work for peace! Everyone is aware of the difficulty of this task. If it is to be effective and long-lasting, work for peace cannot be concerned merely with the external conditions of coexistence; rather, it must affect people's hearts and appeal to a new awareness of human dignity. It must be forcefully repeated: authentic peace is only possible if the dignity of the human person is promoted at every level of society and every individual is given the chance to live in accordance with this dignity. "Any human society, if it is to be well-ordered and productive, must lay down as a foundation this principle, namely, that every human being is a person, that is, his nature is endowed with intelligence and free will. Indeed, precisely because he is a person he has rights and obligations which flow directly and immediately from his very nature. And these rights and obligations are universal, inviolable and inalienable."[2]

The truth about man is the keystone in the resolution of all the problems involved in promoting peace. To teach people this truth is one of the most fruitful and lasting ways to affirm the value of peace.

Women and the Teaching of Peace

2. To educate in the ways of peace means to open minds and hearts to embrace the values which Pope John XXIII indicated in the Encyclical *Pacem in Terris* as essential to a peaceful society: truth, justice, love, and freedom. This is an educational program which involves every aspect of life and is lifelong. It trains individuals to be responsible for themselves and for others, capable of promoting, with boldness and wisdom, the welfare of the whole person and of all people, as Pope Paul VI emphasized in the Encyclical *Populorum Progressio*. The effectiveness of this education for peace will depend on the extent to which it involves the cooperation of those who, in different ways, are responsible for education and for the life of society. Time dedicated to education is time truly well spent, because it determines a person's future and therefore the future of the family and of the whole of society.

In this context, I wish to direct my Message for this year's World Day of Peace especially to women, and to invite them to become teachers of peace with their whole being and in all their actions. May they be witnesses, messengers, and teachers of peace in relations between individuals and between generations, in the family, in the cultural, social, and political life of nations, and particularly in situations of conflict and war. May they continue to follow the path which leads to peace, a path which many courageous and far-sighted women have walked before them!

In Communion of Love

3. This invitation to become teachers of peace, directed particularly to women, is based on a realization that to them God "entrusts the human being in a special way." This is not to be understood in an exclusive sense, but rather according to the logic of the complementary roles present in the common vocation to love, which calls men and women to seek peace with one accord and to work together in building it. Indeed, from the very first pages of the Bible God's plan is marvelously expressed: he willed that there should be a relationship of profound communion between man and wom-

an, in a perfect reciprocity of knowledge and of the giving of self. In woman, man finds a partner with whom he can dialogue in complete equality. This desire for dialogue, which was not satisfied by any other living creature, explains the man's spontaneous cry of wonder when the woman, according to the evocative symbolism of the Bible, was created from one of his ribs: "This at last is bone of my bones and flesh of my flesh" (Gen 2:23). This was the first cry of love to resound on the earth!

Even though man and woman are made for each other, this does not mean that God created them incomplete. God "created them to be a communion of persons, in which each can be a 'helpmate' to the other, for they are equal as persons ('bone of my bones …') and complementary as masculine and feminine." Reciprocity and complementarity are the two fundamental characteristics of the human couple.

4. Sadly, a long history of sin has disturbed and continues to disturb God's original plan for the couple, for the male and the female, thus standing in the way of its complete fulfillment. We need to return to this plan, to proclaim it forcefully, so that women in particular—who have suffered more from its failure to be fulfilled—can finally give full expression to their womanhood and their dignity.

In our day women have made great strides in this direction, attaining a remarkable degree of self-expression in cultural, social, economic, and political life, as well as, of course, in family life. The journey has been a difficult and complicated one and, at times, not without its share of mistakes, but it has been substantially a positive one, even if it is still unfinished because of the many obstacles which, in various parts of the world, still prevent women from being acknowledged, respected, and appreciated in their own special dignity. The work of building peace can hardly overlook the need to acknowledge and promote the dignity of women as persons, called to play a unique role in educating for peace. I urge everyone to reflect on the critical importance of the role of women in the family and in society, and to heed the yearning for peace which they express in words and deeds and, at times of greatest tragedy, by the silent eloquence of their grief.

Women of Peace

5. In order to be a teacher of peace, a woman must first of all nurture peace within herself. Inner peace comes from knowing that one is loved by God and from the desire to respond to his love. History is filled with marvelous examples of women who, sustained by this knowledge, have been able successfully to deal with difficult situations of exploitation, discrimination, violence, and war.

Unfortunately, many women, especially as a result of social and cultural conditioning, do not become fully aware of their dignity. Others are victims of a materialistic and hedonistic outlook which views them as mere objects of pleasure, and does not hesitate to organize the exploitation of women, even of young girls, into a despicable trade. Special concern needs to be shown for these women, particularly by other women who, thanks to their own upbringing and sensitivity, are able to help them discover their own inner worth and resources. Women need to help women, and to find support in the valuable and effective contributions which associations, movements, and groups, many of them of a religious character, have proved capable of making in this regard.

6. In rearing children, mothers have a singularly important role. Through the special relationship uniting a mother and her child, particularly in its earliest years of life, she gives the child that sense of security and trust without which the child would find it difficult to develop properly its own personal identity and, subsequently, to establish positive and fruitful relationships with others. This primary relationship between mother and child also has a very particular educational significance in the religious sphere, for it can direct the mind and heart of the child to God long before any formal religious education begins.

In this decisive and sensitive task, no mother should be left alone. Children need the presence and care of both parents, who carry out their duty as educators above all through the influence of the way they live. The quality of the relationship between the spouses has profound psychological effects on children and greatly conditions both the way they relate to their surroundings and the other relationships which they will develop throughout life.

This primary education is extremely important. If relationships with parents and other family members are marked by affectionate and positive interaction, children come to learn from their own experience the values which promote peace: love of truth and justice, a sense of responsible freedom, esteem and respect for others. At the same time, as they grow up in a warm and accepting environment, they are able to perceive, reflected in their own family relationships, the love of God himself; this will enable them to mature in a spiritual atmosphere which can foster openness to others and to the gift of self to their neighbor. Education in the ways of peace naturally continues throughout every period of development; it needs particularly to be encouraged during the difficult time of adolescence, when the passage from childhood to adulthood is not without some risks for young people, who are called to make choices which will be decisive for life.

7. Faced with the challenge of education, the family becomes "the first and fundamental school of social living," the first and fundamental school of peace. It is not difficult to imagine the tragic consequences which occur when the family experiences profound crises which undermine or even destroy its inner equilibrium. Often, in these circumstances, women are left alone. It is then, however, that they most need to be assisted, not only by the practical solidarity of other families, of communities of a religious nature, and of volunteer groups but also by the State and by International Organizations through appropriate structures of human, social, and economic support which will enable them to meet the needs of their children without being forced to deprive them unduly of their own indispensable presence.

8. Another serious problem is found in places where the intolerable custom still exists of discriminating, from the earliest years, between boys and girls. If, from the very beginning, girls are looked down upon or regarded as inferior, their sense of dignity will be gravely impaired and their healthy development inevitably compromised. Discrimination in childhood will have lifelong effects and will prevent women from fully taking part in the life of society.

In this regard, how can we fail to acknowledge and encourage the invaluable efforts of so many women, including so many congregations of women religious, who on different continents and in every cultural context make the education of girls and women the principal goal of their activity? Similarly, how can we fail to acknowledge with gratitude all those women who have worked and continue to work in providing health services, often in very precarious circumstances, and who are frequently responsible for the very survival of great numbers of female children?

Women, Teachers of Peace in Society

9. When women are able to share their gifts fully with the whole community, the very way in which society understands and organizes itself is improved and comes to reflect in a better way the substantial unity of the human family. Here we see the most important condition for the consolidation of authentic peace. The growing presence of women in social, economic, and political life at the local, national, and international levels is thus a very positive development. Women have a full right to become actively involved in all areas of public life, and this right must be affirmed and guaranteed, also, where necessary, through appropriate legislation.

This acknowledgment of the public role of women should not detract from their unique role within the family. Here their contribution to the welfare and progress of society, even if its importance is not sufficiently appreciated, is truly incalculable. In this regard, I will continue to ask that more decisive steps be taken in order to recognize and promote this very important reality.

10. With astonishment and concern we are witnessing today a dramatic increase in all kinds of violence. Not just individuals but whole groups seem to have lost any sense of respect for human life. Women and even children are unfortunately among the most frequent victims of this blind violence. We are speaking of outrageous and barbaric behavior which is deeply abhorrent to the human conscience.

We are all called upon to do everything possible to banish from society not only the tragedy of war but also every violation of human rights, beginning with the indisputable right to life, which every person enjoys from the very moment of conception. The violation of the individual human being's right to life contains the seeds of the extreme violence of war. For this reason, I appeal to all women ever to take their place on the side of life. At the same time, I urge everyone to help women who are suffering, particularly children, and in a special way those scarred by the painful trauma of having lived through war. Only loving and compassionate concern will enable them once again to look to the future with confidence and hope.

11. When my beloved predecessor Pope John XXIII indicated the participation of women in public life as one of the signs of our times, he also stated that, being aware of their dignity, they would no longer tolerate being exploited. Women have the right to insist that their dignity be respected. At the same time, they have the duty to work for the promotion of the dignity of all persons, men as well as women.

In view of this, I express the hope that the many international initiatives planned for 1995—of which some will be devoted specifically to women, such as the Conference sponsored by the United Nations in Beijing on work for equality, development, and peace—will provide a significant opportunity for making interpersonal and social relationships ever more human, under the banner of peace.

Mary, Model of Peace

12. Mary, Queen of Peace, is close to the women of our day because of her motherhood, her example of openness to others' needs, and her witness of suffering. Mary lived with a deep sense of responsibility the plan which God willed to carry out in her for the salvation of all humanity. When she was made aware of the miracle which God had worked in her by making her the Mother of his Incarnate Son, her first thought was to visit her elderly kinswoman Elizabeth in order to help her. That meeting gave Mary the chance to express, in the marvelous canticle of the *Magnificat* (Lk 1:46-55), her gratitude to God who, with her and through her, had begun a new creation, a new history.

I implore the Most Holy Virgin Mary to sustain those men and women who, in the service of life, have committed themselves to building peace. With her help, may they bear witness before all people, especially those who live in darkness and suffering and who hunger and thirst for justice, to the loving presence of the God of peace!

From the Vatican, December 8, 1994.

READING 17 (MARCH 19, 1995):
The Feminine Presence in the Family[1]

Dear Brothers and Sisters,

1. My pilgrimage today is taking place on the feast of St. Joseph, and naturally my thoughts turn to the world of work marked this year in particular by my meeting with craftsmen. How could we not think, then, of the home in Nazareth where Joseph and Mary helped each other in managing their family and caring for the child Jesus? As a carpenter, Joseph was a craftsman in the truest sense of the term. Mary, who looked after the household chores, could today be considered a housewife and, as such, the model for all those women who are true "homemakers."

2. After a period marked by a certain ideological confusion and pressure, many today are asking that the relationship between women, the family, and work be dealt more calmly and objectively, so that the feminine presence in the family can be reevaluated. "Experience confirms," I wrote in the encyclical *Laborem Exercens*, "that there must be a social reevaluation of the mother's role, of the toil connected with it, and of the need that children have for care, love and affection" (no. 19).

In this regard, too, the Family of Nazareth provides a meaningful example: Mary worked at Joseph's side in a personal, feminine manner, which the Gospel accounts allow us to glimpse. Doubtless their harmony was greatly fostered by the husband's trade; Joseph could work close to his family and introduce the young Jesus to his skilled labor as a carpenter. It is to Mary that we now wish to address our prayer, entrusting to her the hopes and anxieties of every family, especially those at risk from the problems connected with work.

3. O Mary, Mother of Jesus and spouse of Joseph the craftsman, in your heart are gathered the joys and labors of the Holy Family. You offered even your moments of pain to God, always trusting in his Providence. We beg you, protect all women who daily toil so that the domestic community can live in active harmony. Grant that they may be women of Christian wis-

dom, skilled in prayer and human kindness, strong in hope and affection, artisans, like you, of authentic peace.

Amen.

READING 18 (MARCH 25, 1995): *Evangelium Vitae* (The Gospel Life)[1]

"Walk as children of light" (Eph 5:8): Bringing about a transformation of culture.

99. In transforming culture so that it supports life, women occupy a place, in thought and action, which is unique and decisive. It depends on them to promote a "new feminism" which rejects the temptation of imitating models of "male domination" in order to acknowledge and affirm the true genius of women in every aspect of the life of society and overcome all discrimination, violence, and exploitation.

Making my own the words of the concluding message of the Second Vatican Council (Closing Message of the Council: To Women [December 8, 1965]), I address to women this urgent appeal: "Reconcile people with life." You are called to bear witness to the meaning of genuine love, of that gift of self and of that acceptance of others which are present in a special way in the relationship of husband and wife, but which ought also to be at the heart of every other interpersonal relationship. The experience of motherhood makes you acutely aware of the other person and, at the same time, confers on you a particular task (Apostolic Letter *Mulieris Dignitatem* [August 15, 1988], 18: AAS 80 [1988], 1696): "Motherhood involves a special communion with the mystery of life, as it develops in the woman's womb.... This unique contact with the new human being developing within her gives rise to an attitude towards human beings not only towards her own child, but every human being, which profoundly marks the woman's personality." A mother welcomes and carries in herself another human being, enabling it to grow inside her, giving it room, respecting it in its otherness. Women first learn and then teach others that human relations are authentic if they are open to accepting the other person: a person who is recognized and loved because of the dignity which comes from being a person and not from other considerations, such as usefulness, strength, intelligence, beauty, or health. This is the fundamental contribution which the Church and humanity expect from women, and it is the indispensable prerequisite for an authentic cultural change.

I would now like to say a special word to women who have had an abortion. The Church is aware of the many factors which may have influenced your decision, and she does not doubt that in many cases it was a painful and even shattering decision. The wound in your heart may not yet have healed.

Certainly what happened was and remains terribly wrong, but do not give in to discouragement and do not lose hope. Try rather to understand what happened and face it honestly. If you have not already done so, give yourselves over with humility and trust to repentance. The Father of mercies is ready to give you his forgiveness and his peace in the Sacrament of Reconciliation. To the same Father and his mercy you can with sure hope entrust your child. With the friendly and expert help and advice of other people, and as a result of your own painful experience, you can be among the most eloquent defenders of everyone's right to life. Through your commitment to life, whether by accepting the birth of other children or by welcoming and caring for those most in need of someone to be close to them, you will become promoters of a new way of looking at human life.

READING 19 (APRIL 7, 1995):
Letter to Priests for Holy Thursday 1995[1]

"Honor to Mary, honor and glory honor to the Blessed Virgin! (…)
He who created the marvelous world honored in her his own Mother (…).
He loved her as his Mother, he lived in obedience.
Though he was God, he respected her every word."

Dear Brother Priests!

Do not be surprised if I begin this Letter, which I traditionally address to you on Holy Thursday, with the words of a Polish Marian hymn. I do so because this year I wish to speak to you *about the importance of women in the life of the priest,* and these verses which I have sung since my childhood can serve as a meaningful introduction to this subject.

The hymn speaks of Christ's love for his Mother. The first and most basic relationship which any human being establishes with a woman is precisely the relationship of the child to its mother. Each of us can express his love for his earthly mother just as the Son of God did and still does for his. Our mother is *the woman to whom we owe our life*.

She conceived us in her womb and brought us into the world amid the pains which are part of the experience of every woman who gives birth. Through childbirth a special and almost *sacred* bond is established between a human being and his mother.

Having brought us into the world, our parents then enabled us to become in Christ, through the *Sacrament of Baptism*, adopted children of God. All this further deepened the bond between us and our parents, and in particular between us and our mothers. *The prototype here is Christ himself, Christ the Priest*, who addresses his Eternal Father in these words: "Sacrifices and offerings you have not desired, but a body you have prepared for me. In burnt offerings and sin offerings you have taken no pleasure. Then I said, 'Lo, I have come to do your will, O God'" (Heb 10:5-7). *These words in some way also involve his Mother*, since the Eternal Father formed Christ's body by the power of the Holy Spirit in the womb of the Virgin Mary, thanks also to her consent: "Let it be to me according to your word" (Lk 1:38).

How many of us also owe to our mothers our very vocation to the priesthood? Experience shows that very often it is the mother who for years nurtures in her own heart a desire for a priestly vocation for her son, and *obtains it by praying with persevering trust and deep humility*; thus, without imposing her own will, she favors with the effectiveness typical of faith the blossoming of an aspiration to the priesthood in the soul of her son, an aspiration which will bear fruit in due season.

2. In this Letter, I wish to reflect on the relationship between priests and women, taking as my point of departure the fact that *the subject of women calls for special attention this year*, just as last year the subject of the family did. In fact, the important *International Conference called by the United Nations Organization in Beijing* next September will be devoted to women. This is a new subject with respect to last year's, but closely related to it.

Dear Brothers in the priesthood, with this Letter I also wish to make reference to another document. Just as in the Holy Thursday Message of last year I referred to my Letter to Families, so this time *I would like to redirect your attention to* the Apostolic Letter *Mulieris Dignitatem*, issued on August 15, 1988. As you will recall, this text was prepared at the end of the Marian Year of 1987–1988, during which I published the Encyclical *Redemptoris Mater* (March 25, 1987). It is my fervent hope that during this year you will reread *Mulieris Dignitatem*, making it the subject of special meditation and giving particular consideration to its Marian aspects.

A link with the Mother of God is fundamental for Christian "thinking." This is true first of all on the theological level because of the very special relationship of Mary with the Incarnate Word and the Church, his Mystical Body, but it is also true on the historical, anthropological, and cultural levels. In Christianity, in fact, the figure of the Mother of God represents a great source of inspiration not only for the life of piety but also for Christian culture and even for love of country. Proofs of this exist in the history of many nations. In Poland, for example, the most ancient literary monument is the hymn *Bogurodzica* (Mother of God), which inspired our forefathers not only in shaping the life of the nation but even in defending the just cause on the battlefield. The Mother of the Son of God has become the "great inspiration" for individuals and for whole Christian nations. This, too, in its own way, *tells us much about the importance of women in human life* and, in a special way, in the life of the priest.

I have already had occasion to deal with this subject in the Encyclical *Redemptoris Mater* and in the Apostolic Letter *Mulieris Dignitatem*, where I paid homage to those women— mothers, wives, daughters, or sisters— who for their respective sons, husbands, parents, and brothers were an effective inspiration for good. Not without reason do we speak of the "feminine genius," and what I have written thus far confirms the validity of this expression. In dealing with priestly life, the presence of women has a particular character and calls for a specific analysis.

3. Meanwhile let us return to Holy Thursday, the day when the words of the liturgical hymn take on special meaning:

Ave verum Corpus natum de Maria Virgine: Vere passum, immolatum in cruce pro homine. Cuius latus perforatum fluxit aqua et sanguine: Esto nobis praegustatum mortis in examine. O Iesu dulcis! O Iesu pie! O Iesu, fili Mariae!

These words, although they do not belong to the Liturgy of Holy Thursday, are closely connected with it. The Last Supper, at which Christ instituted the sacraments of the Sacrifice and the Priesthood of the New Covenant, is the beginning of the *Triduum Paschale. At its center is the Body of Christ.* It is precisely this Body which before being subjected to suffering and death is offered at the Last Supper as food in the institution of the Eucharist. Christ takes bread in his hands, breaks it, and gives it to his Apostles with the words: "Take; eat: this is my Body" (Mt 26:26). In this way, he institutes the sacrament of his *Body, that Body which, as the Son of God, he had taken from his Mother, the Immaculate Virgin.* Then, taking the cup, he offers to the Apostles his own Blood under the species of wine, saying: "Drink of it, all of you; for this is my Blood of the covenant, which is poured out for many for the forgiveness of sins" (Mt 26:27-28).

Here, too, it is the Blood which gave life to the Body received from the Virgin Mother: Blood which had to be shed, in fulfillment of the mystery of the Redemption, in order that the Body received from his Mother could—as *Corpus immolatum in cruce pro homine*—become for us and for all mankind the sacrament of eternal life, the *viaticum* for eternity. In the *Ave verum,* which is at once a Eucharistic hymn and a Marian hymn, we ask: *Esto nobis praegustatum mortis in examine.* Even though the Holy Thursday liturgy does not speak of Mary—rather we find her on Good Friday at the foot of the Cross with the Apostle John—*it is difficult not to sense her presence at the institution of the Eucharist,* the anticipation of the Passion and Death of the Body of Christ, that Body which the Son of God had received from the Virgin Mother at the moment of the Annunciation.

For us, as priests, the Last Supper is an especially holy moment. Christ, who says to the Apostles: "Do this in remembrance of me" (1 Cor 11:24), institutes the Sacrament of Holy Orders. With respect to our lives as priests, *this is an eminently Christocentric moment:* for we receive the priesthood from Christ the priest, the one priest of the New Covenant. As we think of the sacrifice of the Body and Blood, which we offer in *persona Christi, we find it difficult not to recognize therein the presence of the Mother*. Mary gave life to the Son of God so that he might offer himself, even as our mothers gave us life, that we, too, through the priestly ministry, might offer ourselves in sacrifice together with him. Behind this mission there is the vocation received from God, but there is also hidden the great love of our mothers, just as behind the sacrifice of Christ in the Upper Room there was hidden the ineffable love of his Mother. *Oh how truly and yet how discreetly is motherhood and thus womanhood present in the Sacrament of Holy Orders* which we celebrate anew each year on Holy Thursday!

4. Christ Jesus is the *only son of Mary Most Holy*. We clearly understand the meaning of this mystery; it was fitting that he should be such: a Son so unique by reason of his divinity had to be the only son of his Virgin Mother. Precisely *this uniqueness serves in some way as the best "guarantee" of a spiritual "multiplicity."* Christ, true man and yet Eternal and Only-Begotten Son of the Heavenly Father, *has, on the spiritual plane, a countless number of brothers and sisters*. For the family of God includes everyone: not just those who through Baptism become God's adopted children but in a certain sense all mankind, since Christ has redeemed all men and all women and offered them the possibility of becoming adopted sons and daughters of the Eternal Father. Through adoption, we have all become brothers and sisters in Christ.

At this point in our reflection on the relationship between priests and women, beside the figure of the mother there emerges the figure of the *sister*. Thanks to the Redemption, the priest shares in a special way in the *relationship of brotherhood* offered by Christ to all the redeemed.

Many of us priests have sisters in our families. In any event, every priest from childhood onward has met girls, if not in his own family at least in the neighborhood, in childhood games, or at school. A type of mixed community has *enormous importance for the formation of the personalities of boys and girls*.

Here we encounter the original plan of the Creator, who in the beginning created man "male and female" (cf. Gen 1:27). This divine creative act continues from generation to generation. The Book of Genesis speaks of it in the context of the vocation to marriage: "Therefore a man leaves his father and his mother and cleaves to his wife" (Gen 2:24). The vocation to marriage obviously assumes and requires that the environment in which one lives is made up of both men and women.

In this setting, there arise not only vocations to marriage but also *vocations to the priesthood and the consecrated life*. These do not develop in isolation. Every candidate for the priesthood, when he crosses the threshold of the seminary, has behind him the experience of his own family and of school, where he was able to meet many young people of his own age, of both sexes. In order to live as a celibate in a mature and untroubled way, it seems particularly important that the priest should develop deep within himself *the image of women as sisters*. In Christ, men and women are brothers and sisters, independently of any bonds of family relationship. This is a universal bond thanks to which the priest can be open to every new situation, even the most foreign, from an ethnic or cultural standpoint, knowing that he must exercise toward the men and women to whom he is sent a ministry of authentic *spiritual fatherhood*, which gains him "sons" and "daughters" in the Lord (cf. 1 Thes 2:11, Gal 4:19).

5. Certainly "woman as sister" represents *a specific manifestation of the spiritual beauty of women*; but it is at the same time a revelation that they are in a certain sense "set apart." If the priest, with the help of divine grace and under the special protection of Mary, Virgin and Mother, gradually develops such an attitude toward women, he will see his ministry met by a sense of great trust precisely on the part of women whom he regards, in the variety of their ages and life situations, as sisters and mothers.

The figure of woman as sister has considerable importance in our Christian civilization, in which countless women have become *sisters to everyone*, thanks to their exemplary attitude toward their neighbor, especially to those most in need. *A "sister" is a guarantee of selflessness*: in the school, in the hospital, in prison, and in other areas of social service. When a woman remains single, in her "gift of self as sister" by means of apostolic commitment or generous dedication to neighbor, she develops a particular *spiritual motherhood*. This selfless gift of femininity "as sister" lights up human existence, evokes the best sentiments of which human beings are capable, and always leaves behind gratitude for the good freely offered.

The dimensions of mother and sister *are the two fundamental dimensions* of the relationship between women and priests. If this relationship develops in a serene and mature way, women will find no particular difficulties in their contact with priests. For example, they will not find difficulties in confessing their faults in the Sacrament of Penance. Even less will they encounter any in undertaking various kinds of *apostolic activities* with priests. Every priest thus has the great *responsibility of developing an authentic way of relating to women* as a *brother*, a way of relating which does not admit of ambiguity. In this perspective, Saint Paul exhorts his disciple Timothy to treat "older women like mothers, younger women like sisters, in all purity" (1 Tm 5:2).

When Christ stated—as the Evangelist Matthew writes—that *man can remain celibate for the Kingdom of God*, the Apostles were disturbed (cf. 19:10-12). A little earlier Jesus had declared that marriage is indissoluble, and this truth had caused in them a significant reaction: "If such is the case of a man with his wife, it is not expedient to marry" (Mt 19:10). As is evident, their reaction went contrary to the notion of fidelity which Jesus had in mind, but the Master makes use even of this lack of understanding, in order to introduce into their narrow and limited way of thinking the perspective of celibacy for the sake of the Kingdom of heaven. He thereby wishes to affirm that marriage has a specific dignity and sacramental holiness, and that nevertheless there exists another path for the Christian: a path which is not a flight from marriage but rather a *conscious choice of celibacy* for the sake of the Kingdom of heaven.

In view of this, women can only be sisters for the priest, and their dignity as sisters needs to be consciously fostered by him. The Apostle Paul, who lived a celibate life, writes in the First Letter to the Corinthians: "I wish that all were as I myself am. *But each one has his own special gift from God*, one of one kind and one of another" (7:7).

For him there is no doubt: marriage and celibacy are both gifts of God, to be protected and fostered with great care. While emphasizing the superiority of virginity, he does not in any way diminish the value of marriage. Each has its own specific *charism*, each of them is a *vocation* which individuals, with the help of God's grace, must learn to discern in their own lives.

The vocation to celibacy needs to be consciously protected by keeping special watch over one's feelings and over one's whole conduct. In particular, it must be protected by those priests who, following the discipline in force in the Western Church and so highly esteemed by the Eastern Church, have chosen celibacy for the sake of the Kingdom of God. If in a relationship with a woman the gift and the choice of celibacy should become endangered, the priest cannot but strive earnestly to remain faithful to his own vocation. Such a defense would not mean that marriage in itself is something bad, but that for him the path is a different one. For him to abandon that path would be to break the word he has given to God.

The Lord's prayer: "And lead us not into temptation, but deliver us from evil," takes on a specific meaning in the context of *contemporary civilization*, steeped as it is in elements of hedonism, self-centeredness, and sensuality. Pornography is unfortunately rampant, debasing the dignity of women and treating them exclusively as objects of sexual pleasure. *These aspects of present-day civilization certainly do not favor either marital fidelity or celibacy for the sake of the Kingdom of God.* Therefore if the priest does not foster in himself genuine dispositions of faith hope and love of God, he can easily yield to the allurements coming to him from the world. On this Holy Thursday, then, dear Brother Priests, how can I fail to address you in order to *exhort you to remain faithful to the gift of celibacy* which Christ has given us? In it is contained a spiritual treasure which belongs to each of us and to the whole Church.

Today our thoughts and prayers turn in a special way to *our brothers in the priesthood who meet with difficulties in this area*, and to all those who precisely because of a woman *have abandoned the priestly ministry*. Let us commend to Mary Most Holy, Mother of Priests, and to the intercession of the countless holy priests in the Church's history the difficult time which they are experiencing, and let us implore for them *the grace of a return to their first fervor* (cf. Rv 2:4-5). The experience of my own ministry, and I believe that this is true of every Bishop, confirms that such returns do occur and that even today they are not rare. God remains faithful to his covenant with man in the Sacrament of Holy Orders.

6. At this point, I would like to touch on the even wider issue of the role which women are called to play *in the building up of the Church*. The Sec-

ond Vatican Council fully grasped the logic of the Gospel, in chapters 2 and 3 of the Constitution *Lumen Gentium*, when it presented the Church first as the People of God and only afterward as a hierarchical structure. The Church is first and foremost the People of God, since all her members, men and women alike, *share*—each in his or her specific way—in the prophetic, priestly, and royal mission of Christ. While I invite you to reread those texts of the Council, I will limit myself here to some brief reflections drawn from the Gospel.

Just before his Ascension into heaven, Christ commands the Apostles: "Go into all the world and preach the Gospel to the whole creation" (Mk 16:15). To preach the Gospel is to carry out the prophetic mission which has different forms in the Church, according to the charism granted to each individual (cf. Eph 4:11-13). In that circumstance, since it was a question of the Apostles and their own particular mission, this task was entrusted to certain men, but if we read the Gospel accounts carefully, especially that of John, we cannot but be struck by the fact that the *prophetic mission*, considered in all its breadth and diversification, is *given to both men and women*. Suffice it to mention, for example, *the Samaritan woman* and a sinner, that Jesus reveals the depths of the true worship of God, who is concerned not about the place but rather about the attitude of worship "in spirit and truth."

What shall we say of *the sisters of Lazarus, Mary and Martha*? The Synoptics, speaking of the "contemplative" Mary, note the preeminence which Christ gives to contemplation over activity (cf. Lk 10:42). Still more important is what Saint John writes in the context of the raising of their brother Lazarus. In this case it is to Martha, the more "active" of the two, that Jesus reveals the profound mysteries of his mission: "I am the resurrection and the life; he who believes in me, though he dies, yet shall he live, and whoever lives and believes in me shall never die" (Jn 11:25-26). The Paschal Mystery is summed up in these words addressed to a woman.

Let us proceed in the Gospel account and enter into the Passion narrative. Is it not an incontestable fact that women were the ones closest to Christ along the way of the cross and at the hour of his death? A man, Simon of Cyrene, is forced to carry the cross (cf. Mt 27:32), but many women of Jerusalem spontaneously show him compassion along the "*via crucis*" (cf. Lk 23:27). The figure of Veronica, albeit not biblical, expresses well the feelings of the women of Jerusalem along the *via dolorosa*. Beneath the cross there is only one Apostle, John, the son of Zebedee, whereas there are several women (cf. Mt 27:55-56): the Mother of Christ who, according to tradition, had followed him on his journey to Calvary; Salome, the mother of the sons of Zebedee, John, and James; Mary, the mother of James the Less and Joseph; and Mary Magdalene.

All these women were fearless witnesses of Jesus' agony; all were present at the anointing and the laying of his body in the tomb. After his burial, as the day before the Sabbath draws to a close, they depart, but with the intention of returning as soon as it is allowed. It is they who will be the first to go to the tomb, early in the morning on the day after the feast. They will be the first witnesses of the empty tomb, and again they will be the ones to tell the Apostles (cf. Jn 20:1-2). Mary Magdalene, lingering at the tomb in tears, is the first to meet the Risen One, who sends her to the Apostles as the first herald of his Resurrection (cf. Jn 20:11-18). With good reason, the Eastern tradition places Mary Magdalene almost on a par with the Apostles since she was the first to proclaim the truth of the Resurrection, followed by the Apostles and Christ's disciples.

Women, too, together with men, have a part in the prophetic mission of Christ, and the same can be said of their sharing in his priestly and royal mission. The universal priesthood of the faithful and the royal dignity belong to both men and women. Most enlightening in this regard is a careful reading of the passages of the First Letter of St. Peter (2:9-10) and of the Conciliar Constitution *Lumen Gentium* (nn10-12; 34-36).

7. In that Dogmatic Constitution, the chapter on the People of God is followed by the one on the hierarchical structure of the Church. Here reference is made to the ministerial priesthood, to which by the will of Christ only men are admitted. Today in some quarters the fact that women cannot be ordained priests is being interpreted as a form of discrimination. Is this really the case?

Certainly, the question could be put in these terms if the hierarchical priesthood granted a social position of privilege characterized by the exercise of "power." This is not the case: the ministerial priesthood, in Christ's plan, is an expression not of *domination* but of *service*! Anyone who interpreted it as "domination" would certainly be far from the intention of Christ, who in the Upper Room began the Last Supper by washing the feet of the Apostles. In this way, he strongly emphasized the "ministerial" character of the priesthood which he instituted that very evening. "For the Son of Man came not to be served but to serve, and to give his life as a ransom for many" (Mk 10:45).

Yes, dear Brothers, the priesthood which today we recall with such veneration as our special inheritance is *a ministerial priesthood! We are at the service of the People of God! We are at the service of its mission! This priesthood of ours must guarantee the participation of everyone*—men and women alike—in the threefold prophetic, priestly, and royal mission of Christ. Not only is the Sacrament of Holy Orders ministerial: *above all else the Eucharist itself is ministerial.* When Christ affirms that "[t]his is my Body which is given for you.... This cup which is poured out for you is the new covenant in my Blood" (Lk 22:19, 20), he reveals his greatest service: *the service of the Redemption*, in which the Only Begotten and Eternal Son of God becomes the *Servant of man* in the fullest and most profound sense.

8. Beside *Christ the Servant*, we cannot forget the one who is "the Handmaid," Mary.

St. Luke tells us that, at the decisive moment of the Annunciation, the Virgin expressed her "*fiat*" in these words: "Behold, I am the handmaid of the Lord" (Lk 1:38). The relationship of priests to women as mothers and sisters is enriched, thanks to the Marian tradition, by another aspect: that of service in imitation of Mary *the Handmaid*. If the priesthood is by its nature ministerial, we must live it in union with *the Mother who is the Handmaid of the Lord*. Then our priesthood will be kept safe in her hands, indeed in her heart, and we shall be able to open it to everyone. In this way, our priesthood, in all its dimensions, will be fruitful and salvific.

May the Blessed Virgin look with special affection upon us all, her well-beloved sons, on this annual celebration of our priesthood. May she especially inspire in our hearts a burning desire for holiness. As I wrote in the Apostolic Exhortation *Pastores dabo vobis*: "The new evangelization needs new evangelizers and these are the priests who are serious about living their priesthood as a specific path towards holiness" (n82).

Holy Thursday, by taking us back to the origins of our priesthood, reminds us also of the duty to strive for holiness, to be "ministers of holiness" to the men and women entrusted to our pastoral service. In this light we see how very fitting is the suggestion put forward by the Congregation for the Clergy that every diocese should celebrate a "Day for the Sanctification of Priests" on the Feast of the Sacred Heart or on another date better suited to local needs and pastoral usage. I make this suggestion my own, and I express my hope that this day will help priests to live in ever greater conformity to the heart of the Good Shepherd.

Upon all of you I invoke the protection of Mary, Mother of the Church, Mother of Priests, and with great affection I give you my blessing.

From the Vatican, March 25, 1995, the Solemnity of the Annunciation of the Lord.

READING 20 (MAY 26, 1995): Papal Message on Women's Conference[1]

On Friday, May 26, the Holy Father met Mrs. Gertrude Mongella, secretary general of the UN Fourth World Conference on Women, to be held next September in Beijing, China. At the end of their meeting, the Pope gave Mrs. Mongella the following English-language message.

To Mrs. Gertrude Mongella, Secretary General of the Fourth World Conference on Women of the United Nations,

1. It is with genuine pleasure that I welcome you to the Vatican, at a time when you and your collaborators are engaged in preparing the United Nations Fourth World Conference on Women, to be held in Beijing in September. There, the attention of the world community will be focused on important, urgent questions regarding the dignity, the role, and the rights of women. Your visit enables me to express deep appreciation for your efforts to make the conference, on the theme of "Action for Equality, Development and Peace," the occasion for a serene and objective reflection on these vital goals, and the role of women in achieving them.

The conference has raised high expectations in large sectors of public opinion. Conscious of what is at stake for the well-being of millions of women around the world, the Holy See, as you are aware, has taken an active part in the preparatory and regional meetings leading up to the conference. In this process, the Holy See has discussed both local and global issues of particular concern to women not only with other delegations and organizations but especially with women themselves. The Holy See's delegation, which has itself consisted mostly of women, has heard with keen interest and appreciation the hopes and fears, the concerns and demands, of women all over the world.

Solutions Must be Based on Inherent Dignity of Women

2. Solutions to the issues and problems raised at the conference, if they are to be honest and permanent, cannot but be based on the *recognition of the inherent inalienable dignity of women*, and the importance of women's presence and participation in all aspects of social life. The conference's success will depend on whether or not it will offer *a true vision of women's dignity and aspirations*, a vision capable of inspiring and sustaining objective and realistic responses to the suffering, struggle, and frustration that continue to be a part of all too many women's lives.

In fact, the recognition of the dignity of every human being is the foundation and support of the concept of *universal human rights*. For believers, that dignity and the rights that stem from it are solidly grounded in the truth of the human being's creation in the image and likeness of God. The United Nations Charter refers to this dignity in the same instance as it acknowledges the equal rights of men and women (cf. Preamble, par. 2), a concept prominent in almost every international human rights instrument. If the potential and aspirations of many of the world's women are not realized, this is due in great part to the fact that their human rights, as acknowledged by these instruments, are not upheld. In this sense, the conference can sound a needed warning and call governments and organizations to work effectively to ensure the legal guarantee of women's dignity and rights.

3. As most women themselves point out, *equality of dignity* does not mean "sameness with men." This would only impoverish women and all of society, by deforming or losing the unique richness and the inherent value of femininity. In the Church's outlook, women and men have been called by the Creator to live in profound communion with one another with re-

ciprocal knowledge and giving of self, acting together for the common good with the complementary characteristics of that which is feminine and masculine.

A Unique Role in Humanizing Society

At the same time, we must not forget that at the personal level one's dignity is experienced not as a result of the affirmation of rights on the juridical and international planes but as the natural consequence of the concrete material, emotional, and spiritual care received *in the heart of one's family*. No response to women's issues can ignore women's role in the family or take lightly the fact that every new life is *totally entrusted* to the protection and care of the woman carrying it in her womb (cf. Encyclical Letter *Evangelium Vitae*, n58). In order to respect this natural order of things, it is necessary to counter the misconception that the role of motherhood is oppressive to women, and that a commitment to her family, particularly to her children, prevents a woman from reaching personal fulfillment, and women as a whole from having an influence in society. It is a disservice not only to children, but also to women and society itself, when a woman is made to feel guilty for wanting to remain in the home and nurture and care for her children. A mother's presence in the family, so critical to the stability and growth of that basic unity of society, should instead be recognized, applauded, and supported in every possible way. By the same token, society needs to *call husbands and fathers to their family responsibilities*, and ought to strive for a situation in which they will not be forced by economic circumstances to move away from the home in search of work.

4. Additionally, in today's world, when so many children are facing crises that threaten not only their long-term development but also their very life, it is imperative that the security afforded by responsible parents—mother and father—within the context of the family be reestablished and reaffirmed. Children need the positive environment of a stable family life that will ensure their development to human maturity—girls on an equal basis with boys. The Church historically has demonstrated in action, as well as in word, the importance of educating the girl-child and providing her with health care, particularly where she may not otherwise have had

these benefits. In keeping with the Church's mission and in support of the goals of the Women's Conference, Catholic institutions and organizations around the world will be encouraged to continue their care and special attention to the girl-child.

5. In this year's World Day of Peace Message, on the theme of "Women: Teachers of Peace," I wrote that the world urgently needs "to heed the yearning for peace which they [women] express in words and deeds and, at times of greatest tragedy, by the silent eloquence of their grief" (1995 World Day of Peace Message, n4). It should in fact be clear that "when women are able fully to share their gifts with the whole community, the very way in which society understands and organizes itself is improved" (n9). This is a recognition of the *unique role which women have in humanizing society* and directing it toward the positive goals of solidarity and peace.

It is far from the Holy See's intentions to try to limit the influence and activity of women in society. On the contrary, without detracting from their role in relation to the family, the Church recognizes that women's contribution to the welfare and progress of society is incalculable, and the Church looks to women to do even more to save society from the deadly virus of degradation and violence which is today witnessing a dramatic increase.

There should be no doubt that on the basis of their equal dignity with men "women have a full right to become actively involved in all areas of public life, and this right must be affirmed and guaranteed, also where necessary, through appropriate legislation" (1995 World Day of Peace Message, n9). In truth, in some societies, women have made great strides in this direction, being involved in a more decisive way, not without overcoming many obstacles in cultural, social, economic, and political life (cf. ibid., n4). This is a positive and hopeful development which the Beijing Conference can help to consolidate, in particular by calling on all countries to overcome situations which prevent women from being acknowledged, respected, and appreciated in their dignity and competence. Profound changes are needed in the attitudes and organization of society in order to facilitate the participation of women in public life, while at the same time providing for the special obligations of women and of men with regard to their families. In some cases, changes have also to be made to render it possible for women to have access to property and to the management of their assets, nor should the special difficulties and problems faced by single women living alone or those who head families be neglected.

Women Bear Hardest Burden of Abortion

6. In fact, development and progress imply access to resources and opportunities, equitable access not only between the least developed, developing, and richer countries, and between social and economic classes, but also *between women and men* (cf. Second Vatican Ecumenical Council, Constitution on the Church in the Modern World *Gaudium et Spes*, n9). Greater efforts are needed to eliminate discrimination against women in areas that include education, health care, and employment. Where certain groups or classes are systematically excluded from these goods, and where communities or countries lack basic social infrastructures and economic opportunities, women and children are the first to experience marginalization. Even so, where poverty abounds, or in the face of the devastation of conflict and war, or the tragedy of migration, forced or otherwise, it is very often women who maintain the vestiges of human dignity, defend the family, and preserve cultural and religious values. History is written almost exclusively as the narrative of men's achievements, when in fact its better part is most often molded by women's determined and persevering action for good. Elsewhere I have written about man's debt to woman in the realm of life and the defense of life (cf. Apostolic Letter *Mulieris Dignitatem*, n18). How much still needs to be said and written about man's enormous debt to woman in every other realm of social and cultural progress! The Church and human society have been, and continue to be, measurelessly enriched by the unique presence and gifts of women, especially those who have consecrated themselves to the Lord and in him have given themselves in service to others.

7. The Beijing Conference will undoubtedly draw attention to *the terrible exploitation of women and girls* which exists in every part of the world. Public opinion is only beginning to take stock of the inhuman conditions in which women and children are often forced to work, especially in less developed areas of the globe, with little or no recompense, no labor rights,

no security. What about the sexual exploitation of women and children? The trivialization of sexuality, especially in the media, and the acceptance in some societies of a sexuality without moral restraint and without accountability are deleterious above all to women, increasing the challenges that they face in sustaining their personal dignity and their service to life. In a society which follows this path, the temptation to use abortion as a so-called "solution" to the unwanted results of sexual promiscuity and irresponsibility is very strong. Here again it is the woman who bears the heaviest burden: often left alone or pressured into terminating the life of her child before it is born, she must then bear the burden of her conscience which forever reminds her that she has taken the life of her child (cf. *Mulieris Dignitatem*, n14).

A radical solidarity with women requires that the underlying causes which make a child unwanted be addressed. There will never be justice, including equality, development, and peace, for women or for men, unless there is an unfailing determination to *respect, protect, love, and serve life*—every human life, at every stage and in every situation (cf. *Evangelium Vitae*, nn5 and 87). It is well known that this is a primary concern of the Holy See, and it will be reflected in the positions taken by the Holy See delegation at the Beijing Conference.

8. The challenge facing most societies is that of upholding, indeed strengthening, woman's role in the family while at the same time making it possible for her to use all her talents and exercise all her rights in building up society. Women's greater presence in the work force, in public life, and generally in the decision-making processes guiding society, on an equal basis with men, will continue to be problematic as long as the costs continue to burden the private sector. In this area, the State has a duty of subsidiarity to be exercised through suitable legislative and social security initiatives. In the perspective of uncontrolled free-market policies, there is little hope that women will be able to overcome the obstacles on their path.

Many challenges face the Beijing Conference. We must hope that the conference will set a course that avoids the reefs of exaggerated individualism, with its accompanying moral relativism, or—on the opposite side—the reefs of social and cultural conditioning which does not permit women to become aware of their own dignity, with drastic consequences for the proper balance of society, and with continuing pain and despair on the part of so many women.

⋙

9. Madame Secretary General, it is my hope and prayer that the participants in the conference will appreciate the importance of what is to be decided there, and its implications for millions of women throughout the world. A great sensitivity is required in order to avoid the risk of prescribing action which will be far removed from the real-life needs and aspirations of women, which the conference is supposed to serve and promote. With almighty God's help may you and all involved work with enlightened mind and upright heart so that the goals of equality, development, and peace may be more fully realized.

READING 21 (JUNE 18, 1995): Culture Must Respect Femininity[1]

Dear Brothers and Sisters,

1. In the course of the Fourth World Conference on Women, organized by the United Nations in Beijing for next September, the international community will be called to reflect on a sense of problems concerning the status of women in our time. I would like to express immediately my deep appreciation of this initiative. The theme chosen is, in fact, extraordinarily important, not only for women but for the very future of the world, which depends so much on the awareness women have of themselves and on the proper recognition which should be guaranteed to them. The Church looks hopefully to all that is being done in this regard and considers it a true "sign of the times," as my venerable predecessor John XXIII pointed out in his encyclical *Pacem in Terris* (no. 22),— a "sign of the times" that highlights an aspect of the full truth about the human being which cannot be ignored.

Unfortunately, awareness of the identity and value of women has been obscured in the past—and still is today, in many cases—by various forms of conditioning. Indeed they have been and are often culpably disregarded and offended by unjust and even violent practices and behavior. All this, on the threshold of the Third Millennium, is really intolerable! As the Church joins in denouncing all injustices that weigh on women's condition, she intends to proclaim God's plan in a positive way, so that a culture may develop that respects and welcomes "femininity."

2. As I have had more than one occasion to stress, and particularly in the Apostolic Letter *Mulieris Dignitatem*, the affirmation of women's dignity must be the basis of this new culture, since she, like man and with man, is a person, that is, a creature made in the image and likeness of God (no. 6) —a creature endowed with a subjectivity from which stems her responsible autonomy in leading her own life. This subjectivity, far from isolating people and setting them in opposition, is on the contrary a source of constructive relationships and finds its fulfillment in love. Women, no less than men, are fulfilled "in a sincere giving of self" (*Gaudium et Spes*, no. 24). This subjectivity is the basis of a specific way of being for women, a way of "being feminine," which is enriching and indeed indispensable for harmonious human coexistence, both within the family and in society.

3. May the Blessed Virgin help men and women in our time clearly understand God's plan for femininity. Called to the highest vocation of divine motherhood, Our Lady is the exemplary woman who developed her authentic subjectivity to the full. May Mary obtain for women throughout the world an enlightened and active awareness of their dignity, gifts, and mission.

READING 22 (JUNE 25, 1995): Culture of Equality Is Urgently Needed Today[1]

Dear Brothers and Sisters,

1. Respect for the full equality of man and woman in every walk of life is one of civilization's great achievements. Women themselves, with their deeply felt and generous daily witness, have contributed to this, as have the organized movements which, especially in our century, have put this subject before world attention.

Unfortunately, even today there are situations in which women live, *de facto* if not legally, in a condition of inferiority. It is urgently necessary to cultivate everywhere a culture of equality which will be lasting and constructive to the extent that it reflects God's plan.

Equality between man and woman is, in fact, asserted from the first page of the Bible in the stupendous narrative of creation. The Book of Genesis says: "God created man in his own image, in the image of God he created him; male and female he created them" (Gen 1:27). In these brief lines we see the profound reason for man's grandeur: he bears the image of God imprinted on him! This is true to the same degree for male and female, both marked with the Creator's imprint.

2. This original biblical message is fully expressed in Jesus' words and deeds. In his time, women were weighed down by an inherited mentality in which they were deeply discriminated. The Lord's attitude was a "consistent *protest* against whatever offends the dignity of women" (*Mulieris Dignitatem*, n15). Indeed, he established a relationship with women which was distinguished by great freedom and friendship. Even if he did not assign the Apostles' role to them, he nevertheless made them the first witnesses of his Resurrection and utilized them in proclaiming and spreading God's kingdom. In his teaching, women truly find "their own subjectivity and dignity" (ibid., n14).

In the footprints of her divine Founder, the Church becomes the convinced bearer of this message. If down the centuries some of her children have at times not lived it with the same consistency, this is a reason for deep regret. The Gospel message about women has lost none of its timeliness. This is why I wanted to present it once again with all its richness in the Apostolic Letter *Mulieris Dignitatem*, which I published on the occasion of the Marian year.

3. One can already perceive the immense dignity of women by the sole fact that God's eternal Son chose, in the fullness of time, to be born of a woman, the Virgin of Nazareth, the mirror and measure of femininity. May Mary herself help men and women to perceive and to live the mystery dwelling within them, by mutually recognizing one another without discrimination as living "images" of God!

Once again I thank you all, Romans and pilgrims, for your presence, and I invite you to the great Solemnity of SS. Peter and Paul, which will be celebrated next Thursday in the presence of His Holiness Bartholomew, Patriarch of Constantinople.

Welcome to Rome, dear Brother from Constantinople! Praised be Jesus Christ.

INTRODUCTION TO READING 23 BY BROOKE WILLIAMS DEELY AND FR. EDWARD J. BAENZIGER, CSB

John Paul II wrote this Letter to Women on the eve of the Fourth World Congress on Women, held in Beijing by the United Nations, in 1995. In anticipation of this event, he declared 1995 the "Year of the Woman," and he dedicated over fifteen Sunday Angelus reflections to the conference theme, "Action for Equality, Development and Peace," in relation to the dignity and vocation of woman. His Letter to Women is the central missive for the purpose of opening dialogue between the Church and the United Nations in order to promote the welfare of women globally, in all areas of life. In seeking to dispel confusion or misrepresentation of the Church's stance on women, he reflects on the "problems" as well as the "promising prospects" of being a woman at this time in history.

John Paul II's letter is a missive of thanks and of love for all women. It stands out as the first papal letter written directly to women, both collectively and to every woman worldwide. He intends in this dialogue that the letter to be used for reflecting on what he emphasizes as the "full truth" about femininity (what he refers to as the "genius" of woman) in that women by nature, in dynamic relation with any given culture, are especially attuned to human relationship and thereby contribute vitally to shaping culture in the direction of the "civilization of love."

At the same time, since Christianity itself gives primacy to the spiritual order of being, so John Paul II gives primacy to love overflowing from contemplation as the innermost vocation of every human being of either gender. That is, the primacy of the spiritual transcends gender. In this letter, John Paul II calls upon woman, as unique sign of such love, to participate in society in a way that cultivates social and ethical values that are truly humane, in every walk of life, wherein women play a vital role especially in the social and ethical dimension.

In this letter, he is profoundly mindful of the relation between nature and culture that constitutes human history, wherein women need to collaborate with men in social relations that promote the common good, yet women's contributions in these relations have been screened out of written history as merely mundane daily interactions. He calls for a continued rewriting of history, one that acknowledges not only exceptional women in the written record—such as, for example, women saints, including Doctors of the Church, who offer pertinent remedies for insufficiencies within and outside of the Church—but also ordinary women's true contributions. His own vision of what constitutes human history goes far beyond the purview of the historian, in that the pope recognizes the spiritual effect of women's collaboration with men.

As pointed out in the general introduction to this volume, John Paul II is remarkably attentive in this letter to obstacles women have faced in history that have stood in the way of their own full development as persons. In this regard, he refers to particular women in particular places, whether an individual woman be married or single, rich or poor, educated or illiterate. His letter intrepidly speaks out against the long-prevailing marginalization of women, which is traceable to the presuppositions of a patriarchal mindset. He speaks of the pressing need to redress any practice that continues to marginalize women in exploitive ways as objects rather than as human subjects who are inherently equal to men in human nature, as the teaching of Jesus exemplifies.

In reflecting in this letter on both mistakes and true gains of the "women's liberation" movement, John Paul II envisions a future that enables women to embrace motherhood, rather than reject it, with the needed support of society. A specific concern of John Paul II, in the context of the Beijing Conference, is that the potential realization of the equal rights of women be in consonance with the Universal Declaration of Human Rights, including the sanctioning of the family as "the natural and fundamental group unit of society" to be protected by society and the State. In standing his ground against a shifting paradigm of human rights that would bring into opposition motherhood and citizenship rather than publically support women's roles in child-raising, John Paul II takes a definitive stance: universal human rights, based upon the inalienable dignity of the person, include both women's rights in the public sphere and the protection of life and family in the private sphere.

Although the purpose of the Beijing Conference was to promote the status of women worldwide in order to allow for full and equal participation in culture, a UN conference held the year before in Cairo proved to be a disastrous meeting that denigrated marriage and motherhood as being impediments to women's well-being. The United States' delegation had aggressively championed contraception and abortion, even to the complete denial of some components of the fundamental Declaration of Human Rights. There was some hope that the Beijing Conference would avoid the widespread denial of marriage, motherhood, and family as goods in themselves. Alas, such was not quite the case. Even though John Paul's letter had no dramatic effect on the general assemblies and even less effect on the working groups, his letter and Third-World repugnance about Cairo helped avoid more dire consequences, especially when joined with the valiant and concerted labor of the Vatican delegates headed by Mary Ann Glendon, the Learned Hand Professor of Law at Harvard University. She reported that the end of the conference was "mixed," in relation to consonance with Catholic teachings in the context of universal human rights. Surely many provisions, such as, for one vital example, championing women's equal access to education, are promising for the future human good and for women at all levels of society. She pointed out that John Paul II seeks to build on what is sound in human enterprises—such as progress toward women's liberation—while at the same time recognizing and addressing error in the sense of what is likely to counter the true human good of both women and men.

Indeed, John Paul II moves in the direction of a true integral humanism grounded in universal human rights. The results of John Paul II's papal letter are being felt throughout the world, and not only in Catholic circles, because the letter deals with the truth in a resolute, straightforward fashion.

Fr. Edward J. Baenziger, CSB, is a past director of the Women, Culture and Society Program (2007–2009), succeeded in the position by Brooke Williams Deely. He teaches French and Honors at the University of St. Thomas.

READING 23 (JUNE 29, 1995): Letter to Women[1]

I greet you all most cordially, women throughout the world!

1. I am writing this letter to each one of you as a sign of solidarity and gratitude on the eve of the Fourth World Conference on Women, to be held in Beijing this coming September.

Before all else, I wish to express my *deep appreciation* to the United Nations Organization for having sponsored this very significant event. The Church desires for her part to contribute to upholding the dignity, role, and rights of women, not only by the specific work of the Holy See's official delegation to the conference in Beijing but also by speaking directly to the heart and mind of every woman. Recently, when Mrs. Gertrude Mongella, the Secretary General of the conference, visited me in connection with the Beijing meeting, I gave her a written message which stated some basic points of the Church's teaching with regard to women's issues. That message, apart from the specific circumstances of its origin, was concerned with a broader vision of the situation and problems of *women in general*, in an attempt to promote the *cause* of women in the Church and in today's world. For this reason, I arranged to have it forwarded to every Conference of Bishops, so that it could be circulated as widely as possible.

Taking up the themes I addressed in that document, I would now like to *speak directly to every woman*, to reflect with her on the problems and the prospects of what it means to be a woman in our time. In particular, I wish to consider the essential issue of the dignity and rights of women, as seen in the light of the word of God.

This "dialogue" really needs to begin with a word of thanks. As I wrote in my Apostolic Letter *Mulieris Dignitatem*, the Church "desires to give thanks to the Most Holy Trinity for the 'mystery of woman and for every woman—for all that constitutes the eternal measure of her feminine dignity, for the 'great works of God', which throughout human history have been accomplished in and through her" (no. 31).

2. This word of thanks to the Lord for his mysterious plan regarding the vocation and mission of women in the world is at the same time a concrete

and direct word of thanks to women, to every woman, for all that they represent in the life of humanity.

Thank you, *women who are mothers!* You have sheltered human beings within yourselves in a unique experience of joy and travail. This experience makes you become God's own smile upon the newborn child, the one who guides your child's first steps, who helps it to grow, and who is the anchor as the child makes its way along the journey of life.

Thank you, *women who are wives!* You irrevocably join your future to that of your husbands, in a relationship of mutual giving, at the service of love and life.

Thank you, women who are daughters and *women who are sisters!* Into the heart of the family, and then of all society, you bring the richness of your sensitivity, your intuitiveness, your generosity and fidelity.

Thank you, *women who work!* You are present and active in every area of life—social, economic, cultural, artistic, and political. In this way, you make an indispensable contribution to the growth of a culture which unites reason and feeling, to a model of life ever open to the sense of "mystery," to the establishment of economic and political structures ever more worthy of humanity.

Thank you, *consecrated women!* Following the example of the greatest of women, the Mother of Jesus Christ, the Incarnate Word, you open yourselves with obedience and fidelity to the gift of God's love. You help the Church and all mankind to experience a "spousal" relationship to God, one which magnificently expresses the fellowship which God wishes to establish with his creatures.

Thank you, *every woman*, for the simple fact of *being a woman!* Through the insight which is so much a part of your womanhood you enrich the world's understanding and help to make human relations more honest and authentic.

3. I know, of course, that simply saying thank you is not enough. Unfortunately, we are heirs to a history which has *conditioned* us to a remarkable extent. In every time and place, this conditioning has been an obstacle to the progress of women. Women's dignity has often been unacknowledged and their prerogatives misrepresented; they have often been relegated to

the margins of society and even reduced to servitude. This has prevented women from truly being themselves, and it has resulted in a spiritual impoverishment of humanity. Certainly it is no easy task to assign the blame for this, considering the many kinds of cultural conditioning which down the centuries have shaped ways of thinking and acting. If objective blame, especially in particular historical contexts, has belonged to not just a few members of the Church, for this I am truly sorry. May this regret be transformed, on the part of the whole Church, into a renewed commitment of fidelity to the Gospel vision. When it comes to setting women free from every kind of exploitation and domination, the Gospel contains an ever-relevant message which goes back to the *attitude of Jesus Christ himself.* Transcending the established norms of his own culture, Jesus treated women with openness, respect, acceptance, and tenderness. In this way, he honored the dignity which women have always possessed according to God's plan and in his love. As we look to Christ at the end of this Second Millennium, it is natural to ask ourselves: how much of his message has been heard and acted upon?

Yes, it is time to *examine the past with courage*, to assign responsibility where it is due in a review of the long history of humanity. Women have contributed to that history as much as men and, more often than not, they did so in much more difficult conditions. I think particularly of those women who loved culture and art and devoted their lives to them in spite of the fact that they were frequently at a disadvantage from the start, excluded from equal educational opportunities, underestimated, ignored, and not given credit for their intellectual contributions. Sadly, very little of women's achievements in history can be registered by the science of history. Even though time may have buried the documentary evidence of those achievements, their beneficent influence can be felt as a force which has shaped the lives of successive generations, right up to our own. To this great, immense feminine "tradition" humanity owes a debt which can never be repaid. How many women have been and continue to be valued more for their physical appearance than for their skill, their professionalism, their intellectual abilities, their deep sensitivity; in a word, the very dignity of their being!

4. What shall we say of the obstacles which in so many parts of the world still keep women from being fully integrated into social, political, and economic life? We need only think of how the gift of motherhood is often penalized rather than rewarded, even though humanity owes its very survival to this gift. Certainly, much remains to be done to prevent discrimination against those who have chosen to be wives and mothers. As far as personal rights are concerned, there is an urgent need to achieve *real equality* in every area: equal pay for equal work, protection for working mothers, fairness in career advancements, equality of spouses with regard to family rights, and the recognition of everything that is part of the rights and duties of citizens in a democratic State.

This is a matter of justice but also of necessity. Women will increasingly play a part in the solution of the serious problems of the future: leisure time, the quality of life, migration, social services, euthanasia, drugs, health care, the ecology, etc. In all these areas a greater presence of women in society will prove most valuable, for it will help to manifest the contradictions present when society is organized solely according to the criteria of efficiency and productivity, and it will force systems to be redesigned in a way which favors the processes of humanization which mark the "civilization of love."

5. Then, too, when we look at one of the most sensitive aspects of the situation of women in the world, how can we not mention the long and degrading history, albeit often an "underground" history, of violence against women in the area of sexuality? At the threshold of the Third Millennium, we cannot remain indifferent and resigned before this phenomenon. The time has come to condemn vigorously the types of *sexual violence* which frequently have women for their object and to pass laws which effectively defend them from such violence, nor can we fail, in the name of the respect owed to the human person, to condemn the widespread hedonistic and commercial culture which encourages the systematic exploitation of sexuality and corrupts even very young girls into letting their bodies be used for profit.

In contrast to these sorts of perversion, what great appreciation must be shown to those women who, with a heroic love for the child they have conceived, proceed with a pregnancy resulting from the injustice of rape. Here we are thinking of atrocities perpetrated not only in situations of war, still so common in the world, but also in societies which are blessed by prosperity and peace and yet are often corrupted by a culture of hedonistic permissiveness which aggravates tendencies to aggressive male behavior. In these cases, the choice to have an abortion always remains a grave sin. Before being something to blame on the woman, it is a crime for which guilt needs to be attributed to men and to the complicity of the general social environment.

6. My word of thanks to women thus becomes a *heartfelt appeal* that everyone, and in a special way States and international institutions, should make every effort to ensure that women regain full respect for their dignity and role. Here I cannot fail to express my admiration for those women of good will who have devoted their lives to defending the dignity of womanhood by fighting for their basic social, economic, and political rights, demonstrating courageous initiative at a time when this was considered extremely inappropriate, the sign of a lack of femininity, a manifestation of exhibitionism, and even a sin!

In this year's World Day of Peace Message, I noted that when one looks at the great process of women's liberation, "the journey has been a difficult and complicated one and, at times, not without its share of mistakes, but it has been substantially a positive one, even if it is still unfinished, because of the many obstacles which, in various parts of the world, still prevent women from being acknowledged, respected, and appreciated in their own special dignity" (no. 4).

This journey must continue! I am convinced that the secret of making speedy progress in achieving full respect for women and their identity involves more than simply the condemnation of discrimination and injustices, necessary though this may be. Such respect must first and foremost be won through an effective and intelligent *campaign for the promotion of women*, concentrating on all areas of women's life and beginning with a *universal recognition of the dignity of women*. Our ability to recognize this dignity, in spite of historical conditioning, comes from the use of reason itself, which is able to understand the law of God written in the heart of every human being. More than anything else, the word of God enables us to grasp clearly the ultimate *anthropological basis* of the dignity of women, making it evident as a part of God's plan for humanity.

7. Dear sisters, together let us reflect anew on the magnificent passage in Scripture which describes the creation of the human race and which has so much to say about your dignity and mission in the world.

The Book of Genesis speaks of creation in summary fashion, in language which is poetic and symbolic yet profoundly true: "God created man in his own image, in the image of God he created him; *male and female he created them*" (Gen 1:27). The creative act of God takes place according to a precise plan. First of all, we are told that the human being is created "in the image and likeness of God" (cf. Gen 1:26). This expression immediately makes clear *what is distinct about the human being with regard to the rest of creation.*

We are then told that, from the very beginning, man has been created "male and female" (Gen 1:27). Scripture itself provides the interpretation of this fact: even though man is surrounded by the innumerable creatures of the created world, he realizes that *he is alone* (cf. Gen 2:20). God intervenes in order to help him escape from this situation of solitude: "*It is not good that the man should be alone; I will make him a helper fit for him*" (Gen 2:18). The creation of woman is thus marked from the outset by the principle of help: a help which is not one-sided but *mutual.* Woman complements man, just as man complements woman: men and women are *complementary.* Womanhood expresses the "human" as much as manhood does, but in a different and complementary way.

When the Book of Genesis speaks of "help," it is not referring merely to acting but also to being. Womanhood and manhood are complementary *not only from the physical and psychological points of view* but also from the *ontological.* It is only through the duality of the "masculine" and the "feminine" that the "human" finds full realization.

8. After creating man male and female, God says to both: "*Fill the earth and subdue it*" (Gen 1:28). Not only does he give them the power to procreate as a means of perpetuating the human species throughout time, but *he*

also gives them the earth, charging them with the responsible use of its resources. As a rational and free being, man is called to transform the face of the earth. In this task—which is essentially that of culture—*man and woman alike* share equal responsibility from the start. In their fruitful relationship as husband and wife, in their common task of exercising dominion over the earth, woman and man are marked neither by a static and undifferentiated equality nor by an irreconcilable and inexorably conflictual difference. Their most natural relationship, which corresponds to the plan of God, is the "unity of the two," a relational "uni-duality" which enables each to experience their interpersonal and reciprocal relationship as a gift which enriches and which confers responsibility.

To this "unity of the two," God has entrusted not only the work of procreation and family life but the creation of history itself. While the 1994 International Year of the Family focused attention on *women as mothers*, the Beijing Conference, which has as its theme "Action for Equality, Development and Peace," provides an auspicious occasion for heightening awareness of the many contributions made by women to the life of whole societies and nations. This contribution is primarily spiritual and cultural in nature, but sociopolitical and economic as well. The various sectors of society, nations and states, and the progress of all humanity are certainly deeply indebted to the contribution of women!

9. Progress usually tends to be measured according to the criteria of science and technology. Nor from this point of view has the contribution of women been negligible. Even so, this is not the only measure of progress, nor in fact is it the principal one. Much more important is *the social and ethical dimension*, which deals with human relations and spiritual values. In this area, which often develops in an inconspicuous way beginning with the daily relationships between people, especially within the family, society certainly owes much to the "*genius of women*."

Here I would like to express particular appreciation to those women who are involved in the various *areas of education* extending well beyond the family: nurseries, schools, universities, social service agencies, parishes, associations, and movements. Wherever the work of education is called for, we can note that women are ever ready and willing to give themselves generously to others, especially in serving the weakest and most defenseless. In this work, they exhibit a kind of *affective, cultural, and spiritual motherhood* which has inestimable value for the development of individuals and the future of society. At this point, how can I fail to mention the witness of so many Catholic women and religious congregations of women from every continent who have made education, particularly the education of boys and girls, their principal apostolate? How can I not think with gratitude of all the women who have worked and continue to work in the area of health care, not only in highly organized institutions but also in very precarious circumstances, in the poorest countries of the world, thus demonstrating a spirit of service which not infrequently borders on martyrdom?

10. It is thus my hope, dear sisters, that you will reflect carefully on what it means to speak of the "*genius of women*," not only in order to be able to see in this phrase a specific part of God's plan which needs to be accepted and appreciated but also in order to let this genius be more fully expressed in the life of society as a whole, as well as in the life of the Church. This subject came up frequently during the Marian Year and I myself dwelt on it at length in my Apostolic Letter *Mulieris Dignitatem* (1988). In addition, this year in the Letter which I customarily send to priests for Holy Thursday I invited them to reread *Mulieris Dignitatem* and reflect on the important roles which women have played in their lives as mothers, sisters, and coworkers in the apostolate. This is another aspect— different from the conjugal aspect, but also important—of that "help" which women, according to the Book of Genesis, are called to give to men.

The Church sees in Mary the highest expression of the "feminine genius" and she finds in her a source of constant inspiration. Mary called herself the "handmaid of the Lord" (Lk 1:38). Through obedience to the Word of God she accepted her lofty yet not easy vocation as wife and mother in the family of Nazareth. Putting herself at God's service, she also put herself at the service of others: a *service of love.* Precisely through this service Mary was able to experience in her life a mysterious but authentic "reign." It is not by chance that she is invoked as "Queen of heaven and earth." The entire community of believers thus invokes her; many nations and peoples call upon her as their "Queen." *For her, "to reign" is to serve! Her service is "to reign"!*

This is the way in which authority needs to be understood, both in the family and in society and the Church. Each person's fundamental vocation is revealed in this "reigning," for each person has been created in the "image" of the One who is Lord of heaven and earth and called to be his adopted son or daughter in Christ. Man is the only creature on earth "which God willed for its own sake," as the Second Vatican Council teaches; it significantly adds that man "cannot fully find himself except through a sincere gift of self" (*Gaudium et Spes*, 24).

The maternal "reign" of Mary consists in this. She who was, in all her being, a gift for her Son, *has also become a gift for the sons and daughters of the whole human race*, awakening profound trust in those who seek her guidance along the difficult paths of life on the way to their definitive and transcendent destiny. Each one reaches this final goal by fidelity to his or her own vocation; this goal provides meaning and direction for the earthly labors of men and women alike.

11. In this perspective of "service"—which when it is carried out with freedom, reciprocity, and love expresses the truly "royal" nature of mankind—one can also appreciate that the presence of *a certain diversity of roles* is in no way prejudicial to women, provided that this diversity is not the result of an arbitrary imposition but is rather an expression of what is specific to being male and female. This issue also has a particular application within the Church. If Christ—by his free and sovereign choice is clearly attested to by the Gospel and by the Church's constant Tradition—entrusted only to men the task of being an *"icon" of his countenance as "shepherd" and "bridegroom" of the Church through the exercise of the ministerial priesthood*, this in no way detracts from the role of women, or for that matter from the role of the other members of the Church who are not ordained to the sacred ministry, since all share equally in the dignity proper to the "*common priesthood*" based on Baptism. These role distinctions should not be viewed in accordance with the criteria of functionality typical in human societies. Rather they must be understood according to the particular criteria of the *sacramental economy* (i.e., the economy of "signs" which God freely chooses in order to become present in the midst of humanity).

Precisely in line with this economy of signs, even if apart from the sacramental sphere, there is great significance to that "womanhood" which was lived in such a sublime way by Mary. In fact, there is present in the "womanhood" of a woman who believes, and especially in a woman who is "consecrated," a kind of inherent "prophecy" (cf. *Mulieris Dignitatem* 29), a powerfully evocative symbolism, a highly significant "iconic character," which finds its full realization in Mary and which also aptly expresses the very essence of the Church as a community consecrated with the integrity of a "*virgin*" heart to become the "*bride*" of Christ and "*mother*" of believers. When we consider the "iconic" complementarity of male and female roles, two of the Church's essential dimensions are seen in a clearer light: the "Marian" principle and the Apostolic-Petrine principle (cf. ibid., 27).

On the other hand—as I wrote to priests in this year's Holy Thursday Letter—the ministerial priesthood, according to Christ's plan, "is an expression not of domination but of service" (no. 7). The Church urgently needs, in her daily self-renewal in the light of the Word of God, to emphasize this fact ever more clearly, both by developing the spirit of communion and by carefully fostering all those means of participation which are properly hers, and also by showing respect for and promoting the diverse personal and communal charisms which the Spirit of God bestows for the building up of the Christian community and the service of humanity.

In this vast domain of service, the Church's two-thousand-year history, for all its historical conditioning, has truly experienced the "genius of woman"; from the heart of the Church there have emerged women of the highest caliber who have left an impressive and beneficial mark in history. I think of the great line of woman martyrs, saints, and famous mystics. In a particular way, I think of Saint Catherine of Siena and of Saint Teresa of Avila, whom Pope Paul VI of happy memory granted the title of Doctors of the Church. How can we overlook the many women, inspired by faith, who were responsible for initiatives of extraordinary social importance, especially in serving the poorest of the poor? The life of the Church in the Third Millennium will certainly not be lacking in new and surprising manifestations of "the feminine genius."

12. You can see then, dear sisters, that the Church has many reasons for hoping that the forthcoming United Nations Conference in Beijing *will bring out the full truth about women*. Necessary emphasis should be placed on the "*genius of women,*" not only by considering great and famous women of the past or present but also those *ordinary* women who reveal the gift of their womanhood by placing themselves at the service of others in their everyday lives. For in giving themselves to others each day women fulfill their deepest vocation. Perhaps more than men, women *acknowledge the person*, because they see persons with their hearts. They see them independently of various ideological or political systems. They see others in their greatness and limitations; they try to go out to them and *help them*. In this way, the basic plan of the Creator takes flesh in the history of humanity and there is constantly revealed, in the variety of vocations, that beauty—not merely physical but above all spiritual—which God bestowed from the very beginning on all, and in a particular way on women.

While I commend to the Lord in prayer the success of the important meeting in Beijing, I invite ecclesial communities to make this year an occasion of heartfelt thanksgiving to the Creator and Redeemer of the world for the gift of *this great treasure* which is womanhood. In all its expressions, womanhood is part of the essential heritage of mankind and of the Church herself.

May Mary, Queen of Love, watch over women and their mission in service of humanity, of peace, of the spread of God's Kingdom!

With my Blessing. From the Vatican, June 29, 1995, the Solemnity of Saints Peter and Paul.

JULY 1995–SEPTEMBER 1995

READING 24 (JULY 9, 1995): Men and Women Must Live for the Other[1]

Dear Brothers and Sisters,

1. Tomorrow my Letter to Women will be published. In it I have wished to address all the women of the world, directly and almost confidentially, to express to them the Church's esteem and gratitude, and at the same time to propose once again the main lines of the Gospel message concerning them. Today, continuing the topic I began a few Sundays ago, I wish particularly to reflect on the "complementarity and reciprocity" which mark the relationship between the persons of the two sexes.

In the biblical account of creation, we read that after creating man God took pity on his loneliness and decided to give him "a helper fit for him" (Gen 2:18), but no creature was able to fill this void. Only when the woman taken from his own body was presented to him could the man express his deep and joyful amazement, recognizing her as "flesh of [his] flesh and bone of [his] bones" (Gen 2:23).

In the vivid symbolism of this narrative, the difference between the sexes is interpreted in a deeply unitive key: it is, in fact, a question of the "one human being" who exists in two distinct and complementary forms: the "male" and the "female." Precisely because the woman is different from the man, nevertheless putting herself at the same level, she can really be his "helper." On the other hand, the help is anything but unilateral: the woman is "a helper" for the man, just as the man is a "helper" for the woman!

2. This complementarity and reciprocity emerges in every context of coexistence. "In the 'unity of the two,'" I wrote in my Apostolic Letter *Mulieris Dignitatem*, "man and woman are called from the beginning not only to exist 'side by side' or 'together', but they are also called to exist mutually 'one for the other'" (n7).

The most intense expression of this reciprocity is found in the "spousal encounter" in which the man and the woman live in a relationship which is strongly marked by biological complementarity, but which, at the same time, "goes far beyond biology." Sexuality, in fact, reaches the deep structures of the human being, and the nuptial encounter, far from being reduced to the satisfaction of a blind instinct, becomes a language through which the "deep union of the two persons, male and female," is expressed. They give themselves to one another and in this intimacy, precisely to express the total and definitive communion of their persons, they make themselves at the same time the responsible coworkers of God in the gift of life.

3. We ask the Blessed Virgin to help us to be aware of the beauty of God's plan. In the special mission entrusted to her, Mary brought all her feminine richness, first to the family of Nazareth and later to the first community of believers. May the men and women of our time learn from her the joy of being fully themselves, establishing mutual relations of respectful and genuine love.

READING 25 (JULY 16, 1995): The Vocation to Motherhood[1]

Dear Brothers and Sisters,

1. Today, too, in this splendid place in the mountains, I would like to continue the talks I have been developing over the past few weeks. The fact can never be sufficiently stressed that woman must be appreciated in every area of her life; it must be recognized, however, that, among the gifts and tasks proper to her, her vocation to motherhood stands out particularly clearly.

With this gift woman assumes almost a "foundational" role with regard to society. It is a role she shares with her husband, but it is indisputable that nature has assigned to her the greater part. I wrote about this in *Mulieris Dignitatem*: "Parenthood—even though it belongs to both—is realized much more fully in the woman, especially in the prenatal period. It is the woman who pays directly for this shared generation, which literally absorbs the energies of her body and soul. It is therefore necessary that the man be fully aware that in their shared parenthood he owes a special debt to the woman" (n18).

Woman's singular relationship with human life derives from her vocation to motherhood. Opening herself to motherhood, she feels the life in her womb unfolding and growing. This indescribable experience is a privilege of mothers, but all women have in some way an intuition of it, predisposed as they are to this miraculous gift.

2. The maternal mission is also the basis of a particular responsibility. The mother is appointed guardian of life. It is her task to accept it with care, encouraging the human being's first dialogue with the world, which is carried out precisely in the symbiosis with the mother's body. It is here that the history of every human being begins. Each one of us, retracing this history, cannot fail to reach that moment when he began to exist within his mother's body, with an exclusive and unmistakable plan of life. We were "in" our mother, but without being confused with her: in need of her body and her love but fully autonomous in our personal identity.

The woman is called to offer the best of herself to the baby growing within her. It is precisely by making herself "gift" that she comes to know herself better and is fulfilled in her femininity. One could say that the fragility of her creature demands the best of her emotional and spiritual resources. It is a real exchange of gifts! The success of this exchange is of inestimable value for the child's serene growth.

3. Mary, whom we invoke today under the title of Our Lady of Mount Carmel, experienced this to the full, having received the task of generating, in time, the eternal Son of God. In her the vocation to motherhood reached the summit of its dignity and potential. May the Blessed Virgin help women to be ever more aware of their mission and encourage the whole of society to express every possible form of gratitude and active closeness to mothers!

READING 26 (JULY 23, 1995): Society and Church Need Genius of Woman[1]

Dear Brothers and Sisters,

1. It is a "sign of the times" that woman's role is increasingly recognized, not only in the family circle but also in the wider context of all social activities. Without the contribution of women, society is less alive, culture impoverished, and peace less stable. Situations where women are prevented from developing their full potential and from offering the wealth of their gifts should therefore be considered profoundly unjust, not only to women themselves but to society as a whole.

Of course, the employment of women outside the family, especially during the period when they are fulfilling the most delicate tasks of motherhood, must be done with respect for this fundamental duty. Apart from this requirement, it is necessary to strive convincingly to ensure that the widest possible space is open to women in all areas of culture, economics, politics, and ecclesial life itself, so that all human society is increasingly enriched by the gifts proper to masculinity and femininity.

2. In fact, woman has a genius all her own, which is vitally essential to both society and the Church. It is certainly not a question of comparing woman to man, since it is obvious that they have fundamental dimensions and values in common; however, in man and in woman these acquire different strengths, interests, and emphases, and it is this very diversity which becomes a source of enrichment.

In *Mulieris Dignitatem*, I highlighted one aspect of feminine genius that I would like to stress today: Woman is endowed with a particular capacity for accepting the human being in his concrete form (cf. n18). Even this singular feature which prepares her for motherhood, not only physically but also emotionally and spiritually, is inherent in the plan of God who entrusted the human being to woman in an altogether special way (cf. ibid, n30). The woman, of course, as much as the man, must take care that her sensitivity does not succumb to the temptation to possessive selfishness and must put it at the service of authentic love. On these conditions she gives of her best, everywhere adding a touch of generosity, tenderness, and joy of life.

3. Let us look at the Blessed Virgin's example. In the narrative of the wedding at Cana, John's Gospel offers us a vivid detail of her personality when it tells how, in the busy atmosphere of a wedding feast, she alone realized that the wine was about to run out. To avoid the spouses' joy becoming embarrassment and awkwardness, she did not hesitate to ask Jesus for his first miracle. This is the "genius" of the woman! May Mary's thoughtful sensitivity, totally feminine and maternal, be the ideal mirror of all true femininity and motherhood!

READING 27 (JULY 30, 1995): Initial Education in Family Relies on "Feminine Genius"[1]

Dear Brothers and Sisters,

1. In the message which last May 26 I addressed to Mrs. Gertrude Mongella, Secretary General of the forthcoming Beijing Conference, I made the observation that, because of a new appreciation of woman's role in society, it would be appropriate to rewrite history in a less one-sided way. Unfortunately, a certain way of writing history has paid greater attention to extraordinary and sensational events than to the daily rhythm of life, and the resulting history is almost only concerned with the achievements of men. This tendency should be reversed. "How much still needs to be said and written about man's enormous debt to woman in every other realm of social and cultural progress!" (ibid., n6; *L'Osservatore Romano*, English edition, May 31, 1995). With the intention of helping to fill this gap, I would like to speak on behalf of the Church and to pay homage to the manifold, immense, although frequently silent, contribution of women in every area of human life.

2. Today in particular, I would like to call to mind woman as teacher. It is an extremely positive fact that in countries where the school system is more developed, the presence of women teachers is constantly increasing. We can, of course, hope that this greater involvement of women in education will lead to a qualitative leap in the educational process itself. It is a well-founded hope, if one considers the deep meaning of education, which

cannot be reduced to the dry imparting of concepts but must aim at the full growth of man in all his dimensions. In this respect, how can we fail to understand the importance of the "feminine genius"? It is also indispensable for the initial education in the family. Its "educational" effect on the child begins when he is still in his mother's womb.

Woman's role in the rest of the formational process is just as important. She has a unique capacity to see the person as an individual, to understand his aspirations and needs with special insight, and she is able to face up to problems with deep involvement. The universal values themselves, which any sound education must always present, are offered by feminine sensitivity in a tone complementary to that of man. The whole educational process will certainly be enriched when men and women work together in training projects and institutions.

3. May the Holy Virgin guide this rediscovery of the feminine mission in the field of education. Mary had a unique relationship with her divine Son: on the one hand she was a docile disciple, meditating on his words in the depths of her heart; on the other, as his mother and teacher, she helped his human nature to grow "in wisdom and in stature, and in favor with God and man" (Lk 2:52). May the women and men who work in the field of education and are committed to building man's future look to her!

READING 28 (AUGUST 6, 1995): Culture Needs Women's Genius[1]

Dear Brothers and Sisters,

1. Today I would like to introduce our reflection on woman's role, a reflection accompanying us during the weeks of preparation for the Beijing meeting, with a mention of the Servant of God, Paul VI, who died here in Castel Gandolfo exactly seventeen years ago.

Speaking of Maria Montessori in 1970, on the occasion of the centenary of her birth, he remarked that the secret of her success, in a certain sense the very origin of her scientific merits, should be sought in her soul or in that spiritual sensitivity and feminine outlook which enabled her to make the "vital discovery" of the child and led her to conceive of an original form of education on this basis (cf. *Insegnamenti di Paolo VI*, VIII [1970], 88). The name of Montessori is clearly representative of all women who have made important contributions to cultural progress.

Unfortunately, in looking objectively at historical reality, we are compelled to notice with regret that, even at this level, women have suffered the effects of systematic marginalization. For too long their opportunities for expression outside the family have been denied or restricted, and the women who, despite being thus penalized, succeeded in asserting themselves have had to be very enterprising.

2. It is time, therefore, to close the gap between the cultural opportunities for men and women. I deeply hope that the forthcoming Beijing Conference will provide a decisive impetus in this direction.

This will benefit not only women but culture itself, since the vast and variegated world of thought and art has a greater need of their "genius" than ever. Let this not seem a gratuitous assertion! Cultural activity calls into question the human person as a whole, in the twofold complementary sensitivity of man and woman.

This is always important, but especially when the ultimate questions about life are at stake. Who is man? What is his destiny? What is the meaning of life? These decisive questions do not find a satisfactory answer in the laboratories of positive science, but they profoundly challenge man and require, so to speak, a "global thinking" that can harmonize with the sphere of mystery. To this end, how could the contribution of the feminine mind be undervalued? Women's increasingly qualified entrance, not only as beneficiaries but also as protagonists, into the world of culture in all its branches—from philosophy to theology, from the social to the natural sciences, from the figurative arts to music—is a very hopeful sign for humanity.

3. Let us turn our gaze trustingly to the Blessed Virgin. Like the other women of her time, she bore the burden of an age when little room was allowed them, yet the Son of God did not hesitate, in some ways, to learn from her! May Mary obtain for all the women in the world a full awareness of their potential and their role at the service of a culture which is ever more truly human and in conformity with God's plan.

READING 29 (AUGUST 20, 1995): Equal Opportunity Still Urgently Needed[1]

Dear Brothers and Sisters,

1. Doubtless one of the great social changes of our time is the increasing role played by women, also in an executive capacity, in labor and the economy. This process is gradually changing the face of society, and it is legitimate to hope that it will gradually succeed in changing that of the economy itself, giving it a new human inspiration and removing it from the recurring temptation of dull efficiency marked only by the laws of profit. How can we fail to see that, in order to deal satisfactorily with the many problems emerging today, special recourse to the feminine genius is essential? Among other things, I am thinking of the problems of education, leisure time, the quality of life, migration, social services, the elderly, drugs, health care, and ecology. "In all these areas a greater presence of women in society will prove most valuable," and it will force systems to be redesigned in a way which favors the processes of humanization which mark the "civilization of love" (Letter to Women, n4).

2. It is clear that increasing the role of women in the frequently harsh and demanding structures of economic activity must take into account their temperament and particular needs. Above all, it is necessary to respect the right and duty of woman as mother to carry out her specific tasks in the family, without being forced by need to take on an additional job. What would society truly gain—even at the economic level—if a short-sighted labor policy were to prejudice the family's endurance and functions?

The safeguarding of this basic good cannot be a rationalization for failing to apply the principle of equal opportunity for men and women also in work outside the family. Flexible and balanced solutions should be found which can harmonize the different needs. In fact—as I wrote in my recent Letter to Women—"[m]uch remains to be done to prevent discrimination against those who have chosen to be wives and mothers. As far as personal rights are concerned, there is an urgent need to achieve real equality in every area: equal pay for equal work, protection for working mothers, fairness in career advancements, equality of spouses with regard to family rights and the recognition of everything that is part of the rights and duties of citizens in a democratic State" (n4).

⁂

3. Dear brothers and sisters, let us entrust this great challenge of our era to the Blessed Virgin's intercession! Her home in Nazareth was a place of work. Mary, like any good housewife, was busy with domestic tasks while Joseph, with Jesus beside him, worked as a carpenter. May working women look to the hard-working and holy family of Nazareth, and may society be able to find suitable ways to increase their role to the full.

READING 30 (AUGUST 27, 1995): Women Have Much to Offer in Political Life[1]

Dear Brothers and Sisters,

1. As the Beijing Conference is now close at hand, today I would like to stress the importance of a greater involvement of women in public life. A long tradition has seen mostly men involved in politics. Today, more and more women are asserting themselves even at the highest levels of representation, national and international.

This process should be encouraged. Politics, in fact, geared as it is to promoting the common good, can only benefit from the complementary gifts of men and women. Of course, it would be naive to expect "miracles" from this alone. It is especially true that for women no less than for men, the quality of politics is measured by the authenticity of the values which inspire them, as well as by the competence, commitment, and moral consistency of those who dedicate themselves to this important service.

In every case, women are showing that they can make as skilled a contribution as men, a contribution which indeed is proving particularly significant, especially with regard to the aspects of politics that concern the basic areas of human life.

⁂

2. How great, for example, is the role they can play on behalf of peace, precisely by being involved in politics, where the fate of humanity is largely decided. Dear brothers and sisters, peace is the most pressing need of our time. A collective effort is more than ever necessary to restrain the fren-

zy of arms; however, peace is not limited to the silence of cannons. It becomes concrete with justice and freedom. It needs a spiritual atmosphere rich in basic elements such as the sense of God, a taste for the beautiful, love for the truth, the option for solidarity, the capacity for tenderness, and the courage of forgiveness. How can we not recognize the valuable contribution which woman can make in promoting this atmosphere of peace!

3. Let us call upon the Blessed Virgin, Queen of Peace, so that she may turn her gaze to those countries of the world where unbridled hatred has caused destruction and death for too long. In this regard, my thoughts cannot but turn to the thousands of mothers, wives, and daughters, who in the countries of the former Yugoslav Republic—whether they are Croats, Serbs, or Muslims—are still forced to abandon their homes and their loved ones and are often the object of inhuman treatment and exposed to a very uncertain future. I am particularly troubled by the grave news from Banja Luka. I am close to the zealous and generous Bishop Franjo Komarica, who is almost helplessly witnessing the forced expulsion of his priests, religious and faithful. It is their desire and their right to be able to continue living in their own homes, remaining there as a sign of the reconciliation for which they long and of the coexistence of peoples of different nationalities and religions, which is still possible.

May those responsible for all this suffering open their eyes! May the women on opposing sides, especially the mothers, give one another their hand symbolically in a chain of peace, as if to compel the governments, those fighting, and the people to regain their trust in the validity of negotiations and the prospects of peaceful coexistence.

I greet the English-speaking visitors who are here with us for this Angelus prayer. As we invoke the Queen of Peace, my thoughts turn in a special way to Northern Ireland where a year has passed since a cease-fire was declared and where the people of both communities eagerly hope for the advancement of the peace process. May God enlighten all those involved to find the way forward to lasting mutual reconciliation and harmony.

God bless you all!

READING 31 (AUGUST 29, 1995):
Address to the Vatican Delegation to the Fourth World Conference on Women[1]

Dear Mrs. Glendon and Members of the
Delegation of the Holy See to the Fourth World
Conference on Women,

As you prepare to leave for Beijing, I am happy to meet you, the head of the Delegation of the Holy See to the Fourth World Conference on Women, and the other members of the delegation. Through you, I extend my best wishes and prayers to the Secretary General of the conference, to the participant nations and organizations, as well as to the authorities of the host country, the People's Republic of China. My wishes are for the success of this conference in its aim to guarantee all the women of the world "equality, development and peace," through full respect for their equal dignity and for their inalienable human rights, so that they can make their full contribution to the good of society.

Over the past months, on various occasions, I have drawn attention to the positions of the Holy See and to the teaching of the Catholic Church on the dignity, rights, and responsibilities of women in today's society: in the family, in the workplace, in public life. I have drawn inspiration from the life and witness of great women within the Church throughout the centuries who have been pioneers within society, as mothers, as workers, as leaders in the social and political fields, in the caring professions, and as thinkers and spiritual leaders.

The Secretary General of the United Nations has asked the participating nations at the Beijing Conference to announce concrete commitments for the improvement of the condition of women. Having looked at the various needs of women in today's world, the Holy See wishes to make a specific option regarding such a commitment: an option in favor of girls and young women; therefore, I call all Catholic caring and educational institutions to adopt a concerted and priority strategy directed to girls and young women, especially to the poorest, over the coming years.

It is disheartening to note that in today's world, the simple fact of being a female, rather than a male, can reduce the likelihood of being born or of surviving childhood; it can mean receiving less adequate nutrition and health care, and it can increase the chance of remaining illiterate and having only limited access, or none at all, even to primary education.

Investment in the care and education of girls, as an equal right, is a fundamental key to the advancement of women. It is for this reason that today:

- I appeal to all the educational services linked to the Catholic Church to guarantee equal access for girls, to educate boys to a sense of women's dignity and worth, to provide additional possibilities for girls who have suffered disadvantage, and to identify and remedy the reasons which cause girls to drop out of education at an early stage;
- I appeal to those institutions which are involved in health care, especially primary health care, to make improved basic health care and education for girls a hallmark of their service;
- I appeal to the Church's charitable and development organizations to give priority in the allocation of resources and personnel to the special needs of girls;
- I appeal to congregations of religious sisters, in fidelity to the special charism and mission given to them by their founders, to identify and reach out to those girls and young women who are most on the fringes of society, who have suffered most, physically and morally, who have the least opportunity. Their work of healing, caring, and educating, and of reaching to the poorest, is needed in every part of the world today;
- I appeal to Catholic universities and centers of higher education to ensure that, in the preparation of future leaders in society, they acquire a special sensitivity to the concerns of young women;
- I appeal to women and women's organizations within the Church and active in society to establish patterns of solidarity so that their leadership and guidance can be put at the service of girls and young women.

As followers of Jesus Christ, who identifies himself with the least among children, we cannot be insensitive to the needs of disadvantaged girls, especially those who are victims of violence and suffer a lack of respect for their dignity.

In the spirit of those great Christian women who have enlightened the life of the Church throughout the centuries and who have often called the

Church back to her essential mission and service, I make an appeal to the women of the Church today to assume new forms of leadership in service, and I appeal to all the institutions of the Church to welcome this contribution of women.

I appeal to all men in the Church to undergo, where necessary, a change of heart and to implement, as a demand of their faith, a positive vision of women. I ask them to become more and more aware of the disadvantages to which women, and especially girls, have been exposed and to see where the attitude of men, their lack of sensitivity, or lack of responsibility may be at the root.

Once again, through you, I wish to express my good wishes to all those who have responsibility for the Beijing Conference and to assure them of my support, as well as that of the Holy See and the institutions of the Catholic Church, for a renewed commitment of all to the good of the world's women.

READING 32 (SEPTEMBER 3, 1995): Enhance Women's Role in Church Life[1]

Dear Brothers and Sisters,

1. Last Tuesday, as I met the Holy See's Delegation to the Fourth World Conference on Women, which starts in Beijing tomorrow, I confirmed the Church's commitment on behalf of women and I asked the communities and institutions of the Church to make concrete gestures, particularly in service to girls and adolescents, especially the poorest.

Today, I appeal to the whole Church community to be willing to foster feminine participation in every way in its internal life. This is certainly not a new commitment, since it is inspired by the example of Christ himself. Although he chose men as his Apostles—a choice which remains normative for their successors—nevertheless, he also involved women in the cause of his kingdom; indeed, he wanted them to be the first witnesses and heralds of his Resurrection. In fact, there are many women who have distinguished themselves in the Church's history by their holiness and hardworking ingenuity. The Church is increasingly aware of the need for enhancing their role. Within the great variety of different and complementary gifts that enrich ecclesial life, many important possibilities are open to them.

The 1987 Synod on the laity expressed precisely this need and asked that "without discrimination women should be participants in the life of the Church and also in consultation and the process of coming to decisions" (*Propositio* 47; cf. *Christifideles Laici*, n51).

2. This is the way to be courageously taken. To a large extent, it is a question of making full use of the ample room for a lay and feminine presence recognized by the Church's law. I am thinking, for example, of theological teaching, the forms of liturgical ministry permitted, including service at the altar, pastoral and administrative councils, diocesan synods and particular councils, various ecclesial institutions, curias, and ecclesiastical tribunals, many pastoral activities, including the new forms of participation in the care of parishes when there is a shortage of clergy, except for those tasks that belong properly to the priest. Who can imagine the great advantages to pastoral care and the new beauty that the Church's face will assume when the feminine genius is fully involved in the various areas of her life?

3. May the Blessed Virgin, model of the Church and ideal of femininity, accompany and sustain the efforts of all the people of goodwill who are involved in the Beijing Conference. May the Mother of the Lord help all humanity to progress in their respect for and promotion of women's true dignity! May she obtain for the Christian community to be ever more faithful to God's plan, following the example of the great women who have embellished its history!

NOVEMBER 1995–NOVEMBER 1999

READING 33 (NOVEMBER 29, 1995): Mary Shows Us God's Respect for Women[1]

The Church holds that a proper reading of the figure of Mary in the Gospels provides a model of authentic emancipation for women according to God's plan: "The figure of Mary shows that God has such esteem for woman that any form of discrimination lacks a theoretical basis." The pope's catechesis on Mary and the value of woman at the General Audience of November 29, 1995, was the seventh in the series on the Blessed Mother.

1. The theological and spiritual aspects of the Church's teaching on Mary, which have been amply developed in our century, have recently acquired a new importance from the sociological and pastoral standpoint, due also to a clearer understanding of woman's role in the Christian community and in society, as we see in many significant interventions of the Magisterium.

The message to women addressed by the Fathers at the conclusion of the Second Vatican Council on December 8, 1965, are well known: "But the hour is coming, in fact has come, when the vocation of woman is being achieved in its fullness, the hour in which woman acquires in the world an influence, an effect and a power never hitherto achieved" (*Enchiridion Vat.*, I, 307). I confirmed these affirmations a few years later in the Encyclical *Mulieris Dignitatem:* "The dignity and the vocation of women—a subject of constant human and Christian reflection—have gained exceptional prominence in recent years" (n1).

The role and dignity of woman have been particularly championed in this century by the feminist movement which has sought to react, sometimes in forceful ways, against everything in the past and present that has hindered the full appreciation and development of the feminine personality as well as her participation in the many expressions of social and political life.

These demands were in large part legitimate and contributed to building up a more balanced view of the feminine question in the contemporary world. The Church, especially in recent times, has paid special attention to these demands, encouraged by the fact that the figure of Mary, if seen in the light of her Gospel life, is a valid response to woman's desire for emancipation: Mary is the only human person who eminently fulfils God's plan of love for humanity.

Every Woman Shares in Mary's Sublime Dignity

2. This plan is already manifest in the Old Testament, with the creation narrative that introduces the first couple created in the image of God himself: "So God created man in his own image, in the image of God he created him, male and female he created them" (Gen 1:27). Woman, no less than man, bears God's image in herself. This means that, since her appearance on the earth is a result of the divine action, she, too, is appreciated: "God saw everything that he had made, and behold, it was very good" (Gen 1:31). According to this view, the difference between man and woman does not imply the inferiority of the latter nor her inequality but is a new element which enriches God's plan, and is "very good."

God's intention goes well beyond what is revealed in the Book of Genesis. In fact, in Mary God created a feminine personality which greatly surpasses the ordinary condition of woman as it appears in the creation of Eve. Mary's unique excellence in the world of grace and her perfection are fruits of the particular divine benevolence which seeks to raise everyone, men and women, to the moral perfection and holiness which are proper to the adopted children of God. Mary is "blessed among women"; however, every woman shares in some way in her sublime dignity in the divine plan.

3. The remarkable gift to the Mother of the Lord not only testifies to what we could call God's respect for woman but also emphasizes the profound regard in God's plans for her irreplaceable role in human history.

Women need to discover this divine esteem in order to be ever more aware of their lofty dignity. The historical and social situations which caused the reaction of feminism were marked by a lack of appreciation of woman's worth; frequently she was relegated to a second rate or even marginal role. This did not allow her to express fully the wealth of intelligence and wisdom contained in her femininity. Indeed, throughout history women have not infrequently suffered from scant esteem for their abilities, and sometimes even scorn and unjust prejudice. This is a state of affairs that, despite important changes, unfortunately continues even today in many nations and in many parts of the world.

4. The figure of Mary shows that God has such esteem for woman that any form of discrimination lacks a theoretical basis. The marvelous work which the Creator achieved in Mary gives men and women the possibility to discover dimensions of their condition which before were not sufficiently perceived. In beholding the Mother of the Lord, women will be able to understand better their dignity and the greatness of their mission. Men, too, in the light of the Virgin Mother, will be able to acquire a fuller and more balanced view of their identity, of the family and of society.

Attentive consideration of the figure of Mary, as she is presented to us in Sacred Scripture as read in faith by the Church, is still more necessary in view of the disparagement she sometimes receives from certain feminist currents. The Virgin of Nazareth has, in some cases, been presented as the symbol of the female personality imprisoned in a narrow, confining domesticity. Mary on the contrary, is the model of the full development of woman's vocation, since, despite the objective limits imposed by her social condition, she exercised a vast influence on the destiny of humanity and the transformation of society.

In Mary All Are Called to Trust the Lord

5. Marian doctrine can shed light on the multiple ways in which the life of grace promotes woman's spiritual beauty. In view of the shameful exploitation that sometimes makes woman an object without dignity, destined for the satisfaction of base passions, Mary reaffirms the sublime meaning of feminine beauty, a gift and reflection of God's beauty.

It is true that feminine perfection, as it was fully realized in Mary, can at first sight seem to be an exceptional case and impossible to imitate, a model too lofty for imitation. In fact, the unique holiness of her, who from the very first moment received the privilege of the Immaculate Conception, is sometimes considered unreachably distant.

Far from being a restraint on the way of following the Lord, Mary's exalted holiness is, on the contrary, destined in God's plan to encourage all Christians to open themselves to the sanctifying power of the grace of God, for whom nothing is impossible. In Mary all are called to put total trust in the divine omnipotence, which transforms hearts, guiding them toward full receptivity to his providential plan of love.

READING 34 (DECEMBER 6, 1995): Mary Sheds Light on Role of Women[1]

God's saving plan which is revealed in creation attributes equal dignity and worth to women, but it also affirms the uniqueness of the gift of femininity. At the General Audience of December 6, 1995, the Holy Father continued his catechesis on the Virgin Mary, calling particular attention to her as the model for woman's role in the contemporary world. His address was the eighth in the series on the Blessed Virgin.

1. As I have already explained in the preceding catechesis, the role entrusted to Mary by the divine plan of salvation sheds light on the vocation of woman in the life of the Church and society by defining its difference in relation to man. The model represented by Mary clearly shows what is specific to the feminine personality.

In recent times, some trends in the feminist movement, in order to advance women's emancipation, have sought to make her like man in every way; however, the divine intention manifested in creation, though desiring woman to be man's equal in dignity and worth, at the same time, clearly affirms her diversity and specific features. Woman's identity cannot consist in being a copy of man, since she is endowed with her own qualities and prerogatives, which give her a particular uniqueness that is always to be fostered and encouraged.

These prerogatives and particular features of the feminine personality attained their full development in Mary. The fullness of divine grace actually fostered in her all the natural abilities typical of woman.

"Let It Be Done to Me According to Your Word"

Mary's role in the work of salvation is totally dependent on Christ's. It is a unique function, required by the fulfillment of the mystery of the Incarnation: Mary's motherhood was necessary to give the world its Savior, the true Son of God, but also perfectly man.

The importance of woman's cooperation in the coming of Christ is emphasized by the initiative of God, who, through the angel, communicates his plan of salvation to the Virgin of Nazareth so that she can consciously and freely cooperate by giving her own generous consent. Here the loftiest model of woman's collaboration in the Redemption of man—every man—is fulfilled, and this model represents the transcendent reference point for every affirmation of woman's role and function in history.

2. In carrying out this sublime form of cooperation, Mary also shows the style in which woman must concretely express her mission. With regard to the angel's message, the Virgin makes no proud demands nor does she seek to satisfy personal ambitions. Luke presents her to us as wanting only to offer her humble service with total and trusting acceptance of the divine plan of salvation. This is the meaning of her response: "Behold, I am the handmaid of the Lord, let it be done to me according to your word" (Lk 1:38).

It is not a question of a purely passive acceptance, since her consent is given only after she has expressed the difficulty that arose from her intent to remain a virgin, inspired by her will to belong more completely to the Lord. Having received the angel's response, Mary immediately expresses her readiness, maintaining an attitude of humble service. It is the humble, valuable service that so many women, following Mary's example, have offered and continue to offer in the Church for the growth of Christ's kingdom.

3. The figure of Mary reminds women today of the value of motherhood. In the contemporary world, the appropriate and balanced importance is not always given to this value. In some cases, the need for women to work in order to provide for the needs of their family and an erroneous

concept of freedom, which sees child care as a hindrance to woman's autonomy and opportunities, have obscured the significance of motherhood for the development of the feminine personality. On the contrary, in other cases the biological aspect of childbirth becomes so important as to overshadow the other significant opportunities woman has for expressing her innate vocation to being a mother.

In Mary we have been given to understand the true meaning of motherhood, which attains its loftiest dimension in the divine plan of salvation. For her, being a mother not only endows her feminine personality, directed toward the gift of life, with its full development, but also represents an answer of faith to woman's own vocation, which assumes its truest value only in the light of God's covenant (cf. *Mulieris Dignitatem*, n19).

4. In looking attentively at Mary, we also discover in her the model of virginity lived for the kingdom. The Virgin par excellence, in her heart she grew in her desire to live in this state in order to achieve an ever deeper intimacy with God.

For women called to virginal chastity, Mary reveals the lofty meaning of so special a vocation and thus draws attention to the spiritual fruitfulness which it produces in the divine plan: a higher order of motherhood, a motherhood according to the Spirit (cf. *Mulieris Dignitatem*, n21).

Women Sow the Seeds of the Civilization of Love

Mary's maternal heart, open to all human misfortune, also reminds women that the development of the feminine personality calls for a commitment to charity. More sensitive to the values of the heart, woman shows a high capacity for personal self-giving.

To all in our age who offer selfish models for affirming the feminine personality, the luminous and holy figure of the Lord's Mother shows how only by self-giving and self-forgetfulness toward others is it possible to attain authentic fulfillment of the divine plan for one's own life. Mary's presence therefore encourages sentiments of mercy and solidarity in women for situations of human distress and arouses a desire to alleviate the pain of those who suffer: the poor, the sick and all in need of help.

In virtue of her special bond with Mary, woman has often in the course of history represented God's closeness to the expectations of goodness and tenderness of a humanity wounded by hatred and sin, by sowing in the world seeds of a civilization that can respond to violence with love.

READING 35 (JANUARY 24, 1996): THE MEDIA: Modern Forum for Promoting the Role of Women in Society[1]

Dear Brothers and Sisters,

This year, the theme for World Communications Day, "The Media: Modern Forum for Promoting the Role of Women in Society," recognizes that the communications media play a crucial role not only in promoting justice and equality for women but in fostering appreciation for their specific feminine gifts, which elsewhere I have called the "genius" of women (cf. *Mulieris Dignitatem*, 30; Letter to Women, 10).

Last year, in my Letter to Women I sought to advance a dialogue, especially with women themselves, on what it means to be a woman in our time (cf. no. 1). I also pointed out some of "the obstacles which in so many parts of the world still keep women from being fully integrated into social, political and economic life" (no. 4). This is a dialogue which people in the communications media can, indeed have an obligation to, foster and support. People in the media often become advocates, and commendably so, of the voiceless and the marginalized. They are in a unique position also to stimulate public consciousness with regard to two serious issues concerning women in today's world.

First, as I noted in my Letter, motherhood is often penalized rather than rewarded, even though humanity owes its very survival to those women who have chosen to be wives and mothers (cf. no. 4). It is certainly an injustice that such women should be discriminated against, economically or socially, precisely for following that fundamental vocation. I also pointed out that there is an urgent need to achieve real equality in every area: equal pay for equal work, protection for working mothers, fairness in career advancement, equality of spouses with regard to family rights, and the recognition of everything that is part of the rights and duties of citizens in a democratic state (cf. no. 4).

Secondly, the advancement of women's genuine emancipation is a matter of justice which can no longer be overlooked; it is also a question of society's welfare. Fortunately, there is a growing awareness that women must be enabled to play their part in the solution of the serious problems of society and of society's future. In every area, "a greater presence of women in society will prove most valuable, for it will help to manifest the contradictions present when society is organized solely according to the criteria of efficiency and productivity, and it will force systems to be redesigned in a way which favors the processes of humanization which mark the 'civilization of love'" (ibid., no. 4).

The "civilization of love" consists, most particularly, in a radical affirmation of the value of life and of the value of love. Women are especially qualified and privileged in both of these areas. Regarding life, although not alone responsible for affirming its intrinsic value, women enjoy a unique capacity for doing so because of their intimate connection with the mystery of life's transmission. Regarding love, women can bring to every aspect of life, including the highest levels of decision-making, that essential quality of femininity which consists in objectivity of judgment, tempered by the capacity to understand in depth the demands of interpersonal relationships.

The communications media, including the press, the cinema, radio and television, the music industry, and computer networks, represent the modern forum where information is received and transmitted rapidly to a global audience, where ideas are exchanged, where attitudes are formed—and, indeed, where a new culture is being shaped. The media are therefore destined to exercise a powerful influence in determining whether society fully recognizes and appreciates not only the rights but also the special gifts of women.

Sadly though, we often see not the exaltation but the exploitation of women in the media. How often are they treated not as persons with an inviolable dignity but as objects whose purpose is to satisfy others' appetite for pleasure or for power? How often is the role of woman as wife and mother undervalued or even ridiculed? How often is the role of women in business or professional life depicted as a masculine caricature, a denial of the specific gifts of feminine insight, compassion, and understanding, which so greatly contribute to the "civilization of love"?

Women themselves can do much to foster better treatment of women in the media: by promoting sound media education programs, by teaching others, especially their families, to be discriminating consumers in the media market, by making known their views to production companies, publishers, broadcasting networks, and advertisers with regard to programs and publications which insult the dignity of women or debase their role in society. Moreover, women can and should prepare themselves for positions of responsibility and creativity in the media, not in conflict with or imitation of masculine roles but by impressing their own "genius" on their work and professional activity.

The media would do well to focus on the true heroines of society, including the saintly women of the Christian tradition, as role models for the young and for future generations. Nor can we forget, in this respect, the many consecrated women who have sacrificed all to follow Jesus and to dedicate themselves to prayer and to the service of the poor, the sick, the illiterate, the young, the old, the handicapped. Some of these women are themselves involved in the communications media—working so that "the poor have the Gospel preached to them" (cf. Lk 4:18).

"My soul proclaims the greatness of the Lord" (Lk 1:46). The Blessed Virgin Mary used these words in responding to the salutation of her cousin Elizabeth, thus acknowledging the "great things" that God had done in her. The image of women communicated by the media should include the recognition that every feminine gift proclaims the greatness of the Lord, the Lord who has communicated life and love, goodness and grace, the Lord who is the source of the dignity and equality of women, and of their special "genius."

My prayer is that this Thirtieth World Communications Day will encourage all those involved in the media of social communication, especially the sons and daughters of the Church, to promote the genuine advancement of women's dignity and rights by projecting a true and respectful image of their role in society, and by bringing out "the full truth about women" (Letter to Women, no. 12).

READING 36 (JANUARY 24, 1996):
Victory over Sin Comes through a Woman[1]

Editorial note. This General Audience itself had for its opening header "*Maria nel Protovangelo*" (i.e., the foreshadowing or [adumbration] of Mary in Genesis 3:15).

The main title as here assigned, accordingly, is an editorial interpretation of the theme of the text. Through her cooperation with Christ in the work of salvation, the Blessed Virgin contributes in a unique way to the triumph over Satan. The Holy Father's concluding remark in this General Audience affirms that "Mary's unique vocation is inseparable from humanity's vocation and, in particular, from that of every woman, on which light has been shed by the mission of Mary, proclaimed God's first ally against Satan and evil." The audience was the twelfth in a series and was given in Italian.

1. "The books of the Old Testament describe the history of salvation, by which the coming of Christ into the world was slowly prepared. The earliest documents, as they are read in the Church and are understood in the light of a further and full revelation, bring the figure of a woman, Mother of the Redeemer, into a gradually clearer light" (*Lumen Gentium*, n55).

With these statements, the Second Vatican Council reminds us how the figure of Mary gradually took shape from the very beginning of salvation history. She is already glimpsed in the Old Testament texts but is fully understood only when these "are read in the Church" and understood in the light of the New Testament. The Holy Spirit, by inspiring the various human authors, oriented Old Testament Revelation to Christ, who was to come into the world from the Virgin Mary's womb.

2. Among the biblical accounts which foretold the Mother of the Redeemer, the Council particularly cites those in which God revealed his plan of salvation after the fall of Adam and Eve. The Lord says to the serpent, the personification of the spirit of evil: "I will put enmity between you and the woman, and between your seed and her seed; he shall bruise your head, and you shall bruise his heel" (Gen 3:15).

These statements, called the *Proto-gospel* (i.e., the first Good News), by Christian tradition since the sixteenth century enable us to see God's saving will from the very origins of humanity. Indeed according to the sacred author's narrative, the Lord's first reaction to sin was not to punish the guilty but to offer them the hope of salvation and to involve them actively in the work of redemption, showing his great generosity even to those who had offended him.

The *Proto-gospel's* words also reveal the unique destiny of the woman who, although yielding to the serpent's temptation before the man did, in virtue of the divine plan later becomes God's first ally. Eve was the serpent's accomplice in enticing man to sin. Overturning this situation, God declares that he will make the woman the serpent's enemy.

3. Exegetes now agree in recognizing that the text of Genesis, according to the original Hebrew, does not attribute action against the serpent directly to the woman, but to her offspring. Nevertheless, the text gives great prominence to the role she will play in the struggle against the tempter: in fact, the one who defeats the serpent will be her offspring.

Who is this woman? The biblical text does not mention her personal name but allows us to glimpse a new woman, desired by God to atone for Eve's fall; in fact, she is called to restore woman's role and dignity, and to contribute to changing humanity's destiny, cooperating through her maternal mission in God's victory over Satan.

4. In the light of the New Testament and the Church's tradition, we know that the new woman announced by the *Proto-gospel* is Mary, and in "her seed" we recognize her Son, Jesus, who triumphed over Satan's power in the paschal mystery.

We also observe that in Mary the enmity God put between the serpent and the woman is fulfilled in two ways. God's perfect ally and the devil's enemy, she was completely removed from Satan's domination in the Immaculate Conception, when she was fashioned in grace by the Holy Spirit and preserved from every stain of sin. In addition, associated with her Son's saving work, Mary was fully involved in the fight against the spirit of evil.

Thus the titles "Immaculate Conception" and "Cooperator of the Redeemer," attributed by the Church's faith to Mary, in order to proclaim her spiritual beauty and her intimate participation in the wonderful work of Redemption, show the lasting antagonism between the serpent and the New Eve.

5. Exegetes and theologians claim that the light of the New Eve, Mary, shines from the pages of Genesis onto the whole economy of salvation. In that text, they already see the bond between Mary and the Church. Here

we point out with joy that the term "woman," used in its generic form in the Genesis text, spurs women especially to join the Virgin of Nazareth and her task in the work of salvation, for they are called to take part in the fight against the spirit of evil.

Women who, like Eve, could succumb to Satan's seduction, through solidarity with Mary receive superior strength to combat the enemy, becoming God's first allies on the way of salvation.

God's mysterious alliance with woman can also be seen in a variety of ways in our day: in women's assiduous personal prayer and liturgical devotion, in their catechetical service and in their witness to charity, in the many feminine vocations to the consecrated life, in religious education in the family, etc.

All these signs are a very concrete fulfillment of the *Proto-gospel's* prediction. Indeed, by suggesting a universal extension of the word "woman" within and beyond the visible confines of the Church, the *Proto-gospel* shows that Mary's unique vocation is inseparable from humanity's vocation and, in particular, from that of every woman, on which light has been shed by the mission of Mary, proclaimed God's first ally against Satan and evil.

READING 37 (MARCH 6, 1996): Motherhood Is God's Special Gift[1]

The Old Testament not only shows that motherhood is a gift of God but also suggests a special link between the destiny of mothers and their sons. "The Bible's message regarding motherhood reveals important and ever timely aspects: indeed, it sheds light on the dimension of gratuitousness, which is especially apparent in the case of barren women, God's particular covenant with woman and the special bond between the destiny of the mother and that of the son," the Holy Father concluded his General Audience on Wednesday, March 6, focusing on the Old Testament's treatment of motherhood. Here is a translation of the Pope's catechesis, which was the fourteenth in his series on the Blessed Virgin and was given in Italian.

1. Motherhood is a gift of God. "I have gotten a man with the help of the Lord!" (Gen 4: 1), Eve exclaims after giving birth to Cain, her first-born son. With these words, the Book of Genesis presents the first motherhood in human history as a grace and joy that spring from the Creator's goodness.

2. The birth of Isaac is similarly described, at the origin of the chosen people. God promises Abraham, who has been deprived of children and is now advanced in years, descendants as numerous as the stars of heaven (cf. Gen 15:5). The promise is welcomed by the patriarch with the faith that reveals God's plan to this man: "He believed the Lord; and he reckoned it to him as righteousness" (Gen 15: 6).

This promise was confirmed in the words spoken by the Lord on the occasion of the covenant he made with Abraham: "Behold, my covenant is with you, and you shall be the father of a multitude of nations" (Gen 17:4).

Extraordinary and mysterious events emphasize how Sarah's motherhood was primarily the fruit of the mercy of God, who gives life beyond all human expectation: "I will bless her, and moreover I will give you a son by her; I will bless her, and she shall be a mother of nations; kings of peoples shall come from her" (Gen 17:15-16).

Motherhood is presented as a decisive gift of the Lord. The patriarch and his wife will be given a new name to indicate the unexpected and marvelous transformation that God is to work in their life.

The Lord Gladdens with the Gift of Motherhood

3. The visit of the three mysterious persons, whom the Fathers of the Church interpreted as a prefiguration of the Trinity, announced the fulfillment of the promise to Abraham more explicitly: "The Lord appeared to him by the oaks of Mamre, as he sat at the door of his tent in the heat of the day. He lifted up his eyes and looked, and behold, three men stood in front of him" (Gen 18:1-2). Abraham objected, "Shall a child be born to a man who is a hundred years old? Shall Sarah, who is ninety years old, bear a child?" (Gen 17:17; cf. 18:11-13). The divine guest replied: "Is anything too hard for the Lord? At the appointed time I will return to you, about this time next year, and Sarah shall have a son" (Gen 18:14; cf. Lk 1:37).

The narrative stresses the effect of the divine visit, which makes fruitful a conjugal union that had been barren until then. Believing in the promise, Abraham becomes a father against all hope, and "father in the faith" because from his faith "descends" that of the chosen people.

4. The Bible relates other stories of women released from sterility and gladdened by the Lord with the gift of motherhood. These are often situations of anguish, which God's intervention transforms into experiences of joy by receiving the heartfelt prayers of those who are humanly without hope. "When Rachel saw that she bore Jacob no children," for example, "she envied her sister; and she said to Jacob, 'Give me children, or I shall die!'. Jacob's anger was kindled against Rachel, and he said, 'Am I in the place of God, who has withheld from you the fruit of the womb?'" (Gen 30:1-2).

The biblical text immediately adds: "Then God remembered Rachel, and God hearkened to her and opened her womb. She conceived and bore a son" (Gen 30:22-23). This son, Joseph, would play a very important role for Israel at the time of the migration to Egypt.

In this as in other narratives, the Bible intends to highlight the marvelous nature of God's intervention in these specific cases by stressing the initial condition of the woman's sterility; however, at the same time, it allows us to grasp the gratuitousness inherent in all motherhood.

5. We find a similar process in the account of the birth of Samson. The wife of Manoah, who had never been able to conceive a child, hears the Lord's announcement from the angel: "Behold, you are barren and have no children; but you shall conceive and bear a son" (Jgs 13:3). The conception, unexpected and miraculous, announces the great things that the Lord will do through Samson.

In the case of Hannah, Samson's mother, the special role of prayer is underlined. Hannah suffers the humiliation of being barren, but she is full of great trust in God, to whom she turns insistently, that he may help her to overcome this trial. One day, at the temple, she makes a vow: "Oh Lord of hosts, if you will indeed look on the affliction of your maidservant, and remember me, and not forget your maidservant, but will give to your maidservant a son, then I will give him to the Lord all the days of his life" (1 Sm 1: 11).

Her prayer was answered: "The Lord remembered her" and "Hannah conceived and bore a son, and she called his name Samuel" (1 Sm 1:19-20). Keeping her promise, Hannah offered her son to the Lord: "For this child I prayed; and the Lord has granted me my petition which I made to him.

Therefore I have lent him to the Lord; as long as he lives, he is lent to the Lord" (1 Sm 1:27-28). Given by God to Hannah and then given by Hannah to God, the little Samuel becomes a living bond of communion between Hannah and God.

Samuel's birth is thus an experience of joy and an occasion for thanksgiving. The First Book of Samuel contains a hymn known as Hannah's *Magnificat*, which seems to anticipate Mary's: "My heart exults in the Lord; my strength is exalted in the Lord" (1 Sm 2:1).

The grace of motherhood that God granted to Hannah because of her ceaseless prayers filled her with a new generosity. Samuel's consecration is the grateful response of a mother who, recognizing in her child the fruit of God's mercy, returns his gift, entrusting the child she had so longed for to the Lord.

God Intervenes in Important Moments

6. In the accounts of miraculous motherhood which we have recalled, it is easy to discover the important place the Bible assigns to mothers in the mission of their sons. In Samuel's case, Hannah has a determining role in deciding to give him to the Lord. An equally decisive role is played by another mother, Rebecca, who procures the inheritance for Jacob (Gen 27). That maternal intervention, described by the Bible, can be interpreted as the sign of being chosen as an instrument in God's sovereign plan. It is he who chooses the youngest son, Jacob, to receive the paternal blessing and inheritance, and therefore as the shepherd and leader of his people.... It is he who by a free and wise decision, determines and governs each one's destiny (Wis 10:10-12).

The Bible's message regarding motherhood reveals important and ever-timely aspects: indeed, it sheds light on the dimension of gratuitousness, which is especially apparent in the case of barren women, God's particular covenant with woman and the special bond between the destiny of the mother and that of the son.

At the same time, the intervention of God, who, at important moments in the history of his people, causes certain barren women to conceive, prepares for belief in the intervention of God who, in the fullness of time, will make a Virgin fruitful for the Incarnation of his Son.

READING 38 (MARCH 27, 1996): Woman's Indispensable Role in Salvation History[1]

Editorial note: The Old Testament presents the figures of some extraordinary women who, prompted by God's Spirit, played an active part in Israel's history. The role of certain Old Testament women in the salvation of God's chosen people was the theme of the Holy Father's catechesis at this General Audience. The Pope considered the indispensable role of these women as a prefiguring of Mary's mission in salvation history. Here is a translation of his talk which was the fifteenth in the series on the Blessed Virgin and was given in Italian.

1. The Old Testament holds up for our admiration some extraordinary women who, impelled by the Spirit of God, share in the struggles and triumphs of Israel or contribute to its salvation. Their presence in the history of the people is neither marginal nor passive: they appear as true protagonists of salvation history. Here are the most significant examples.

After the crossing of the Red Sea, the sacred text emphasizes the initiative of a woman inspired to make this decisive event a festive celebration: "Then Miriam, the prophetess, the sister of Aaron took a timbrel in her hand; and all the women went out after her with timbrels and dancing. And Miriam sang to them: 'Sing to the Lord, for he has triumphed gloriously; the horse and his rider he has thrown into the sea'" (Ex 15:20-21). This mention of feminine enterprise in the context of a celebration stresses not only the importance of woman's role but also her particular ability for praising and thanking God.

Positive Contribution of Women to Salvation History

2. The action of the prophetess Deborah, at the time of the Judges, is even more important. After ordering the commander of the army to go and gather his men, she guarantees by her presence the success of Israel's army, predicting that another woman, Jael, will kill their enemy's general.

To celebrate the great victory, Deborah also sings a long canticle praising Jael's action: "Most blessed of women be Jael ... of tent-dwelling women most blessed" (Jgs 5:24). In the New Testament, this praise is echoed in the words Elizabeth addresses to Mary on the day of the Visitation: "Blessed are you among women ..." (Lk 1:42).

The significant role of women in the salvation of their people, highlighted by the figures of Deborah and Jael, is presented again in the story of another prophetess named Huldah, who lived at the time of King Josiah. Questioned by the priest Hilkiah, she made prophecies announcing that forgiveness would be shown to the king who feared the divine wrath. Huldah thus becomes a messenger of mercy and peace (cf. 2 Kgs 22:14-20).

3. The Books of Judith and Esther, whose purpose is to idealize the positive contribution of woman to the history of the chosen people, present—in a violent cultural context—two women who win victory and salvation for the Israelites.

The Book of Judith, in particular, tells of a fearsome army sent by Nebuchadnezzar to conquer Israel. Led by Holofernes, the enemy army is ready to seize the city of Bethulia, amid the desperation of its inhabitants, who, considering any resistance to be useless, ask their rulers to surrender. The city's elders, who in the absence of immediate aid declare themselves ready to hand Bethulia over to the enemy, are rebuked by Judith for their lack of faith as she professes her complete trust in the salvation that comes from the Lord.

After a long invocation to God, she who is a symbol of fidelity to the Lord, of humble prayer, and of the intention to remain chaste, Judith goes to Holofernes, the proud, idolatrous and dissolute enemy general.

Left alone with him and before striking him, Judith prays to Yahweh, saying: "Give me strength this day, O Lord God of Israel!" (Jdt 13:7). Then, taking Holofernes' sword, she cuts off his head.

Here, too, as in the case of David and Goliath, the Lord used weakness to triumph over strength. On this occasion, however, it was a woman who brought victory: Judith, without being held back by the cowardice and unbelief of the people's rulers, goes to Holofernes and kills him, earning the gratitude and praise of the High Priest and the elders of Jerusalem. The latter exclaimed to the woman who had defeated the enemy: "You are the exaltation of Jerusalem, you are the great glory of Israel, you are the great pride of our nation! You have done all this single-handed; you have done great good to Israel, and God is well pleased with it. May the Almighty Lord bless you forever!" (Jdt 15:9-10).

4. The events narrated in the Book of Esther occurred in another very difficult situation for the Jews. In the kingdom of Persia, Haman, the king's superintendent, decrees the extermination of the Jews. To remove the danger, Mordecai, a Jew living in the citadel of Susa, turns to his niece Esther, who lives in the king's palace where she has attained the rank of queen. Contrary to the law in force, she presents herself to the king without being summoned, thus risking the death penalty, and she obtains the revocation of the extermination decree. Haman is executed, Mordecai comes to power, and the Jews delivered from menace thus get the better of their enemies.

Judith and Esther both risk their lives to win the salvation of their people. The two interventions, however, are quite different: Esther does not kill the enemy but, by playing the role of mediator, intercedes for those who are threatened with destruction.

Holy Spirit Sketches Mary's Role in Human Salvation

5. This intercessory role is later attributed to another female figure, Abigail, the wife of Nabal, by the First Book of Samuel. Here, too, it is due to her intervention that salvation is once again achieved. She goes to meet David, who has decided to destroy Nabal's family, and asks forgiveness for her husband's sins. In doing so, she delivers his house from certain destruction (1 Sm 25).

As can be easily noted, the Old Testament tradition frequently emphasizes the decisive action of women in the salvation of Israel, especially in the writings closest to the coming of Christ. In this way, the Holy Spirit, through the events connected with Old Testament women, sketches with ever greater precision the characteristics of Mary's mission in the work of salvation for the entire human race.

READING 39 (APRIL 10, 1996): The Ideal Woman Is a Precious Treasure[1]

Although the Bible does give examples of women who led others astray, the predominant image is one of strong individuals who work with and for God. "In these figures of woman, in whom the marvels of divine grace are manifest, we glimpse the one who will be the greatest: Mary, Mother of the Lord," the Holy Father said at this General Audience, as he returned to his catechesis on the Blessed Virgin Mary. This talk was the sixteenth in the series and was given in Italian.

1. The Old Testament and the Judaic tradition are full of acknowledgments of woman's moral nobility, which is expressed above all in an attitude of trust in the Lord, in prayer to obtain the gift of motherhood, and in imploring God for Israel's salvation from the assaults of its enemies. Sometimes, as in Judith's case, this quality is celebrated by the entire community, becoming the object of common admiration.

Beside the shining examples of the biblical heroines, the negative witnesses of some women are not lacking, such as Delilah, who destroys Samson's prophetic ability (Jgs 16:4-21); the foreign women, who in Solomon's old age turn the king's heart away from the Lord and make him worship other gods (1 Kgs 11:1-8); Jezebel, who kills all "the prophets of the Lord" (1 Kgs 18:13) and has Naboth killed, to give his vineyard to Ahab (1 Kgs 21); and Job's wife who insults him in his misfortune and spurs him to rebel (Jb 2:9). In these cases, the woman's conduct is reminiscent of Eve's; however, the prevailing outlook in the Bible is that inspired by the *Proto-gospel*, which sees in woman an ally of God.

The Feminine Figure Is a Precious Gift of the Lord

2. In fact, if foreign women were accused of turning Solomon away from his devotion to the true God, the Book of Ruth presents us instead with the most noble figure of a foreign woman: Ruth, the Moabite, an example of piety to her relatives and of sincere and generous humility. Sharing Israel's life and faith, she was to become David's great-grandmother and an ancestor of the Messiah. Matthew, inserting her in Jesus' genealogy (Mt 1:5), makes her a sign of universality and a proclamation of God's mercy which extends to all humanity.

Among Jesus' forebears, the first Evangelist also mentions Tamar, Rahab, and Uriah's wife, three sinful but not wicked women who are listed among the female ancestors of the Messiah, in order to proclaim that divine goodness is greater than sin. Through his grace, God causes their irregular matrimonial situations to contribute to his plans of salvation, thereby also preparing for the future.

Another example of humble dedication, different from Ruth's, is represented by Jephthah's daughter, who agrees to pay for her father's victory over the Ammonites with her own death (Jgs 11:34-40). Lamenting her cruel destiny, she does not rebel but gives herself up to death in fulfillment of the thoughtless vow made by her parent in the context of primitive customs that were still prevalent (cf. Jer 7:31; Mi 6:6-8).

3. Although sapiential literature frequently alludes to woman's defects, it perceives in her a hidden treasure: "He who finds a wife finds a good thing, and obtains favor from the Lord" (Prv 18:22), says the Book of Proverbs, expressing convinced appreciation of the feminine figure, a precious gift of the Lord. At the end of the same book, the portrait of the ideal woman is sketched. Far from representing an unattainable model, she is a concrete image born from the experience of women of great value: "A good wife who can find? She is far more precious than jewels ..." (Prv 31:10).

Sapiential literature sees in woman's fidelity to the divine covenant the culmination of her abilities and the greatest source of admiration. Indeed, although she can sometimes disappoint, woman transcends all expectations when her heart is faithful to God: "Charm is deceitful, and beauty is vain, but a woman who fears the Lord is to be praised" (Prv 31:30).

Mother Was Worthy of Honorable Memory

4. In this context, the Book of the Maccabees, in the story of the mother of the seven brothers martyred during Antiochus Epiphanes' persecution, holds up to us the most admirable example of nobility in trial.

After describing the death of the seven brothers, the sacred author adds: "The mother was especially admirable and worthy of honorable memory. Though she saw her seven sons perish within a single day, she bore it with good courage because of her hope in the Lord. She encouraged each of them in the language of their fathers. Filled with a noble spirit, she fired her woman's reasoning with a man's courage," thus expressing her hope in a future resurrection: "Therefore the Creator of the world, who shaped the beginning of man and devised the origin of all things, will in his mercy give life and breath back to you again, since you now forget yourselves for the sake of his laws" (2 Mc 7:20-23).

Urging her seventh son to submit to death rather than disobey the divine law, the mother expresses her faith in the work of God who creates all things from nothing: "I beseech you, my child, to look at the heaven and the earth and see everything that is in them, and recognize that God did not make them out of things that existed. Thus also mankind comes into being. Do not fear this butcher, but prove worthy of your brothers. Accept death, so that in the time of mercy I may get you back again with your brothers" (2 Mc 7:28-29). She then gives herself up to a bloody death, after suffering torture of the heart seven times, witnessing to steadfast faith, boundless hope, and heroic courage.

In these figures of woman, in whom the marvels of divine grace are manifest, we glimpse the one who will be the greatest: Mary, Mother of the Lord.

READING 40 (DECEMBER 7, 1996): Motherhood: Woman's Gift to Society[1]

I joyfully welcome you to this meeting entitled Women, organized by the Pontifical Council for the Laity. A year ago, the Fourth World Conference on Women took place in Beijing. It opportunely shed light on the moral, cultural, and social challenges still facing the international community. Prominent among the areas still in need of reflection for finding suitable solutions are the legal and practical norms that guarantee the rights of the individual, universal access to education, respect for human dignity and family units, and the recognition of male and female identity.

It is no exaggeration to say that the work of the conference, an event followed with interest on all represented continents, rightly stressed the close connection between issues affecting women and the value that the contemporary world puts upon life. I am consequently delighted that during your days of study you will be able to examine these themes in greater depth and thus show the Church's constant concern that women should renew and continue their involvement in social life. With your reflections you will be making an original contribution to the Church's mission in the service of man, created in God's image, "the only creature on earth that God has wanted for its own sake," and to whom he entrusted the whole of creation.

Human Being Has Infinite Value from the Start

A renewed commitment by all to the well-being of all the world's women: this was the theme you chose in accordance with the mandate I gave the members of the Holy See's delegation—led by a woman—on the eve of their departure for Beijing. Today, I would like to pay tribute once again to the achievements of the delegation, which was constantly concerned with the true good of all women while taking into account the sociocultural context and attaching importance above all to respect for the individual. Further, the delegation forcefully reminded political leaders and all who work in international organizations that every person must be respected for himself, in his physical, intellectual, and spiritual integrity, so that a person will never be treated as an object or be exploited by political or economic interests that are often inspired by neo-Malthusian ideologies. Your initiative fits within the framework of the post-synodal exhortation *Christifideles Laici*, in which I described a necessary condition for ensuring women their rightful place in the Church and in society, for the full development of their particular genius: "a more penetrating and accurate consideration of the anthropological foundation of masculinity and femininity for the purpose of clarifying woman's personal identity in relation to man."

The legitimate quest for equality between men and women in such important areas as education, the workplace, and parental responsibility has led research to the question of the equality of rights. In principle, at least, this has enabled many discriminatory practices to be abolished, although it has yet to be universally implemented and further action will be necessary.

In the sphere of human rights, it is more appropriate than ever to ask our contemporaries to question themselves on what is mistakenly called "reproductive health." The expression contains a contradiction that distorts the very meaning of subjectivity: actually, it includes the alleged right to abortion, which denies the basic right of every human being to life, and in harming one of its members it injures the whole human race. "The roots of the contradiction between the solemn affirmation of human rights and their tragic denial in practice lies in a notion of freedom which exalts the isolated individual in an absolute way, and gives no place to solidarity, openness to others and service of them." Recognition of someone as human being is never based on the awareness or experience we may have of him but by the certitude that he has an infinite value from conception, which comes to him from his relationship with God. A human being has primacy over the ideas others have of him, and his existence is absolute and not relative.

At the moment, it should be noted that insistence on equality is also accompanied by renewed attention to the difference between men and women and a great respect for their distinctive traits. A true reflection might suggest that the foundations of difference and equality have been well laid. In this perspective, the Church does not only make a theological contribution but is also involved in anthropological research. The role played by the twentieth-century Christian philosophers who exalted the greatness of the human being cannot be forgotten. The Church takes part in the creation of a common cultural base for men and women of goodwill, so as to offer a systematic answer to our contemporaries' questions and to recall that equality goes hand in hand with the recognition of differences inherent in them since creation (cf. Gen 1:27).

In our societies, deeply marked by the individual pursuit of success, each person will nonetheless realize that he cannot live without openness to others, for, as Mons. Maurice Nedoncelle commented, "[A]n individual exists for himself through others" (*La personne humaine et sa nature* 5). He does not find himself, and does not consciously develop, except by being linked to specific culture, and through it, to all humanity. The advancement of individuals and their interpersonal relations therefore includes the advancement of cultures, which are like a jewel box in which every human being finds his proper place for the protection and growth of his being.

Trinity Is Model of Perfect Loving and Giving

Conjugal love is the loftiest and most beautiful expression of human relations and self-giving, for it is essentially a desire for mutual growth. In this encounter based on reciprocal love, each is recognized for what he is and is called to express his personal talents and achieve his potential. The "logic of the sincere gift of self" (Letter to Families II) is a source of joy, help, and understanding.

Human love finds in Trinitarian love a model of perfect loving and giving. Through the total gift of himself, Jesus gives birth to the people of the New Covenant. On the cross, the Lord entrusted the disciple he loved and his Mother to each other (cf. Jn 19:26-27). Does not the Apostle compare the love of Christ and His Church to the love between man and woman? (cf. Eph 5:25-32). The biblical texts also reveal to us the profound meaning of the motherhood of woman "introduced into the order of the Covenant that God made with humanity in Jesus Christ" (*Mulieris Dignitatem* 19). In its personal and ethical sense, this motherhood shows a creativity on which the humanity of each human being largely depends; it also invites man to learn and to express his own fatherhood; thus women contribute to society and to the Church their ability to nurture human beings.

The Church is our mother. We are her children and are called to share in giving birth to a new people for God. We learn this motherhood from Mary, for to all those who are working for the rebirth of man through their participation in the apostolic mission she is an "exemplar both of virgin and mother." You are providentially holding your meeting on the eve of the feast of the Immaculate Conception. This is certainly an occasion for everyone, priests, religious, laity, men, and women, to contemplate Mary and to ask her help so that each, according to his own vocation, may contribute to the witness given by the Church, Bride of Christ, "in splendor, without spot or wrinkle or any such thing, that she might be holy and without blemish" (Eph 5:27).

At the close of our meeting, I am delighted with this initiative taken by the Pontifical Council for the Laity, and I hope that your work here may be fruitful and give the Church a precious means to carry out her pastoral mission and service in society. I encourage you to continue your activities in the Catholic organizations, ecclesiastical communities, and the various associations in which you are involved. As I commend you to the intercession of the holy women who throughout history have shared in the Church's journey, I cordially give you my apostolic blessing, which I extend to all your dear ones.

READING 41 (JANUARY 8, 1997): Christ Calls Women to Share His Mission[1]

Editor's note. Simeon's words and Anna's example at the presentation in the Temple shed light on the role women will have in Jesus' work of Redemption. "The resurrection of many is a marvelous effect of the Redemption. This proclamation alone kindles great hope in the hearts of those to whom the fruit of the sacrifice already bears witness," the Holy Father said at this General Audience, as he focused on the cooperation of women in the work of Redemption. Here is a translation of the pope's catechesis, which was the forty-first in the series on the Blessed Virgin and was given in Italian.

1. The words of the aged Simeon, announcing to Mary her sharing in the Messiah's saving mission, shed light on woman's role in the mystery of Redemption. Indeed, Mary is not only an individual person but she is also the "daughter of Zion," the new woman standing at the Redeemer's side in order to share his Passion and to give birth in the Spirit to the children of God. This reality is expressed by the popular depiction of the "seven swords" that pierce Mary's heart: this image highlights the deep link between the mother, who is identified with the daughter of Zion and with the Church, and the sorrowful destiny of the Incarnate Word.

Giving back her Son, whom she had just received from God, to consecrate him for his saving mission, Mary also gives herself to this mission. It is an act of interior sharing that is not only the fruit of natural maternal affection but above all expresses the consent of the new woman to Christ's redemptive work.

Mary Will Be Involved in Jesus' Suffering

2. In his words, Simeon indicates the purpose of Jesus' sacrifice and Mary's suffering: these will come about so "that thoughts out of many hearts may be revealed" (Lk 2:35). Jesus, "a sign that will be opposed" (Lk 2:34), who involves his mother in his suffering, will lead men and women to take a stand in his regard, inviting them to make a fundamental decision. In fact, he "is set for the fall and rising of many in Israel" (Lk 2:34).

Mary is united to her divine Son in this "contradiction," in view of the work of salvation. Certainly there is a risk of ruin for those who reject Christ, but the resurrection of many is a marvelous effect of the Redemption. This proclamation alone kindles great hope in the hearts of those to whom the fruit of the sacrifice already bears witness.

Directing the Blessed Virgin's attention to these prospects of salvation before the ritual offering, Simeon seems to suggest to Mary that she perform this act as a contribution to humanity's ransom. In fact, he does not speak *to* Joseph or *about* Joseph: his words are addressed to Mary, whom he associates with the destiny of her Son.

3. The chronological priority of Mary's action does not obscure Jesus' primacy. In describing Mary's role in the economy of salvation, the Second Vatican Council recalled that she "devoted herself totally ... to the person and work of her Son, *under and with him*, serving the mystery of Redemption" (*Lumen Gentium*, n56).

At the presentation of Jesus in the Temple, Mary serves the mystery of Redemption under Christ and with Christ: indeed he has the principal role in salvation and must be ransomed by a ritual offering. Mary is joined to the sacrifice of her Son by the sword that will pierce her soul.

4. The primacy of Christ does not rule out but supports and demands the proper, irreplaceable role of woman. By involving his mother in his own sacrifice, Christ wants to reveal its deep human roots and to show us an anticipation of the priestly offering of the cross. The divine intention to call for the specific involvement of woman in the work of Redemption can be seen by the fact that Simeon's prophecy is addressed to Mary alone, although Joseph also took part in the offering rite.

The conclusion of the episode of Jesus' presentation in the temple seems to confirm the meaning and value of the feminine presence in the economy of salvation. The meeting with a woman, Anna, brings to a close these special moments when the Old Testament, as it were, is handed over to the New.

Like Simeon, this woman has no special status among the chosen people, but her life seems to have a lofty value in God's eyes. St. Luke calls her a "prophetess," probably because many consulted her for her gift of discernment and the holy life she led under the inspiration of the spirit of the Lord.

Anna is advanced in age, being eighty-four years old, and has long been a widow. Totally consecrated to God, "she never left the Temple, serving God day and night with fasting and prayer" (cf. Lk 2:37). She represents those who, having intensely lived in expectation of the Messiah, are able to accept the fulfillment of the promise with joyous exultation. The evangelist mentions that "coming up at that very hour she gave thanks to God" (2:38). Staying constantly in the temple, she could, perhaps more easily than Simeon, meet Jesus at the end of a life dedicated to the Lord and enriched by listening to the Word and by prayer.

At the dawn of Redemption, we can glimpse in the prophetess Anna all women who, with holiness of life and in prayerful expectation, are ready to accept Christ's presence and to praise God every day for the marvels wrought by his everlasting mercy.

Anna Is Symbol of Women Who Spread the Gospel

5. Chosen to meet the Child, Simeon and Anna have a deep experience of sharing the joy of Jesus' presence with Mary and Joseph and spreading it where they live. Anna, in particular, shows wonderful zeal in speaking about Jesus, thus witnessing to her simple and generous faith. This faith prepares others to accept the Messiah in their lives. Luke's expression, "she ... spoke of him to all who were looking for the redemption of Jerusalem" (2:38), seems to credit her as a symbol of the women who, dedicated to spreading the Gospel, will arouse and nourish the hope of salvation.

To the English-speaking visitors and pilgrims, the Holy Father said: "I am pleased to greet all the English-speaking visitors, especially the pilgrims from Korea and the United States. I also thank the choirs for their praise of God in song. Upon you and your families I cordially invoke the joy and peace of Jesus Christ our Savior."

READING 42 (FEBRUARY 20, 1998): Address to the International Conference on Women's Health Issues[1]

Distinguished Ladies and Gentlemen,

1. I wish to express my appreciation to the Catholic University of the Sacred Heart, represented here by the rector, Prof. Adriano Bausola, to the director of the Institute of Bioethics of the same university, Bishop Elio Sgreccia, and to the director of the Center for Medical Ethics of Georgetown University, for having organized this international conference on such a timely theme for society and for the Church: women's health issues. To reflect on this topic is, in fact, a duty and a debt of recognition not only for the dignity of every woman, whose right to treatment and access to means for improving health must be acknowledged, but also in relation to the special role that women are called to exercise in the family and in so-

ciety. In this respect, we cannot fail to remember a great number of women—children, adolescents, wives, mothers of families, the elderly—who live in conditions of poverty, with a total lack of health services, and who are burdened by the difficulties involved in supporting a family in vast areas of the world, often aggravated by disaster and war.

2. In my Message to the Secretary General of the Fourth World Conference on Women, held in Beijing, I mentioned the "terrible exploitation of women and girls which exists in every part of the world." I added, "Public opinion is only beginning to take stock of the inhuman conditions in which women and children are often forced to work, especially in less developed areas of the globe" (n7, May 26, 1995; *L'Osservatore Romano*, English edition, May 31, 1995, 2). No true development occurs without respect for life at every stage. It is essential for every society that such rights be guaranteed and that societies which enjoy full economic development and sometimes a superfluous level of goods turn their attention and their assistance to these people. This cannot be done without an appropriate and corresponding recognition of the role of women, of their dignity, and of the importance of their specific contribution to the society in which they live: "When women are able fully to share their gifts with the whole community, the very way in which society understands and organizes itself is improved" (Message for 1995 World Day of Peace, n9; *L'Osservatore Romano*, English edition, December 14, 1994, 2).

3. In particular, I consider it significant that at your international conference you wished to examine all aspects of women's health: the prevention and treatment of illness, respect for their integrity and their procreative capacities, and the psychological and spiritual aspects of the various situations in which they find themselves. In fact, an idea of health is spreading that, paradoxically, exalts and at the same time impoverishes its meaning and this particularly applies to women. Indeed, health has been defined as a striving for "complete physical, psychological and social well-being and not just the absence of illness." When, however, well-being is taken in a hedonistic sense without any reference to moral, spiritual, and religious values, this aspiration, in itself noble, can be confined to a narrow horizon that sti-

fles its zeal with negative consequences for health itself. Interpreted in this reductive sense, the quest for health as well-being has reached the point that, even in important political documents, motherhood itself is regarded as a burden and illness, thus creating the pretext, in the name of health and quality of life, for the justification of contraception, sterilization, abortion, and even euthanasia. This distortion must be rectified because "there will never be justice, including equality, development and peace, for women or for men, unless there is an unfailing determination to respect, protect, love and serve life—every human life at every stage and in every situation" (Message for the Fourth World Conference on Women, n7; cf. Encyclical *Evangelium Vitae*, n87).

4. Promoting the authentic, balanced, overall health of women means helping them to harmonize their physical, psychological, and social well-being with moral and spiritual values. In this perspective of personal and specifically feminine fulfillment, in which spousal and maternal self-giving is lived in the family or in consecrated life and a sense of social solidarity is expressed, health represents both a fundamental condition and a dimension of the person. For this reason, the concept of health must be based on a complete anthropological vision that considers respect for life and for the dignity of every person to be indispensable values. The quest for health cannot, therefore, ignore the ontological value of the person and his personal dignity: even where physical and mental health are deficient, the person still preserves his full dignity.

5. In promoting women's health, procreation has a special role from the standpoint of the fulfillment of both the feminine personality and possible motherhood. To promote the procreative health of women will therefore imply the primary prevention of those illnesses that can jeopardize fertility, as well as treatment, counseling, and assistance aimed at preserving the female organism in its integrity or at restoring its functionality; but it can never mean offending the personal dignity of the woman or the dignity of the newly conceived life. The Church recognizes women's contribution to society. In this regard, the moral commitment of the woman herself will always have great importance: in her daily conduct, she must assume and

respect the values of her own corporality, trying to assure their conformity with the demands of health. This promotion of woman's overall health must also involve society, and this will only take place with the contribution of women themselves: "The Church," I wrote to the Secretary General of the United Nations Fourth World Conference on Women, "recognizes that women's contribution to the welfare and progress of society is incalculable, and the Church looks to women to do even more to save society from the deadly virus of degradation and violence which is today witnessing a dramatic increase" (n5).

6. The whole dimension of culture and society, and in the first place health care, must be measured against the dignity of women in joint responsibility with men and for the good of families and the human community itself. I wish here to repeat the gratitude I expressed to women in the Letter addressed specifically to them in 1995 during International Women's Year: Thank you to women who are mothers, to women who are wives, to women who are daughters, to working women, and to consecrated women. Today, I would also like to thank women who practice medicine: More and more of them help to promote the health of others, becoming guardians of life in a special capacity. I hope that all people, society as a whole and political authorities, will make their contribution to the achievement of health for every woman and every man, as a guarantee of a civilization that conforms to the dignity of the human person.

With these wishes, I impart my Blessing to all.

READING 43 (NOVEMBER 24, 1999): The Fatherhood of God and the Dignity of Women[1]

Dear Brothers and Sisters,

1. Among the challenges of this historical moment on which the Great Jubilee spurs us to reflect, I drew attention in my Apostolic Letter *Tertio Millennio Adveniente* to the issue of respect for women's rights (cf. *Tertio Millennio Adveniente*, n51). Today, I would like to recall certain aspects of the women's question, which I have also spoken of on other occasions.

Sacred Scripture sheds great light on the theme of women's advancement, pointing out God's plan for man and woman in the two accounts of creation. The first one says: "God created man in his own image, in the image of God he created him; male and female he created them" (Gen 1: 27). This statement is the basis of Christian anthropology, because it identifies the foundation of man's dignity as a person in his creation "in the likeness" of God. At the same time, the passage clearly says that neither man nor woman separately is the image of the Creator, but man and woman in their reciprocity. Both are equally God's masterpiece. In the second account of creation, through the symbolism of the creation of woman from man's rib, Scripture stresses that humanity is not, in fact, complete until woman is created (cf. Gen 2: 18-24).

She is given a name whose verbal assonance in Hebrew indicates a relationship to man (*'iš-'iššah*). "God created man and woman together and willed each for the other" (Catechism of the Catholic Church, n371). That woman is presented as a "helper fit for him" (Gen 2: 18) should not be interpreted as meaning that woman is man's servant—"helper" is not the equivalent of "servant"; the psalmist says to God: "You are my help" (Ps(s) 70: 5; cf. Ps(s) 115: 9, 10, 11; Ps(s) 118: 7; Ps(s) 146: 5); rather, the whole statement means that woman is able to collaborate with man because she complements him perfectly. Woman is another kind of "ego" in their common humanity, which consists of male and female in perfectly equal dignity.

2. There is good reason to rejoice in the fact that in contemporary culture reflection on what it means to be feminine has led to a deeper understanding of the human person in terms of his "being for others" in interpersonal communion. Today, to think of the person in his self-giving dimension is becoming a matter of principle. Unfortunately, it is often disregarded at the practical level; thus, among the many assaults on human dignity, that widespread violation of woman's dignity manifested in the exploitation of her person and her body should be strongly condemned. All practices that offend woman's freedom or femininity must be vigorously opposed: so-called "sexual tourism," the buying and selling of young girls, mass sterilization, and, in general, every form of violence to the other sex.

A very different attitude is required by the moral law, which proclaims the dignity of woman as a person created in the image of God-Communion! Today, it is more necessary than ever to present the biblical anthropology of relationality, which helps us genuinely understand the human being's identity in his relationship to others, particularly between man and woman. In the human person considered in his "relationality," we find a vestige of God's own mystery revealed in Christ as a substantial unity in the communion of three divine Persons. In the light of this mystery, it is easy to understand the statement of *Gaudium et Spes* that the human being, who "is the only creature on earth that God has wanted for its own sake, can fully discover his true self only in a sincere giving of himself" (*Gaudium et Spes*, n24). The difference between man and woman calls for interpersonal communion, and meditation on the dignity and vocation of woman strengthens the concept of the human being based on communion (cf. *Mulieris Dignitatem*, n7).

3. Precisely this capacity for communion, which the feminine dimension strongly evokes, enables us to reflect on God's fatherhood, thus avoiding the imaginative projections of a patriarchal sort that are so challenged, and not without reason, in some currents of contemporary literature. It is a question, in fact, of discerning the Father's face within the mystery of God as Trinity, that is, as perfect unity in distinction. The figure of the Father must be reconsidered in his relationship to the Son, who is turned toward him from all eternity (cf. Jn 1: 1) in the communion of the Holy Spirit. It should also be stressed that the Son of God became man in the fullness of time and was born of the Virgin Mary (cf. Gal 4: 4), and this, too, sheds light on the feminine dimension, showing Mary as the model of woman as willed by God. The greatest event in human history took place in her and through her. The fatherhood of God the Father is related not only to God the Son in his eternal mystery but also to his Incarnation in a woman's womb. If God the Father, who 'begets' the Son from all eternity, turned to a woman, Mary, to 'beget' him in the world, thus making her '*Theotókos*,' Mother of God, this is not without significance for understanding woman's dignity in the divine plan.

4. The Gospel message about God's fatherhood, far from restricting woman's dignity and role, serves instead as a guarantee of what the "feminine" humanly symbolizes, that is, to welcome, to care for the human person, and to give birth to life. All this is rooted, in a transcendent way, in the mystery of the eternal divine "begetting." Certainly, God's fatherhood is entirely spiritual; nevertheless, it expresses that eternal reciprocity and relationality which are truly Trinitarian and are the origin of all fatherhood and motherhood and the basis of the riches common to male and female.

Reflection on woman's role and mission is particularly appropriate this year, which is dedicated to God the Father, and spurs us to work with ever greater effort so that all the possibilities that are proper to woman in the Church and in society will be acknowledged.

CONCLUDING SECTION

Fr. Edward J. Baenziger, CSB

PROCLAMATION OF ST. THÉRÈSE OF LISIEUX AS DOCTOR OF THE CHURCH

We include the October 19, 1997, proclamation of Thérèse of Lisieux to be a Doctor of the Church, because her "little way" of trust and spiritual childhood is thereby highlighted as an historically fresh set of ideas and ideals on the "science of love" that are open equally for all souls to become saints of God. Her focus is that of the micro-sign, the tiniest and seemingly unnoticed action which can lead to sanctity. Recognized for her teachings, she models contemplation both for religious and laity as the mystical union with Christ overflowing into acts of pure love, however small and inconsequential they might seem. She provides for the counter-cultural soul the inner authority that is especially helpful to women but not limited to women alone. Rather, the "little way" transcends patriarchal values and feminism, since the longing of the soul for the infinite comes about through any person having empty hands. The "little way" is applicable to any believer, empty-handed before God, who revels in one's own weakness, trusting in the infinite merciful love of God. Although others suggested to John Paul II that he investigate the possibility of her becoming a Doctor, it was he who made it happen, through his own direct action.

As with the naming of Thérèse as Doctor of the Church, so also for the canonizations and beatifications: John Paul II did them in a joyous manner. With both the proclamation and with the canonizations and beatifications, his actions were done in the face of much criticism, both in the secular press and among some in the curia. He changed the rules and pushed the process to bring it about that the Church's statements *about* women are shown to have been realized in these women's *actions*. He thereby emphasized that there are saints, even now, and that we, the Church, must recognize these women saints in order to help us along our own little way.

APOSTOLIC LETTER

On August 15, 1996, the pope urged the youth of the world to take up the "little way" of Thérèse of Lisieux, and at the World Youth Day recitation of the Angelus, August 24, 1997, he announced his intention to name her a Doctor of the Church.[1] Here is the text of his Apostolic Letter of October 19 in that same year of 1997.

Saint Thérèse of the Child Jesus and the Holy Face Is Proclaimed a Doctor of the Universal Church[2]

1. THE SCIENCE OF DIVINE LOVE, which the Father of mercies pours out through Jesus Christ in the Holy Spirit, is a gift granted to the little and the humble so that they may know and proclaim the secrets of the kingdom, hidden from the learned and the wise; for this reason, Jesus rejoiced in the Holy Spirit, praising the Father who graciously willed it so (cf. Lk 10:21-22; Mt 11:25-26).

Mother Church also rejoices in noting that throughout history the Lord has continued to reveal himself to the little and the humble, enabling his chosen ones, through the Spirit who "searches everything, even the depths of God" (1 Cor 2:10), to speak of the gifts "bestowed on us by God ... in words not taught by human wisdom but taught by the Spirit, interpreting spiritual truths in spiritual language" (1 Cor 2:12-13). In this way, the Holy Spirit guides the Church into the whole truth, endowing her with various gifts, adorning her with his fruits, rejuvenating her with the power of the Gospel, and enabling her to discern the signs of the times in order to respond ever more fully to the will of God (cf. *Lumen Gentium*, nn4, 12; *Gaudium et Spes*, n4).

Shining brightly among the little ones to whom the secrets of the kingdom were revealed in a most special way is Thérèse of the Child Jesus and the Holy Face, a professed nun of the Order of Discalced Carmelites, the one hundredth anniversary of whose entry into the heavenly homeland occurs this year. During her life, Thérèse discovered "new lights, hidden and mysterious meanings" (Ms A, 83v) and received from the divine Teacher that "science of love" which she then expressed with particular originality in her writings (cf. Ms B, 1r). This science is the luminous expression of her knowledge of the mystery of the kingdom and of her personal experience of grace. It can be considered a special charism of Gospel wisdom which Thérèse, like other saints and teachers of faith, attained in prayer (cf. Ms C, 36r·).

2. The reception given to the example of her life and Gospel teaching in our century was quick, universal, and constant. As if in imitation of her precocious spiritual maturity, her holiness was recognized by the Church in the space of a few years. In fact, on June 10, 1914, Pius X signed the decree introducing her cause of beatification; on August 14, 1921, Benedict XV declared the heroic virtues of the Servant of God, giving an address for the occasion on the way of spiritual childhood; and Pius XI proclaimed her blessed on April 29, 1923. Shortly afterward, on May 17, 1925, the same Pope canonized her before an immense crowd in St. Peter's Basilica, highlighting the splendor of her virtues and the originality of her doctrine. Two years later, on December 14, 1927, in response to the petition of many missionary Bishops, he proclaimed her patron of the missions, along with St. Francis Xavier.

Beginning with these acts of recognition, the spiritual radiance of Thérèse of the Child Jesus increased in the Church and spread throughout the world. Many institutes of consecrated life and ecclesial movements, especially in the young Churches, chose her as their patron and teacher, taking their inspiration from her spiritual doctrine. Her message, often summarized in the so-called "little way," which is nothing other than the Gospel way of holiness for all, was studied by theologians and experts in spirituality. Cathedrals, basilicas, shrines, and churches throughout the world were built and dedicated to the Lord under the patronage of the Saint of Lisieux. The Catholic Church venerates her in the various Eastern and Western rites. Many of the faithful have been able to experience the power of her intercession. Many of those called to the priestly ministry or the consecrated life, especially in the missions and the cloister, attribute the divine grace of their vocation to her intercession and example.

3. The Pastors of the Church, beginning with my predecessors, the Supreme Pontiffs of this century, who held up her holiness as an example for all, also stressed that Thérèse is a teacher of the spiritual life with a doctrine both spiritual and profound, which she drew from the Gospel sources under the guidance of the divine Teacher and then imparted to her brothers and sisters in the Church with the greatest effectiveness (cf. Ms B, 2v-3). This spiritual doctrine has been passed on to us primarily by her autobiography which, taken from three manuscripts she wrote in the last years of her life and published a year after her death with the title *Histoire d'une âme* (Lisieux 1898), has aroused an extraordinary interest down to our day. This autobiography, translated along with her other writings into about fifty languages, has made Thérèse known in every part of the world, even outside the Catholic Church. A century after her death, Thérèse of the Child Jesus continues to be recognized as one of the great masters of the spiritual life in our time.

4. It is not surprising then that the Apostolic See received many petitions to confer on her the title of Doctor of the Universal Church. In recent years, especially with the happy occasion of the first centenary of her death close at hand, these requests became more and more numerous, including on the part of Episcopal conferences; in addition, study conferences were held and numerous publications have pointed out how Thérèse of the Child Jesus possesses an extraordinary wisdom and with her doctrine helps so many men and women of every state in life to know and love Jesus Christ and his Gospel. In the light of these facts, I decided to study carefully whether the Saint of Lisieux had the prerequisites for being awarded the title of Doctor of the Universal Church.

5. In this context, I am pleased to recall briefly some events in the life of Thérèse of the Child Jesus. Born in Alençon, France, on January 2, 1873, she is baptized two days later in the Church of Notre Dame, receiving the name

Marie-Françoise-Thérèse. Her parents are Louis Martin and Zélie Guérin, whose heroic virtues I recently recognized. After her mother's death on August 28, 1877, Thérèse moves with her whole family to the town of Lisieux where, surrounded by the affection of her father and sisters, she receives a formation both demanding and full of tenderness.

Toward the end of 1879 she receives the Sacrament of Penance for the first time. On the day of Pentecost in 1883, she has the extraordinary grace of being healed from a serious illness through the intercession of Our Lady of Victories. Educated by the Benedictines of Lisieux, she receives First Communion on May 8, 1884, after an intense preparation crowned with an exceptional experience of the grace of intimate union with Jesus. A few weeks later, on June 14 of that same year, she receives the Sacrament of Confirmation with a vivid awareness of what the gift of the Holy Spirit involves in her personal sharing in the grace of Pentecost. On Christmas Day of 1886, she has a profound spiritual experience that she describes as a "complete conversion." As a result, she overcomes the emotional weakness caused by the loss of her mother and begins "to run as a giant" on the way of perfection (cf. Ms A, 44v45v).

Thérèse wishes to embrace the contemplative life, like her sisters Pauline and Marie in the Carmel of Lisieux, but is prevented from doing so by her young age. During a pilgrimage to Italy, after visiting the Holy House of Loreto and places in the Eternal City, at an audience granted by the Pope to the faithful of the Diocese of Lisieux on November 20, 1887, she asks Leo XIII with filial boldness to be able to enter Carmel at the age of fifteen years.

On April 9, 1888, she enters the Carmel of Lisieux, where she receives the habit of the Blessed Virgin's order on January 10 of the following year and makes her religious profession on September 8, 1890, the feast of the Birth of the Virgin Mary. At Carmel, she undertakes the way of perfection marked out by the Mother Foundress, Teresa of Jesus, with genuine fervor and fidelity in fulfilling the various community tasks entrusted to her. Illumined by the Word of God, particularly tried by the illness of her beloved father, Louis Martin, who dies on July 29, 1894, Thérèse embarks on the way of holiness, insisting on the centrality of love. She discovers and imparts to the novices entrusted to her care the little way of spiritual childhood, by which she enters more and more deeply into the mystery of the Church and, drawn by the love of Christ, feels growing within her the apostolic and missionary vocation which spurs her to bring everyone with her to meet the divine Spouse.

On June 9, 1895, the feast of the Most Holy Trinity, she offers herself as a sacrificial victim to the merciful Love of God. On April 3 of the following year, on the night between Holy Thursday and Good Friday, she notices the first symptoms of the illness which will lead to her death. Thérèse welcomes it as a mysterious visitation of the divine Spouse. At the same time, she undergoes a trial of faith which will last until her death. As her health deteriorates, she is moved to the infirmary on July 8, 1897. Her sisters and other religious collect her sayings, while her sufferings and trials, borne with patience, intensify to the moment of her death on the afternoon of September 30, 1897. "I am not dying; I am entering life," she had written to one of her spiritual brothers, Fr. Bellière (*Lettres* 244). Her last words, "My God, I love you," are the seal of her life.

6. Thérèse of the Child Jesus left us writings that deservedly qualify her as a teacher of the spiritual life. Her principal work remains the account of her life in three autobiographical manuscripts (*Manuscrits autobiographiques A, B, C*), first published with the soon-to-be-famous title of *Histoire d'une Âme*.

In Manuscript A, written at the request of her sister Agnes of Jesus, then Prioress of the monastery, and given to her on January 21, 1896, Thérèse describes the stages of her religious experience: the early years of childhood, (especially the time of her First Communion and Confirmation), adolescence up to her entrance into Carmel and her first profession.

Manuscript B, written during her retreat that same year at the request of her sister Marie of the Sacred Heart, contains some of the most beautiful, best-known, and oft-quoted passages from the Saint of Lisieux. They reveal the Saint's full maturity as she speaks of her vocation in the Church, the Bride of Christ and Mother of souls.

Manuscript C, composed in June and the first days of July 1897, a few months before her death and dedicated to the Prioress, Marie de Gonzague, who had requested it, completes the recollections in Manuscript

A on life in Carmel. These pages reveal the author's supernatural wisdom. Thérèse recounts some sublime experiences during this final period of her life. She devotes moving pages to her trial of faith: a grace of purification that immerses her in a long and painful dark night, illuminated by her trust in the merciful, fatherly love of God. Once again, and without repeating herself, Thérèse makes the light of the Gospel shine brightly. Here we find the most beautiful pages she devoted to trusting abandonment into God's hands, from unity between love of God and love of neighbor, to her missionary vocation in the Church.

In these three different manuscripts, which converge in a thematic unity and in a progressive description of her life and spiritual way, Thérèse has left us an original autobiography which is the story of her soul. It shows how in her life God has offered the world a precise message, indicating an evangelical way, the "little way," which everyone can take, because everyone is called to holiness. In the 266 *Lettres* we possess, addressed to family members, women religious, and missionary "brothers," Thérèse shares her wisdom, developing a teaching that is actually a profound exercise in the spiritual direction of souls.

Her writings also include fifty-four *Poésies*, some of which have great theological and spiritual depth inspired by sacred scripture. Worthy of special mention are *Vivre d'Amour! …* (*Poésies* 17) and *Pourquoi je t'aime, ô Marie!* (*Poésies* 54), an original synthesis of the Virgin Mary's journey according to the Gospel. To this literary production should be added eight *Récréations Pieyses*: poetic and theatrical compositions, conceived and performed by the Saint for her community on certain feast days, in accordance with the tradition of Carmel. Among those writings should be mentioned a series of twenty-one *Prières*. Nor can we forget the collection of all she said during the last months of her life. These sayings, of which there are several editions, known as the *Novissima Verba*, have also been given the title *Derniers Entretiens*.

7. From careful study of the writings of St. Thérèse of the Child Jesus and from the resonance they have had in the Church, salient aspects can be noted of her "eminent doctrine," which is the fundamental element for conferring the title of Doctor of the Church. First of all, we find a special

charism of wisdom. This young Carmelite, without any particular theological training, but illumined by the light of the Gospel, feels she is being taught by the divine Teacher who, as she says, is "the Doctor of Doctors" (Ms A, 83v), and from him she receives "divine teachings" (Ms B, 1r). She feels that the words of Scripture are fulfilled in her: "Whoever is a little one, let him come to me.... For to him that is little, mercy shall be shown" (Ms B, 1v; cf. Prv 9:4; Ws 6:6), and she knows she is being instructed in the science of love, hidden from the wise and prudent, which the divine Teacher deigned to reveal to her, as to babes (Ms A, 49r; cf. Lk 10:21-22).

Pius XI, who considered Thérèse of Lisieux the "Star of his pontificate," did not hesitate to assert in his homily on the day of her canonization, May 17, 1925: "The Spirit of truth opened and made known to her what he usually hides from the wise and prudent and reveals to little ones; thus she enjoyed such knowledge of the things above—as Our immediate Predecessor attests—that she shows everyone else the sure way of salvation" (*AAS* 17 [1925], 213). Her teaching not only conforms to Scripture and the Catholic faith but excels ("*eminet*") for *the depth and wise synthesis it achieved.* Her doctrine is at once a confession of the Church's faith, an experience of the Christian mystery and a way to holiness. Thérèse offers a mature synthesis of Christian spirituality: she combines theology and the spiritual life; she expresses herself with strength and authority, with a great ability to persuade and communicate, as is shown by the reception and dissemination of her message among the People of God.

Thérèse's teaching expresses with coherence and harmonious unity the dogmas of the Christian faith as a doctrine of truth and an experience of life. In this regard, it should not be forgotten that the understanding of the deposit of faith transmitted by the Apostles, as the Second Vatican Council teaches, makes progress in the Church with the help of the Holy Spirit: "There is growth in insight into the realities and words that are passed on ... through the contemplation and study of believers who ponder these things in their hearts (cf. Lk 2:19 and 51). It comes from the intimate sense of spiritual realities which they experience. And it comes from the preaching of those who have received, along with their right of succession in the episcopate, the sure charism of truth" (*Dei Verbum*, n8).

In the writings of Thérèse of Lisieux, we do not find perhaps, as in other

Doctors, a scholarly presentation of the things of God, but we can discern an enlightened witness of faith which, while accepting with trusting love God's merciful condescension and salvation in Christ, reveals the mystery and holiness of the Church. We can rightly recognize in the Saint of Lisieux the charism of a Doctor of the Church, because of the gift of the Holy Spirit she received for living and expressing her experience of faith, and because of her particular understanding of the mystery of Christ. In her are found the gifts of the new law, that is, the grace of the Holy Spirit, who manifests himself in living faith working through charity (cf. St. Thomas Aquinas, *Summa Theol.*, I-II, q. 106, art. 1; q. 108, art. 1).

We can apply to Thérèse of Lisieux what my Predecessor Paul VI said of another young Saint and Doctor of the Church, Catherine of Siena: "What strikes us most about the Saint is her infused wisdom, that is to say, her lucid, profound and inebriating absorption of the divine truths and mysteries of faith .... That assimilation was certainly favored by the most singular natural gifts, but it was also evidently something prodigious, due to a charism of wisdom from the Holy Spirit" (*AAS* 62 [1970], 675).

⇝

8. With her distinctive doctrine and unmistakable style, Thérèse appears as an *authentic teacher of faith and the Christian life*. In her writings, as in the sayings of the Holy Fathers, is found that life-giving presence of Catholic tradition whose riches, as the Second Vatican Council again says, "are poured out in the practice and life of the Church, in her belief and prayer" (*Dei Verbum*, n8).

If considered in its literary genre, corresponding to her education and culture, and if evaluated according to the particular circumstances of her era, the doctrine of Thérèse of Lisieux appears in providential harmony with the Church's most authentic tradition, both for its confession of the Catholic faith and for its promotion of the most genuine spiritual life, presented to all the faithful in a living, accessible language.

She has made the Gospel shine appealingly in our time; she had the mission of making the Church, the Mystical Body of Christ, known and loved; she helped to heal souls of the rigors and fears of Jansenism, which tended to stress God's justice rather than his divine mercy. In God's mercy she contemplated and adored all the divine perfections, because "even his justice (and perhaps even more so than the other perfections) seems to me clothed in love" (Ms A, 83v.). Thus she became a living icon of that God who, according to the Church's prayer, "shows his almighty power in his mercy and forgiveness" (cf. *Roman Missal*, Opening prayer, Twenty-sixth Sunday in Ordinary Time).

Even though Thérèse does not have a true and proper doctrinal corpus, nevertheless a *particular radiance of doctrine* shines forth from her writings which, as if by a charism of the Holy Spirit, grasp the very heart of the message of Revelation in a fresh and original vision, presenting a teaching of eminent quality. The core of her message is actually the mystery itself of God—Love, of the Triune God, infinitely perfect in himself. If genuine Christian spiritual experience should conform to the revealed truths in which God communicates himself and the mystery of his will (cf. *Dei Verbum*, n2), it must be said that Thérèse experienced divine revelation, going so far as to contemplate the fundamental truths of our faith united in the mystery of Trinitarian life. At the summit, as the source and goal, is the merciful love of the three Divine Persons, as she expresses it, especially in her *Act of Oblation to Merciful Love*. At the root, on the subject's part, is the experience of being the Father's adoptive children in Jesus; this is the most authentic meaning of spiritual childhood, that is, the experience of divine filiation, under the movement of the Holy Spirit. At the root again, and standing before us, is our neighbor, others, for whose salvation we must collaborate with and in Jesus, with the same merciful love as his.

Through spiritual childhood one experiences that everything comes from God, returns to him, and abides in him, for the salvation of all, in a mystery of merciful love. Such is the doctrinal message taught and lived by this Saint.

As it was for the Church's Saints in every age, so also for her, in her spiritual experience Christ is the center and fullness of Revelation. Thérèse knew Jesus, loved him, and made him loved with the passion of a bride. She penetrated the mysteries of his infancy, the words of his Gospel, the passion of the suffering Servant engraved on his holy Face, in the splendor of his glorious life, in his Eucharistic presence. She sang of all the expressions of Christ's divine charity, as they are presented in the Gospel (cf. *PN* 24, *Jésus, mon Bien-Aimé, rappelle-toi!*).

Thérèse received particular light on the reality of Christ's Mystical Body, on the variety of its charisms, gifts of the Holy Spirit, and on the eminent power of love, which in a way is the very heart of the Church, where she found her vocation as a contemplative and missionary (cf. Ms B, 2r-3v·).

Lastly, among the most original chapters of her spiritual doctrine we must recall Thérèse's wise delving into the mystery and journey of the Virgin Mary, achieving results very close to the doctrine of the Second Vatican Council in chapter eight of the Constitution *Lumen Gentium*, and to what I myself taught in the Encyclical Letter *Redemptoris Mater* of March 25, 1987.

9. The primary source of her spiritual experience and her teaching is the Word of God in the Old and New Testaments. She herself admits it, particularly stressing her passionate love for the Gospel (cf. Ms A, 83v). Her writings contain over one thousand biblical quotations: more than four hundred from the Old Testament and over six hundred from the New Testament.

Despite her inadequate training and lack of resources for studying and interpreting the sacred books, Thérèse immersed herself in meditation on the Word of God with exceptional faith and spontaneity. Under the influence of the Holy Spirit, she attained a profound knowledge of Revelation for herself and for others. By her loving concentration on Scripture—she even wanted to learn Hebrew and Greek to understand better the spirit and letter of the sacred books—she showed the importance of the biblical sources in the spiritual life; she emphasized the originality and freshness of the Gospel; she cultivated with moderation the spiritual exegesis of the Word of God in both the Old and New Testaments. Thus she discovered hidden treasures, appropriating words and episodes, sometimes with supernatural boldness, as when, in reading the texts of St. Paul (cf. 1 Cor 12-13), she realized her vocation to love (cf. Ms B, 3r-3v). Enlightened by the revealed Word, Thérèse wrote brilliant pages on the unity between love of God and love of neighbor (cf. Ms C, 11v-19r), and she identified with Jesus' prayer at the Last Supper as the expression of her intercession for the salvation of all (cf. Ms C, 34r-35r).

Her doctrine, as was said, conforms to the Church's teaching. From childhood, she was taught by her family to participate in prayer and liturgical worship. In preparation for her first Confession, first Communion, and the Sacrament of Confirmation, she gave evidence of an extraordinary love for the truths of the faith, and she learned the *Catechism* almost word for word (cf. Ms A, 37r-37v). At the end of her life, she wrote the Apostles' Creed in her own blood, as an expression of her unreserved attachment to the profession of faith.

In addition to the words of Scripture and the Church's doctrine, Thérèse was nourished as a youth by the teaching of the *Imitation of Christ*, which, as she herself acknowledges, she knew almost by heart (cf. Ms A, 47r). Decisive for fulfilling her Carmelite vocation were the spiritual texts of the Mother Foundress, Teresa of Jesus, especially those explaining the contemplative and ecclesial meaning of the charism of the Teresian Carmel (cf. Ms C, 33v). But in a very special way, Thérèse was nourished on the mystical doctrine of St. John of the Cross, who was her true spiritual master (cf. Ms A, 83r). It should cause no surprise, then, if she who had been an outstanding pupil in the school of these two Saints, later declared Doctors of the Church, should later become a master of the spiritual life.

10. The *spiritual doctrine of Thérèse of Lisieux has helped extend the kingdom of God.* By her example of holiness, of perfect fidelity to Mother Church, of full communion with the See of Peter, as well as by the special graces obtained by her for many missionary brothers and sisters, she has rendered a particular service to the renewed proclamation and experience of Christ's Gospel and to the extension of the Catholic faith in every nation on earth. There is no need to dwell at length on the *universality of Thérèse's doctrine and on the broad reception of her message* during the century since her death: it has been well documented in the studies made in view of conferring on her the title of Doctor of the Church.

A particularly important fact in this regard is that the Church's Magisterium has not only recognized Thérèse's holiness but has also highlighted the wisdom of her doctrine. Pius X had already said that she was "the greatest saint of modern times." On joyfully receiving the first Italian edition of the *Story of a Soul*, he extolled the fruits that had resulted from Thérèse's spirituality. Benedict XV, on the occasion of proclaiming the Servant of

God's heroic virtues, explained the way of spiritual childhood and praised the knowledge of divine realities which God granted to Thérèse in order to teach others the ways of salvation (cf. *AAS* 13 [1921], 449–452). On the occasion of both her beatification and canonization, Pius XI wished to expound and recommend the Saint's doctrine, underscoring her special divine enlightenment (*Discorsi di Pio XI*, vol. I, Turin 1959, 91) and describing her as a teacher of life (cf. *AAS* 17 [1925], 211–214). When the Basilica of Lisieux was consecrated in 1954, Pius XII said, among other things, that Thérèse penetrated to the very heart of the Gospel with her doctrine (cf. *AAS* 46 [1954], 404–408). Cardinal Angelo Roncalli, the future Pope John XXIII, visited Lisieux several times, especially when he was Nuncio in Paris. On various occasions during his pontificate, he showed his devotion to the Saint and explained the relationship between the doctrine of the Saint of Avila and her daughter, Thérèse of Lisieux (*Discorsi, Messaggi, Colloqui*, vol. II [1959–1960], 771–72). Many times during the celebration of the Second Vatican Council, the Fathers recalled her example and doctrine. On the centenary of her birth, Paul VI addressed a letter on January 2, 1973, to the Bishop of Bayeux and Lisieux, in which he extolled Thérèse's example in the search for God, offered her as a teacher of prayer and theological virtue of hope, and a model of communion with the Church, calling the attention of teachers, educators, pastors, and theologians themselves to the study of her doctrine (cf. *AAS* 65 [1973], 12–15). I myself on various occasions have had the joy of recalling the person and doctrine of the saint, especially during my unforgettable visit to Lisieux on June 2, 1980, when I wished to remind everyone: "One can say with conviction about Thérèse of Lisieux that the Spirit of God allowed her heart to reveal directly to the people of our time the *fundamental mystery*, the reality of the Gospel ... Her 'little way' is the way of 'holy childhood'. There is something unique in this way, the genius of St. Thérèse of Lisieux. At the same time, there is the confirmation and renewal of the most *basic* and most *universal* truth. What truth of the Gospel message is really more basic and more universal than this: God is our Father and we are his children?" (*Insegnamenti di Giovanni Paolo II*, vol. III/1 [1980], 1659). These simple references to an uninterrupted series of testimonies from the Popes of this century on the holiness and doctrine of St. Thérèse of the Child Jesus and to the universal dissemination of her message clearly express to what extent the Church, in her pastors and her faithful, has accepted the spiritual doctrine of this young Saint.

A sign of the ecclesial reception of the Saint's teaching is *the appeal to her doctrine in many documents of the Church's ordinary Magisterium*, especially when speaking of the contemplative and missionary vocation, of trust in the just and merciful God, of Christian joy, and of the call to holiness. Evidence of this fact is the presence of her doctrine in the recent *Catechism of the Catholic Church* (nn127, 826, 956, 1011, 2011, 2558). She who so loved to learn the truths of the faith in the catechism deserved to be included among the authoritative witnesses of Catholic doctrine. *Thérèse possesses an exceptional universality*. Her person, the Gospel message of the "little way" of trust and spiritual childhood have received and continue to receive a remarkable welcome, which has transcended every border.

The influence of her message extends first of all to men and women whose holiness and heroic virtues the Church herself has recognized, to the Church's pastors, to experts in theology and spirituality, to priests and seminarians, to men and women religious, to ecclesial movements and new communities, to men and women of every condition and every continent. To everyone Thérèse gives her personal confirmation that the Christian mystery, whose witness and Apostle she became by making herself in prayer "the apostle of the apostles," as she boldly calls herself (Ms A, 56r·), must be taken literally, with the greatest possible realism, because it has a value for every time and place. The power of her message lies in its concrete explanation of how all Jesus' promises are fulfilled in the believer who knows how confidently to welcome in his own life the saving presence of the Redeemer.

11. All these reasons are clear evidence of how *timely* is the Saint of Lisieux's doctrine and of the *particular impact* her message has had on the men and women of our century. Moreover, some circumstances contribute to making her designation as a Teacher for the Church of our time even more significant.

First of all, Thérèse is a *woman*, who in approaching the Gospel knew how to grasp its hidden wealth with that practicality and deep resonance of life and wisdom which belong to the feminine genius. Because of her universality, she stands out among the multitude of holy women who are resplendent for their Gospel wisdom.

Thérèse is also a *contemplative*. In the hiddenness of her Carmel, she lived the great adventure of Christian experience to the point of knowing the breadth, length, height, and depth of Christ's love (cf. Eph 3:18-19). God did not want his secrets to remain hidden but enabled Thérèse to proclaim the secrets of the King (cf. Ms C, 2v·). By her life, Thérèse offers a witness and theological illustration of the beauty of the contemplative life as the total dedication to Christ, Spouse of the Church, and as an affirmation of God's primacy over all things. Hers is a hidden life which possesses a mysterious fruitfulness for spreading the Gospel and fills the Church and the world with the sweet odor of Christ (cf. *LT* 169, 2v).

Lastly, Thérèse of Lisieux is a *young person*. She reached the maturity of holiness in the prime of youth (cf. Ms C, 4r). As such, she appears as a Teacher of evangelical life, particularly effective in illumining the paths of young people who must be the leaders and witnesses of the Gospel to the new generations.

Thérèse of the Child Jesus is not only the youngest Doctor of the Church but is also the closest to us in time, as if to emphasize the continuity with which the Spirit of the Lord sends his messengers to the Church, men and women as teachers and witnesses to the faith. In fact, whatever changes can be noted in the course of history and despite the repercussions they usually have on the life and thought of individuals in every age, we must never lose sight of the continuity which links the Doctors of the Church to each other: in every historical context they remain witnesses to the unchanging Gospel and, with the light and strength that come from the Holy Spirit, they become its messengers, returning to proclaim it in its purity to their contemporaries. Thérèse is a Teacher for our time, which thirsts for living and essential words, for heroic and credible acts of witness. For this reason, she is also loved and accepted by brothers and sisters of other Christian communities and even by non-Christians.

12. This year, when the centenary of the glorious death of Thérèse of the Child Jesus and the Holy Face is being celebrated, as we prepare to celebrate the Great Jubilee of the Year 2000, after receiving a great number

of authoritative petitions, especially from many Episcopal Conferences throughout the world, and after accepting the official petition, or *Supplex Libellus*, addressed to me on March 8, 1997, by the Bishop of Bayeux and Lisieux, as well as from the Superior General of the Discalced Carmelites of the Blessed Virgin Mary of Mount Carmel and from the Postulator General of the same order, I decided to entrust the Congregation for the Causes of Saints, which has competence in this matter, with the special study of the cause for conferring the title of Doctor on this Saint, "after hearing the opinion of the Congregation for the Doctrine of the Faith regarding the eminent doctrine" (Apost. Const. *Pastor Bonus*, n73).

After the necessary documentation had been collected, the two aforementioned Congregations addressed the question in the meetings of their respective consultors: the Congregation for the Doctrine of the Faith on May 5, 1997, with regard to the "eminent doctrine," and the Congregation for the Causes of Saints on May 29 of the same year, to examine the special "*Positio*." On June 17 of the same year, the Cardinals and Bishops who are members of these Congregations, following a procedure approved by me for this occasion, met in a plenary interdicasterial session and discussed the cause, giving a unanimously favorable opinion on granting the title of Doctor of the Universal Church to St. Thérèse of the Child Jesus and the Holy Face. I was personally informed of this opinion by Cardinal Joseph Ratzinger, Prefect of the Congregation for the Doctrine of the Faith, and by the Pro-Prefect of the Congregation for the Causes of Saints, Archbishop Alberto Bovone, titular Archbishop of Caesarea in Numidia. In view of this, on August 24 last, during the Angelus prayer in the presence of hundreds of Bishops and before a vast throng of young people from around the world, gathered in Paris for the Twelfth World Youth Day, I wanted personally to announce my intention to proclaim Thérèse of the Child Jesus and the Holy Face a Doctor of the Universal Church during the celebration of World Mission Sunday in Rome.

Today, October 19, 1997, in St. Peter's Square, filled with faithful from every part of the world, and in the presence of a great many Cardinals, Archbishops, and Bishops, during the solemn Eucharistic celebration I proclaimed Thérèse of the Child Jesus and the Holy Face a Doctor of the Universal Church in these words: "Fulfilling the wishes of many Brothers in the Episcopate and of a great number of the faithful throughout the world, after consulting the Congregation for the Causes of Saints and hearing the opinion of the Congregation for the Doctrine of the Faith regarding her eminent doctrine, with certain knowledge and after lengthy reflection, with the fullness of Our apostolic authority We declare Saint Thérèse of the Child Jesus and the Holy Face, virgin, to be a Doctor of the Universal Church. In the name of the Father, and of the Son and of the Holy Spirit."

This having been duly enacted, We decree that this Apostolic Letter is to be religiously preserved and to have full effect both now and in the future; furthermore, it is thus to be judged and defined as right, and whatever to the contrary may be attempted by anyone, on whatever authority, knowingly or unknowingly, is null and void.

Given in Rome, at St Peter's, under the Fisherman's ring, the nineteenth day of the month of October in the year of the Lord 1997, the twentieth of the Pontificate.

APPENDIX

JOHN PAUL II: WOMEN'S CANONIZATION AND BEATIFICATION

Fr. Edward J. Baenziger, CSB

I have given a course on Saints and Sanctity at the University of Saint Thomas for ten years, and it is from my database that I began this report, beginning from French sources, but ultimately drawing from *Acta Apostolica Sedis* for information on John Paul II's activity conferring canonization and beatification on these women. For the period of John Paul II's papacy, I have counted ninety-five named women *sanctae* and about two hundred forty-nine *beatae* (some of whom, as of 2012, have since been canonized). Although some names may be missing, especially among the Korean and Chinese martyrs, where the names are difficult, the Appendix contains a record of what John Paul II has done, proclaiming heroic sanctity for a vastly larger number of women and men than in any other papacy until the present.[1] The names in the Appendix are arranged by the date of promulgation, first of canonizations, then beatifications.

Feast	*Name*	*Origin*	*Born*	*Died*	*Status*	*Canonized*	*Beatified*
08 17	Jeanne Delanoue	from Saumur (Maine-et-Loire)	1666 vi 18	1736 viii 17	hermit, then then founder	1982 x 31 JP II	1947 xi 09 Pius XII
01 12	Marguerite Bourgeoys	France	1620 iv 17	1700 I 12	religious and founder	1982 x 31 JP II	1971 Paul VI
06 11	Paola Frassinetti	Italy	1809 iii 03	1892 vi 11	religious and founder	1984 iii 11 JP II	1947 Pius XII
09 20	Agatha Kim Agi	Korea	1789	1839 v 04	martyr	1984 v 06	1925 or 1968
09 20	Agatha Yi Sosa	Korea	1839 v 24		martyr	1984 v 06	1925 or 1968
09 20	Anna Pak Agi	Korea	1839 v 24		martyr	1984 v 06	1925 or 1968
09 20	Barbara Han Agi	Korea	1792	1839 v 24	martyr	1984 v 06	1925 or 1968
09 20	Barbara Kim	Korea	1805	1839 v 07	martyr	1984 v 06	1925 or 1968
09 20	Barbara Yi	Korea	1839 v 07		martyr	1984 v 06	1925 or 1968
09 20	Cecilia Yu Sosa	Korea	1839		martyr	1984 v 06	1925 or 1968
09 20	Elisabeth Chung Junghye	Korea	1839		martyr	1984 v 06	1925 or 1968
09 20	Lucy Kim	Korea	1839 vii 20		martyr	1984 v 06	1925 or 1968
09 20	Lucy Park Huisun	(Lucia) Korea	1839 v 24		martyr	1984 v 06	1925 or 1968
09 20	Magdalena Yi	Korea	1839 vii 20		martyr	1984 v 06	1925 or 1968
09 20	Magdalene Kim Obi	Korea	1774	1839 v 24	martyr	1984 v 06	1925 or 1968
09 20	Maria Won Kwi-im	Korea	1839 vii 20		martyr	1984 v 06	1925 or 1968
09 20	Martha Kim Songim (1787–1839)	Korea	1797	1839 vii 20	martyr	1984 v 06	1925 or 1968
09 20	Rosa Kim	Korea	1839 vii 20		martyr	1984 v 06	1925 or 1968
09 20	Theresa Yi Mae-im	Korea	1839 vii 20		martyr	1984 v 06	1925 or 1968

Feast	*Name*	*Origin*	*Born*	*Died*	*Status*	*Canonized*	*Beatified*
01 20	Eustochia Smeralda Calafato / Eustochia de Messina	from Messina in Italy	1434 iii 25	1485 i 20	abbess	1988 vi 11 JP II	1975 Paul VI
11 18	Rose-Philippine Duchesne	from Grenoble, France	1769 viii 29	1852 xi 18	founder	1988 vii 03 JP II	1950 Pius XII
05 08	Maddelena di Canossa	Magdalen of Canossa	1774 iii 01	1835 iv 10	religious	1988 x 02 JP II	1976 Paul VI
06 11	Maria Rosa Molas y Vallvee	Spain	1815 iii 24	1876 vi 11	religious and founder	1988 xii 11 JP II	1930 Pius XI
07 13	Clelia Barbieri	also as Cloelia Barbieri	1847 ii 13	1870 vii 13	religious and founder	1989 iv 09 JP II	1925 Pius XI and 1968 Paul VI
03 02	Anežka de Bohème	also as Agnes of Prague	1211	1282 iii 02	princess, religious and founder	1989 xi 12 JP II	1951 Pius XII
02 03	Marie-Marguérite d'Youville	also as Mary of of Saint Ignatius	1701 x 15	1771 ii 03		1990 xii 09 JP II	1803 Pius VII
02 03	Claudine Thénevet	Lyon, France	1774 iii 30	1837 ii 03	founder	1993 iii 21 JP II	1977 Paul VI
06 13	Teresa Fernández Solar	Teresa de los Andes; Juana Enriqueta Josefina de los Sagragos Corazones Fernández Solar (1st) Chile	1900 vii 13	1920 iv 13	discalced Carmelite	1993 iii 21 JP II	1987 iv 03 JP II
01 01	Zdislava Berka	Zdisava of Lemberk	1220 ca	1252 i 01	married	1995 v 21 JP II	1981 JP II
02 28	Hedwige / Jadwiga d'Anjou	France/ Poland 1375 ii 18	1374 x 03–1399 vii 17	king / queen	1997 vi 08 JP II	1997 vi 08 JP II	1975 Paul VI

table continues

Feast	*Name*	*Origin*	*Born*	*Died*	*Status*	*Canonized*	*Beatified*
08 09	Édith Stein	(Theresia Benedikta) Teresa Benedicta of the Cross (Teresia)	1891 x 12	1942 viii 09	religious	1998 x 11 JP II	1981 JP II
11 13	Agostina Piustrantoni	also as Agostina Petrantoni or Livia Piustranton	1864 iii 27	1894 xi 13	religious	1999 iv 18 JP II	1975 Paul VI
07 24	Kinga / Conégonde / Cunegunda	Cunegunda, Kinga in Polish	1224 iii 05	1292 vii 24	princess and religious	1999 vi 16 JP II	1690 Alexander VIII
10 05	Maria Faustyna Kowalska	saint of Divine Mercy	1905 viii 25	1938 x 05	religious	2000 iv 30 JP II	1983 iv 18
07 30	Maria Navidad [Natividad] Venegas de la Torre	María de Jesús Sacramentado	1868 xii 08	1959 vii 30	religious and founder	2000 v 21 JP II	1900 Leo XIII, then 1906 Pius X, 1909 Benedict XV, then 1951 Pius XII
02 08	Josephine Bakhita / Giuseppina Marguerita Bhakita	Sudan (1st)	1869 ca.	1947 ii 08	religious	2000 x 01 JP II	1782 Pius VI
01 28 09 28	Agatha Lin	Lin Zhao Agatha	1817	1858 i 28	lay woman, teacher	2000 x 01 JP II	1909 v 02 Pius X
03 03	Katherine Drexel / Katherine Mary	Philadelphia, Pennsylvania	1858 xi 26	1955 iii 03	founder	2000 x 01 JP II	1934 Pius XI
11 18	Marie-Joseph Sancho de Guerra / María Josefa	Basque country, Spain	1842 ix 07	1912 iii 20	religious and founder	2000 x 01 JP II	1940 Pius XII
09 28	Agnes Tsao Kouy	China	1856	1900 v 27	widow	2000 x 01 JP II	1946 xi 24 Pius XII
09 28	Anna Dierk	Maria Adolfina	1866	1900 vii 09	religious F.M.M.	2000 x 01 JP II	1946 xi 24 Pius XII
09 28	Elisabeth Tsinn	China		1900		2000 x 01 JP II	1946 xi 24 Pius XII
07 08	Jeanne-Marie Kerguin	China	1864 v 05	1900 vii 09	religious	2000 x 01 JP II	1946 xi 24 Pius XII

Feast	Name	Origin	Born	Died	Status	Canonized	Beatified
09 28	Maria Anna Giuliani	Maria della Pace	1875	1900	religious F.M.M.	2000 x 01 JP II	1946 xi 24 Pius XII
09 28	Maria Chaira	Clelia Nanette	1872 I 09	1900 vii 09	religious	2000 x 01 JP II	1946 xi 24 Pius XII
09 28	Marie Adolphine Dierks	Anne-Catherine Dierks	1866 iii 08	1900 vii 09	religious	2000 x 01 JP II	1946 xi 24 Pius XII
09 28	Marie Amandine	Maria Amandina	1872 xii 28	1900 vii 09	religious	2000 x 01 JP II	1946 xi 24 Pius XII
09 28	Marie de Saint Just	Maria di San Giusto; Anne-Francoise Moreau	1866 iv 09	1900 vii 09	religious	2000 x 01 JP II	1946 xi 24 Pius XII
09 28	Mary Hermina Grivot	Marie Hermine de Jésus	1866 iv 28	1900 vii 09	religious	2000 x 01 JP II	1946 xi 24 Pius XII
09 29	Paola Jeuris	Pauline Jeuris	1872	1900 vii 09	religious F.M.M.	2000 x 01 JP II	1946 xi 24 Pius XII
09 28	Anna Nan-Sinn-Cheu	China		1900		2000 x 01 JP II	1955 iv 17 Pius XII
09 28	Anna Nan-Tsiao-Cheu	China		1900		2000 x 01 JP II	1955 iv 17 Pius XII
09 28	Anna Wang	China		1900		2000 x 01 JP II	1955 iv 17 Pius XII
09 28	Barbara Ts'Oei-Lien-Cheu	China		1900		2000 x 01 JP II	1955 iv 17 Pius XII
09 28	Lang-Yang-Cheu	China		1900		2000 x 01 JP II	1955 iv 17 Pius XII
09 28	Lucy Wang-Tcheng	China		1900		2000 x 01 JP II	1955 iv 17 Pius XII
09 28	Lucy Wang-Wang-Cheu	China		1900		2000 x 01 JP II	1955 iv 17 Pius XII
09 28	Lucy Y	China	1862	1909 v 02		2000 x 01 JP II	1955 iv 17 Pius XII
09 28	Magdalene Tou-Fong-Kiu	China		1900		2000 x 01 JP II	1955 iv 17 Pius XII
09 28	Martha Ouang	China		1909 v 02		2000 x 01 JP II	1955 iv 17 Pius XII
09 28	Mary Fan-K'Ounn	China		1900		2000 x 01 JP II	1955 iv 17 Pius XII
09 28	Mary Fou	China		1900		2000 x 01 JP II	1955 iv 17 Pius XII
09 28	Mary Kouo-Li-Cheu	China		1900		2000 x 01 JP II	1955 iv 17 Pius XII

table continues

Feast	Name	Origin	Born	Died	Status	Canonized	Beatified
09 28	Mary Nan	China		1900		2000 x 01 JP II	1955 iv 17 Pius XII
09 28	Mary Nan-Kouo-Cheu	China		1900		2000 x 01 JP II	1955 iv 17 Pius XII
09 28	Mary Tchao	China		1900		2000 x 01 JP II	1955 iv 17 Pius XII
09 28	Mary Tchao-Kouo-Cheu	China		1900		2000 x 01 JP II	1955 iv 17 Pius XII
09 28	Mary Tcheng-Su	China		1900		2000 x 01 JP II	1955 iv 17 Pius XII
09 28	Mary Tchou-Ou-Cheu	China		1900		2000 x 01 JP II	1955 iv 17 Pius XII
09 28	Mary Tou-Tchao-Cheu	China		1900		2000 x 01 JP II	1955 iv 17 Pius XII
09 28	Mary Tou-T'Ien-Cheu	China		1900		2000 x 01 JP II	1955 iv 17 Pius XII
09 28	Mary Ts'I-U	China		1900		2000 x 01 JP II	1955 iv 17 Pius XII
09 28	Mary Wang-Li-Cheu	China		1900		2000 x 01 JP II	1955 iv 17 Pius XII
09 28	Rose Tchao	Rosa Tchao		1900		2000 x 01 JP II	1955 iv 17 Pius XII
09 28	Rose Tch'enn-Kai-Tsie	Rosa Chen Aijieh		1900		2000 x 01 JP II	1955 iv 17 Pius XII
09 28	Rose Wang-Hoei	Rosa Fan Hui		1900		2000 x 01 JP II	1955 iv 17 Pius XII
09 28	Teresa Kinn-Tsie	China		1900		2000 x 01 JP II	1955 iv 17 Pius XII
09 28	Teresa Tchang-Hene-Cheu	China		1900		2000 x 01 JP II	1955 iv 17 Pius XII
03 03	Teresa Eustochio Verzeri	Bergamo, Italie. Ignazia Verzeri	1801 vii 31	1852 iii 03	religious and founder	2001 vi 10 JP II	1766 Clément XIII
03 23	Rafqā Shabaq ar-Rayes	Anissa (Agnes)	1832 vi 29	1859 iii 23	religious	2001 vi 10 JP II	1981 JP II
04 05	Maria Crescentia Hoss	Crescentia Hoss	1682 x 20	1744 iv 05	religious	2001 xi 25 JP II	1900 x 07 Leo XIII
01 11	Francisca Salesia	Leonia Aviat	1844 ix 16	1914 i 10	religious and founder	2001 xi 25 JP II	1978 xii 01
02 26	Paula of Saint Joseph of Calasanz	Paula Montal Fornés De San José De Calasanz	1799 x 11	1889 ii 26	religious and founder	2001 xi 25 JP II	1993 iv 18

Feast	*Name*	*Origin*	*Born*	*Died*	*Status*	*Canonized*	*Beatified*
03 21	Benedicta Cambiagio Frassinello	Benedetta	1791 x 02	1858 iii 21	religious and founder	2002 v 18 JP II	1987 v 10 JP II
07 09	Paulina do Coração Agonizante de Jesus	Pauline Visintainer	1865 xii 16	1942 vii 09	religious and founder	2002 v 19 JP II	1991 x 18 JP II
03 02	Angela of the Cross Guerrero	Angela of the Cross Guerrero y González	1846 i 30	1932 iii 02	religious and founder	2003 v 04 JPII	1982 xi 05 JPII
01 05	Genoveva Torres Morales		1870 I 03	1956 I 05	religious and founder	2003 v 04 JPII	1995 I 29 JPII
12 11	María Maravillas de Jesús	Maravillas Pidal y Chico de Guzmán	1891 xi 04	1974 xii 11	religious	2003 v 04 JPII	1998 v 10 JPII
05 08	Ursule Ledochowska	Cracovie	1865 iv 17	1939 v 29	religious and founder	2003 v 04 JP II	1941 Pius XII
02 04	Maria de Mattias	Mary de Matthias	1805 ii 04	1866 viii 20	religious and founder	2003 v 18 JPII	1950 x 01 Pius XII
05 26	Ursula Ledochowska	Julia	1865 iv 17	1939 v 29	religious and founder	2003 v 18 JPII	1983 vi 20 JPII
12 15	Virginia Centurione Bracelli		1587 iv 02	1651 xii 15	widow and founder	2003 v 18 JPII	1985 ix 22 JP II
12 24	Paola Elisabetta Cerioli		1816 I 28	1865 xii 24	mother and founder	2004 v 16 JP II	1950 iii 19 Pius XII
04 28	Gianna Beretta Molla		1922 x 04	1962 iv 28	mother	2004 v 16 JP II	1994 ix 24 JP II
05 19	Maria Bernarda Butler	Verena Bütler	1848 v 28	1924 v 19	religious and founder	2008 x 12 Benedict XVI	1995 JP II
02 18	Geltrude Comesoli		1847 I 18	1903 ii 18	religious and founder	2009 iv 26 Benedict XVI	1989 JP II
12 28	Catherine Volpicelli / Catarina	Naples	1859 I 21	1894 xii 28	religious and founder	2009 iv 26 Benedict XVI	2001 JP II
08 29	Jeanne Jugan		1792 x 25	1879 viii 29	religious and founder	2009 x 11 Benedict XVI	1982 JP II
05 17	Giulia Salzano		1846 x 13	1929 v 17	religious and founder	2010 x 17 Benedict XVI	2003 iv 27 JPII

table continues

Feast	*Name*	*Origin*	*Born*	*Died*	*Status*	*Canonized*	*Beatified*
08 08	Bonifacia Rodríguez y Castro	1837 vi 06	1905 viii 08		religious and founder	2011 x 23 Benedict XVI	2001 iv 09 JPII
04 17	Kateri Tekawitha		1656	1680 iv 17	virgin, lay religious	2012 x 12 canonization	1980 vi 22 JP II
06 20	Margareta Ebner	Germany	1291	1351 v 20	religious		1979 11 24 JP II
10 05	Anna Schäffer		1882	1925 x 05	laywoman	2012 x 12 canonization	1999 iii 07 JP II
04 30	Marie Guyart de l'Incarnation	France	1599 x 28	1672 iv 30	widow and founder		1980 vi 22 JP II
	María Anna Sala	France	1829	1891	religious		1980 x 26 JP II
01 05	Maria Repetto	Italy	1807 x 31	1890 i 05	religious		1981 x 04 JP II
02 03	Anne-Marie Rivier	France	1768 xii 19	1838 ii 03	religious		1982 v 23 JP II
12 02	María Ángela Astorch	Spain	1592 ix 01	1665 xii 02	religious		1982 v 23 JP II
10 06	Marie Rose Durocher	Canada	1811 x 06	1849 x 06	religious		1982 v 23 JP II
04 22	Maria Gabriella Sagheddu	Italy	1914	1939 iv 23	religious		1983 i 25 JP II
07 26	Maryam Bawārdī of Jesus Crucified	St. Mary of the Crucified Jesus (Gallilee/ Bethlehem)	1846 i 05	1878 viii 26	religious		1983 xi 13 JP II
01 02	Anne Françoise de Villeneuve	France	1741 ix 11	1794 ii 01	laywoman and martyr		1984 ii 19 JP II
01 02	Anne Hamard	Anger, France	1742 ca.	1794 ii 01	laywoman and martyr		1984 ii 19 JP II
01 02	Anne Maugrain	France	1769 iv 12	1794 iv 16	laywoman and martyr		1984 ii 19 JP II
01 02	Catherine Cottanceau	France	1733 ca.	1794 ii 01	laywoman and martyr		1984 ii 19 JP II
01 02	Charlotte Davy	France	1760 x 19	1794 ii 01	laywoman and martyr		1984 ii 19 JP II
01 02	Charlotte Lucas	France	1752 iv 01	1794 i 18	laywoman and martyr		1984 ii 19 JP II

Feast	*Name*	*Origin*	*Born*	*Died*	*Status*	*Canonized*	*Beatified*
01 02	Félicité Pricet	France	1744 ca.	1794 i 18	laywoman and martyr		1984 ii 19 JP II
01 02	Gabrielle Androuin	France	1755 xii 06	1794 ii 01	laywoman and martyr		1984 ii 19 JP II
01 02	Jacquine Monnier	France	1726 i 16	1794 ii 01	laywoman and martyr		1984 ii 19 JP II
01 02	Jeanne Fouchard épouse Chalonneau	France	1747 ix 10	1794 ii 01	laywoman and martyr		1984 ii 19 JP II
01 02	Jeanne Sailland d'Epinatz	France	1769 vii 03	1794 ii 01	laywoman and martyr		1984 ii 19 JP II
02 10	Louise Bessay de la Voûte	France	1721 viii 21	1794 ii 10	laywoman and martyr		1984 ii 19 JP II
01 02	Madeleine Saillard d'Epinatz	France	1770 viii 09	1794 ii 01	laywoman and martyr		1984 ii 19 JP II
01 02	Marguerite Rivière épouse Huau	France	1756 viii 20	1794 ii 01	laywoman and martyr		1984 ii 19 JP II
01 02	Marie Anne Pichery épouse Delahaye	France	1754 vii 30	1794 ii 01	laywoman and martyr		1984 ii 19 JP II
01 02	Marie Lenée épouse Lepage de Varancé	France	1749 vii 14	1794 ii 01	laywoman and martyr		1984 ii 19 JP II
01 02	Marie Leroy épouse Brevet	France	1755 ca.	1794 ii 01	laywoman and martyr		1984 ii 19 JP II
01 02	Marie Rouault épouse Bouju	France	1744 x 26	1794 ii 01	laywoman and martyr		1984 ii 19 JP II
01 02	Marie-Anne Vaillot	France	1736 v 13	1794 ii 01	religious and martyr		1984 ii 19 JP II
01 02	Odile Baumgarten	Anger, France	1750 xi 15	1794 ii 01	religious and martyr		1984 ii 19 JP II
01 02	Perrine Besson	France	1742 ca.	1794 ii 01	laywoman and martyr		1984 ii 19 JP II
01 02	Perrine-Charlotte Phellipeaux épouse Saillard d'Epinatz	France	1740 v 13	1794 ii 01	laywoman and martyr		1984 ii 19 JP II
01 02	Renée Martin épouse Martin	France	1752 ca.	1794 ii 01	laywoman and martyr		1984 ii 19 JP II

table continues

Feast	*Name*	*Origin*	*Born*	*Died*	*Status*	*Canonized*	*Beatified*
01 02	Renée Valin	France	1760 iii 08	1794 ii 01	laywoman and martyr		1984 ii 19 JP II
01 02	Rosalie du Verdier de la Sorinière	France		1794 ii 01	religious and martyr		1984 ii 19 JP II
05 04	Marie Léonie Paradis	Québec	1840 v 12	1912 v 03	founder		1984 ix 11 JP II
02 23	Rafaela Ybarra de Villalonga		1843 i 16	1900 ii 23	mother and founder		1984 ix 30 JP II
11 08	Élizabeth Catez de la Trinité	Dijon	1880 vii 18	1906 xi 09	religious		1984 xi 25 JP II
06 12	Mercedes Molina Ayala		1828 ix 24	1883 vi 12	religious and founder		1985 ii 01 JP II
01 10	Ana Monteagudo de los Ángeles		1602 vii 26	1686 i 10	religious		1985 ii 02 JP II
06 21	Maria Caterina Troiani	Maria Caterina di S. Rosa da Viterbo	1813 i 19	1887 v 06	religious and founder		1985 iv 14 JP II
04 30	Pauline von Mallinckrodt		1817 vi 03	1881 iv 30	religious and founder		1985 iv 14 JP II
12 01	Anuarite Nengapeta	Marie-Clémentine	1914 xii 29	1964 xii 01	religious		1985 viii 15 JP II
05 09	Maria Theresia Gerhardinger	Blessed Theresa of Jesus Gerhardinger	1797 vi 20	1879 v 09	religious and founder		1985 xi 17 JP II
04 23	Teresia Maria Manetti		1846 iii 02	1910 iv 23	religious and founder		1986 x 19 JP II
07 24	Maria Angeles of St. Joseph	Carmélites de Guadalajara	1905 iii 06 Guadalajara	1936 vii 24	religious and martyr		1987 iii 29 JP II
07 24	Maria Pilar of St. Francis Borgia	Carmélites de Guadalajara	1877 xii 30	1936 vii 24	religious and martyr		1987 iii 29 JP II
07 24	Teresa of the Child Jesus	Carmélites de Guadalajara	1909 iii 05	1936 vii 24	religious and martyr		1987 iii 29 JP II
11 18	Caroline Kózka	Karolina	1898 viii 02	1914 xi 18	teenager		1987 vi 10 JP II
05 17	Antonia Mesina		1919 vi 21	1935 v 17	teenager		1987 x 04 JP II

Feast	Name	Origin	Born	Died	Status	Canonized	Beatified
04 06	Piusrina Morosini		1931 i 07	1957 iv 04	laywoman		1987 x 04 JP II
05 08	Ulrika Franziska Nisch		1882 ix 18	1913 v 08	religious		1987 xi 01 JP II
05 18	Blandina Merten	Mary Magdalene Merten	1883 vii 10	1918 v 18	religious		1987 xi 18 JP II
01 22	Laura Vicuna		1891	1904 Ii22	laywoman		1988 JP II
04 18	Savina Petrilli		1851	1923 iv 18	religious and founder		1988 JP II
08 14	Élizabeth Renzi	Elizabetta	1786	1859 viii 14	religious and founder		1989 JP II
02 25	Francinaina Cirer Carbonell	Francinaina of the Sorrowful Mother of God	1781	1855 ii 25	religious		1989 JP II
08 08	Maria Marguerita Caiani		1863	1921 viii 08	religious and founder		1989 JP II
02 27	Marie Deluil-Martiny		1841	1884 ii 27 martyr	religious and founder,		1989 JP II
05 08	Marie-Catherine de Saint-Augustin (Simon de Longpré)	Québec	1632 v 03	1668 v 08	religious		1989 JP II
08 21	Victoire Rasoamanarivo	Madagascar	1848	1894 viii 21	widow		1989 JP II
04 02	Élizabeth Vendramini	Elisabetta	1790	1860 iv 02	religious and founder		1990 JP II
06 27	Louise-Thérèse Montaignac de Chauvance		1820	1885 vi 27	religious and founder		1990 JP II
06 10	Maria Schininà		1844	1910 vi 10	religious and founder		1990 JP II
07 24	Marie Merce Prat	Maria Mercedes	1890	1936 vii 24	martyr		1990 JP II
03 18	Marthe Le Bouteiller		1816	1883 iii 18	religious		1990 JP II
03 12	Aniela Salawa		1881	1922 iii 12	laywoman, 3rd order Franciscan		1991 JP II

table continues

Feast	*Name*	*Origin*	*Born*	*Died*	*Status*	*Canonized*	*Beatified*
03 23	Annunciata Cocchetti		1800	1882 iii 23	religious and founder		1991 JP II
01 29	Bolesława Maria Lament		1862	1946 i 29	religious and founder		1991 JP II
04 20	Chiara Bosatta	Clara	1858	1887 iv 20	religious and founder		1991 JP II
01 07	Marie-Thérèse Haze		1782	1876 i 07	religious		1991 JP II
07 06	Nazaria Ignacia March Mesa		1889	1943 vii 06	religious		1992 JP II
09 24	Colomba Gabriel		1858	1926 ix 24	religious founder		1993 JP II
09 04	Dina Belánger		1897	1929 ix 04	religious		1993 JP II
06 12	Florida Cevoli		1685	1767 vi 12	abbess		1993 JP II
10 09	Maria Angela Truszkowska		1825	1899 x 09	religious		1993 JP II
11 08	Maria Crocifissa Satellico		1706	1745 xi 08	abbess		1993 JP II
08 06	Marie-Françoise Rubatto		1844	1904 viii 06	founder		1993 JP II
04 28	Marie-Louise de Jésus Trichet	Poitiers	1684	1759 iv 28	founder		1993 JP II
10 10	Victoria Díez Bustos de Molina		1903	1936	laywoman, martyr		1993 JP II
10 19	Agnès de Jésus Galand	Langeac	1602	1634 x 16	religious		1994 JP II
02 05	Élizabeth Canori Mora	Elisabetta	1774	1825 ii 05	mother, Trinitarian		1994 JP II
07 02	Eugénie Joubert		1876	1904 vii 02	religious		1994 JP II
02 23	Josephine Vannini	Giuseppina	1859	1911 ii 23	religious and founder		1994 JP II
11 15	Maddalena Caterina Morano	Madeleine Catherine	1847	1908 ix 15	religious		1994 JP II
08 30	Maria Rafols Bruna		1781	1853 viii 30	religious and founder		1994 JP II

Feast	Name	Origin	Born	Died	Status	Canonized	Beatified
10 14	Marie Poussepin		1653	1744 x 14	religious and founder		1994 JP II
	Petra Pérez Florido		1845	1906			1994 JP II
02 08	Josephine Gabrielle Bonino	Giuseppina Gabriella	1843	1906 ii 08	religious and founder		1995 JP II
04 02	Laura Alvarado Cardozo	Maria of St. Joseph	1875	1967 iv 02	religious and founder		1995 JP II
06 27	Marguerite Bays		1815	1879 vi 27	laywoman		1995 JP II
05 22	Maria Domenica Brun Barbantini		1789	1868 v 22	Mother, religious and founder		1995 JP II
02 03	Maria Helena Stollenwerk		1852	1900 ii 03	religious		1995 JP II
06 16	Maria Theresia Scherer		1825	1888 vi 16	religious		1995 JP II
08 09	Mary Helen MacKillop		1842	1909 viii 09	religious and founder		1995 JP II
08 09	Cándida María de Jesús Cipitria y Barriola	Juana Josefa	1845	1912 viii 09	religious and founder		1996 JP II
07 04	Catherine Jarrige		1754	1836 vii 04	lay religious		1996 JP II
07 03	María Ana Mogas Fontcuberta		1827	1886 vii 03	religious and founder		1996 JP II
04 27	María Antonia Bandrés Elósegui		1898	1919 iv 27	religious		1996 JP II
01 05	Maria Marcelina Darowska		1827	1911 i 05	religious and founder		1996 JP II
07 04	Maria Raffaela Cimatti		1861	1945 vi 23	religious		1996 JP II
	Bernardyna Jabłońska		1878	1940	religious and founder		1997 JP II
10 27	María Encarnación Rosal Vásquez		1820	1886 viii 24	religious, reformer		1997 JP II
06 06	Maria Karłowska		1865	1935 iii 24	religious and founder		1997 JP II
01 18	Maria Teresa Fasce		1881	1947	abbess		1997 JP II

table continues

Feast	Name	Origin	Born	Died	Status	Canonized	Beatified
07 30	María Vicenta Chávez Orozco		1867	1949 vii 07	religious and founder		1997 JP II
09 03	Brigit Morello	Brigida de Gesú Morello	1610	1679	religious and founder		1998 JP II
07 25	Maria del Carmen Sallés Barangueras	Sister Carmen of Jesus	1848	1911	religious and founder		1998 JP II
07 20	Francisca Aldea Araujo	Francisca del Sagrado Corazón de Jesús (of the Sacred Heart of Jesus)	1881	1936	religious and martyr		1998 v 10 JP II
11 18	Josefa Maria	(María del Carmen Barrera y Izaguirre)	1881	1936	religious and martyr		1998 v 10 JP II
11 18	María Angela	(Martina Olaizola y Garagarza)	1893	1936	religious and martyr		1998 v 10 JP II
11 18	María Cecilia	(María Felicitas Cendoya y Arraquistain)	1910	1936	religious and martyr		1998 v 10 JP II
11 18	María Engracia	(Josefa Joachima Lecuona y Aramburu)	1897	1936	religious and martyr		1998 v 10 JP II
11 18	María Gabriela Hinojosa Naveros and 6 companions	(María of Refuge Hinojosa y Naveros)	1872 vii 24	1936 xi 18	religious and martyr		1998 v 10 JP II
11 18	María Inés	(Inés Zudaire y Galdeano)	1900	1936	religious and martyr		1998 v 10 JP II
08 15	María Sagrario Moragas Cantarero	(Elvira Moragas Cantarero)	1881	1936	religious and martyr		1998 v 10 JP II

Feast	Name	Origin	Born	Died	Status	Canonized	Beatified
07 20	Rita Josefa Pujalte Sánchez	Rita Dolores (of the Sorrowful Virgin)	1853	1936	religious and martyr		1998 v 10 JP II
11 18	Teresa María	(Laura Cavestany y Anduaha)	1888	1936	religious and martyr		1998 v 10 JP II
01 25	Maria Antonia Grillo Michel	Sister Teresa	1855	1944 i 25	widow, religious and founder		1998 v 24 JP II
08 28	Thérèse Bracco / Teresa		1924	1944 viii 08	young laywoman martyr		1998 v 24 JP II
03 30	Maria Restituta Kafka	Austria	1894	1943	religious and martyr		1998 vi 21 JP II
06 12	Alicja Maria Jadwiga Kotowska	(108 Martyrs of Poland)	1899	1939	religious and martyr		1999 vi 13 JP II
12 19	Ewa Noiszewska (108 Martyrs of Poland)	Sister Maria Jesus	1885	1942 xii 19	religious and martyr		1999 vi 13 JP II
06 12	Julia Rodzińska	(108 Martyrs of Poland)	1899	1945 ii 20	religious and martyr		1999 vi 13 JP II
06 12	Katarzyna Celestyna Faron	(108 Martyrs of Poland)	1913	1944	religious and martyr		1999 vi 13 JP II
06 12	Maria Antonina Kratochwil	(108 Martyrs of Poland)	1881	1942	religious and martyr		1999 vi 13 JP II
06 12	Maria Klemensa Staszewska (108 Martyrs of Poland)	(108 Martyrs of Poland)	1890	1943	religious and martyr		1999 vi 13 JP II
06 12	Marianna Biernacka	(108 Martyrs of Poland)	1888	1943 vii 13	religious and martyr		1999 vi 13 JP II
06 12	Marta Wołowska (108 Martyrs of Poland)	Sister Marta Maria Jesus	1879	1942 xii 19	religious and martyr		1999 vi 13 JP II
06 12	Mieczysława Kowalska (108 Martyrs of Poland)	Sister Theresa of the Child Jesus	1902	1941 vii 25	religious and martyr		1999 vi 13 JP II

table continues

Feast	*Name*	*Origin*	*Born*	*Died*	*Status*	*Canonized*	*Beatified*
06 12	Natalia Tułasiewicz	(108 Martyrs of Poland)	1906	1945 iii 31	religious and martyr		1999 vi 13 JP II
01 18	Regina Protmann	Poland	1552	1613 i 18	religious and founder		1999 vi 13 JP II
08 01	Maria Boromea & 10 Compagnons	Weronika Narmontowicz	1916 xiii 18	1943 viii 01	religious and martyr		2000 iii 05 JP II
08 01	Maria Daniela & 10 Compagnons	Eleonora Aniela Jóźwik	1895 i 25	1943 viii 01	religious and martyr		2000 iii 05 JP II
08 01	Maria Felicyta & 10 Compagnons	Paulina Borowik	1905 viii 30	1943 viii 01	religious and martyr		2000 iii 05 JP II
08 01	Maria Gwidona & 10 Compagnons	Helena Cierpka	1900 iv 18	1943 viii 01	religious and martyr		2000 iii 05 JP II
08 01	Maria Heliodora & 10 Compagnons	Leokadia Matuszewska	1906 ii 08	1943 viii 01	religious and martyr		2000 iii 05 JP II
08 01	Maria Imelda of the Eucharistic Jesus & 10 Compagnons	Jadwiga Karolina Zak	1892 xii 02	1943 viii 01	religious and martyr		2000 iii 05 JP II
08 01	Maria Kanizja & 10 Compagnons	Eugenia Mackiewicz	1903 xi 27	1943 viii 01	religious and martyr		2000 iii 05 JP II
08 01	Maria Kanuta & 10 Compagnons	Józefa Chrobot	1896 v 22	1943 viii 01	religious and martyr		2000 iii 05 JP II
08 01	Maria Rajmunda & 10 Compagnons	Anna Kokołowicz	1892 viii 24	1943 viii 01	religious and martyr		2000 iii 05 JP II
08 01	Maria Sergia & 10 Compagnons	Julia RaPiusj	1900 viii 18	1943 viii 01	religious and martyr		2000 iii 05 JP II
08 01	Marie Stella & 10 Compagnons	Adela Mardosewicz	1888 xii 14	1943 viii 01	religious and martyr		2000 iii 05 JP II
05 06	Anna Rosa Gattorno	Italy	1841 x 14	1900 v 06	widow, religious and founder		2000 iv 09 JP II

Feast	*Name*	*Origin*	*Born*	*Died*	*Status*	*Canonized*	*Beatified*
04 08	Mariam Thresia Chiramel Mankidiyan	Kerala, India	1876 iv 26	1926 vi 08	religious and founder		2000 iv 09 JP II
06 04	Mary Elizabeth Hesselblad	Maria Elisabetta	1870 vi 04	1957 iv 24	religious		2000 iv 09 JP II
	Agueda Hernández Amorós de Nuestra Señora de las Virtudes	Valencia, Spain	1893	1936	religious and martyr		2001 iii 11 JP II
	Amalia Abad Casasempere	Valencia, Spain	1897	1936	widow and martyr		2001 iii 11 JP II
	Ana María Aranda Riera	Valencia, Spain	1888	1936	martyr		2001 iii 11 JP II
	Antonia Gosens Sáez de Ibarra de San Timoteo	Valencia, Spain	1870	1936	religious and martyr		2001 iii 11 JP II
	Ascensión Lloret Marco de San José de Calasanz	Valencia, Spain	1879	1936	religious and martyr		2001 iii 11 JP II
	Cándida Cayuso González de Nustra Señora de los Ángeles	Valencia, Spain	1901	1936	religious and martyr		2001 iii 11 JP II
	Carmen de San Felipe Neri	(Nazaria Gómez Lezáun)	1869	1936	religious and martyr		2001 iii 11 JP II
	Clara Ezcurra Urrutia de Nuestra Señora de la Esperanza	Valencia, Spain	1896	1936	religious and martyr		2001 iii 11 JP II
	Clemencia de San Juan Bautista	(Antonia Riva Mestres)	1893	1936	religious and martyr		2001 iii 11 JP II
	Concepción Odriozola Zabalia de San Ignacio	Valencia, Spain	1882	1936	religious and martyr		2001 iii 11 JP II

table continues

Feast	Name	Origin	Born	Died	Status	Canonized	Beatified
	Concepción Rodríguez Fernández de Santa Magdalena	Valencia, Spain	1895	1936	religious and martyr		2001 iii 11 JP II
	Consuelo Aguilar-Mella Díaz	Uruguay	1898	1936	religious and martyr		2001 iii 11 JP II
	Consuelo Cuñado González del Santísimo Sacramento	Valencia, Spain	1884	1936	religious and martyr		2001 iii 11 JP II
	Crescencia Valls Espí	Valencia, Spain	1863	1936	martyr		2001 iii 11 JP II
	Daría Campillo Paniagua de Santa Sofia	Valencia, Spain	1873	1936	religious and martyr		2001 iii 11 JP II
	Dolores Aguilar-Mella Díaz	Uruguay	1897	1936	religious and martyr		2001 iii 11 JP II
	Dolores de Santa Eulalia Puig Bonany	Valencia, Spain	1857	1936	religious and martyr		2001 iii 11 JP II
	Elvira Torrentallé Paraire	Valencia, Spain	1883	1936	religious and martyr		2001 iii 11 JP II
	Encarnación Gil Valls	Valencia, Spain	1888	1936	martyr		2001 iii 11 JP II
	Erundina Colino Vega de Nuestra Señora del Carmen	Valencia, Spain	1883	1936	religious and martyr		2001 iii 11 JP II
	Feliciana de Uribe Orbe de Nustra Señore del Carmen	Valencia, Spain	1893	1936	religious and martyr		2001 iii 11 JP II
	Florencia Caerols Martínez	Valencia, Spain	1890	1936	martyr		2001 iii 11 JP II
	Francisca Cualladó Baixauli	Valencia, Spain	1890	1936	martyr		2001 iii 11 JP II

Feast	Name	Origin	Born	Died	Status	Canonized	Beatified
	Francisca de Amézua Ibaibarriaga de Santa Teresa	Valencia, Spain	1881	1936	religious and martyr		2001 iii 11 JP II
	Herminia Martínez Amigó	Valencia, Spain	1887	1936	martyr		2001 iii 11 JP II
	Isabel Calduch Rovira	Valencia, Spain	1882	1937	religious and martyr		2001 iii 11 JP II
	Josefa de San Juan Ruano García	Valencia, Spain	1854	1936	religious and martyr		2001 iii 11 JP II
	Josefina Moscardó Montalvá	Valencia, Spain	1880	1936	martyr		2001 iii 11 JP II
	Justa Maiza Goicoechea de la Inmaculada	Valencia, Spain	1897	1936	religious and martyr		2001 iii 11 JP II
	Luisa María Frías Cañizares	Valencia, Spain	1896	1936	martyr		2001 iii 11 JP II
	Manuela Fernández Ibero	Valencia, Spain	1872	1936	Third order capuchin, martyr		'l2001 iii 11 JP II
	María Amparo Carbonell Muñoz	Valencia, Spain	1893	1936	religious and martyr		2001 iii 11 JP II
	María Calaf Miracle de Nuestra Señora de la Providencia	Valencia, Spain	1871	1936	religious and martyr		2001 iii 11 JP II
	María Climet Mateu	Valencia, Spain	1887	1936	martyr		2001 iii 11 JP II
	María de Jesús	(María de Encarnaciún de la Yglesia de Varo)	1891	1936	religious and martyr		2001 iii 11 JP II
	María de la Purificación Vidal Pastor	Valencia, Spain	1892	1936	martyr		2001 iii 11 JP II

table continues

Feast	*Name*	*Origin*	*Born*	*Died*	*Status*	*Canonized*	*Beatified*
	María de la Purificación Ximénez Ximénez de San José	Valencia, Spain	1871	1936	religious and martyr		2001 iii 11 JP II
	María de las Nieves Crespo López de la Santísima Trinidad	Valencia, Spain	1897	1936	religious and martyr		2001 iii 11 JP II
	María del Carmen Moreno Benítez	Valencia, Spain	1885	1936	religious and martyr		2001 iii 11 JP II
	María del Carmen Viel Ferrando	Valencia, Spain	1893	1936	martyr		2001 iii 11 JP II
	María del Niño Jesús	(María Baldillou Bullit)	1905	1936	religious and martyr		2001 iii 11 JP II
	María del Olvido Noguera Albelda	Valencia, Spain	1903	1936	martyr		2001 iii 11 JP II
	María Desamparados Giner Líster del Santísimo Sacramento	Valencia, Spain	1877	1936	religious and martyr		2001 iii 11 JP II
	María Dolores Vidal Cervera de San Francisco Javier	Valencia, Spain	1895	1936	religious and martyr		2001 iii 11 JP II
	Mariá Felicidad (Mariá Felicidad Masiá Ferragud)	Valencia, Spain	1890	1936	religious and martyr		2001 iii 11 JP II
	María Fenollosa Alcaina	Valencia, Spain	1901	1936	Third order capuchin, martyr		2001 iii 11 JP II
	María Guadalupe Ricart Olmos	Valencia, Spain	1891	1936	religious and martyr		2001 iii 11 JP II
	Mariá Jesús (Mariá Vicenta Masiá Ferragud)	Valencia, Spain	1882	1936	religious and martyr		2001 iii 11 JP II

Feast	Name	Origin	Born	Died	Status	Canonized	Beatified
	María Jordá Botella	Valencia, Spain	1905	1936	martyr		2001 iii 11 JP II
	María Josefa del Río Messa de Santa Sofia	Valencia, Spain	1895	1936	religious and martyr		2001 iii 11 JP II
	María Luisa de Jesús Romera)	(María Luisa Girón 1887)	1936		religious and martyr		2001 iii 11 JP II
	María Luisa Montesinos Orduña	Valencia, Spain	1901	1937	martyr		2001 iii 11 JP II
	María Patrocinio Giner Gómis de San Juan	Valencia, Spain	1874	1936	religious and martyr		2001 iii 11 JP II
	María Teresa Ferragut Roig	Valencia, Spain	1853	1936	martyr		2001 iii 11 JP II
	Mariá Verónica (Mariá Joaquina Masiá Ferragud)	Valencia, Spain	1884	1936	religious and martyr		2001 iii 11 JP II
	Milagro Ortells Gimeno	Valencia, Spain	1882	1936	religious and martyr		2001 iii 11 JP II
	Niceta Plaja Xifra de San Prudencia	Valencia, Spain	1863	1936	religious and martyr		2001 iii 11 JP II
	Paula Isla Alonso de Santa Anastasia	Valencia, Spain	1863	1936	religious and martyr		2001 iii 11 JP II
	Pilar Villalonga Villalba	Valencia, Spain	1891	1936	martyr		2001 iii 11 JP II
	Presentación de la Sagrada Familia	(Pascuala Presentación Gallén Martí)	1872	1936	religious and martyr		2001 iii 11 JP II
	Rosa Pedret Rull de Nuestra Señora del Buen Consejo	Valencia, Spain	1864	1936	religious and martyr		2001 iii 11 JP II
	Sofía Ximénez Ximénez	Valencia, Spain	1876	1936	widow and martyr		2001 iii 11 JP II

table continues

Feast	*Name*	*Origin*	*Born*	*Died*	*Status*	*Canonized*	*Beatified*
	Társila Córdoba Belda	Valencia, Spain	1861	1936	widow and martyr		2001 iii 11 JP II
	Teresa Chambó Palés de la Divina Pastora	Valencia, Spain	1889	1936	religious and martyr		2001 iii 11 JP II
	Victoria Quintana Argos	Valencia, Spain	1866	1936	Third order capuchin, martyr		2001 iii 11 JP II
	Josaphata	Michaelina Hordashevska	1869	1919	religious and founder		2001 iv 27 JP II
	Laurentia (Leukadia Harasymiv) (1911–1952)	Martyrs of Ukraine	1911	1952	religious and martyr		2001 iv 27 JP II
	Olympia (Olha Bidà)	Martyrs of Ukraine	1903	1952	religious and martyr		2001 iv 27 JP II
	Tarsykia (Olha Mackiv)	Martyrs of Ukraine	1919	1944	religious and martyr		2001 iv 27 JP II
05 05	Caterina Cittadini	Bergamo, Italy	1801 ix 28	1857 v 05	religious and founder		2001 iv 29 JP II
04 18	Marie Anne Blondin	Terrebonne, Québec	1809 iv 18	1890 i 02	religious and founder		2001 iv 29 JP II
09 23	Émilie Tavernier Gamelin	Montréal	1800 ii 19	1852 ix 23	widow, religious and founder		2001 JP II
02 25	Adeodata Pisani	Malte	1806 xii 29	1855 ii 25	religious		2001 v 09 JP II
11 25	Luigi et Maria Corsini Beltrame Quattrocchi	Rome	1880, 1884	1951	married couple (first beatified couple)		2001 v 21 JP II
09 07	Anna Eugenia Picco	Milan	1867 xi 08	1921 ix 07	religious		2001 x 07 JP II
09 09	Maria Euthymia Üffing	Münster, Germany	1914 iv 08	1955 ix 09	religious		2001 x 07 JP II
	Gaetana Sterni	Italy	1827	1889	religious		2001 xi 04 JP II
08 27	María Pilar Izquierdo Albero	Zaragoza, Spain	1906 vii 27	1945 viii 27	religious and founder		2001 xi 04 JP II
	Juana María Condesa Lluch	Spain	1862	1916	religious and founder		2002 iii 23 JP II

Feast	Name	Origin	Born	Died	Status	Canonized	Beatified
	María Caridad	(María Josefa Carolina Brader) Switzerland/ Colombia	1860	1943	religious and founder		2002 iii 23 JP II
	María Dolores Rodríguez Sopeña	Spain	1848	1915	religious and founder		2002 iii 23 JP II
	Artemide Zatti	Italy/ Argentina	1880	1951	religious		2002 iv 14 JP II
	María del Transito de Jesús Sacramentado	Argentina (1st)	1821	1885	religious and founder		2002 iv 14 JP II
	María Romero Meneses	Nicaragua (1st from Central America)	1902	1977	religious		2002 iv 14 JP II
	Eugenia Ravasco	Italy	1845	1900	religious and founder		2002 iv 27 JP II
	Maria Cristina Brando	Italy	1856	1906	religious and founder		2002 iv 27 JP II
	Maria Domenica Mantovani	Italy	1862	1934	religious and founder		2002 iv 27 JP II
	Sancja Szymkowiak	Poland	1910	1942	religious		2002 viii 18 JP II
	Liduina Meneguzzi	Italy/ Ethiopia	1901	1941	religious		2002 x 20 JP II
	Mary of the Passion	(Hélène Marie de Chappotin de Neuville)	1839	1904	religious and founder		2002 x 20 JP II
	Zdenka Schelingová	(Cecilia)	1916 xii 24	1955	religious and martyr		2003 ix 14 JP II
07 09	Marija of Jesus Crucified Petkovic	Croatia	1892 xii 10	1966 vii 09	religious and founder		2003 vi 06 JP II
09 05	Teresa of Calcutta	Agnes Gonxha Bojaxhiu	1910 viii 26	1997 ix 05	religious and founder		2003 x 19 JP II
02 07	Rosalie Rendu	(Jeanne Marie Rendu) France	1786 ix 09	1856 ii 07	religious		2003 xi 09 JP II

table continues

Feast	*Name*	*Origin*	*Born*	*Died*	*Status*	*Canonized*	*Beatified*
10 13	Alexandria Maria da Costa	Portugal	1904 iii 30	1955 x 13	laywoman		2004 iv 25 JP II
02 10	Eusebia Palomino Yenes	Spain	1899 xii 15	1935 ii 10	religious		2004 iv 25 JP II
10 21	Laura Montoya y Upegui	(María Laura de Jesus Montoya Upegui) Colombia (1st)	1874 v 26	1949 x 29	religious and founder		2004 iv 25 JP II
06 24	Maria Guadalupe Garcia Zavala	Mexico	1878 iv 27	1963 vi 24	religious and founder		2004 iv 25 JP II
12 18	Julia Nemesia Valle	Italy	1847 vi 26	1916 xii 18	religious		2004 iv 25 JP II
02 09	Anna Katharina Emmerich	Münster	1774 ix 08	1824 ii 09	religious		2004 x 03 JP II
06 12	Maria Candida dell'Eucaristia	(Maria Barba)	1884 i 16	1949 vi 12	religious		2004 x 03 JP II
02 25	Maria Ludovica De Angelis	(Antonina) Italy/ Argentina	1880 x 24	1962 ii 25	religious		2004 x 03 JP II
12 17	Matilde del Sagrado Corazón	(Matilde Téllez Robles)	1841 v 30	1902 xii 17	religious and founder		2004 x 03 JP II
02 26	Piedad de la Cruz Ortiz Real	(Tomasa Ortiz Real)	1842 xi 12	1916 ii 26	religious and founder		2004 x 03 JP II
	Louis and Zelie Martin	France	1823 viii 22 1831 xii 23	1894 vii 29 1877 viii 28	married couple (second beatified couple)		2008 x 19
10 22	**John Paul II**	**Karol Józef Wojtyła**	**1920 v 18**	**2005 iv 02**	**pope**		**2011 v 01 Benedict XIV**[3]

NOTES

Foreword by John P. Hittinger

1. John Paul II, *The Feminine Presence in the Family*, Angelus Reflections on Women, 1995, Molise, Italy.

2. See Rocco Buttiglione, *Karol Wojtyła: The Thought of the Man Who Became Pope John Paul II* (Grand Rapids, Mich.: Eerdmans, 1997); and Kenneth Schmitz, *At the Center of the Human Drama: The Philosophical Anthropology of Karol Wojtyła /Pope John Paul II* (Washington, D.C.: The Catholic University of America Press, 1993).

General Introduction by Brooke Williams Deely

1. On the topic of women in history, see my essay "The Feminist Revolution in 'Ultramodern' Perspective," in *Cross Currents*, XXXI, no. 3 (1981): 307–19. See also my further essays: "Toward a Semiotic: Beyond Feminism," in *Semiotics 1980*, ed. Michael Herzfeld and Margot D. Lenhart (New York: Plenum Press, 1980); "Feminism, Postmodernism, and Mystical Contemplation," in *Semiotics 1999*, ed. Scott Simpkins, C. W. Spinks, and John Deely (New York: Peter Lang, 1999); "The Anthroposemiosis of Contemplation," in *Semiotics 2011*, ed. Scott Simpkins (New York: Legas, 2002); "Time for a Semiosis beyond Feminism," in *Semiotics* 2009, ed. John Deely (New York: Legas, 2009); and "Teresa of Avila as Sign of a Postmodern World View," in *Semiotics 2011*, ed. Karen Haworth (New York: Legas, 2012).

For my work on Jacques Maritain, see my book, Brooke Williams Smith [Deely], *Jacques Maritain: Antimodern or Ultramodern? An Historical Analysis of His Critics, His Thought, and His Life* (New York: Elsevier Scientific Publishing Company, Inc., 1976). See also my essays: "Mystical Contemplation in the Thought of Jacques Maritain and Yves R. Simon," *Notes et Documents* (Rome: Journal of International Maritain Association, 1979); "Jacques Maritain's Reflections on America," in *Semiotics 2003*, ed. Rodney Williamson, Leonard Sbrocchi, and John Deely (New York: Legas, 2004); "Contemplation Overflowing the Roads of the World: Love and Friendship in the Life and Work of Jacques and Raissa Maritain," *Love and Friendship: Maritain and the Tradition*, ed. Montague Brown (Washington, D.C.: The Catholic University Press of America, 2013).

2. The work of Sister Prudence Allen, RSM, on the history of the concept of woman in relation to man is developed through three volumes on *The Concept of Woman*: Volume I, *The Aristotelian Revolution, 750<sc>bce</sc>–<sc>ce</sc>1250* (Grand Rapids, Mich.: William B. Eerdmans Publishing Co., 1985); Volume II, *The Early Humanist Reformation, 1250–1500* (Grand Rapids, Mich.: William B. Eerdmans Publishing Co., 2002); Volume III,

Search for Communion of Persons 1500–2000+ (forthcoming; projected for 2015). In advance of the projected third volume, Sr. Prudence has published several articles on Pope John Paul II's writing on women, two of particular interest in the context of the present work: "Philosophy of Relation in John Paul II's New Feminism" and "Can Feminism Be a Humanism?" in *Women in Christ: Toward a New Feminism*, ed. Michele M. Schumacher (Grand Rapids, Mich.: Eerdmans, 2004), 67–104 and 251–84, respectively.

Sr. Prudence serves as mentor for *Endow* (Educating on the Nature and Dignity of Women), a Catholic study program for women and teenage girls rooted in the teachings of John Paul II's "New Feminism." See www.endowgroups.org.

3. Romero Carrasquilla and Troyer de Romero provide an overview of the controversial and problematic defining of woman offered by Aquinas. See Francisco J. Romero Carrasquillo and Hilaire K. Troyer de Romero, "Aquinas on the Inferiority of Woman, *American Catholic Philosophical Quarterly* 87, no. 4 (2013): 685–710, 2013.

4. See Jacques Maritain, "Let Us Make for Him a Helpmate Like to Himself," in *Untrammeled Approaches*, trans. Bernard Doering (vol. 20 in *The Collected Works of Jacques Maritain*; Notre Dame, Ind.: University of Notre Dame Press, 1997), 151–64. Cf. "Faisons-lui une aide semblable a lui," *Nova et Vetera*, XLII, no. 4 (October-December 1967), 241–54.

5. See the Introduction to Reading 10, *Mulieris Dignitatem* ("On the Dignity and Vocation of Woman"), from August 15, 1988.

6. See two of my articles on this point. "Feminism, Postmodernism, and Mystical Contemplation," in *Semiotics 1999*, ed. Scott Simpkins, C. W. Spinks, and J. Deely (New York: Peter Lang, 2000), 389–401; and "Teresa of Avila: Time for a Semiosis beyond Feminism," in *Semiotics 1982*, ed. J. Deely and Jonathan Evans (Lanham, Md.: University Press of America, 1987), 13–25. Regarding this second article, further application to the present context can be found in J. Deely's *Semiotic Animal*, 103–06.

7. See Karol Wojtyla, "Doctrina de fide apud S. Joannem a Cruce." Presented as a doctoral dissertation at the Pontifical University of St. Thomas Aquinas, Rome. Trans. Jordan Aumann, OP, under the title *Faith According to Saint John of the Cross* (San Francisco, Calif.: Ignatius Press, 1981).

8. See Jacques Maritain, "A Note on the Bourgeois World," *Commonweal* XVIII (June 2, 1933), 120.

9. For an overview of Edith Stein's philosophy of woman, see Kathleen Haney, "Edith Stein: Woman and Essence," in *Feminist Phenomenology*, ed. Linda Fisher and Lester Embree (New York: Kluwer Academic Publishing, 2000), 213–35.

10. Here we touch on a point that joins Pope John Paul II's thought on women with the personalist thought of his successor, Pope Benedict XVI. This bridging is profiled in John Deely's book, *Semiotic Animal* (South Bend, Ind.: St. Augustine's Press, 2010). On reading that work in the manuscript phase, I pointed out to the author (see page v of the book) that what he was proposing amounted to "a postmodern definition of human being transcending patriarchy and feminism," a quotation which then became the subtitle of the published volume. See my article "Teresa of Avila as Sign of a Postmodern Worldview: The Semiotic Animal," in *Semiotics 2011*, ed. Karen Haworth, Jason Hogue, and Leonard G. Sbrocchi (Ottawa, Canada: Legas, 2012), 113–21.

Semiotic Animal examines the history of the problem of defining the human, in particular the traditional "rational animal" definition (which dates from Porphyry, not, as is commonly but mistakenly assumed, from Aristotle). Sorely needed is a complete survey of the definitional question in terms which at once retain the original ancient and medieval meaning of "rational" as signifying difference in kind, while at the same time overcoming "rational" in the modern sense which reduces to difference in degree. That survey, based directly on the views of Maritain and John Paul II's successor as Pope, Benedict XVI, is what the book in question provides.

Reading 1 (November 7, 1979): Original Unity of Man and Woman

1. General Audience; Catechesis No. 8 from the Theology of the Body series: http://www.vatican.va/holy_father/john_paul_ii/audiences/catechesis_genesis/documents/hf_jp-ii_aud_19791107_e n.html.

2. The Hebrew term *'adam* expresses the collective concept of the human species, that is, man who represents humanity. (The Bible defines the individual using the expression: "son of man," *ben-'adam*). The contraposition, *'is-'issah*, underlines the sexual difference (as in Greek *anergyne*).

After the creation of the woman, the Bible text continues to call the first man *'adam* (with the definite article), thus expressing his "corporate personality," since he has become "father of mankind," its progenitor and representative, just as Abraham was recognized as "father of believers" and Jacob was identified with Israel—the Chosen People

3. Adam's sleep (in Hebrew, *tardemah*) is a deep one (in Latin, *sopor*), into which man falls without consciousness or dreams (the Bible has another term to define a dream: *halom*, cf. Gen 15:12, 1 Sm 26:12).

Freud examines, on the other hand, the content of dreams (Latin: *somnium*), which being formed with physical elements "pushed back into the subconscious," makes it possible, in his opinion, to allow the unconscious contents to emerge. The latter, he claims, are in the last analysis always sexual. This idea is, of course, quite alien to the biblical author.

In the theology of the Yahwist author, the sleep into which God caused the first man to fall emphasizes the exclusivity of God's action in the work of the creation of the woman; the man had no conscious participation in it. God uses his "rib" only to stress the common nature of man and of woman.

4. *Tardemah* (Italian *torpore*, English "sleep") is the term that appears in Sacred Scriptures when, during sleep or immediately afterward, extraordinary events are to happen (cf. Gen 15:12; 1 Sm 26:12; Is 29:10; Jb 4:13, 33:15). The Septuagint translates *tardemah* with *ekstasis* (ecstasy).

In the Pentateuch, *tardemah* appears only once more in a mysterious context. On God's command, Abram has prepared a sacrifice of animals, driving away birds of prey from them. "As the sun was going down, a deep sleep fell on Abram, and lo, a dread fell upon him" (Gen 15:12). Just then, God begins to speak and concludes a covenant with him, which is the summit of the revelation made to Abram.

This scene is similar in a way to the one in the garden of Gethsemane. Jesus "begins to be greatly distressed and troubled" (Mk 14:33) and found the apostles "sleeping for sorrow" (Lk 22:45).

The biblical author admits in the first man a certain sense of privation and solitude, even if not of fear ("It is not good that the man should be alone"; "For the man there was not found a helper fit for him"). Perhaps this state brings about "a sleep caused by sorrow," or, perhaps, as in Abram, by "a dread" of non-being, as on the threshold of the work of creation: "The earth was without form and void, and darkness was upon the face of the deep" (Gen 1:2).

In any case, according to both texts, in which the Pentateuch or rather Genesis speaks of the deep sleep *tardemah*, a special divine action takes place, that is, a "covenant pregnant with consequences for the whole history of salvation: Adam begins mankind, Abram the Chosen People.

5. It is interesting to note that for the ancient Sumerians the cuneiform sign to indicate the noun "rib" coincided with the one used to indicate the word "life." As for the Yahwist narrative, according to a certain interpretation of Genesis 2:21, God rather covers the rib with flesh (instead of closing up its place with flesh) and in this way "makes the woman, who comes from the "flesh and bones" of the first man (male).

In biblical language, this is a definition of consanguinity or descent from the same lineage (cf. Gen 29:14). The woman belongs to the same species as the man, different from the other living beings created before.

In biblical anthropology, the term "bones" expresses a very important element of the body. Since for the Jews there was no precise distinction between "body" and "soul" (the body was considered an exterior manifestation of the personality), "bones" meant simply, by synecdoche, the human "being" (cf., for example, Ps(s) 139:15: "My frame was not hidden from you"; in Italian, "*Non ti erano nascoste le mie ossa*" [bones]).

"Bone of my bones" can therefore be understood in the relational sense, as "being of my being." "Flesh of my flesh" means that, though she has different physical characteristics, the woman has the same personality as the man possesses.

In the first man's "nuptial song," the expression "bone of my bones, flesh of my flesh" is a form of superlative, stressed, moreover, by the repetition of "this," "she" (in Italian there are three feminine forms: *questa, essa, la*).

6. It is difficult to translate exactly the Hebrew expression *cezer kenegdo*, which is translated in various ways in European languages, for example:

Latin: *Adiutorium ei conveniens sicut oportebat iuxta eum*;
German: *eine Hilfe . . . die ilum entspricht*;
French: *égal vis-à-vis de lui*;
Spanish *como él que le ayude*;
English: a helper fit for him
Polish: *Odopowicdnia alla niego pomoc.*

Since the term *aiuto* (help) seems to suggest the concept of "complementarity," or better, of "exact correspondence," the term "*simile*" is connected rather with that of "similarity," but in a different sense from man's likeness to God.

Reading 2 (November 14, 1979): Man Becomes the Image of God by Communion of Persons

1. General Audience; Catechesis No. 9 from the "Theology of the Body" series: <http://www.vatican.va/holy_father/john_paul_ii/audiences/catechesis_genesis/documents/hf_jp-ii_aud_19791114_e n.html>.

2. "But God did not create man as a solitary being, for from the beginning "male and female he created them" (Gen 1:27). Their companionship produces the primary form of interpersonal communion" (*Gaudium et Spes* 12).

3. The dualistic contraposition "soul-body" does not appear in the conception of the most ancient books of the Bible. As has already been stressed (cf. *L'Osservatore Romano*, English edition, November 5, 1979, 15n1), we can speak rather of a complementary combination of "body-life." The body is the expression of man's personality, and if it does not fully exhaust this concept, it must be understood in biblical language as a *pars pro toto*; cf., for example, "Flesh and blood has not revealed this to you, but my Father ..." (Mt 16:17), that is, it was not a man who revealed it to you.

4. "For no man ever hates his own flesh, but nourishes it and cherishes it, as Christ does the Church, because we are members of his body. For this reason a man shall leave his father and mother and be joined to his wife, and the two shall become one flesh. This mystery is a profound one, and I am saying that it refers to Christ and the Church" (Eph 5:29-32). This will be the subject of our reflections in the part titled "The Sacrament."

Reading 3 (December 19, 1979): Fullness of Interpersonal Communication

1. General Audience; Catechesis No. 12 from the "Theology of the Body" series: <http://www.vatican.va/holy_father/john_paul_ii/audiences/catechesis_genesis/documents/hf_jp-ii_aud_19791114_e n.html>.

2. According to the words of Holy Scripture, God penetrates the creature, who is completely "naked" before him. "And before him no creature is hidden, but all are open (*panta gymn*) and laid bare to the eyes of him with whom we have to do" (Heb 4:13). This characteristic belongs in particular to divine Wisdom: "Wisdom ... because of her pureness pervades and penetrates all things" (Ws 7:24).

Reading 4 (February 13, 1980): Original Innocence and Man's Historical State

1. General Audience; Catechesis No. 18 from the "Theology of the Body" series: <http://www.vatican.va/holy_father/john_paul_ii/audiences/catechesis_genesis/documents/hf_jp-ii_aud_19800213_e n.html>.

2. "If one should not acknowledge that the first man Adam, on transgressing God's command in paradise, did not immediately lose the holiness and justice in which he had been constituted ... let him be anathema" (Council of Trent, Sess. V, con. 1, 2: D.B. 788, 789).

3. "The first parents had been constituted in a state of holiness and justice ... The state of original justice conferred on the first parents was gratuitous and truly supernatural ... The first parents were constituted in a state of integral nature, i.e., immune from concupiscence, ignorance, pain and death ... and they enjoyed a unique happiness.... The gifts of integrity granted to the first parents were gratuitous and preternatural" (A. Tanquerey, *Synopsis Theologiae Dogmaticae* [Paris: 1943], 24, 545–49).

Reading 5 (October 15, 1980): Gospel Values and Duties of the Human Heart

1. General Audience; Catechesis No. 44 from the "Theology of the Body" series: <http://www.vatican.va/holy_father/john_paul_ii/audiences/1980/documents/hf_jp-ii_aud_19801015_it.html>.

2. Manichaeism contains and brings to maturation the characteristic elements of all *gnosis*,

that is, the dualism of two coeternal and radically opposed principles and the concept of a salvation which is realized only through knowledge (*gnosis*) or self-understanding. In the whole Manichaean myth, there is only one hero and only one situation which is always repeated: the fallen soul is imprisoned in matter and is liberated by knowledge. The present historical situation is negative for man, because it is a provisional and abnormal mixture of spirit and matter, good and evil, which presupposes *a priori*, an original state, in which the two substances were separate and independent. There are, therefore, three "Times": *initium*, or the original separation; the *medium*, that is, the present mixture; and the *finis*, which consists in return to the original division, in salvation, implying a complete break between Spirit and Matter.

Matter is, fundamentally, concupiscence, an evil instinct for pleasure, the instinct of death, comparable, if not identical, with sexual desire, libido. It is a force that tries to attack Light; it is disorderly movement, bestial, brutal, and semiconscious desire.

Adam and Eve were begotten by two demons; our species was born from a series of repelling acts of cannibalism and sexuality and keeps signs of this diabolical origin, which are the body, which is the animal form of the "Archons of hell" and libido, which drives man to copulate and reproduce himself, that is, to keep his luminous soul always in prison.

If he wants to be saved, man must try to liberate his "living self" (*nous*) from the flesh and from the body. Since Matter has its supreme expression in concupiscence, the capital sin lies in sexual union (fornication), which is brutality and bestiality, and makes men instruments and accomplices of Evil for procreation.

The elect constitute the group of the perfect, whose virtue has an ascetic characteristic, practicing the abstinence commanded by the three "seals": the "seal of the mouth" forbids all blasphemy and also commands fasting, and abstention from meat, blood, wine, and all alcoholic drinks; the "seal of the hands" commands respect of the life (the "light") enclosed in bodies, in seeds, in trees, and forbids the gathering of fruit, the tearing up of plants, the taking of the life of men and of animals; the "seal of the womb" prescribes total continence. Cf. H. Ch. Puech, *Le Manicheisme; son fondateur—sa doctrine* (Paris: Musée Guimet, LVI, 1949), 73–88; H. Ch. Puech, Le Manichéisme, in "*Histoire des Religions*," *Encyclopédie de la Pleiade II* (Gallimard: 1972), 522–645; J. Ties, "*Manichéisme*," in *Catholicisme hier, aujourd'hui, demain*, Vol. 34 (Lille: Letouzey-Ané, 1977), 314–20.

Introduction to Reading 6 by Diane and Dominic Aquila

1. <http://www.vatican.va/holy_father/john_paul_ii/apost_exhortations/documents/hf_jp-ii_exh_19811122_familiaris-consortio_en.html>.

2. Francis de Sales, *Practical Piety* (Louisville: Webb & Levering, 1853), 297.

3. http://www.barna.org/culture-articles/615-christians-on-leadership-calling-and-career?q=leadership.

4. As Edmund Morgan points out in his study of *The Puritan Family* (New York: Harper & Row, 1966), 68–73.

Reading 6 (November 22, 1980): *Familiaris Consortio* ("On the Role of the Christian Family in the Modern World")

1. Apostolic Exhortation to the Whole Church on the Role of the Christian Family in the "Modern World": The Plan of God for Marriage and the Family, Nos. 11–16; Role of the Christian Family, Nos. 22–27, 45–48. <http://www.vatican.va/holy_father/john_paul_ii/apost_exhortations/documents/hf_jp-ii_exh_19811122_familiaris- consortio_en.html>.

Reading 7 (August 11, 1982): Reverence for Christ: The Basis of the Relationship between Spouses

1. General Audience: <http://www.vatican.va/holy_father/john_paul_ii/audiences/1982/documents/hf_jp-ii_aud_19820811_sp.html>.

Reading 8 (December 15, 1982): The Redemptive and Spousal Dimensions of Love

1. General Audience: Catechesis no. 103 from the Theology of the Body series: <http://www.vatican.va/holy_father/john_paul_ii/audiences/1982/documents/hf_jp-ii_aud_19821215_it.html>.

Introduction to Reading 9 by Virginia Galloway

1. Encyclical Letter: http://www.vatican.va/holy_father/john_paul_ii/encyclicals/documents/hf_jp-ii_enc_25031987_redemptoris-mater_en.html: Sect. 20, 23.

2 Encyclical Letter http://www.vatican.va/holy_father/john_paul_ii/encyclicals/documents/hf_jp-ii_enc_25031995_evangelium-vitae_en.html: Sect. 1:2ff.

3. *Redemptoris Mater*, Sect. 4:10.

Reading 9 (March 25, 1987): *Redemptoris Mater* (Mother of the Redeemer)

1. Encyclical Letter: <http://www.vatican.va/holy_father/john_paul_ii/encyclicals/documents/hf_jp-ii_enc_25031987_redemptoris-mater_en.html>.

Introduction to Reading 10 by Brooke Williams Deely

1. Vincent Guagliardo, OP, "Father and Son in the Trinity: Metaphor or Analogy?" *The American Journal of Semiotics* 27.1–4 (2011): 159–86.

Reading 10 (August 15, 1988): *Mulieris Dignitatem* (On the Dignity and Vocation of Women)

1. Apostolic Letter: <http://www.vatican.va/holy_father/john_paul_ii/apost_letters/documents/hf_jp-ii_apl_15081988_mulieris-dignitate m_it.html>.

Reading 11 (September 4, 1988): Discovery of a New Feminine Identity

1. On occasion of a pastoral visit: <http://www.vatican.va/holy_father/john_paul_ii/speeches/1988/september/documents/hf_jp-ii_spe_19880904_religi ose-valdocco_it.html>.

Reading 12 (December 30, 1988): *Christifideles Laici* (The Lay Members of Christ's Faithful People)

1. Post-synodal Apostolic Exhortation, nos. 9, 14–17, 49–52, 55, 64. <http://www.vatican.va/holy_father/john_paul_ii/apost_exhortations/documents/hf_jp-ii_exh_30121988_christifidele s-laici_en.html>.

Reading 13 (September 25, 1993): True Human Love Reflects the Divine

1. On occasion of pastoral visit: <http://www.vatican.va/holy_father/john_paul_ii/speeches/1993/september/documents/hf_jp-ii_spe_19930925_famig lie-asti_it.html>.

Reading 14 (March 18, 1994): Population Conference Draft Document Criticized

1. Letter to Mme. Nafis Sadik, secretary general of the International Conference on Population: <http://www.vatican.va/holy_father/john_paul_ii/letters/1994/documents/hf_jp-ii_let_19940318_cairo-population-sad ik_it.html>.

Reading 15 (May 22, 1994): *Ordinatio Sacerdotalis* (On Ordination to the Priesthood)

1. Apostolic Letter on the Reservation of Ordination to Male Human Beings ("men alone"): <http://www.vatican.va/holy_father/john_paul_ii/apost_letters/documents/hf_jp-ii_apl_22051994_ordinatio-sacerdota lis_en.html>.

Reading 16 (January 1, 1995): Women: Teachers of Peace

1. Message for the Twenty-eighth "World Day of Peace": <http://www.vatican.va/holy_father/john_paul_ii/messages/peace/documents/hf_jp-ii_mes_08121994_xxviii-world-d ay-for-peace_en.html>.

2. John XXIII, *Pacem in Terris*, Aprill 11, 1963.

Reading 17 (March 19, 1995): The Feminine Presence in the Family

1. John Paul II, *The Feminine Presence in the Family*, Angelus Reflections on Women, 1995, Molise, Italy.

Reading 18 (March 25, 1995): *Evangelium Vitae* (The Gospel Life)

1. Encyclical Letter: <http://www.vatican.va/holy_father/john_paul_ii/encyclicals/documents/hf_jp-ii_enc_25031995_evangelium-vitae_en.html>.

Reading 19 (April 7, 1995): Letter to Priests for Holy Thursday 1995

1. <http://www.vatican.va/holy_father/john_paul_ii/letters/documents/hf_jp-ii_let_25031995_priests_en.html>.

Reading 20 (May 26, 1995): Papal Message on Women's Conference

1. <http://www.vatican.va/holy_father/john_paul_ii/letters/1995/documents/hf_jp-ii_let_19950526_mongella-pechino_it.html>.

Reading 21 (June 18, 1995): Culture Must Respect Femininity

1. <http://www.vatican.va/holy_father/john_paul_ii/angelus/1995/documents/hf_jp-ii_ang_19950618_it.html>.

Reading 22 (June 25, 1995): Culture of Equality Is Urgently Needed Today

1. <http://www.vatican.va/holy_father/john_paul_ii/angelus/1995/documents/hf_jp-ii_ang_19950625_it.html>.

Introduction to Reading 23 by Brooke Williams Deely and Fr. Edward J. Baenziger, CSB

1. See Mary Ann Glendon's report, "What Happened at Beijing," 99–108, as reprinted in The Endow study guide for the Pope's Letter to Women (which provides context for further appreciation of the components and positive effects of this papal letter, both in the Beijing context and subsequently). *Pope John Paul II's Letter to Women: An Introduction to the New Feminism*, with a commentary by Erica Laethem and appendices on the historical context of the World Congress on Women in Beijing (West Chester, Pa.: Ascension Press, 2006); published for *Endow* Catholic Women's Studies.

Reading 23 (June 29, 1995): Letter to Women

1. http://www.vatican.va/holy_father/john_paul_ii/letters/documents/hf_jp-ii_let_29061995_women_en.html.

Reading 24 (July 9, 1995): Men and Women Must Live for the Other

1. http://www.vatican.va/holy_father/john_paul_ii/angelus/1995/documents/hf_jp-ii_ang_19950709_it.html.

Reading 25 (July 16, 1995): The Vocation to Motherhood

1. http://www.vatican.va/holy_father/john_paul_ii/angelus/1995/documents/hf_jp-ii_ang_19950716_it.html.

Reading 26 (July 23, 1995): Society and Church Need Genius of Woman

1. http://www.vatican.va/holy_father/john_paul_ii/angelus/1995/documents/hf_jp-ii_ang_19950723_it.html.

Reading 27 (July 30, 1995): Initial Education in Family Relies on "Feminine Genius"

1. http://www.vatican.va/holy_father/john_paul_ii/angelus/1995/documents/hf_jp-ii_ ang_19950730_it.html.

Reading 28 (August 6, 1995): Culture Needs Women's Genius

1. http://www.vatican.va/holy_father/john_paul_ii/angelus/1995/documents/hf_jp-ii_ang_19950806_it.html.

Reading 29 (August 20, 1995): Equal Opportunity Still Urgently Needed

1. http://www.vatican.va/holy_father/john_paul_ii/angelus/1995/documents/hf_jp-ii_ang_19950820_it.html.

Reading 30 (August 27, 1995): Women Have Much to Offer in Political Life

1. http://www.vatican.va/holy_father/john_paul_ii/angelus/1995/documents/hf_jp-ii_ang_19950827_it.html.

Reading 31 (August 29, 1995): Address to the Vatican Delegation to the Fourth World Conference on Women

1. http:// www.vatican.va/holy_father/john _paul_ii/speeches.1995/august/documents/hf_jp-ii_spe_19950829_glendon_en.html.

Reading 32 (September 3, 1995): Enhance Women's Role in Church Life

1. http://www.vatican.va/holy_father/john_paul_ii/angelus/1995/documents/hf_jp-ii_ang_19950903_it.html.

Reading 33 (November 29, 1995): Mary Shows Us God's Respect for Women

1. General Audience: http://www.vatican.va/holy_father/john_paul_ii/audiences/1995/documents/hf_jp-ii_aud_19951129_it.html.

Reading 34 (December 6, 1995): Mary Sheds Light on Role of Women

1. General Audience:
http://www.vatican.va/holy_father/john_paul_ii/audiences/1995/documents/hf_jp-ii_aud_19951206_it.html.

Reading 35 (January 24, 1996): The Media: Modern Forum for Promoting the Role of Women in Society

1. Message for the Thirtieth "World Communications Day":
http://www.vatican.va/holy_father/john_paul_ii/messages/communications/documents/hf_jp-ii_mes_24011996_world-communications-day_en.html.

Reading 36 (January 24, 1996): Victory over Sin Comes through a Woman

1. http://www.vatican.va/holy_father/john_paul_ii/audiences/1996/documents/hf_jp-ii_aud_19960124_it.html.

Reading 37 (March 6, 1996): Motherhood Is God's Special Gift

1. http://www.vatican.va/holy_father/john_paul_ii/audiences/1996/documents/hf_jp-ii_aud_19960306_it.html.

Reading 38 (March 27, 1996): Woman's Indispensable Role in Salvation History

1. http://www.vatican.va/holy_father/john_paul_ii/audiences/1996/documents/hf_jp-ii_aud_19960327_it.html.

Reading 39 (April 10, 1996): The Ideal Woman Is a Precious Treasure

1. http://www.vatican.va/holy_father/john_paul_ii/audiences/1996/documents/hf_jp-ii_aud_19960410_it.html

Reading 40 (December 7, 1996): Motherhood: Woman's Gift to Society

1. http://www.vatican.va/holy_father/john_paul_ii/speeches/1996/december/documents/ hf_jp-ii_spe_19961207_motherhood_en.html.

Reading 41 (January 8, 1997): Christ Calls Women to Share His Mission

1. http://www.vatican.va/holy_father/john_paul_ii/audiences/1997/documents/hf_jp-ii_aud_08011997_en.html

Reading 42 (February 20, 1998): Address to the International Conference on Women's Health Issues

1. http://www.vatican.va/holy_father/john_paul_ii/speeches/1998/february/documents/ hf_jp-ii_spe_19980220_women's-health-issues_en.html.

Reading 43 (November 24, 1999): The Fatherhood of God and the Dignity of Women

1. http://www.vatican.va/holy_father/john_paul_ii/audiences/1999/documents/hf_jp-ii_aud_24111999_en.html.

Concluding Section by Fr. Edward J. Baenziger, CSB

1. http://catholicpreaching.com/content/docs/JP2Youth.pdf (accessed April 25, 2012).

2. http://www.vatican.va/holy_father/john_paul_ii/apost_letters/documents/hf_jp-ii_apl_ 19101997_divini-amoris_en.html (accessed April 25, 2012). Pope John Paul II, *Divini Amoris Scientia*, English, Aust. ed. (Kew, Vic.: Carmelite Monastery, 1997).

Appendix

1. http://www.catholic-forum.com/saints; http://myfaith.brainerd-mn.info/pope/travels/beatifications/saints.html

BIBLIOGRAPHY

John Paul II. *On the Family*. Washington, D.C.: United States Catholic Conference, 1981.

———. "Address to Women Religious in Turin, Italy, Praying that Mary Will Inspire the Church to Discover a New Feminine Identity." *Osservatore Romano* 1060 (10/17, 1988): 3–4.

———. *On the Dignity and Vocation of Women*. Washington, D.C.: United States Catholic Conference, 1988.

———. *The Vocation and the Mission of the Lay Faithful in the Church and in the World*. Washington, D.C.: United States Catholic Conference, 1988.

———. "Family and Population Issues Require Ethical Principles." *Pope Speaks* 39 (Jul 1994): 253–58.

———. *The Gospel of Life*. Boston: Pauline Books & Media, 1995.

———. "Media's Role in Women's Emancipation." *Pope Speaks* 41 (Jul 1996): 205–207.

———. "Christ Calls Women to Share His Mission." *Osservatore Romano* 1474 (01/15 1997): 11.

———. "Closing the Gap between Cultural Opportunities for Men and Women." In *The Genius of Women*. Washington, D.C.: United States Conference of Catholic Bishops, 1997, 30–32.

———. "Complementarity and Reciprocity between Women and Men." In *The Genius of Women*. Washington, D.C.: United States Conference of Catholic Bishops, 1997, 24–25.

———. "Culture Must Respect Femininity." In *The Genius of Women*. Washington, D.C.: United States Conference of Catholic Bishops, 1997, 20–22.

———. "Culture of Equality is Urgently Needed Today." In *The Genius of Women*. Washington, D.C.: United States Conference of Catholic Bishops, 1997, 22–23.

———. "Equal Opportunity in the World of Work." In *The Genius of Women*. Washington, D.C.: United States Conference of Catholic Bishops, 1997, 32–33.

———. "The Feminine Genius." In *The Genius of Women*. Washington, D.C.: United States Conference of Catholic Bishops, 1997, 27–28.

———. "The Feminine Presence in the Family." In *The Genius of Women*. Washington, D.C.: United States Conference of Catholic Bishops, 1997, 19–20.

———. "History Needs to Include Women's Contributions." In *The Genius of Women*. Washington, D.C.: United States Conference of Catholic Bishops, 1997, 28–30.

———. "Letter to Mary Ann Glendon and the Holy See's Delegation to the Fourth World Conference on Women." In *The Genius of Women*. Washington, D.C.: United States Conference of Catholic Bishops, 1997, 59–62.

———. "Letter to Women." In *The Genius of Women*. Washington, D.C.: United States Conference of Catholic Bishops, 1997, 45–58.
———. "Motherhood, Woman's Gift to Society." *Osservatore Romano* 1475 (01/22, 1997): 8.
———. "The Vocation of Motherhood." In *The Genius of Women*. Washington, D.C.: United States Conference of Catholic Bishops, 1997, 25–27.
———. "Welcome to Gertrude Mongella, Secretary General of the Fourth World Conference on Women." In *The Genius of Women*. Washington, D.C.: United States Conference of Catholic Bishops, 1997, 37–44.
———. "Woman's Role in the Church." In *The Genius of Women*. Washington, D.C.: United States Conference of Catholic Bishops, 1997, 35–36.
———. "Women in Political Life." In *The Genius of Women*. Washington, D.C.: United States Conference of Catholic Bishops, 1997, 33–34.
———. "World Day of Peace Message." In *The Genius of Women*. Washington, D.C.: United States Conference of Catholic Bishops, 1997, 9–18.
———. "Apostolic Letter on Reserving Priestly Ordination to Men Alone." In *From "Inter Insigniores" to "Ordinatio Sacerdotalis": Documents and Commentaries*. Washington, D.C.: United States Catholic Conference, 1998, 185–91.
———. "Justice Demands Respect for Human Life." *L'Osservatore Romano (English)* (3/4, 1998): 4.
———. "Commitment to Promoting Women's Dignity." *L'Osservatore Romano (English)* (12/1, 1999): 11.
———. "True Human Love Reflects the Divine." *Catholic Dossier* 5, no. 1 (Jan/Feb 1999): 28–30.
———. "The Ideal Woman Is a Precious Treasure." In *Theotókos: Woman, Mother, Disciple*. Boston: Pauline Books & Media, 2000, 76–78.
———. "Mary Sheds Light on the Role of Woman." In *Theotókos: Woman, Mother, Disciple*. Boston: Pauline Books & Media, 2000, 45–48.
———. "Mary Shows Us Respect for Women." In *Theotókos: Woman, Mother, Disciple*. Boston: Pauline Books & Media, 2000, 41–44.
———. "Motherhood Is God's Special Gift." In *Theotókos: Woman, Mother, Disciple*. Boston: Pauline Books & Media, 2000, 68–71.
———. "Victory Over Sin Comes through a Woman." In *Theotókos: Woman, Mother, Disciple*. Boston: Pauline Books & Media, 2000, 61–63.
———. "Woman's Indispensable Role in Salvation History." In *Theotókos: Woman, Mother, Disciple*. Boston: Pauline Books & Media, 2000, 72–75.
———. "Letter to Priests for Holy Thursday 1995." In *Letters to My Brother Priests: Holy Thursday (1979–2001)*. Edited by James P. Socias. Princeton, N.J.: Scepter Publishers, 2001.
———. "Attempted Reconstruction." In *Man and Woman He Created Them: A Theology of the Body*. Translated and edited by Michael Waldstein. Boston: Pauline Books & Media, 2006, 173–77.
———. "Gospel Values and Duties of the Human Heart." In *Man and Woman He Created Them: A Theology of the Body*. Translated and edited by Michael Waldstein. Boston: Pauline Books & Media, 2006, 301–305.
———. "Man Becomes the Image of God by the Communion of Persons." In *Man and*

Woman He Created Them: A Theology of the Body. Translated and edited by Michael Waldstein. Boston: Pauline Books & Media, 2006, 161–65.

———. "The Spousal and Redemptive Meaning of Love." In *Man and Woman He Created Them: A Theology of the Body*. Translated and edited by Michael Waldstein. Boston: Pauline Books & Media, 2006, 525–29.

———. "The Spouses: 'Reciprocally Subject in the Fear of Christ.'" In *Man and Woman He Created Them: A Theology of the Body*. Translated and edited by Michael Waldstein. Boston: Pauline Books & Media, 2006, 472–75.

———. "Theology of Original Innocence." In *Man and Woman He Created Them: A Theology of the Body*. Translated and edited by Michael Waldstein. Boston: Pauline Books & Media, 2006, 198–201.

———. "The Unity of the Two." In *Man and Woman He Created Them: A Theology of the Body*. Translated and edited by Michael Waldstein. Boston: Pauline Books & Media, 2006, 156–60.

INDEX OF NAMES

This index does not include the chart of names in the Appendix.

Pope John Paul II Speaks on Women was designed in Garamond Premier Pro and composed by Kachergis Book Design of Pittsboro, North Carolina. It was printed on 50-pound Natures recycled and bound by Sheridan Books of Ann Arbor, Michigan.